S0-BYQ-533

ROME, FLORENCE AND VENICE 2024

9th Edition

By Donald Strachan, Elizabeth Heath, Stephen Keeling

FrommerMedia LLC

Frommer's Rome, Florence and Venice 2024, 9th Edition

Published by:
Frommer Media LLC

ISBN 978-1-62887-583-6 (paper), 978-1-62887-584-3 (e-book)

Editorial Director: Pauline Frommer
Editor: Melinda Quintero
Production Editor: Kelly Dobbs Henthorne
Cartographer: Liz Puhl

Photo Editor: Meghan Lamb
Indexer: Kelly Dobbs Henthorne
Compositor: Lissa Auciello-Brogan
Cover Design: Dave Riedy

For information on our other products or services, see www.frommers.com.

Frommer Media LLC also publishes its books in a variety of electronic formats. Some content that appears in print may not be available in electronic formats.

Manufactured in Malaysia

5   4   3   2   1

HOW TO CONTACT US

In researching this book, we discovered many wonderful places—hotels, restaurants, shops, and more. We're sure you'll find others. Please tell us about them, so we can share the information with your fellow travelers in upcoming editions. If you were disappointed with a recommendation, we'd love to know that, too. Please write to: Support@FrommerMedia.com

FROMMER'S STAR RATINGS SYSTEM

Every hotel, restaurant and attraction listed in this guide has been ranked for quality and value. Here's what the stars mean:

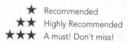

★ Recommended
★★ Highly Recommended
★★★ A must! Don't miss!

AN IMPORTANT NOTE

The world is a dynamic place. Hotels change ownership, restaurants hike their prices, muse-ums alter their opening hours, and buses and trains change their routings. And all of this can occur in the several months after our authors have visited, inspected, and written about these hotels, restaurants, museums, and transportation services. Though we have made valiant efforts to keep all our information fresh and up-to-date, some few changes can inevitably occur in the periods before a revised edition of this guidebook is published. So please bear with us if a tiny number of the details in this book have changed. Please also note that we have no responsibility or liability for any inaccuracy or errors or omissions, or for inconve-nience, loss, damage, or expenses suffered by anyone as a result of assertions in this guide.

CONTENTS

LIST OF MAPS

ABOUT THE AUTHORS

Elizabeth Heath, a longtime contributor to Frommer's guides, is a writer and editor based in Umbria, central Italy, from where she writes about travel and culture in Italy, Europe, and farther afield. Her work has appeared in *The Washington Post, Travel + Leisure, Discover Magazine*, Frommers.com, and many other outlets. When not traveling and writing about it, she enjoys rural life with her extended Italian family and houseful of pets.

Stephen Keeling has been traveling to Italy since 1985 (when a serving of gelato was 1,000 lire), and covering his favorite nation for Frommer's since 2007. He has written for *The Independent, Daily Telegraph*, various travel magazines, and numerous travel guides. Stephen resides in New York City.

Donald Strachan has written about Italy and Europe for publications worldwide, including *National Geographic Traveller, The Guardian, Sunday Telegraph*, and *The Independent*. He resides in London, England.

ABOUT THE FROMMER TRAVEL GUIDES

For most of the past 50 years, Frommer's has been the leading series of travel guides in North America, accounting for as many as 24% of all guidebooks sold. I think I know why.

Though we hope our books are entertaining, we nevertheless deal with travel in a serious fashion. Our guidebooks have never looked on such journeys as a mere recreation, but as a far more important human function, a time of learning and introspection, an essential part of a civilized life. We stress the culture, lifestyle, history, and beliefs of the destinations we cover, and urge our readers to seek out people and new ideas as the chief rewards of travel.

We have never shied from controversy. We have, from the beginning, encouraged our authors to be intensely judgmental, critical—both pro and con—in their comments, and wholly independent. Our only clients are our readers, and we have triggered the ire of countless prominent sorts, from a tourist newspaper we called "practically worthless" (it unsuccessfully sued us) to the many rip-offs we've condemned.

And because we believe that travel should be available to everyone regardless of their incomes, we have always been cost-conscious at every level of expenditure. Though we have broadened our recommendations beyond the budget category, we insist that every lodging we include be sensibly priced. We use every form of media to assist our readers, and are particularly proud of our feisty daily website, the award-winning Frommers.com.

I have high hopes for the future of Frommer's. May these guidebooks, in all the years ahead, continue to reflect the joy of travel and the freedom that travel represents. May they always pursue a cost-conscious path, so that people of all incomes can enjoy the rewards of travel. And may they create, for both the traveler and the persons among whom we travel, a community of friends, where all human beings live in harmony and peace.

Arthur Frommer

THE BEST OF ROME, FLORENCE & VENICE

By Donald Strachan

taly is never far from the top of the world's must-see list, and it's easy to understand why. The name alone conjures up vivid, postcard images: the grand ruins of ancient **Rome,** the paintings and panoramas of **Florence,** the secret canals and noble palaces of **Venice.** For centuries, visitors have come to Italy for a slice of the good life *(La dolce vita)*, and these three cities can be the highpoints of any trip here.

Rome, a city mythically founded by twins Romulus and Remus in 753 B.C., once ruled much of the "known world." Today, the modern capital thrives on top of, within, and around the ancient city's ruins. A 90-minute train ride north takes you to Florence. Nowhere else in Europe carries the legacy of the Renaissance more than this city, its birthplace and unrivaled repository of iconic art by Michelangelo, Masaccio, Botticelli, Leonardo da Vinci, and many others. As if all these artistic and historic monuments weren't enough, the impossible floating city of Venice, a two-hour train ride north from Florence, rises from the Adriatic with a distinct beauty and history shaped by centuries of trade with the Byzantine world to the east.

And there's more. Long before Italy was a country, it was a loose collection of city-states. Centuries of alliances and rivalries left a legacy dotted across the hinterlands of Rome, Florence, and Venice. Many of these historic smaller cities are within easy day-trip distance. It is a short hop from Venice to the "Venetian Arc": **Verona,** where Shakespearean romance echoes through an intact Roman Arena, and **Padua** with its sublime Giotto paintings. In **Siena,** an hour or so from Florence, ethereal art and Gothic palaces have barely changed since the city's heyday in the 1300s. South of Rome, **Pompeii**—preserved under volcanic ash for two millennia after Vesuvius's eruption in A.D. 79—remains the best place to get a hint of everyday life in the ancient world.

ITALY'S best AUTHENTIC EXPERIENCES

o **Dining Italian Style:** On the one hand, no Italian pastime is more cherished than eating—even better, eating a multi-course meal outdoors, preferably with a view of a Renaissance piazza. On the other hand, Italians—especially city dwellers—don't linger in a piazza sipping their morning cappuccino. For them, *un caffè* (specifically, an espresso) is a pitstop: They stand at the counter (*al banco*), throw back the bitter elixir, and continue on their way. Bonus for visitors giving it a try: The Italian-style morning ritual costs less, maybe half of the sit-down price.

o **Exploring Beyond the Tourist Trail:** There is no shame in seeing all the classic sights of Rome, Florence, and Venice. But Italy is much more than one giant museum tour. Step off Main Street to wander atmospheric neighborhoods beyond the historic core—Testaccio in Rome, the Oltrarno backstreets of Florence, Cannaregio in Venice. Each will give you a glimpse of daily life in a country that effortlessly blends modern cool with ancient ways.

o **Taking a Moment for Peaceful Prayer:** Even the most historic churches celebrate mass daily (almost always Roman Catholic). On Sunday mornings, bells toll across every city, town, and village. Doors are open to all, of

St. Mark's Square in Venice.

The vendors in Florence's Mercato Centrale sell simple meals showcasing the best of Italy's regional cuisines.

course, and in big city cathedrals like in Florence (p. 204), you may even find a weekly service in English.

o **Shopping at Rome's Working Food Markets:** Testaccio's reborn historic market is a culinary and cultural treat, where acclaimed chefs jostle with feisty *signore* for the day's best *pomodori, mozzarella di bufala,* and *trippa* (tripe). Sustain yourself with street food as you soak up a genuine Roman neighborhood south of the Aventine. See p. 153.

THE best TASTES OF ITALY

o **Bonci Pizzarium, Rome:** Chef-entrepreneur Gabriele Bonci elevates the simple slice to extraordinary levels. There's nothing fussy about the place, or the prices, but every single ingredient is carefully sourced and expertly prepared. You can taste it from the very first bite. See p. 82.

o **Mercato Centrale, Florence:** Not simply a restaurant … more the food hall of your dreams, with a constant buzz from noon until nighttime. Pick and choose from multiple street food vendors preparing the best modern Italian soul food; wash it down with fine wine from a well-stocked enoteca. Downstairs is a Tuscan ingredient emporium—much of which can be vacuum-sealed for taking home. See p. 239.

o **Florence's Vegetarian Dining Scene:** The days when you had to be a carnivore to fully enjoy a meal in the Renaissance city are long gone. **iO** (p. 201) reinvents Tuscan flavors in a contemporary, inclusive style. Vegans, as well as anyone gluten intolerant, are looked after by an inventive menu at **Brac** (p. 200).

o **Cicchetti & a Spritz in Venice:** *Cicchetti*—tapas-like small plates, usually eaten while standing at a bar—are a local tradition. To complete the Venetian experience, accompany them with a spritz made from Aperol and sparkling prosecco wine from the Veneto hills, at **Osteria Al Squero** (p. 298) or **Bacareto Da Lele** (p. 300).

o **Osteria dell'Enoteca, Florence:** When successful wine-bar owners open a restaurant, you know the *vino* will be first rate. Osteria dell'Enoteca's food unites traditional Tuscan ingredients with light, contemporary cooking. Their stone-and-slate dining room is atmospheric enough for any special occasion. See p. 203.

Cicchetti, Venetian-style small plates, pair well with sparkling wine.

o **A Tasty Tasting Trail Around Siena:** The shell-shaped Piazza del Campo is the heart of this preserved Gothic city. A **Taste Siena** walk shows you the sights via five different encounters with Sienese gastronomy—from sweet treats and artisanal cheese to hand-rolled *pici* pasta and, of course, wine. See p. 253.

o **The Humble Artichoke, Rome:** One of the joys of visiting in winter and early spring? Artichoke season. This edible thistle flower is great as a pizza topping; in traditional dishes like *carciofi alla romana* or *alla guidia*; or carpaccio style, with just a splash of oil, a grind of pepper, and some shavings of hard cheese.

o **Wistèria, Venice:** Part of a new wave of contemporary restaurants opening in Venice, this place features innovative riffs on traditional *cicchetti* and seafood from the lagoon and farther out in the Adriatic. See p. 298.

MOST memorable HOTELS

o **Villa Spalletti Trivelli, Rome:** Recent upgrades have only enhanced the unique experience of staying in an Italian noble mansion in the middle of

Be an Italian noble for a night at Villa Spalletti Trivelli.

the capital. Opulence and impeccable service come at a price, of course. When we win the lottery, we'll be booking a stay here. See p. 75.

o **Soggiorno Battistero, Florence:** Room with a view … and then some. You can almost touch Florence's famous old Baptistery from piazza-facing rooms at this simple guesthouse with an enviable address. Off-season rates are very affordable. See p. 186.

o **Hotel Mediterraneo, Rome:** Upscale and Art Deco, Mediterraneo is the flagship of a trio of hotels near Termini Station run by the Bettoja family. Others are more budget-friendly, but all offer vintage charm, old-school comforts, and warm service from a loyal longtime staff. They don't make 'em like this anymore. See p. 77.

o **Metropole, Venice:** The Grand Old Lady of Venetian hospitality, transformed from a medieval building into a luxury hotel in the 19th century, is still a chic choice, filled with antiques and Asian art. See p. 281.

o **Palazzo Tolomei, Florence:** Raphael once stayed in this palace—and perhaps even gave its owners a painting to make rent. The place is as grand as it sounds, with a Renaissance layout and baroque redecoration from the 1600s that remain gloriously intact. See p. 187.

best **FOR FAMILIES**

o **Climbing Pisa's Wonky Tower:** Are we walking up or down? Pleasantly disoriented kids are bound to ask, as you spiral your way to the rooftop viewing balcony atop the world's most famous work of botched engineering. Pisa is an easy day trip from Florence. The minimum age for heading up its *Torre Pendente,* or Leaning Tower, is eight. See p. 255.

o **Boat Tripping on the Venice Lagoon:** Who doesn't like a day boating on a placid lagoon? Throw in the floating city and its bell tower of San Marco on the horizon, and you have one unforgettable family moment. See p. 272.

o **Rooting for Fiorentina at Soccer:** Forget lions battling gladiators in Rome's Colosseum, or Guelphs fighting Ghibellines in dark medieval lanes. For a modern showdown, hit a Florence soccer game. Home team Fiorentina plays Serie A matches at the city's Stadio Comunale on alternate weekends from September to June. Wear something lilac—the team's nickname is *i viola* ("the purples"). See p. 246.

o **Visiting Rome's Centrale Montemartini:** Industrial-meets-ancient marble in this unique museum, where Greek and Roman statues are on display in the restored rooms of Rome's first public electricity plant. The museum always has drawing materials onsite; guided tours for children are often available. See p. 144.

o **Taste-Testing Every Artisanal Gelateria:** When it comes to Italian ice cream, choose carefully. Smurf-blue or bubblegum-pink flavors are eye-catching for kids but are a sure sign of color enhancers; ice crystals and fluffy heaps betray additives and pumped-in air. Artisanal *gelaterie* make good stuff from scratch daily, with fresh seasonal produce: Look for a short,

In a city of bridges, the Ponte di Rialto is the most famous in Venice.

"Sphere Within Sphere" bronze sculpture by Italian sculptor Arnaldo Pomodoro in the Courtyard of the Pigna at the Vatican Museums.

all-natural ingredient list posted proudly for all to see. Believe us, you'll taste the difference. See "Gelato," p. 84, 203, and 302.

best MUSEUMS

o **Vatican Museums, Rome:** Papal treasures accumulated throughout the centuries pack the 100 galleries of the Musei Vaticani. Musts include the Sistine Chapel, such ancient Greek and Roman sculptures as "Laocoön" and "Belvedere Apollo," and room upon room of Raphael frescoes, including his masterful "School of Athens." See p. 106.

o **Galleria degli Uffizi, Florence:** This U-shaped High Renaissance building designed by Giorgio Vasari was the administrative headquarters, or *uffizi* (offices), for the Medici dukes of Tuscany. It's now the crown jewel of European art museums, housing the world's greatest collection of Renaissance paintings, including icons by Botticelli, Leonardo da Vinci, and Michelangelo. See p. 212.

o **Accademia, Venice:** The "Academy" houses an unequalled array of Venetian paintings, exhibited chronologically from the 13th to the 18th century. Walls are hung with works by Bellini, Carpaccio, Giorgione, Titian, and Tintoretto. See p. 317.

The Galleria degli Uffizi at night.

o **Galleria Borghese, Rome:** The frescoes and decor of a 1613 palace in the heart of the Villa Borghese are merely a backdrop for collections that include baroque sculpture by a young Bernini and Canova, plus paintings by Caravaggio and Raphael. See p. 136.

o **Santa Maria della Scala, Siena:** The building is as much the star as its artworks—frescoed wards, ancient chapels, a sacristy, and a labyrinthine basement in a medieval hospital that was treating patients until the 1990s. See p. 253.

o **Museo dell'Opera del Duomo, Florence:** With icons of sculpture in marble and bronze, modern multimedia curation, and a creative layout, this collection is the homage that two Florentine greats—Ghiberti and Brunelleschi—fully deserve. See p. 211.

best FREE THINGS TO DO

o **Watching Sunrise at the Roman Forum:** A short stroll from the Capitoline Hill down Via del Campidoglio to Via di Monte Tarpeo rewards you with a perfect outlook: a terrace behind this Michelangelo-designed square, an ideal photo op when the sun rises behind the Temple of Saturn, illuminating this archaeological complex in pink-orange light. Complete your ideal early start with breakfast in the nearby Jewish Ghetto, today a neighborhood of restaurants and bakeries. See p. 156.

o **Gazing in Wonder at Caravaggio's Greatest Paintings:** Rome's French church, San Luigi dei Francesi, is home to three panels by bad boy of baroque art, Michelangelo Merisi da Caravaggio. His "Calling of St. Matthew," painted at the height of his powers, incorporates uncompromising realism and trademark *chiaroscuro* (extremes of light and dark). See p. 126.

o **Basking in the Lights of the Renaissance:** At dusk, make the steep climb to the ancient church of San Miniato al Monte, Florence. Sit down on the steps and watch the city begin to twinkle. See p. 234.

o **Discovering You're Hopelessly Lost:** You haven't experienced Venice until you have turned a corner,

The Pantheon, Rome: the only ancient Roman building that remains intact.

convinced you're on the way to somewhere, only to find yourself smack against a canal with no bridge, or in a little courtyard with no way out. All

Venice's Canareggio neighborhood.

Aperitivo time in Rome.

you can do is shrug, smile, and give the city's maze of narrow streets another try. Because getting lost in Venice is a pleasure. See p. 262.

undiscovered ITALY

- **San Frediano, Florence:** Most Florentines have abandoned their *centro storico* to the visitors. But the Arno's Left Bank in San Frediano has plenty of local action after dark: Dine at **iO** (p. 201), slurp a gelato by the river at **La Carraia** (p. 204), and then sip fine wines until late at **Il Santino** (p. 244) or catch some offbeat live music at **Libreria-Café La Cité** (p. 242).

- **Cannaregio, Venice:** This residential neighborhood has silent canals, elegantly faded mansions, hidden churches graced by Tiepolo paintings, and the old Ghetto Nuovo, a historic area of Jewish bakeries, restaurants, and synagogues. It's a great escape from the chaos around San Marco. See chapter 9.

- **Byzantine Mosaics Up-close (Really Close), Florence:** Unless you plan on living for another century or two, you will never again have the chance to see the 10 million mosaics of the Florence Baptistery ceiling from just a few inches away. While a major restoration is underway, small groups can ascend the scaffolding for this closer look. Book now. See p. 208.

- **The View from T Fondaco dei Tedeschi:** This Venice department store—renovated by stellar architect Rem Koolhas—was once an elegant *palazzo* beside the Grand Canal. Views from its free rooftop deck are even more spectacular than the opulence inside. See p. 314.
- **A Secret Insight into Brunelleschi's Genius, Florence:** Tucked away at the top of Florence's **Spedale degli Innocenti** is a window with a cutaway view into a Brunelleschi-designed chapel. From this angle, you can check every ceiling strut, joint, and Renaissance nail holding it up. It's fascinating. See p. 230.

SUGGESTED ITINERARIES

By Donald Strachan

2

taly is so vast and treasure-filled, it's hard to resist the temptation to pack too much into your limited time. This is a dauntingly diverse destination, and you can't even skim the surface in 1 or 2 weeks. Relax; don't try. If you're a first-time visitor with limited time, the classic trio of Rome, Florence, and Venice can be packed into one very busy week, better yet in two.

How can you accomplish that? Well, in addition to having one of Europe's better networks of highways (called *autostrade*), Italy has an efficient high-speed rail network. If you're city-hopping, you need never rent a car. Rome is a key hub of this 21st-century transportation empire; with a train from Rome's Termini station, Florence is only 90 minutes away. Comfortable, fast trains serve key routes (including the Venice–Florence–Rome line). You only require a rental car for rural detours. Of course, some people may prefer to travel in their own vehicle than a train car; see p. 356 for rental tips and individual chapters for parking advice. (Spoiler alert: In cities, parking can be a nightmare.)

The following itineraries take you to some of our favorite places. Note that during the pandemic, museums often restricted visitor numbers with compulsory prebooking, and many of these measures remain in place. Reserve ahead and organize the rest of your days around any personal must-sees.

Occasionally, the pace of some of our itineraries may be a bit breathless, so skip a stop occasionally and enjoy chill-out time—after all, you're on vacation. You can use any of the following itineraries as a jumping-off point to develop your own adventure.

ROME, FLORENCE & VENICE IN 1 WEEK

Let's be realistic: It's impossible to really understand Italy's three iconic cities fully in a week. However, a fast, efficient, center-to-center rail network along the Rome–Florence–Venice line means it's surprisingly easy to see much of the best they offer. This week-long itinerary weaves through the familiar highlights, but there's a

Days 1–3 Rome
Days 4–5 Florence
Days 6–7 Venice

reason why these are Italy's most-visited sites: They're sure to provide memories that will last a lifetime.

Days 1, 2 & 3: Rome: The Eternal City ★★★

You could spend a month touring Italy's capital, but 3 days is enough to get the flavor. There are two essential areas to focus on. The first is the legacy of Imperial Rome, including the **Forum, Campidoglio,** and **Colosseum** (p. 109). Bookend your day with the Forum and Colosseum (one first, the other last) to avoid the busiest crowds. On **Day 2,** tackle **St. Peter's Basilica** (p. 100) and the **Vatican Museums** (p. 106), a collection unlike any other in the world (including Michelangelo's **Sistine**

This classic view of Florence is seen from Piazzale Michaelangelo

Chapel). On **Day 3,** it's a toss-up: Choose between visiting the underground catacombs of the **Via Appia Antica** (p. 146) or the well-trod streets of the **Centro Storico** (p. 72) and **Tridente** (p. 131), where you can wander (and shop) from Piazza Navona to the Pantheon, the Spanish Steps, and the Trevi Fountain. Spend your evenings in the bars of **Campo de' Fiori** or **Monti** (p. 157) and the restaurants of **Trastevere** (p. 91) or

Today, (practically) all trains in Italy lead to Rome's Termini Station.

Testaccio (p. 95). Toward the end of Day 3, catch a late train to Florence. Be sure to buy tickets in advance: On the high-speed network, walk-up fares are much more expensive than prebooked tickets.

Days 4 & 5: Florence: Cradle of the Renaissance ★★★

You have 2 whole days to explore the city of Giotto, Leonardo da Vinci, Botticelli, and Michelangelo. Start with their masterpieces at the **Uffizi** (p. 212; prebook tickets, weeks or even months ahead if possible), then explore the **Duomo** complex (p. 209): Scale Brunelleschi's dome (again, reservations are essential) and follow up with a visit to the adjoining **Battistero di San Giovanni,** the **Museo dell'Opera del Duomo,** and the **Campanile di Giotto.** Start the next day with "David" at the **Accademia** (p. 227; another essential advance booking). Spend the rest of your day getting to know the intimate wall paintings of **San Marco** (p. 228), paintings hanging at the **Palazzo Pitti** (p. 232), and Masaccio's revolutionary frescoes in the **Cappella Brancacci** (p. 235). In the evenings, head south of the Arno, to **San Frediano** or **San Niccolò,** for lively wine bars and better restaurants than you generally find in the historic center (p. 242).

Days 6 & 7: Venice: City That Defies the Sea ★★★

Head to Venice on an early morning train. You'll ride into the heart of the city on a *vaporetto* (water bus), taking the **Grand Canal,** the world's greatest main street. Begin your sightseeing at **Piazza San Marco**

Rome's Flavian Amphitheater, better known as the Colosseum.

(p. 314): The **Basilica di San Marco** is right there, and after exploring it, visit the nearby **Palazzo Ducale** (**Doge's Palace;** p. 309) before walking over the **Bridge of Sighs.** Begin your evening with the classic Venetian *aperitivo*, an Aperol spritz (Aperol with sparkling prosecco wine and soda), followed by *cicchetti* (Venetian tapas) before a late dinner. Make your second day all about the city's art—the **Gallerie dell'Accademia** (p. 317), the modern **Peggy Guggenheim Collection** (p. 318), and **San Rocco** (p. 324). Catch the latest train you can back to Rome. Or add another night—you can never stay too long in Venice.

The Bridge of Sighs, Doge's Palace, Venice.

A 2-WEEK ITINERARY

It's still difficult to see the top sights of Italy—and see them properly—in 2 weeks. But in this itinerary, we show you many of the best. We add significant detours from the Rome–Florence–Venice trail, heading south to Pompeii, Europe's most complete Roman ruins, and north to Pisa (for the Leaning Tower and more); and make day trips to Padua (for Giotto art) and Verona (city of lovers since Romeo met Juliet).

Days 1, 2 & 3: Rome ★★★

Follow the Rome itinerary suggested in "Italy in 1 Week," above. Rome will be your base for 5 nights (days 4 and 5 will be day trips from Rome); for this longer stay, consider an apartment rental rather than a hotel room in the capital (see "Self-Catering Apartments," p. 66).

Day 4: Pompeii: A Day Trip to Europe's Best-Preserved Roman Ruins ★★

Early on **Day 4,** take the high-speed Frecciarossa or Italo train from Rome to Naples (1½ hr.), then a Circumvesuviana train 24km (15 miles) southeast of Naples to wander the archaeological remains at **Pompeii** (p. 160). Pack water and a lunch if you can—on-site services aren't great. Buried for almost 2,000 years, after nearby Vesuvius erupted in A.D. 79, Pompeii exhibits some of the great archaeological treasures of Italy, including the patrician **Casa dei Vettii** and the frescoed **Villa dei**

L. Maggiore   L. Como

Aosta   Como

Milan   L. Garda

Turin   Piacenza

Trento   Udine

Verona   ⑭ ⑬ **Venice** ⑪⑫

Padua

Trieste

Gulf of Venice   Pula

Parma

Genoa   Modena

La Spezia   Bologna

Ligurian Sea   Pisa ⑩   **Florence** ⑥⑦   SAN MARINO

Rimini

FRANCE **MONACO**   Livorno ⑨   San Gimignano ⑧ Siena

Ancona

Capraia

Perugia

Ascoli Piceno

Elba

Bastia   Grosseto   Giglio

CORSICA (FRANCE)   Montecristo   Viterbo

Ajaccio

L'Aquila

Pescara

BOSNIA & HERZEGOVINA

CROATIA   Split   Mostar

Dubrovnik

Adriatic Sea

Tivoli

Rome ★ ① ② ③ ⑤

Latina

Campobasso   Foggia   Barletta   Bari

Sassari   Olbia   Ponza   **Naples** *Mt. Vesuvius* ▲ ■ **Pompeii** ④

Brindisi

Taranto

Amalfi Coast

SARDINIA

Oristano

Tyrrhenian Sea

Gulf of Taranto

Cosenza

Catanzaro

Ustica   *AEOLIAN ISLANDS*   Stromboli

Lipari

Trapani   **Palermo**   Messina   Reggio di Calabria

EGADI ISLANDS   *Mt. Etna* ▲

Strait of Sicily   SICILY   Catania

Agrigento

Gela

Ragusa

Siracusa

Ionian Sea

TUNISIA

0   100 mi

0   100 km

Misteri. You'll return to Rome at night. *Tip:* This is a very long day; it may be easier to do as an escorted visit by bus from Rome, especially with kids or mobility-impaired travel companions. Several operators offer Pompeii tours; ask at your hotel or at one of Rome's tourist information points (see "Visitor Information," p. 56). Doing it by rental car is another option, but only for those confident behind the wheel. Driving in and around both Rome and Naples can be hair-raising.

Day 5: Tivoli: A Day Trip to Rome's Imperial Villa ★★

Take your foot off the gas with a more relaxed day trip, 32km (20 miles) northeast of Rome to **Tivoli** (p. 168). Emperor Hadrian's serene rural retreat here, the **Villa Adriana** (p. 168), is the grandest retirement residence you'll ever see, complete with theaters, baths, fountains, and gardens. This emperor had a fine eye for design.

Days 6 & 7: Florence ★★★

Take an early train to Florence, where you will spend the next 5 nights. Follow the 2-day itinerary in "Rome, Florence & Venice in 1 Week," p. 15 and then use Florence as a base for exploring Siena, San Gimignano, and Pisa. We suggest using public transportation for day trips out of Florence. But all three towns are easily reached by rental car, too, if you prefer your own wheels. See p. 176 for parking tips in Florence; discuss options with your accommodation provider.

Michelangelo's "David" in the Accademia, Florence.

The roads of central Tuscany are pretty at any time of year, and there's well-signposted parking just outside the historic core in all three recommended day-trip destinations.

Day 8: A Day Trip to Gothic Siena ★★★

It's just over an hour to **Siena** (p. 250) on the *rapida* bus from Florence. On arrival, set out immediately for **Piazza del Campo,** the shell-shaped main square, including its art-filled **Museo Civico** (inside the **Palazzo Pubblico**). You still have time to squeeze in a look at the **Duomo** and **Museo dell'Opera Metropolitana,** where you'll find Sienese master Duccio's giant "Maestà" painting. Stop on the Campo for a late-afternoon drink and then grab an early dinner at a restaurant in Siena's atmospheric back streets. The last bus back to Florence departs at 8:45pm, arriving back in Florence at 10pm. (**Note:** On weekends, the last bus is usually 7:10pm, so you may want to schedule dinner in Florence.)

Day 9: San Gimignano: A Town Stuck in the 1300s ★★

It's another day on buses, but well worth it to see one of the best-preserved medieval towns in Europe. You change buses in Poggibonsi for the last, outrageously pretty leg through vine-clad hills to **San Gimignano** (p. 257). In its medieval heyday, the "city of beautiful towers" had more than 70 turrets reaching for the sky above its tiny, crowded plot. Now just a handful remain, including the **Torre Grossa** (which you can climb). The frescoed **Collegiata** is the essential art stop. You can dine early at **Chiribiri** (it's open all day) and then leave on the late bus (usually 8:30pm).

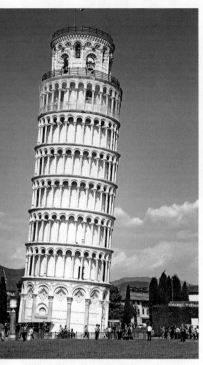
The Leaning Tower of Pisa.

Day 10: Pisa & Its Leaning Tower ★★

A fast train from Florence takes only 1 hour to Pisa, whose set-piece piazza is some of the most photographed real estate on the planet. Pisa's **Campo dei Miracoli** ("Field of Miracles") is home to the **Leaning Tower** (p. 254) of course; book a slot ahead of time if you want to climb it. A combination ticket admits you to the rest of the piazza's sights, including the **Duomo,** behind an Arab-influenced Pisan-Romanesque facade, and the **Battistero,** with a carved pulpit and crazy acoustics. Head away from the piazza for dining *alla pisana*—the "real Pisa" lies in the warren of streets around the market square, **Piazza delle Vettovaglie.** Finish your visit with a stroll on the handsome promenade beside the **River Arno.** Take a late train back to Florence (the last fast service departs at 9:30pm).

Days 11 & 12: Venice ★★★

Set out early the next morning for Venice, where you'll spend the next 4 nights. For the first 2 days, follow the itinerary suggested in "Rome, Florence & Venice in 1 Week," p. 15.

Day 13: Padua & Its Giotto Frescoes ★

Only 40km (25 miles) west of Venice, **Padua** (p. 342) is a relaxed day trip by train. Visit the **Basilica di Sant'Antonio** (p. 344) to see Donatello bronzes and the **Cappella degli Scrovegni** (p. 343) for Giotto frescoes—perhaps the most important paintings in all pre-Renaissance Italian art. Return to Venice for the night.

Day 14: Verona: City of Lovers & Gladiators ★★★

Although he likely never set foot in the place, Shakespeare set his epic love story, "Romeo and Juliet," in Verona. Wander **Piazza dei Signori** and **Piazza delle Erbe** before descending on the **Arena di Verona** (p. 347), the world's best-preserved gladiatorial arena: It's still packed out for monumental opera performances on summer evenings. Aim to

The Roman arch bridge Ponte Pietra crosses the Adige River in Verona.

catch a Regionale Veloce train: It costs the same (under 10€) as a Regionale service, but takes just 1½ hours compared with more than 2 hours for the slower train.

ROME, FLORENCE & VENICE FOR FAMILIES

Italy is probably the friendliest family vacation destination in Europe. Logistically, it presents few challenges. If you're traveling by rental car with young children, request car seats ahead of time, so the rental company can arrange for a seat that complies with EU regulations. Reduced-price family fares are available on much of the high-speed rail network; ask when you buy your tickets. You won't need to hunt for "child-friendly" restaurants or special kids' menus: There is always plenty available for little ones, even dishes not on the grownup menu. If you have a fussy eater, never be afraid to ask; pretty much any request is met with a smile.

A few **tips** from parents who've been here: Space out your museum visits so you get a chance to see the masterpieces, but your youngsters don't suffer a meltdown from too many paintings of saints. You **often must book** major museum targets ahead of arrival; leave plenty of time between them if you are traveling with young children. And punctuate every day with a **gelato** stop—Italy makes the world's best ice cream (you'll easily find soy-milk options for the lactose intolerant). It's a good idea to limit long, tiring day trips out of town, especially by public transportation. End your trip in Venice, which for many kids is every bit as magical as a Disney theme park: It's a city. That floats. (Kinda.)

Days 1–3 Rome
Days 4–5 Florence
Day 6 Pisa
Day 7 Siena
Days 8–10 Venice

Day 1: Rome's Ancient Ruins ★★★

History is on your side here: The wonders of **Ancient Rome** (p. 109) should appeal as much to kids as to adults. There are gory tales to tell at the **Colosseum** (p. 113), where the bookshop also has city guides aimed at kids. (And a new ticketing system has reduced wait times.) After that, little ones can let off steam wandering the **Roman Forum** and **Palatine Hill.** (The roadside ruins of the **Imperial Forums** can be viewed at any time.) Cap the afternoon by exploring the **Villa Borghese** (p. 136), a monumental park in the heart of the city; rent bikes or visit the small zoo in the park's northeast section. For dinner, tuck into crispy crusts at an authentic Roman **pizzeria,** such as **Li Rioni** (p. 84).

Day 2: Rome After the Romans ★★★

Head early to **St. Peter's Basilica** (p. 100) before long lines form. Kids will find it spooky wandering the Vatican grottoes and relish the opportunity to climb up to Michelangelo's dome. After lunch, begin your assault on the **Vatican Museums** (p. 103) and the **Sistine Chapel** (be sure to book tickets way in advance). Even if your kids don't like art museums, they will gawp at the grandeur. Later in the day, head for the iconic **Spanish Steps** (p. 132), then wander over to the **Trevi Fountain** (p. 135). Give the kids coins to toss into the fountain, which is said to guarantee their return to Rome—perhaps when they are older and can better appreciate the city's many more artistic attractions.

Day 3: Rome Underground ★★★

Layers of history survive below the city streets. Kids will love exploring the catacombs of the **Via Appia Antica** (p. 146), the first cemetery of Rome's Christian community, where the devout secretly practiced their faith during periods of persecution. After descending through the layers—and centuries—under **San Clemente** (p. 120), eat more **pizza** before you leave; Rome's pizzerias are bested only by those in Naples, to the south…and our next recommended stops all lie north. *Note:* Rome's cramped underground sites closed completely through the pandemic. It is possible—although unlikely—that restrictions return at short notice.

Overlooking the rooftops of Rome.

Giardino di Boboli.

Day 4: Florence: City of the Renaissance ★★★

Take the early train to Florence. Although it's usually thought of as more of an adult city, there's enough here to fill 2 family days, plus a couple of day trips. (With day trips, you'll be staying 4 nights in Florence: Consider taking an apartment rather than a hotel room, so you have space to spread out; see p. 182.) Begin with the city's monumental main square, **Piazza della Signoria,** an open-air museum of statues with the **Palazzo Vecchio** (p. 218) towering over one side; you can tour the palace on special child-friendly itineraries. Turn your afternoon visit to the **Uffizi** (p. 212; must be prebooked) into a treasure hunt by first researching its key artworks on the revamped museum website.

Day 5: Florence: Cameras at the Ready! ★★★

On the second morning, kids will delight in climbing up Brunelleschi's dome on the **Duomo** (p. 209) for a classic panorama. Book an early slot, when the temperature is cooler. If they still have energy to burn, climb the 414 steps up to the **Campanile di Giotto** (p. 208), run around in the **Giardino di Boboli** (p. 232), eat some of Italy's best gelato (p. 203), and take the bus to **Piazzale Michelangiolo** (p. 234) at dusk. Finish with a *bistecca alla fiorentina,* a huge hunk of flame-grilled beef on the bone which is a Florence specialty. A *fiorentina* is made for sharing: A big one and a couple of sides will fill the family.

Day 6: Pisa & Its Leaning Tower ★★

With children seven or under, you may want to skip **Pisa** (p. 254): Eight is the minimum age for a disorienting ascent up the bell tower of Pisa's cathedral, more commonly known as the **Leaning Tower.** Older kids will appreciate the hyperreal monuments of the **Campo dei Miracoli** and learning about the city's Galileo links: He was born here, and supposedly discovered his law of pendulum motion while watching a swinging lamp inside the **Duomo.** Before returning to Florence, sample a Pisan specialty, *cecina*—a pizzalike flatbread made of garbanzo-bean flour—at **Il Montino** (p. 257). Rail connections between Florence and Pisa are frequent, fast (50–90 min.), and affordable (around 9€ each way).

Day 7: Gothic Siena ★★★

Count yourself lucky if you can visit **Siena** (p. 250) around July 2 or August 16 for the famous 4-day **Palio** celebrations, when horses race around **Piazza del Campo.** Year-round, however, a couple of epic climbs will thrill the kids. The **Torre del Mangia**—the bell tower of the **Palazzo Pubblico**—yields a dramatic view of the city and countryside. Through the **Museo dell'Opera Metropolitana,** they can scale the "Facciatone" for a dizzying view down into the Campo. At **Santa Maria della Scala,** they will find **Bambimus,** the art museum for kids, where paintings hang at child-friendly heights. The zebra-striped **Duomo** is jazzy enough to pique their curiosity, and Siena's bakeries are famous for their sweet treats. Ride the bus back to Florence after an early dinner. (***Note:*** Bus service is reduced on Sundays.)

A dramatic view over Siena and the Tuscan countryside.

Yes, you can rent a kayak to explore Venice from the water.

Days 8, 9 & 10: Venice, City on the Lagoon ★★★

Leave Florence early for Venice, the most kid-pleasing city in Italy. The fun begins the moment you arrive and take a *vaporetto* ride along the **Grand Canal.** Head straight for **Piazza San Marco** (p. 305) and an elevator ride up the **Campanile.** Catch the sparkly mosaics inside the **Basilica di San Marco;** at the **Palazzo Ducale,** walk over the infamous **Bridge of Sighs** after checking out the pint-size knights' armor. Make time for art: Visit the **Gallerie dell'Accademia** (p. 317) and **San Rocco** (p. 324), where kids can "read" the Tintoretto paintings like a comic book. For a modern break, the **Peggy Guggenheim Collection** (p. 318) has pop art, an open courtyard, and a rooftop cafe. In summer, save time for the beach at the **Lido** (p. 331). And yes, splurge on a storybook view of Venice's canals from the seat of a **gondola** (p. 272) or ride the waters DIY-style with a **kayak rental** (p. 332).

ITALY IN CONTEXT

By Donald Strachan

Many of the stereotypes you have heard about this charming country are accurate. Children are fussed over wherever they go; food and soccer are practically religions onto themselves; the north–south divide is alive and well; and (alas) bureaucracy is a frustrating feature of daily life for many families and businesses. Some stereotypes, however, are wide of the mark: Not every Italian you meet will be open and effusive. Just occasionally, they do taciturn pretty well, too.

One important fact to remember is that, for a land so steeped in human history—three millennia and counting—Italy has only a short history *as a country*. In 2021 Italy celebrated its 160th birthday. Prior to 1861, the map of this boot-shaped peninsula was in constant flux. War, alliance, invasion, and disputed successions caused the political map to change color as often as a chameleon in a candy store. Republics, mini-monarchies, client states, Papal states, and city-states, as well as Islamic emirates, colonies, dukedoms, kingdoms, and Christian theocracies, roll on and off the pages of Italian history with regularity. In many places, you'll hear languages and dialects other than Italian. As a result, identity is often more regional than national.

This confusing history explains why your Italian experience will differ wildly if you visit, say, Rome rather than Venice. (And why you should visit both, if you can.) The architecture is different; the food is different; the legends and historical figures are different, as are many local issues of the day. And the people are different: While the north–south schism is most often written about, cities as close as Florence and Siena can feel dissimilar. This chapter tries to help you understand why.

ITALY TODAY

Daily life in 2020 in hill-towns, olive groves, wine cellars, and medieval city streets was profoundly impacted by the novel

The Vittorio Emanuele Monument in Rome.

coronavirus (SARS-CoV-2) and the disease it causes, Covid-19. Italians are a friendly, tactile people; the virus hit at the heart of their social and sociable culture. Italy also has one of the world's oldest populations: Italy's elderly population was hit especially hard.

And yet the Italian people fought back. The government deployed on/off national and local lockdowns, mask mandates bolstered by stiff fines, strict enforcement of social distancing in shops and businesses, quarantines, and a national test-and-trace regime. Virus peaks in 2021 and 2022 grew progressively smaller, while vaccine rollout kept pace with European neighbors—driven both by altruism and by a growing realization that the return of treasured rituals like eating indoors, *aperitivo* hour, social events, inbound and outbound travel, even entering museums, depended on it.

The post-Covid bounce-back has been marked and rapid. Walking around the streets of Florence or Rome today, you could forget the pandemic ever happened. Bars and restaurants are full; hotels have enjoyed a booking boom that shows no sign of relenting. Cafe chatter has returned to favored topics like football—the plight of the local team, or how the Azzurri national team somehow won football's 2021 European Championship and then failed even to qualify for the 2022 World Cup.

Yet pandemic aftershocks are still visible—in politics, especially. The coronavirus caused repeated government crises, which culminated in the 2022 collapse of a unity government. The election that followed was a triumph for the Fratelli d'Italia (FdI), a socially conservative, anti-immigrant political party. FdI's controversial leader, Giorgia Meloni, became Italy's first female prime minister, at the head of an occasionally fractious right-wing coalition. Early government moves have been a mixed bag, from a clampdown on

Soccer (football or calcio) is Italy's national sport.

protest, to renewed emphasis on Italy's commitment to fighting climate change, and a close alliance with the United States regarding Ukraine.

The country's main challenges, as ever, remain economic. In a difficult international climate, the outlook for Italy appears moderately optimistic. Italy has taken the first steps on a bumpy road to recovery—and bouncing back is critical for an economy that needs to draw visitors from around the world.

THE MAKING OF ITALY
Etruscans & Villanovans: Prehistory to the Rise of Rome

Among Italy's earliest inhabitants, the **Etruscans** left the most significant legacy. No one knows exactly where they came from (although some evidence points to origins in what is now Turkey) and inscriptions they left behind—often on tombs in necropolises—are too bland to be of much help. Whatever their origins, within 2 centuries of appearing on the peninsula around 800 B.C., they had subjugated lands in modern **Tuscany** (to which they leave their name), northern Lazio, and Campania, along with the so-called **"Villanovan"** tribes that lived there. They also made Rome the governmental seat of Latium.

THE ESSENTIALS OF italian FOOD

Italians know how to cook—just ask one. But be sure to leave plenty of time: Once Italians start talking food, they don't pause for breath. Italy does not really have a unified national cuisine; it's a loose grouping of delicious regional cuisines that share a few staples, notably pasta, bread, tomatoes, and pork cured in endlessly creative ways.

Rome can be the best place to introduce yourself to Italian food, because it has restaurants from every region. Rome also has its own specialties, such as *saltimbocca alla romana* (literally "jump-in-your-mouth"—thin slices of veal with sage, cured ham, and cheese), *carciofi alla romana* (tender Romanesco artichokes cooked with herbs), and the ubiquitous *carbonara*—pasta coated in a silky sauce of cured pork cheek, egg, and *pecorino Romano* (sheep's milk cheese). Historical migration has also infused Roman food with a strong current of Jewish cuisine.

To the north, in **Florence and Tuscany,** you'll find seasonal ingredients served simply. One main ingredient for almost any savory dish is the local olive oil, feted for its low acidity. The typical Tuscan pasta is wide, flat *pappardelle*, generally tossed with a game sauce such as *lepre* (hare) or *cinghiale* (boar). Tuscans are fond of their own local pecorino, a strong ewe's-milk cheese made in Pienza. The classic main course is a *bistecca alla fiorentina*, a T-bone–like slab of meat from the white Chianina breed of cattle. Sweet treats are also good here, particularly Siena's *panforte* (a dense, sticky cake) and *biscotti di Prato* (hard, almond-flour biscuits for dipping in dessert wine).

While **Venice** is rarely celebrated for its cuisine, the fresh seafood is excellent. Grilled fish is often served with red radicchio, a bitter lettuce that thrives around nearby Treviso. Two classic Venetian non-fish dishes are *fegato alla veneziana* (liver and onions) and *risi e bisi* (rice and fresh peas). The traditional carbohydrate here isn't pasta but *risotto* (rice), enhanced with seasonal vegetables or seafood.

Alfresco dining above the canals in Venice.

"Roma" is an Etruscan name, and the mythical ancient kings of Rome also had Etruscan names: Numa, Ancus, even Romulus.

The Etruscans ruled until the **Roman Revolt** around 509 B.C., which expelled Rome's Etruscan kings. By 250 B.C. Romans and their allies had vanquished or assimilated the Etruscans, wiping out their language and religion. Many of their manners and beliefs remained, however, and are integral to what we now think of as "Roman culture."

Rome's **Museo Nazionale Etrusco** (p. 137) and the Etruscan collection in Rome's **Vatican Museums** (p. 103) are a logical starting point to see

The Arezzo Chimera, star attraction of Florence's archaeological museum.

remnants of Etruscan civilization. Florence's **MAF Museo Archeologico** (p. 228) houses one of the greatest Etruscan bronzes yet unearthed, the "Arezzo Chimera."

The Roman Republic: ca. 509–27 B.C.

After the Roman Republic was established around 509 B.C.—it's impossible to date precisely—the Romans continued to increase their power by conquering neighboring communities in the highlands and forming alliances with other Latins in the lowlands. They gave to their allies and then to conquered peoples, partial or complete Roman citizenship, with a corresponding obligation of military service. This further increased Rome's power and reach. Citizen colonies were established as settlements of Roman farmers or veterans, among them both **Florence** and **Siena.** The all-powerful Senate presided as Rome defeated rival powers one after another and came to rule the Mediterranean Sea.

No figure was more towering during the late Republic, nor more instrumental in its transformation into Empire (see below), than **Julius Caesar,** the charismatic conqueror of Gaul—"the wife of every husband and the husband of every wife," according to scurrilous rumors reported by 1st-century historian Suetonius. After defeating the last resistance of the Pompeiians in 45 B.C., he came to Rome and was made dictator and consul for 10 years. Conspirators, led by Brutus, stabbed him to death at the Theater of Pompey on March 15, 44 B.C., the "Ides of March." The site (now **Largo di Torre Argentina**) is an Instagrammers' hotspot these days, but not for the history: It's home to a photogenic feral cat colony.

The conspirators' motivation was to restore power to the Republic and topple dictatorship. But they failed: **Mark Antony,** a Roman general, assumed control. He made peace with Caesar's willed successor, **Octavian,** and after the Treaty of Brundisium dissolved the Republic, he found himself married to Octavian's sister, Octavia. This didn't prevent him from also marrying Egyptian queen Cleopatra in 36 B.C. A furious Octavian gathered legions and defeated Antony at the **Battle of Actium** on September 2, 31 B.C. Cleopatra fled to Egypt, followed by Antony, who committed suicide in disgrace a year later. Cleopatra, unable to retain her rule of Egypt, followed suit with the help of an asp (or so legend has it).

Many of the standing buildings of Ancient Rome are from later periods, but parts of the **Roman Forum** (p. 116) date to the Republic, including the **Temple of Saturn.** The adjacent **Capitoline Hill** and **Palatine Hill** have been sacred religious and civic spaces since the earliest days of Rome. Rome's best Republican-era artifacts are inside the **Musei Capitolini** (p. 110).

The bust of Julius Caesar.

The Roman Forum and the Colosseum were once the center of life in Ancient Rome.

The Roman Empire in Its Pomp: 27 B.C.–A.D. 395

Born Gaius Octavius in 63 B.C., then known as Octavian, **Augustus** became the first Roman emperor in 27 B.C. and reigned until A.D. 14. His autocratic rule ushered in the so-called *"Pax Romana,"* 2 centuries of peace. In Rome you can still see the remains of the **Forum of Augustus** (p. 115) and admire his statue in the **Vatican Museums** (p. 103).

By now, Rome ruled the entire Mediterranean world, either directly or indirectly. All political, commercial, and cultural pathways led to Rome, a sprawling city set on seven hills: the Capitoline, Palatine, Aventine, Caelian, Esquiline, Quirinal, and Viminal. It was during this period **Virgil** wrote his epic poem "The Aeneid," supplying a grandiose founding myth for the city and empire; **Ovid** composed erotic poetry; and **Horace** wrote his "Odes."

The emperors brought Rome to new heights. Yet without the counterbalance once provided by the Senate and legislatures, success bred corruption. The centuries witnessed a steady decay in the ideals and traditions on which the Empire was founded. The army became a fifth column of unruly mercenaries; tax collectors became the scourge of the countryside; and for every good emperor (Augustus, Claudius, Trajan, Vespasian, and Hadrian, to name a few) there were also cruel, debased, or simply incompetent tyrants (Caligula, Nero, Caracalla, and many others).

After Augustus died (by poison, perhaps), his widow, **Livia**—a shrewd operator who had divorced her first husband to marry Augustus—used intrigues and poisonings to set up her son, **Tiberius,** as ruler. A series of murders ensued and Tiberius, who ruled during Pontius Pilate's trial and the crucifixion of Christ, was eventually murdered in his late 70s. Murder was so common that a short time later, **Domitian** (ruled A.D. 81–96) became so gripped by the fear of assassination, he ordered his palace walls covered in mica, so he could see what was behind him at all times. (He was killed anyway.)

Excesses ruled the day—at least, if you believe surviving tracts written by biased contemporary chroniclers: **Caligula** supposedly committed incest with his sister Drusilla; appointed his horse to the Senate; and proclaimed himself a god. Caligula's successor, his uncle **Claudius,** was poisoned by his final wife—Agrippina the Younger, who was also his niece—to secure the succession of **Nero,** her son by a previous marriage. Nero's thanks were later to murder not only his mother but also his own wife (Claudius's daughter) and his rival, Claudius's 13-year-old son Britannicus. An enthusiastic persecutor of Christians, Nero supposedly committed suicide with the cry, "What an artist I destroy!"

By the 3rd century A.D., corruption and rivalry became so poisonous there were 23 emperors in 73 years. Few were as twisted as **Caracalla,** who to secure control, had his brother Geta slashed to pieces while Geta was in the arms of their mother, former empress Julia Domna.

10 EARLY ROMAN emperors

Augustus (ruled 27 B.C.–A.D.14): First, "divine" emperor to whom all later emperors aspired

Tiberius (r. A.D. 14–37): Former general whose increasingly unpopular reign was infused with paranoia

Caligula (r. A.D. 37–41): This young emperor's reign of spite and terror ended in assassination by his own Praetorian Guard.

Claudius (r. A.D. 41–54): A sickly man who turned into a wise and capable emperor, as well as the conqueror of Britain

Nero (r. A.D. 54–68): Last emperor of the Julio-Claudian dynasty, a cruel megalomaniac who killed his own mother and may have started the Great Fire of Rome (A.D. 64)

Vespasian (r. A.D. 69–79): First emperor of the Flavian dynasty, who built the Colosseum and lived as husband-and-wife with a freed slave, Caenis

Domitian (r. A.D. 81–96): Increasingly paranoid populist and authoritarian who became fixated on the idea he would be assassinated—and was proven right

Trajan (r. A.D. 98–117): Virtuous soldier-ruler who presided over the empire at its widest geographical spread and also rebuilt much of the city

Hadrian (r. A.D. 117–138): Humanist, general, and builder who redesigned the Pantheon and added the Temple of Venus and Roma to the Forum

Marcus Aurelius (r. A.D. 161–180): Philosopher-king, and last of the so-called Five Good Emperors, whose statue is in the Musei Capitolini

Detail of the Arch of Constantine.

Constantine the Great, who became emperor in A.D. 306, made Constantinople (or Byzantium) the new capital of the Empire in 330, moving administrative functions away from Rome altogether, partly because of the growing menace of barbarian attacks. Constantine was the first Christian emperor, allegedly converting after he saw the True Cross in a dream, accompanied by the words, IN THIS SIGN SHALL YOU CONQUER. He defeated rival emperor Maxentius and his followers at the **Battle of the Milvian Bridge** (A.D. 312), a victory memorialized by Rome's triumphal **Arco di Costantino** (p. 109). Constantine formally ended the persecution of Christians with the **Edict of Milan** (A.D. 313).

During the Imperial period, Rome flourished in architecture. **Classical orders** were simplified into forms of column capitals: **Doric** (a plain capital), **Ionic** (a capital with a scroll), and **Corinthian** (a capital with acanthus leaves). Much of this development was enabled by the invention of concrete and fine-tuning the arch, which was used with a logic, rhythm, and ease never before seen. Many of these monumental buildings still stand in Rome, notably **Trajan's Column** (p. 116), the **Colosseum** (p. 113), and Hadrian's **Pantheon** (p. 127). Elsewhere in Italy, Verona's massive **Arena** (p. 347) bears witness to huge crowds the brutal sport of gladiatorial combat could draw. Three **Roman cities** have been preserved, with street plans and in some cases even buildings intact: doomed **Pompeii** (p. 160) and its neighbor **Herculaneum,** both buried by Vesuvius's cataclysmic A.D. 79 eruption; and Rome's ancient seaport, **Ostia Antica** (p. 165). At Herculaneum, one of Rome's greatest writers, **Pliny the Elder** (A.D. 23–79), perished. It's thanks to him; his nephew, **Pliny the Younger,** and satirist **Juvenal;** and historians **Tacitus, Suetonius, Cassius Dio,** and **Livy** that knowledge of ancient Roman life and history was not lost.

Surviving Roman **art** had a major influence on the painters and sculptors of the Renaissance (p. 40). In Rome itself, look for the marble *bas-reliefs* (sculptures projecting slightly from a flat surface) on the **Arco di Costantino** (p. 109); the sculpture and mosaic collections at the **Palazzo Massimo alle Terme** (p. 140); and the gilded equestrian statue of Marcus Aurelius at the **Musei Capitolini** (p. 110). The Florentine Medici were avid collectors of Roman statuary, much of it now at the **Uffizi** (p. 212).

The Fall of the Empire through the "Dark Ages"

The Eastern and Western sections of the Roman Empire split in A.D. 395, leaving the Italian peninsula without the support it once received from east of the Adriatic. When the **Goths** moved toward Rome in the early 5th century, citizens in the provinces, who had grown to hate the bureaucracy set up by **Diocletian,** welcomed the invaders. And then the pillage began.

Rome was first sacked by **Alaric I,** king of the Visigoths, in 410. The populace made no attempt to defend their city (other than trying vainly to buy him off, a tactic that worked 3 years earlier); most people fled into the hills. The feeble Western emperor **Honorius** hid out in **Ravenna,** which in 402 he declared capital of the Western Roman Empire.

More than 40 troubled years passed. Then **Attila the Hun** invaded Italy to besiege Rome. Attila was dissuaded from attacking, thanks largely to a peace mission headed by Pope Leo I in 452. Yet relief was short-lived: In 455, **Gaiseric,** king of the **Vandals,** sailed from Carthage in North Africa to carry out a 2-week sack of unparalleled thoroughness. The empire of the West limped on for another 20 years; finally, in 476, the sacks and chaos ended the once-mighty city. Rome itself was left to the popes, although still ruled nominally from Ravenna.

Little detailed history of Italy in the immediate post-Roman period is known—and few buildings survive—but the spread of **Christianity** was certainly creating a new society. The religion was probably founded in Rome about a decade after the death of Jesus and gradually gained strength despite Roman persecution. To relive the early Christian era, visit Rome's Appian Way and its Catacombs, along the **Via Appia Antica** (p. 146), just outside Rome's ancient walls. A church on the Appian Way marks the spot where the disciple Peter, fleeing persecution, is said to have received a pivotal vision of Christ; the nearby **Catacombs** (p. 146), the first cemeteries of Rome's Christian community, house remains of early popes and martyrs.

ALL ABOUT VINO (& birra, too)

Italy is the largest **wine**-producing country in the world; as far back as 800 B.C., the Etruscans were vintners. In 2021, Italy produced around as much wine as the United States, Australia, and Chile *combined*. However, it was only in 1965 that laws were enacted to guarantee consistency in Italian winemaking. Quality wines are labeled **"DOC"** (Denominazione di Origine Controllata). If you see **"DOCG"** on a label (the "G" stands for *Garantita*), this denotes an even higher-quality wine region (in theory, at least). **"IGT"** (Indicazione Geografica Tipica) indicates a more general wine zone—for example, Umbria—but still with mandatory quality control.

Below we cite a few of the best Italian wines around Venice, Rome, and Florence. Rest assured there are hundreds more—it can be a joy to discover your own favorites. Even a pitcher of a local *vino della casa* (house wine) can be a delight.

Tuscany: Tuscan red wines rank with the world's finest. **Sangiovese** is the king of grapes here; **Chianti** from the hills south of Florence is the most widely known Sangiovese wine. The premium zone is **Chianti Classico,** where a lively ruby-red DOCG wine has a bouquet of violets. More concentrated and powerful are the handful of **Chianti Classico Gran Selezione** wines chosen every year. The Tuscan south houses two even finer DOCGs: mighty, robust **Brunello di Montalcino,** a garnet-colored red ideal for roasts and game; and almost purple **Vino Nobile di Montepulciano,** with its rich, velvet body. End a meal with the Tuscan dessert wine **Vin Santo,** often accompanied by hard *biscotti* to dunk in your glass.

The Veneto: Reds around Venice vary from light, lunchtime-friendly **Bardolino** to **Valpolicella,** which can be particularly intense if grapes are partially dried before fermentation to make an **Amarone.**

White, Garganega-based **Soave** has a pale amber color and a peachlike flavor. **Lugana** at its best has a sparkle of gold and a rich but dry structure. **Prosecco** is the classic Italian sparkling white, the base for both a Bellini and a Spritz (joints that use Champagne are doing it wrong).

Latium: Many of Rome's rustic wines come from the Castelli Romani, hill towns around the capital. These wines are best drunk young and are most often white, mellow, and dry. The golden wines of **Frascati** are the most famous.

Italy's drink isn't all about wine, however. Especially among the young, there's a boom in popularity for artisanal **beer.** Although supermarket shelves are still stacked with mainstream brands Peroni and Moretti, smaller stores and bars increasingly offer craft microbrews. Italy had fewer than 50 breweries in 2000; the count was greater than 1,250 by 2021. Craft-beer consumption has more than tripled since 2012, according to brewers' association, Unionbirrai. Look for Unionbirrai's official seal on the label of genuine craft brewery products. For more on breweries and styles to look out for, browse the annual winners' list at www.birradellanno.it. Ritual Lab Brewery, just outside Rome, have been multiple gold medal winners, including in 2022.

We have Christianity, along with the influence of Byzantium, to thank for the appearance of Italy's next great artistic style: the **Byzantine.** Painting and mosaic work in this era was stylized and static, but also ornate and ethereal. Churches in the Byzantine style include Venice's **Basilica di San Marco** (p. 305) and Rome's **Basilica di San Clemente** (p. 120).

The Middle Ages: 9th–14th Centuries

A ravaged Rome entered the Middle Ages, its population scattered. A modest number of residents continued to live around the swamps of the **Campus Martius.** The Seven Hills—now without water because aqueducts were cut—stood abandoned and crumbling.

The pope turned toward Europe, where he found a powerful ally in **Charlemagne,** king of the Franks. In 800, Pope Leo III crowned him emperor. Although Charlemagne pledged allegiance to the church and made the pope the final arbiter in most religious and cultural matters, he also set Western Europe on a course of bitter opposition to papal meddling in affairs of state.

Italy's climate is perfect for vineyards.

The successor to Charlemagne's empire was a political entity known as the **Holy Roman Empire** (962–1806). The new Empire defined the end of the Dark Ages but ushered in a long period of bloody warfare. Magyars from Hungary invaded Lombardy and, in turn, were defeated by an increasingly powerful **Venice,** which, having defeated its naval rival Genoa in the 1380 Battle of Chioggia, reigned over most of the eastern Mediterranean. Venetian merchants ruled a republic that lasted for a millennium and built a city with imposing architecture like the **Doge's Palace** (p. 309).

While Venice flourished, **Rome** during the Middle Ages was a backwater. Narrow lanes with overhanging buildings filled areas that had once been showcases of Imperial power. The forums, markets, temples, and theaters of the Imperial era slowly disintegrated. It remained the seat of the Roman Catholic Church, a state almost completely controlled by priests who aggressively expanded Church influence and acquisitions. The result was an endless series of power struggles.

Via Appia Antica.

In the mid–14th century, the **Black Death** ravaged Europe, killing perhaps a third of Italy's population; the preservation of Tuscan towns like **San Gimignano** (p. 257) and **Siena** (p. 250) owes much to the fact they never fully recovered from the devastations of this 1348–49 plague. Despite such setbacks, Italian city-states grew wealthy from Crusades' booty, trade, and banking. The **Florin,** a gold coin minted in Florence, became the first truly international currency for centuries, dominating trade all over the continent.

The medieval period marks the beginning of building in stone on a mass scale. Flourishing from 800 to 1300, **Romanesque architecture** took its inspiration and rounded arches from Ancient Rome. Architects built large churches with wide aisles to accommodate the masses. Pisa's **Campo dei Miracoli** (p. 254) is typical of Pisan-Romanesque style, with stacked arcades of mismatched columns in the cathedral facade (and wrapped around the **Leaning Tower of Pisa**) and blind arcading set with diamond-shaped lozenges. The influence of Arab architecture is obvious—Pisa was a city of seafaring merchants.

Romanesque sculpture is often wonderfully childlike in its narrative simplicity, frequently mixing biblical scenes with the myths and motifs of pagan traditions. Among Italy's greatest surviving examples of Romanesque sculpture are 48 relief panels on the bronze doors of the **Basilica di San Zeno Maggiore** in Verona (p. 347).

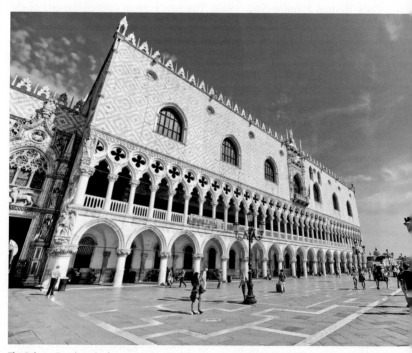

The Palazzo Ducale is the former residence of the doges who ruled Venice for more than 1,000 years.

The hill town of San Gimignano is a 14th-century time capsule.

As the appeal of Romanesque and Byzantine faded, the **Gothic** style flourished between the 13th and 15th centuries. Gothic architecture was characterized by flying buttresses and pointed arches. These engineering developments freed architecture from the heavy, thick walls of the Romanesque and allowed ceilings to soar, walls to thin, and windows to proliferate. Many secular Gothic buildings arose, including palaces designed to show off the prestige of various ruling regimes, like Siena's **Palazzo Pubblico** (p. 252) and many great buildings of **Venice** (see chapter 8). **San Gimignano** (p. 257) has a remarkably preserved Gothic center.

Painters such as **Cimabue** (1251–1302) and **Giotto** (1266–1337) in Florence, **Pietro Cavallini** (1259–ca. 1330) in Rome, and **Duccio di Buoninsegna** (ca. 1255–1319) in Siena lifted art from Byzantine rigidity and set it on the road to realism. Giotto's finest work is his fresco cycle at Padua's **Cappella degli Scrovegni** (p. 343); he was a harbinger of the approaching Renaissance, which would forever change art and architecture. Duccio's "Maestà," now in Siena's **Museo dell'Opera del Duomo** (p. 252), influenced Sienese painters for centuries. Ambrogio Lorenzetti painted the greatest civic frescoes of the Middle Ages—his "Allegories of Good and Bad Government" in Siena's **Palazzo Pubblico** (p. 252)—before he succumbed to the Black Death, along with almost every significant Sienese artist of his generation.

The medieval period saw the birth of literature in the Italian language, which was essentially a written version of the **Tuscan dialect**—primarily because the great writers of the age were Tuscans. Florentine **Dante Alighieri** wrote his "Divine Comedy" in the 1310s, and Boccaccio's "Decameron"—a kind of Florentine "Canterbury Tales"—appeared in the 1350s.

Renaissance & Baroque Italy: 1400s–1700s

The story of Italy from the dawn of the Renaissance in the early 15th century to the Age of Enlightenment in the 17th and 18th centuries is as fascinating and complicated as that of the rise and fall of the Roman Empire.

During this period, **Rome** underwent major physical changes. The old centers of culture reverted to pastures; new churches and palaces were built with the recycled stones of Ancient Rome. This construction boom did more damage to the temples of the Caesars than any barbarian sack ever had. Rare marbles were stripped from Imperial-era baths and used as altarpieces or sent to limekilns. So enthusiastic was the popes' destruction of Imperial Rome, it's a miracle anything is left.

By 1400 the most significant power in Italy was the city where the Renaissance began: **Florence** (see chapter 6). The **Medici** family rose to become the most powerful of the ruling oligarchy, gradually usurping the trades guilds and republicans. They reformed law and commerce, expanded the city's power by taking control of neighbors such as **Pisa** (see chapter 7), and financed a "renaissance," or rebirth, in painting, sculpture, and architecture. Christopher Hibbert's *Rise and Fall of the House of Medici* is the most readable historical account of the era. Netflix's *Medici: Masters of Florence* and *The Magnificent* serve up a fictionalized, sensationalized, but not wholly inaccurate "history" of power plays in the Renaissance city.

Under the patronage of the Medici and other rich Florentine families, innovative painters and sculptors pursued expressiveness and naturalism. In Florence, **Donatello** (1386–1466) cast the first free-standing nude since antiquity (now in the **Museo Nazionale del Bargello;** see p. 215). **Lorenzo Ghiberti** (1378–1455) labored for 50 years on two sets of doors for the **Baptistery** (p. 204), the most famous of which were dubbed the "Gates of Paradise"; and **Masaccio** (1401–28) produced the first painting to realistically portray linear perspective, on the nave wall of **Santa Maria Novella** (p. 226).

Next followed a brief period known as the **High Renaissance.** The epitome of Renaissance Man, Florentine **Leonardo da Vinci** (1452–1519) painted his "Last Supper" in Milan and an "Annunciation," which now hangs in Florence's **Uffizi** (p. 212)

A lion holds Florence's coat of arms in the Museo Nazionale del Bargello.

"Annunciation" by Leonardo da Vinci in the Galleria degli Uffizi, Florence.

alongside countless Renaissance masterpieces from such great painters as Sandro Botticelli and Piero della Francesca. **Raphael** (1483–1520) produced a sublime body of work in his 37 years. Skilled in sculpture, painting, and architecture, **Michelangelo** (1475–1564) marks the apogee of Renaissance. His giant "David" at the **Galleria dell'Accademia** (p. 227) in Florence is the world's most famous statue; his **Sistine Chapel** frescoes have lured millions to the **Vatican Museums** (p. 103) in Rome.

The father of Venice's High Renaissance was **Titian** (1485–1576), known for his mastery of color and tone. Venice (see chapter 8) offers up a trove of Titian's art, along with works by earlier Venetian masters **Gentile Bellini** (1429–1507), **Giorgione** (1477–1510), and **Vittore Carpaccio** (1465–1525).

As in painting, Renaissance **architecture** stressed proportion, order, and classical inspiration. In the early 1400s, **Filippo Brunelleschi** (1377–1446) grasped the mathematics of "perspective" and provided artists with ground rules for creating an illusion of three dimensions on a flat surface. (Read Ross King's *Brunelleschi's Dome* for the story of his greatest achievement, crowning Florence's cathedral with an iconic ochre dome.) Even **Michelangelo** took up architecture late in life, designing the Laurentian Library and New Sacristy at the **Medici Chapels** in Florence (p. 222) and then moving cities to complete the soaring dome of Rome's **St. Peter's Basilica** (p. 100). The third great Renaissance architect—and most influential of them all—**Andrea Palladio** (1508–80) worked in a classical mode of columns, porticoes, pediments, and other ancient-temple-inspired features. His masterpiece is the elegant **Il Redentore** church (p. 327) in Venice.

RENAISSANCE reading

Whole libraries have been written on the Renaissance—and it's worth acquainting yourself with some of the themes and styles before you visit. The most accessible introductions include Peter and Linda Murray's *The Art of the Renaissance* (1963), Michael Levey's *Early Renaissance* (1967), Evelyn Welch's *Art in Renaissance Italy 1350–1500* (2000), and Peter Murray's *The Architecture of* *the Italian Renaissance* (1969). Giorgio Vasari's *Lives of the Artists,* first published in 1550, remains the definitive work on Renaissance artists, written by one who knew some of them personally; it's still a good read. In *The Stones of Florence* (1956), Mary McCarthy mixes architectural insight with no-holds-barred opinion.

In time, the High Renaissance evolved into the **baroque.** Stuccoes, sculptures, and paintings were carefully designed to complement each other—and the space itself—to create a unified whole. The baroque movement's spiritual home was Rome and its towering figure was **Gian Lorenzo Bernini** (1598–1680), the greatest baroque sculptor, a fantastic architect, and a more-than-decent painter. Among many fine sculptures, you'll find his best in Rome's **Galleria Borghese** (p. 136) and **Santa Maria della Vittoria** (p. 141) church.

In **music,** the most famous baroque composer was Venetian **Antonio Vivaldi** (1678–1741), whose "Four Seasons" is among the most performed classical compositions of all time. In **painting,** baroque often mixed a kind of super-realism—using peasants as models, exaggerating light and shadow with a technique called *chiaroscuro*—with complex composition and dynamic explosions of movement and color. The period produced many fine painters, notably **Caravaggio** (1571–1610). Among his masterpieces are a "St. Matthew" cycle in Rome's **San Luigi dei Francesi** (p. 126). The baroque also had an outstanding female painter: **Artemisia Gentileschi** (1593–1652), whose brutal "Judith Slaying Holofernes" hangs in Florence's **Uffizi** (p. 212).

Frothy and ornate, **rococo** art was the baroque taken to flamboyant extremes and had few serious proponents in Italy. **Giambattista Tiepolo** (1696–1770), arguably the best of the rococo painters, specialized in ceiling frescoes and canvases with cloud-filled heavens of light, as in Venice's **Scuola Grande dei Carmini** (p. 322). For rococo building—more a decorative than an architectural movement—look no further than Rome's **Spanish Steps** (p. 132) or **Trevi Fountain** (p. 135).

At Last, a United Italy: the 1800s

By the 1800s Renaissance glories were a fading memory. Chunks of Italy had changed hands many, many times—between the Austrians, the Spanish, and the French, among autocratic thugs and enlightened princes, between the noble and the merchant classes. The 19th century witnessed the final collapse of many Renaissance city-states. The last of the Medici, Gian Gastone, died in 1737, leaving Tuscany in the hands of foreign Lorraine and Habsburg princes. In 1797 French emperor **Napoleon** brought an end to a millennium of republican government in **Venice,** installing puppet rulers across the Italian peninsula. Napoleon's military even oversaw a brief return of the **Roman Republic** (1798–99)—Puccini's opera "Tosca" (see below) is set in the aftermath of its disintegration. After a British/Prussian/Dutch alliance defeated Napoleon, the **Congress of Vienna** (1814–15) parceled out various chunks of Italy once again.

Political unrest became a fact of Italian life, spurred by insurrectionaries like **Giuseppe Mazzini.** Europe's year of revolutions, **1848,** rocked Italy with violent uprisings. After decades of political intrigue, thanks to the efforts of statesman **Camillo Cavour** and rebel general **Giuseppe Garibaldi,** the Kingdom of Italy was proclaimed in 1861 with **Vittorio Emanuele II** of Savoy as its first monarch. The kingdom's first capital was **Turin** (1861–65), followed by **Florence** (1865–71).

The establishment of a kingdom, however, didn't signal a complete unification of Italy—Latium (including Rome) was again under papal control and Venetia was held by Austria. In 1866, Venetia joined the rest of Italy after the **Seven Weeks' War** between Austria and Prussia. Then on September 20, 1870, Rome was taken—present-day **Via XX Settembre** is the very street up which patriots advanced after breaching the gates. It became the capital in 1871. The **Risorgimento**—the "resurgence," Italian unification—was complete.

Political heights in Italy seemed to correspond to creative depths in art and architecture. Among few notable practitioners of this era was Venetian **Antonio Canova** (1757–1822), Italy's major neoclassical sculptor, who became notorious for painting both Napoleon and his sister Pauline as nudes. His best work is in Rome's **Galleria Borghese** (p. 136).

Rome's rococo Trevi Fountain.

Music, however, was experiencing its Italian golden age: **Opera** is the major legacy of the 19th century. *Bel canto* composer **Gioachino Rossini** (1792–1868) found success with his 1816 "The Barber of Seville," and the fame of **Gaetano Donizetti** (1797–1848) was ensured when his "Anna Bolena" premiered in 1830. Both were later overshadowed by **Giuseppe Verdi** (1813–1901), whose works such as "Rigoletto" and "La Traviata" assumed profound nationalist symbolism. At the turn of the century, a dominant Romantic movement gave way to the *verismo* ("realism") of others including **Giacomo Puccini** (1858–1924), whose operas including "La Bohème" and "Madama Butterfly" still pack houses worldwide.

Statue of Giuseppe Verdi in his hometown of Bussetto, just outside Parma, Italy.

The 20th Century: Two World Wars & One Duce

In 1915, Italy entered **World War I** on the side of the Allies, joining Britain, Russia, and France to help defeat Germany and Italy's traditional enemy to the north—now the Austro-Hungarian Empire—and so to "reclaim" Trentino and Trieste. (Mark Thompson's *The White War* [2008] tells the story of Italy's catastrophic, though technically victorious, campaign.) In the aftermath of war's carnage, Italians suffered further with rising unemployment and horrendous inflation. As in Germany, political crisis led to dictatorship.

On October 28, 1922, **Benito Mussolini,** who started his Fascist Party in 1919, gathered 30,000 Black Shirts for his **March on Rome.** Inflation was soaring and workers had called a general strike, but rather than recognize a

---

The A-List of Italian Novels Available in English

- Alessandro Manzoni, *The Betrothed* (1827)
- Alberto Moravia, *The Conformist* (1951)
- Giuseppe Tomasi di Lampedusa, *The Leopard* (1958)
- Elsa Morante, *History: A Novel* (1974)
- Italo Calvino, *If on a Winter's Night a Traveler* (1979)
- Umberto Eco, *Foucault's Pendulum* (1988)
- Niccolò Ammaniti, *I'm Not Scared* (2001)
- Viola di Grado, *Hollow Heart* (2015)
- Elena Ferrante, *Neapolitan Quartet* (2012–15)

state under siege, **King Vittorio Emanuele III** (1900–46) proclaimed Mussolini the new government leader. In 1929 "Il Duce" ("the chief")—a moniker Mussolini began using from 1925—defined the divisions between the Italian government and pope by signing the Lateran Treaty, which granted political, territorial, and fiscal autonomy to the microstate of **Vatican City.** During the Spanish Civil War (1936–39), Mussolini's support for General Franco's Fascists, who had staged a coup against the elected government of Spain, helped seal the Axis alliance between Italy and Nazi Germany. Italy was inexorably and disastrously sucked into **World War II.**

Deeply unpleasant though their politics were, the Fascist regime did sponsor some remarkable **Rationalist architecture,** such as Rome's **EUR** suburb and Florence's **Santa Maria Novella station.** (Today a plaque at the station commemorates Jews sent from the terminus to their deaths in Nazi Germany.)

After defeat in World War II, Italy voted to end its monarchy and establish the **First Republic**—overwhelmingly so in northern and central Italy, who outvoted a southern royalist majority. Italy quickly rebuilt its economy, in part because of U.S. aid under the **Marshall Plan** (1948–1952). By the 1960s, as a member of the European Economic Community (founded by the **Treaty of Rome** in 1957), Italy was one of the world's leading industrialized nations, prominent in the manufacture of automobiles and office equipment. Fiat (from Turin), Ferrari (from Emilia-Romagna), and Olivetti (from northern Piedmont) were known around the world.

The postwar Italian **film industry** gained notice for its innovative directors. **Federico Fellini** (1920–1993) burst onto the scene with a highly individual

Swiss Guards outside Vatican City.

style, starting with *La Strada* (1954) and going on to such classics as *The City of Women* (1980). His *La Dolce Vita* (1961) defined an era in Rome. The gritty "neorealism" of controversial **Pier Paolo Pasolini** (1922–1975) is conveyed most vividly in *Accattone* (1961), which he wrote and directed.

The country continued to be plagued, however, by economic inequality between the prosperous industrial north and depressed south. During the late 1970s and early 1980s, it was rocked by domestic terrorism: These were the so-called **Anni di Piombo (Years of Lead),** when extremists of the political left and right bombed and assassinated with impunity. Conspiracy theories became a staple diet; everyone from a shadow state to Masonic lodges to the CIA was accused of involvement in what became an undeclared civil war. The most notorious incident of the Anni di Piombo was the kidnap and murder of Prime Minister **Aldo Moro** in 1978. A succinct account of these murky years is in Tobias Jones's *The Dark Heart of Italy* (2003).

Into the 21st Century

On the back of a severe economic crisis early in the 21st century—whose effects are still reflected in high levels of government debt—immigration has become a persistent national issue. Italy's population is aging, and the youth vacuum is filled by immigrants, especially those from Eastern Europe, notably Romania and Albania. The plight of migrant refugees from Syria and North Africa through the early 2020s added yet another layer of complexity to Italy's relationship with *stranieri* (foreigners). Italy had scant colonial experience and does not have a "melting pot" history. Tensions were inevitable, and discrimination is a daily fact of life for many minorities (although you are unlikely to experience it overtly as a visitor). Change is coming: In 2013, Cécile Kyenge became Italy's first government minister of African descent. But it is coming too slowly for many, and anti-migrant sentiment is gleefully stoked by populist politicians.

While others arrive, a "brain drain" continues to push young Italians abroad to seek opportunity. The problem is ingrained in rural communities and on Italy's islands, where the old maxim, "it's not what you know, it's who you know," applies more strongly than ever.

It was in this unstable national context—and accompanying political turmoil—that the coronavirus pandemic hit early in 2020, when Italy was the first country outside China to experience the full force of Covid-19.

WHEN TO GO

The best months for traveling in most of Italy are from **April to June** and **mid-September to October:** Temperatures are usually comfortable, rural colors are rich, and crowds aren't too intense (except around Easter). From **July through early September** the country's holiday spots teem with visitors. **Easter, May,** and **June** usually see peak hotel prices in Rome and Florence.

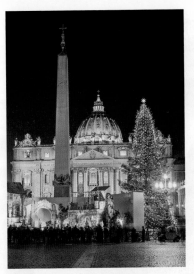

Christmas time at Vatican City.

August is the worst month in many places: Not only is it uncomfortably hot and muggy, but seemingly the entire country goes on vacation for at least 2 weeks (some Italians take off the entire month). Many family-run hotels, restaurants, and shops are closed (except at the spas, beaches, mountains, and islands, where most Italians head). Paradoxically, Florence in August can seem emptied of locals, and hotels there (and in Rome) were once heavily discounted (alas, now less so). Be aware that fashionable urban restaurants and nightspots close for the whole month.

From **late October to Easter,** many attractions operate on shorter (sometimes *much* shorter) winter hours, and some hotels occasionally close for renovation or redecoration, although this inconvenience is unlikely to be a problem in cities. Many family-run restaurants take a week or three off sometime between **November** and **February;** beach destinations become padlocked ghost towns. Deals are often available then, outside of Christmas and New Year.

Weather

It's warm all over Italy in summer; landlocked cities in Tuscany can be stifling during a July or August hot spell. Higher temperatures (measured in Italy in degrees Celsius) usually begin in May, often lasting until early October. Winters in the north of Italy are cold, with rain and snow, and a biting wind whistles over the mountains into Venice and, less often, Florence. In Rome and farther south, the weather is mostly warm (or at least, warm-ish) all year, averaging 10°C (50°F) in winter. Even here chilly snaps are possible, as freezing temperatures and snow in recent winters proved. The rainiest months are October and November.

Italy's Average Daily High Temperature & Monthly Rainfall

		JAN	FEB	MAR	APR	MAY	JUNE	JULY	AUG	SEPT	OCT	NOV	DEC
ROME	Temp. (°F)	55	56	59	63	71	77	83	83	79	71	62	57
	Temp. (°C)	12	13	15	17	21	25	28	28	26	21	16	13
	Rainfall (in.)	3.2	2.8	2.7	2.6	2	1.3	.6	1	2.7	4.5	4.4	3.8
FLORENCE	Temp. (°F)	49	53	60	68	75	84	89	88	81	69	58	50
	Temp. (°C)	9	11	15	20	23	28	31	31	27	20	14	10
	Rainfall (in.)	1.9	2.1	2.7	2.9	3	2.7	1.5	1.9	3.3	4	3.9	2.8
VENICE	Temp. (°F)	42	47	54	61	70	77	81	81	75	65	53	44
	Temp. (°C)	6	8	12	16	21	25	27	27	24	18	11	7
	Rainfall (in.)	2.3	2.1	2.2	2.5	2.7	3	2.5	3.3	2.6	2.7	3.4	2.1

Carnevale in Venice is 2 weeks before Ash Wednesday.

Public Holidays

Offices, government buildings (although not usually tourist information centers), and shops in Italy generally close on January 1 (*Capodanno,* or New Year); January 6 (*La Befana,* or Epiphany); Easter Sunday *(Pasqua);* Easter Monday *(Pasquetta);* April 25 (*Festa della Liberazione,* or Liberation Day); May 1 (*Festa del Lavoro,* or Labor Day); June 2 (*Festa della Repubblica,* or Republic Day); August 15 (*Ferragosto,* or the Assumption of the Virgin); November 1 (All Saints' Day); December 8 (*L'Immacolata,* or the Immaculate Conception); December 25 (*Natale,* Christmas Day); and December 26 (*Santo Stefano,* or St. Stephen's Day). Businesses often close for the annual day dedicated to a local patron saint (for example, Jan 31 in San Gimignano, Tuscany).

Italy Calendar of Events

FEBRUARY

Carnevale, Venice. At this riotous time, theatrical presentations and masked balls take place across Venice and on islands in its lagoon. Balls are by invitation only (except the Doge's Ball), but street events and fireworks are open to everyone.

www.carnevale.venezia.it. Two weeks before Ash Wednesday.

MARCH

Festa di San Giuseppe, Trionfale Quarter, Rome. A decorated statue of St. Joseph graces a fair with food stalls, concerts, and sporting events. Around March 19.

Holy Week, nationwide. Processions and ceremonies are staged—some dating to the Middle Ages. The pope leads the most notable procession, passing the Colosseum and Roman Forum; a torch-lit parade caps the observance. Beginning 4 days before Easter Sunday.

Easter Sunday (Pasqua), Piazza San Pietro, Rome. In an event broadcast around the world, the pope gives his blessing from the balcony of St. Peter's.

Scoppio del Carro (Explosion of the Cart), Florence. White oxen draw a cart laden with flowers and fireworks to the Duomo, where at the 11am Mass a mechanical dove detonates it. Easter Sunday.

MAY

Maggio Musicale Fiorentino (Florentine Musical May), Florence. Italy's most prestigious music festival presents music from the 14th to the 20th centuries. www.maggio fiorentino.com. Late April to June.

Concorso Ippico Internazionale (International Horse Show), Piazza di Siena, Rome. Top-flight show jumping at the Villa Borghese. www.piazzadisiena.it/en. Late May.

JUNE

Festa di San Ranieri, Pisa. The city honors its patron saint with candlelit parades, followed the next day by eight-rower teams competing in 16th-century costumes. June 16 and 17.

Calcio Storico (Historic Football), Florence. A revival of a raucous 15th-century form of football, pitting four teams in medieval costume against one another. Games usually culminate June 24, feast day of St. John the Baptist. www.calciostorico fiorentino.it. Late June.

Gioco del Ponte, Pisa. Teams in Renaissance costume take part in a long-contested push-of-war on the Ponte di Mezzo, which spans the Arno. www.giocodelpontedipisa. it. Last weekend in June.

Il Palio horse race in Siena.

La Biennale di Venezia, Venice. One of the world's most famous recurring contemporary art events shares the limelight with architecture, cinema, and more in alternate years (next in 2024). www.labiennale.org. June to November.

Il Palio, Piazza del Campo, Siena. Palio fever grips this Tuscan hill-town for a wild and exciting horse race from the Middle Ages. Pageantry, costumes, and celebrations for the victorious *contrada* (sort of a neighborhood social club) mark the spectacle. It's a "no rules" event: Even a horse without a rider can win. July 2 and August 16.

Festa del Redentore (Feast of the Redeemer), Venice. This festival marks the lifting of a 1576 plague with fireworks, pilgrimages, and boating. www.redentore venezia.it. Third Saturday and Sunday in July.

Venice International Film Festival, Venice. Ranking just behind Cannes, this festival brings together stars, directors, producers, and filmmakers from all over the world to the Palazzo del Cinema and Palazzo del Casinò on Lido. www.labiennale.org. Late August to early September.

Regata Storica, Grand Canal, Venice. A maritime spectacular: Many gondolas participate in the canal procession, although gondolas don't race in the regatta itself. www.regata storicavenezia.it. First Sunday in September.

Christmas Blessing of the Pope, Piazza San Pietro, Rome. Delivered at noon from the balcony of St. Peter's Basilica, the pope's words are broadcast to the faithful around the globe. December 25.

ROME

By Elizabeth Heath

The partial, scattered ruins of the awesome Roman Empire, which once ruled the Western world, are today among the most overpowering sights on Earth. Wandering the Roman Forum, entering the Colosseum, standing at the foot of the Pantheon, and walking the Appian Way—these are among the most memorable, instructive, and illuminating experiences in all of travel. To see evidence of a once-great civilization that no longer exists is a humbling experience that everyone should have.

Merely being in Rome, you will be reminded constantly of this city's extraordinary history. Yet this is no city stuck in a time warp—Rome is a living, breathing metropolis whose residents just happen to live, work, dine out, and relax in and among ancient ruins, medieval piazzas, Renaissance palaces, and Baroque fountains. Discover the city's ancient wonders, but don't just seek out old Rome—find the innovative bistro, the experimental gelateria, or the modern art exhibit. Get lost in the maze of streets of Rome's centro storico, and stumble upon its monuments, moments, and simpler pleasures.

Walk the streets of Rome, and the city will be yours.

DON'T LEAVE ROME WITHOUT . . .

Exploring the World's Smallest Country: Vatican City is just .2 square miles, but it packs a lot into that tiny space. From one of the finest museums on the planet, to its largest Catholic church, to the architectural masterwork that is St. Peter's Square, your trip isn't complete without at least a day spent here. See p. 98.

Gazing Over the Roman Forum and Palatine from the Capitoline Hill Terraces at Night. Yes, explore the ruins by day, too, but after dark—as spotlights cast dramatic glows over solitary columns and crumbling arches—the view is truly, disarmingly spectacular. See p. 115.

Lingering Over Dinner. Take time to unwind at a typical Roman trattoria, with a steady and wonderfully affordable flow of wine and delicious food. See p. 80.

The view over St. Peter's Square from St. Peter's Basilica.

Mixing with Romans at the Lively Mercato di Testaccio. No other market in the city has such a strong sense of community, coupled with the chance to sample real Roman street food. See p. 153.

Downtime Spent Wandering the Streets of a Roman Neighborhood. It's easy to over program a visit to Rome, but time spent wandering at leisure in Monti, Trastevere, or the Jewish Ghetto might be some of your most memorable. See p. 56.

ESSENTIALS

Arriving

BY PLANE   Most flights arrive at Terminal 3 of Rome's **Leonardo da Vinci International Airport** (www.adr.it; ℭ **06-65951**), popularly known as **Fiumicino,** 30km (19 miles) from the city center. (If you're arriving from other European cities, you might land at Ciampino Airport, discussed below). As you exit baggage claim, you'll see a **tourist information desk** to the right, staffed daily from 8:30am to 6pm. Several *cambio* (currency exchange) desks are in the pre- and post-security areas, but it's just as easy, and possibly less expensive, to withdraw cash from an ATM (*bancomat*) in the airport. See p. 360 for tips on using Italian ATMs.

Follow signs marked TRENI to find the **airport train station,** about a 10-minute walk from the arrivals area. **Pro tip:** If you have a lot of bags and opt for the train, grab a free luggage cart when you get to baggage claim. When you exit into the terminal, turn left instead of right, and take the elevator down to the train station level. If you go right, you must take an escalator and ditch the luggage cart.

From there, catch the delightfully named **Leonardo Express** for a 32-minute shuttle ride) to Rome's main station, **Stazione Termini.** The shuttle runs every 15 minutes (every 30 minutes at off-peak hours) from 5:38am to 11:53pm for 14€ one-way (free for kids 12 and under). You can buy tickets from one of several machines (machines take cash or credit, and you can opt for instructions in English), or buy them at the Trenitalia window near the tracks. You can also buy e-tickets at www.trenitalia.com or use the Trenitalia mobile app.

A **taxi** from Fiumicino airport to the city costs a flat-rate 50€ for the 45-minute to 1-hour trip, depending on traffic (hotels tend to charge 50€–60€ for pickup service). Note that the flat rate is applicable from the airport to central Rome and vice-versa, but only if your central Rome location is inside the Aurelian Walls (most hotels are). Otherwise, standard metered rates apply, which can bump the fare to 75€ or higher. Additional surcharges are tacked on for large luggage, Sunday and holiday rides, more than 4 passengers, and rides after 10pm and before 6am.

If you arrive at **Ciampino Airport** (www.adr.it/ciampino; ☎ **06-65951**), you can take a Terravision bus (www.terravision.eu; ☎ **06-4880086;** first bus 8:45am, last bus 11:40pm) to Stazione Termini. This takes about 45 minutes and costs 6€. (Note that the timetable for buses fluctuates based on current flight schedules.) A **taxi** from Ciampino costs a flat rate of 30€, provided you're going to a destination within the old Aurelian Walls.

Rome in the Post-Covid Era

We've always encouraged readers to buy tickets in advance for the attractions they really want to see; that advice is even more pertinent now. During the tentative days of post-lockdown reopening and social distancing measures, many attractions switched to *advanced ticketing only* to limit crowds. Many have retained these crowd-control systems, which ultimately give visitors a better experience. We've indicated where advanced reservations are required or recommended as of press time.

Train or Taxi?

Whether to take the airport shuttle train or a taxi into Rome from FCO depends on your budget and your tolerance for schlepping. If you're traveling solo and/or traveling light, the train is the most economical option for getting into the city and takes about the same time as a taxi. If you've got a lot of bags, however, bear in mind that the train is a bit of a long walk from the arrival terminal—and that, once your train arrives at Termini station, you'll still have to walk, or take Metro, bus, or taxi to your destination. (See "By Train," p. 54, for more on Termini station options.) Bottom line? If there are 3 or more in your party or you're carrying lots of luggage, go for a taxi.

Roma & OMNIA **PASSES**

If you plan to do serious sightseeing in Rome (and why else would you be here?), the **Roma Pass** (www.romapass.it) is worth considering. For 52€ per card, valid for 3 days, you get free entry to the first two museums or archaeological sites you visit; "express" entry to the Colosseum; discounted entry to all other museums and sites; free use of the city's public transport network (bus, Metro, tram, and railway lines, not including transfers to Fiumucino Airport), free use of P-Stop bathrooms (www.turismoroma.it/en/page/pstop), and a free map.

If your stay in Rome is shorter, you may want to opt for the **Roma Pass 48 Hours** (32€), which offers the same benefits as the 3-day pass, except that only the first museum you visit is free and the ticket is valid for just 48 hours.

The free transportation perk with the Roma Pass is not insignificant, if only because it saves you the hassle of buying digital farecards or paper tickets. In any case, do some quick math; one major museum or attraction entrance is 12€–16€, and each ride on public transportation is 1.50€. Discounts to other sites range from 20–50%. If you plan to visit a lot of sites and dash around the city on public transport, it's probably worth the money.

A glaring disadvantage of the Roma Pass is that it does not include access to the Vatican Museums or the paid areas of St. Peter's. That's where the **OMNIA Card** comes to the rescue. The 72-hour card combines all the benefits of the Roma Pass with skip-the-line entry to the Vatican Museums and St. Peter's, an audioguide

to St. Peter's, a hop-on-hop-off bus pass, and admission to other Vatican properties. At 129€ it's an investment, but worth it if you want to take in all the heavy hitters of Rome and the Vatican. If you just want express entrance to the Vatican Museums and St. Peter's, there's also a 24-hour Omnia Card (69€) that does not include Roma Pass benefits. The cards can be purchased online at www.omniavaticanrome.org and picked up at one of four Omnia Card offices in the city, including at St. Peter's Square.

You can buy Roma passes online (www.romapass.it) and pick them up at one of the Tourist Information Points (see p. 56); you can also order in advance by phone, with a credit card, at ✆ **06-060608**. Roma Passes are also sold directly at Tourist Information Point offices or at participating museums and ATAC subway ticket offices.

Note: Roma Pass holders intending to visit the Colosseum **must reserve timed entry**. We find the easiest way to do this is as follows: On the Roma Pass website, go to the FAQ page and scroll down to question 7.1. Follow the link to Coop-Culture and buy your Roma Pass directly from that site, at the same time reserving entry to the Colosseum. Otherwise, Roma Pass holders can book the 2€ per person timed-entry reservation directly on the CoopCulture website or by calling ✆ **06-39967575,** credit card in hand. Note that other sites included on the Roma Pass may also require advanced booking; check individual websites for the latest on opening hours and Roma Pass reservation requirements.

From either airport, ride-sharing service **Uber** is available—sort of. Because of licensing laws (and strong resistance from Rome's taxi drivers), only Uber Lux, Van, or Black services are available, and they're much more expensive than a taxi.

BY TRAIN OR BUS   Trains and buses (including trains from the airport) arrive in the center of old Rome at **Stazione Termini,** Piazza dei Cinquecento.

This is the train, bus, and transportation hub for all of Rome, and it is surrounded by many hotels, especially budget ones.

The station has lots of services. Currency exchange windows and ATMs are on the platform level, as well as on floor –1 (subway level). **Informazioni Ferroviarie** (in the outer hall) dispenses info on rail travel to other parts of Italy. Also at the station is a **tourist information booth,** plus baggage services, newsstands, clean public toilets (they cost 1€, and snack bars.

To get from Termini to your destination in Rome, you have several options. If you're taking the **Metropolitana** (subway), follow the illuminated red-and-white M signs. To catch a city bus, go straight through the outer hall and enter the sprawling bus lot of **Piazza dei Cinquecento.** See p. 59 for more information about getting around Rome by public transportation.

You will also find a line of **taxis** parked out front. Note that taxis now charge a 2€ supplement for any fares originating at Termini, plus 1€ for each bag in the trunk. Use the official taxi queue right in front of the station; don't go with a driver who approaches you or get into any cab where the meter is "broken." You should be able to pay with a credit or debit card in any official taxi but confirm this before getting in the cab.

BY CAR From the north or south, the main access route is the **Autostrada A1.** This highway runs from Milan to Naples via Bologna, Florence, and Rome. At 754km (469 miles), it is the longest Italian autostrada and is the "spinal cord" of Italy's road network. All the autostrade join with the **Grande Raccordo Anulare (GRA),** a ring road encircling Rome, channeling traffic into and around the congested city. *Tip:* Long before you reach the GRA, you should study your route carefully to see what part of Rome you plan to enter. Route signs along the ring road tend to be confusing.

Warning: If you must drive a car into Rome, return your rental car immediately on arrival, or at least get yourself to your hotel, park your car, and leave it there until you leave the city. Seriously think twice before driving in Rome—the traffic, as well as the parking options, are nightmarish. Plus, most of central Rome is a **ZTL (Zona Traffico Limitato),** off-limits to non-residents and rigorously enforced by cameras. You will almost certainly be fined; the ticket might arrive at your home address months after your trip.

A tram in Rome.

Visitor Information

Information, maps, and the **Roma Pass** (p. 54) are available at 6 Tourist Information Points around the city maintained by **Roma Capitale** (for locations, go to www.turismoroma.it/en). Each kiosk keeps its own hours and none are exactly the same, but you can reliably find them open after 9:30am and until about 6pm (some open earlier and stay open later). Note that the one at Termini (daily 8am–7pm), located next to platform 24, often has a long line. As Rome bloggers go, we like the soup-to-nuts approach of **Romewise** (www.romewise.com) and expat Natalie Kennedy's honest assessments in her blog, **An American in Rome** (www.anamericaninrome.com).

City Layout

The bulk of what you'll want to visit—ancient, Renaissance, and baroque Rome (as well as the train station)—lies on the east side of the **Tiber River (Fiume Tevere),** which curls through the city. However, several important landmarks are on the other side: **St. Peter's Basilica** and the **Vatican, Castel Sant'Angelo,** and the colorful **Trastevere** neighborhood. Even if those last sights are slightly farther afield, Rome has one of the most compact and walkable city centers in Europe.

That doesn't mean you won't get lost from time to time (most newcomers do). Arm yourself with a detailed street map of Rome (or a smartphone with a hefty data plan). Most hotels hand out a pretty good version of a city map.

Rome's Neighborhoods in Brief

Much of the historic core of Rome does not fall under easy or distinct neighborhood classifications. Instead, when describing a location, the frame of reference is the name of the nearest large monument or square, like St. Peter's or Piazza di Spagna. Street numbers usually run consecutively, with odd numbers on one side of the street, evens on the other. However, in centro, the numbers sometimes run up one side and then run back down on the other side (so #50 could be potentially opposite #308).

VATICAN CITY & PRATI Vatican City is technically a sovereign state, although in practice it is just another part of Rome. The **Vatican Museums, St. Peter's,** and the **Vatican Gardens**

St. Peter's Basilica and the Vatican, viewed from the Tiber River.

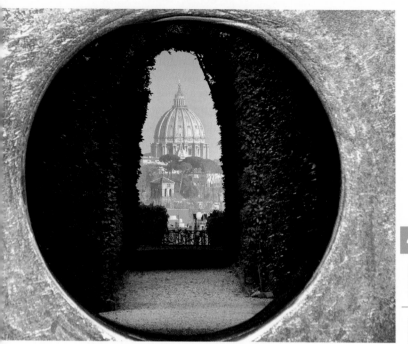

Peek-a-boo views and vistas abound in Rome, if you know where to look (p. 115).

take up most of the land area; the popes have lived here for 7 centuries. If you plan to spend most of your time exploring Vatican City sights, or if you just want to stay outside the city center, **Prati,** a middle-class neighborhood east of the Vatican, has a smattering of affordable hotels and shopping streets, as well as some excellent places to eat.

CENTRO STORICO & THE PANTHEON One of the most desirable (and busiest) areas of Rome, the **Centro Storico** ("Historic Center") is a maze of narrow streets and cobbled alleys dating from the Middle Ages and filled with churches and palaces built during the Renaissance and baroque eras, as well as countless hotels and AirBnB rentals. The only way to explore it is by foot. Its heart is elegant **Piazza Navona,** built over Emperor Domitian's stadium and bustling with overpriced sidewalk cafes and restaurants, street artists, musicians, and milling crowds.

Nearby, the area around the ancient Roman **Pantheon** is abuzz with crowds, a cafe scene, and nightlife. South of Corso Vittorio Emanuele is the lively square of **Campo de' Fiori,** home to the famous produce market. West of Via Arenula lies the old Jewish **Ghetto,** with several good restaurants and a few interesting hotels.

ANCIENT ROME, MONTI & CELIO Although no longer the heart of the city, this is where Rome began, with the **Colosseum, Palatine Hill, Roman Forum, Imperial Forums,** and **Circus Maximus.** This area offers only a few hotels and, in Monti, a handful of very good restaurants. Closer to the Colosseum, many restaurants here are tour-bus traps. Just beyond the Circus Maximus, the **Aventine Hill** is now a posh residential quarter with great city views. For more of a neighborhood feel, stay in **Monti** (Rome's oldest *rione,* or quarter) or **Celio**, respectively located north and southeast of the Colosseum. Monti especially has good dining and plenty of nightlife.

TRIDENTE & THE SPANISH STEPS   The most upscale part of Rome, full of expensive hotels, designer boutiques, and chic restaurants, lies north of Rome's center. It's often called the Tridente, because Via di Ripetta, Via del Corso, and Via del Babuino form a trident leading down from **Piazza del Popolo**. The star here is unquestionably **Piazza di Spagna,** which attracts Romans and tourists alike (though mostly the latter) to linger at its celebrated **Spanish Steps** (just don't eat lunch on the steps! See p. 131). Some of Rome's most high-end shopping streets fan out from here, including **Via Condotti.**

VIA VENETO & PIAZZA BARBERINI   In the 1950s and early 1960s, the tree-lined boulevard **Via Veneto** was the swinging place to be, the haunt of la Dolce Vita celebrities and paparazzi. Luxury hotels, cafes, and restaurants still cluster here, although the restaurants are mostly overpriced tourist traps. To the south, Via Veneto ends at **Piazza Barberini** and the magnificent **Palazzo Barberini,** begun in 1623 by Carlo Maderno and later completed by Bernini and Borromini.

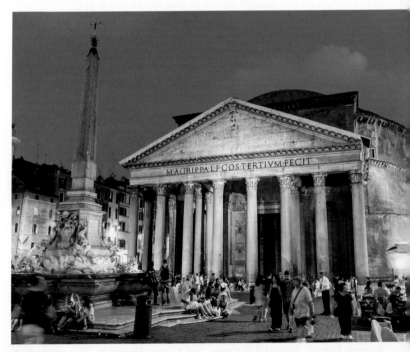

The Pantheon.

VILLA BORGHESE & PARIOLI   Parioli is Rome's most elegant residential section, a setting for excellent restaurants, hotels, museums, and public parks. Bordered by the green spaces of the **Villa Borghese** to the south and the **Villa Glori** and **Villa Ada** to the north, Parioli (and just to its south, Pinciano) is one of the city's safest districts, but it's not exactly central. It's not the best base if you plan to depend on public transportation.

AROUND STAZIONE TERMINI   For many visitors, their first glimpse of Rome is the main train station and the unappealing **Piazza del Cinquecento** out front. There are a lot of affordable hotels in this area (as well as several less-affordable ones), and the location is convenient, near the city's transportation hub and close to ancient Rome. Hotels on the Via Marsala side often occupy floors of a *palazzo* (palace), with clean and decent, sometimes even charming, rooms. The once-seedy neighborhoods on either side of Termini (Esquilino and Tiburtino) have slowly been cleaning up.

TRASTEVERE   In a Roman shift of the Latin *Trans Tiber*, Trastevere means "across the Tiber." Since the 1970s, when expats and other bohemians discovered it, this once-medieval working-class district has been gentrified and is now most definitely on the tourist map. Yet Trastevere retains its colorful appeal, with dance clubs, offbeat shops, pubs, and little *trattorie* and wine bars. Trastevere has places to stay—mostly quaint rentals and Airbnb's—and excellent restaurants and bars, too. The area centers on the ancient churches of **Santa Cecilia** and **Santa Maria in Trastevere**.

TESTACCIO & SOUTHERN ROME   Once home to slaughterhouses and Rome's port on the Tiber, the working-class neighborhood of **Testaccio** was built around one strange feature: A huge, compacted mound of broken amphorae and terracotta roof tiles, begun under Emperor Nero in A.D. 55 and added to over the centuries. Houses were built around the mound; caves were dug into its mass to store wine and foodstuffs. Now known for its authentic Roman restaurants, Testaccio is also one of Rome's liveliest areas after dark. Stay here if you want a taste of a real Roman neighborhood, but bear in mind that you're a bus, tram or subway ride from most touristic sights.

THE APPIAN WAY   Farther south and east, the 2,300-year-old **Via Appia Antica** road once extended from Rome to Brindisi on the southeast coast. This is one of the most historically rich areas of Rome, great for a day trip, but not a convenient place to stay. Its most famous sights are the **Catacombs,** the graveyards of early Christians and patrician families.

Getting Around Rome

Central Rome is perfect for exploring on foot, with sites of interest often clustered together. Much of the inner core is traffic-free, so you will need to walk whether you like it or not. *Tip:* Wear sturdy, comfortable walking shoes. In the most tourist-trod parts of the city, walking can be challenging due to crowds, uneven cobblestones, heavy traffic, and narrow (if any) sidewalks.

Rome's Neighborhoods & Top Attractions

BY SUBWAY   The **Metropolitana (Metro)** is managed by **ATAC** (www.atac.roma.it; ℮ **06-57003**). which also runs the city's buses, trams, and urban trains. The Metro operates daily from 5:30am to 11:30pm (until 12:30am on Sat). A big red M indicates the entrance to the subway. If your destination is close to a Metro stop, hop on, as your journey will be much faster than by taking surface transportation. There are currently three lines: **Line A** (orange) runs southeast to northwest via Termini, Barberini, Spagna, and several stations in Prati near the Vatican; **Line B** (blue) runs north to south via Termini and stops at the Colosseum. A third, **Line C** (green), will ultimately run from Monte Compatri in the southeast to Clodio/Mazzini (just beyond the Ottaviano stop on Line A) and include several stops in the Centro Storico. Completion of Line C has been delayed for years, largely because crews working underground keep stumbling upon new archaeological finds to be researched and excavated.

Tickets are 1.50€ and are available from *tabacchi* (tobacco shops), many newsstands, and vending machines at all stations. Booklets of tickets are available at newsstands, *tabacchi* and in some terminals. You can also buy a **pass** on either a daily or a weekly basis (see "By Bus & Tram," below). To open the subway barrier, insert your ticket. If you have a **Roma Pass** (p. 54), touch it against the yellow dot and the gates will open.

Taking the Metro can be much faster than a bus or tram.

Tickets are valid for 100 minutes from the first time they're used, and can be used to transfer to buses, trams, and urban trains. See the Metro map on the tear-out map in this guide.

BY BUS & TRAM   For 1.50€ you can ride to most parts of Rome on buses or trams, although it can be slow going in all that traffic, and the buses are often very crowded. A ticket is valid for 100 minutes, and you can get on many buses and trams, as well as the Metro, during that time by using the same ticket. Tickets are sold in *tabacchi*, at newsstands, and at bus stops, but there are seldom ticket-issuing machines on the vehicles themselves. Note that if you switch from a bus or tram to Metro within your 100-minute ticket time, you must revalidate your ticket before boarding the subway.

> ### Tap & Go
>
> It's now possible to ride paperless on Rome's Metro. In all stations, ATAC has installed Tap & Go payment machines for credit/debit cards and handheld devices equipped for contactless payment. Machines are in all Metro stations and on most buses and trams. Once you're tapped in, you can ride for up to 100 minutes on all public transport methods.

You can buy **special timed passes:** a 24-hour (ROMA 24H) ticket is 7€; a 48-hour ticket is 12.50€; a 72-hour ticket costs 18€; and a 7-day ticket is 24€. If you plan to ride public transportation a lot—and if you are skipping between the *centro storico*, Roman ruins, and Vatican, you likely will—these passes save time and hassle over buying a new ticket every time you ride. Purchase the appropriate pass for your length of stay in Rome. All the passes allow you to ride on the ATAC network, and are also valid on the Metro (subway). On the first bus you board, place your ticket in a small (typically yellow) machine, which prints the day and hour you boarded, and then withdraw it. The machine will also print your ticket's time of expiration ("*scad.*"—short for scadenza). One-day and weekly tickets are also available at *tabacchi*, many newsstands, and at vending machines at all Metro stations. If you plan to do a lot of sightseeing, however, the **Roma Pass** (p. 54) is a smarter choice. We also like the MyCicero app (www.mycicero.eu), as it allows you to search for transit options, buy e-tickets and passes, and top up your touchless tickets, all on your smartphone.

Buses and trams stop at areas marked *fermata.* Signs will display the numbers of the buses that stop there and a list of all the stops along each bus's route, making it easier to scope out your destination. Digital displays at most stops show how soon the next bus or tram will arrive. Generally, buses run daily from 5am to midnight. From midnight until dawn, you can ride on special night buses (look for the "N" in front of the bus number), which run only on main routes. It's best to take a taxi in the wee hours—if you can find one. Call for one (see "By Taxi," below) in a pinch. **Bus information booths** at Piazza dei Cinquecento, in front of Stazione Termini, offer advice on routes.

BY TAXI   If you've reached your walking limit, don't feel like waiting for a bus, or need to get someplace in a hurry, taking a taxi in Rome is reasonably affordable compared to other major world cities. Just don't count on hailing a taxi on the street. Instead, have your hotel call one, or if you're at a restaurant, ask the waiter or cashier to dial for you. If you want to phone for yourself, try the **city taxi service** at ☏ **06-0609** (Italian only), or one of these **radio taxi numbers**, which may or may not have English-speaking operators on duty: ☏ **06-6645,** 06-3570, or 06-4994. You can also text a taxi at ☏ **366-6730000** by typing the message "Roma [address]" (assuming you know the address in Italian). Taxis on call incur a surcharge of 3.50€. Larger taxi stands are at Piazza Venezia (east side), Piazza di Spagna (Spanish Steps), the Colosseum, Corso Rinascimento (Piazza Navona), Largo Argentina, the Pantheon, Piazza del Popolo, Piazza Risorgimento (near St. Peter's), and Piazza Belli (Trastevere). We always have luck finding a cab at Piazza di San Pantaleo on Corso Vittorio Emanuele II.

Many taxis accept credit cards, but it's best to check before getting in. Between 6am and 10pm, the meter begins at 3€ (4.50€ Sat–Sun) and then it's 1.10€ per kilometer up to 11€. (From 10pm to 6am every day, the meter starts at 6.50€.) After that it's 1.30€ to 1.60€ per kilometer depending on the length of the ride. The first suitcase is free; every additional piece of luggage costs 1€. *Note:* Italians don't tip taxi drivers like Americans do and, at most, will simply round up to the nearest euro. If the driver is really friendly or helpful, a tip of 1€ to 2€ is sufficient.

The main smartphone app for official city taxis is **it Taxi** (www.ittaxi.it), which is run by Rome's largest taxi company, **3570** (www.3570.it). It allows users to pay directly from the app using a credit card or PayPal. Popular throughout Europe, the **MyTaxi** app offers Uber-like convenience for ordering and prepaying a cab. **Uber** is currently available in Rome in a limited capacity only.

BY CAR   All roads might lead to Rome, but you probably won't want to drive once you get here. If you do drive into the city, call or email ahead to your hotel to find out the best route into Rome from wherever you are starting out. You will want to get rid of your rental car as soon as possible, or park it in a garage and leave it there until you depart Rome.

If you want to rent a car to explore the countryside around Rome or drive to another city, you will save money if you reserve before leaving home. If

Walk or Ride?

Rome is such a walkable city, where getting there (on foot) is half the fun. And public transportation doesn't necessarily save that much time. (For example, walking from Piazza Venezia to Piazza di Santa Maria in Trastevere takes about 25 minutes at a leisurely pace; it takes 12 minutes via bus and tram, but that doesn't include potential time spent waiting for the bus or tram to show up.) My take? On a nice day and for relatively short distances, enjoy the stroll. On the other hand, if you want to save your steps (maybe for a marathon tour of the Vatican Museums), then head to the nearest Metro, tram, or bus stop.

First, know that any map of the Roman bus system will likely be outdated before it's printed. Second, take extreme caution when riding Rome's busiest buses—pickpockets abound! This is particularly true on bus no. 64, a favorite of visitors because of its route through the historic districts and thus also a favorite of Rome's pickpocketing community. This bus has earned various nicknames, including the "Pickpocket Express" and "Wallet Eater."

Although routes may change, a few reliable bus routes have remained valid for years in Rome:

o **40 (Express):** Stazione Termini to the Vatican via Via Nazionale, Piazza Venezia and Piazza Pia, by Castel Sant'Angelo

o **64:** The "tourist route" from Termini, along Via Nazionale and through Piazza Venezia and along Via Argentina to Piazza San Pietro in the Vatican

o **75:** Stazione Termini to the Colosseum

o **H:** Stazione Termini via Piazza Venezia and the Ghetto to Trastevere via Ponte Garibaldi

you decide to book a car here, most major car rental companies have desks inside Stazione Termini.

Note that rental cars in Italy may be smaller than what you are used to, including in terms of trunk space. Make sure you consider both luggage size and the number of people when booking your vehicle.

[FastFACTS] ROME

Banks In general, banks are open Monday to Friday 8:30am to 1:30pm and 2:30 or 2:45 to 4pm. Note that many banks do not offer currency exchange.

Business hours Most Roman shops open at 10am and close at 7pm from Monday to Saturday. Smaller shops close for 1 or 2 hours at lunch and may remain closed Monday morning and Saturday afternoon. Many restaurants close for riposo (rest) 1 day per week, usually Sunday or Monday.

Dentists American Dental Arts Rome, Via del Governo Vecchio 73 (near Piazza Navona; www.adadentistsrome.com;

(C) 06-6832613), uses the latest technology.

Doctors Call the U.S. Embassy at (C) **06-46741** for a list of English-speaking doctors. You'll find English-speaking doctors at the privately run Salvator Mundi International Hospital, Viale delle Mura Gianicolensi 67 (in the Gianicolo neighborhood; www.salvatormundi.it; (C) **06-588961.** The International Medical Center is on 24-hour duty at Via Firenze 47 (near Piazza della Repubblica; www.imc84.com; (C) **06-4882371**). Medi-Call Italia, Via Cremera 8 (www.medi-call.it; (C) **06-8840113**) can arrange for a qualified

doctor to make a house call at your hotel or anywhere in Rome.

Emergencies To call the police, dial (C) **113;** for an ambulance (C) **118;** for a fire (C) **115.**

Newspapers & Magazines The English-language expat magazine Wanted in Rome (www.wantedinrome.com) comes out every 2 weeks and lists current events and shows.

Pharmacies Farmacie, recognizable by their neon green or red cross signs, are generally open 8:30am–1pm and 4–7:30pm, though some stay open later. Farmacia Piram at Via Nazionale 228 is open 24 hours. All closed pharmacies have signs in their windows indicating any open pharmacies nearby.

Police Dial ☎ **113.**

Safety Walking alone at night is usually fine anywhere in the centro storico. Violent crime is virtually nonexistent in Rome's touristed areas, though pickpocketing is common. Purse snatching happens on occasion, by perps speeding by on scooters; keep your purse on the wall side of your body with the strap across your chest. Other pickpockets dress like typical businesspeople, so always be suspicious of anyone who tries to "befriend" you in a tourist area. Thieves will also strike where you might least expect it, such as in crowded paid areas like the Colosseum or Vatican Museums.

WHERE TO STAY

Hotels in Rome's *centro storico* are often overpriced and disappointing, and all too often the grand exteriors and lobbies of historic buildings give way to bland modern rooms. Our selections here made the cut because they offer unique experiences, highly personalized service, or extreme value—and in a few cases all of the above.

Room rates vary wildly depending on the season, and last-minute deals are common. For example, a room at a hotel we classify as "expensive" might be had for as low as 99€ if there are empty beds to fill. Always **book directly with the hotel**—you'll usually get a better rate and the chance to build some rapport with reception staff.

Breakfast in all but the highest echelon of hotels is often a buffet with coffee, fruit, rolls, and cheese. It's not always included in the rate, so check the reservation options carefully. If you are budgeting and breakfast is a payable extra, skip it and go to a nearby cafe-bar, where a caffè and *cornetto* (espresso and croissant) will likely be much cheaper.

Many hotels in Rome have rooftop terraces where they serve breakfast and evening drinks.

Though most Roman hotels now have **air-conditioning** (a must during the stifling summer months), some budget options still do not. If it's not listed as a room amenity, double-check.

SELF-CATERING APARTMENTS

Rental apartments have some great virtues: They're often cheaper than standard facilities, and they let you save money by preparing at least some of your own meals.

Nearly every vacation rental in Rome—and there are tens of thousands of them—is owned and maintained by a third party (that is, not the rental agency). That means that the decor and flavor of the apartments, even in the same price range and neighborhood, can vary widely. Every reputable agency, however, puts multiple photos of each property they handle on its website, so you'll have a sense of what you're getting into. The photos should be accompanied by a list of amenities. Goliath booking sites **www.airbnb.com**, **Homeaway.com,** and **vrbo.com,** with platforms that allow individuals to rent their own apartments to guests, have thousands of listings in Rome. These will often be cheaper than apartments rented through local agencies, but they won't be vetted, and sometimes you're on your own if something goes wrong.

If you decide to rent through one of the agencies below, know that its standard practice for them to collect 30% of the total rental amount upfront to secure a booking. When you get to Rome and check in, the balance of your rental fee is often payable in cash only. Upon booking, the agency should provide you with detailed "check-in" procedures. *Tip:* Make sure you ask for a few numbers to call in case of an emergency. Otherwise, most apartments come with information sheets that list neighborhood shops and services.

RECOMMENDED AGENCIES **Cross Pollinate** (www.cross-pollinate. com; *☎* **06-99369799**), is a multi-destination agency with a roster of apartments and B&Bs in Rome. Each property is inspected before it gets listed. **Cities Reference** (www.citiesreference.com/en/rome; *☎* **06-48903612**) offers no-surprises property descriptions (with helpful and diplomatic tags like "better for young people") and even includes the "eco-footprint" for each apartment. You can expect transparency and responsiveness from the plain-dealing staff. **Rental in Rome** (www.rentalinrome.com; *☎* **06-3220068**) has an alluring website—with video clips of the apartments—and the widest selection of midrange and luxury apartments in the *centro storico* (there are less expensive ones, too).

MONASTERIES & CONVENTS

Staying in a convent or a monastery can be a great bargain. But remember, these are religious houses, which means the decor is most often stark and the rules inflexible. Cohabitating is almost always frowned upon—though marriage licenses are rarely required—and unruly behavior is not tolerated (so, no staggering in after too much *vino* at dinner). Plus, there's usually a curfew. Most rooms in convents and monasteries do not have private bathrooms but ask when making your reservation in case some are available. However, if you're planning a low-key trip to Rome, and you can live with these parameters, convents and monasteries are an affordable and often fascinating

> ### A Note on a *Notte* in Rome
>
> The Rome City Council applies a sojourn tax of 3€ to 7€ (depending on hotel class) per person, per night. Many hotels will request this fee in cash upon check-in or check-out; this is perfectly normal. Children ages 10 and under are exempt.

option. The place to start is **www.monasterystays.com**, which lays out all your monastic options for the Eternal City.

Hotels by Price
EXPENSIVE
Anantara Palazzo Naiadi ★★★, p. 77
Babuino 181 ★★, p. 74
Chapter Roma ★★, p. 72
Del Sole al Pantheon ★, p. 72
Raphael ★★★, p. 72
The Inn at the Roman Forum ★★, p. 70
The Inn at the Spanish Steps ★★★, p. 75
Villa Spalletti Trivelli ★★★, p. 75

MODERATE
Coronari Palace ★★, p. 73
Damaso Hotel ★★, p. 73
Duca d'Alba ★★, p. 71
The Glam ★★, p. 71
Hotel Adriano ★★, p. 73
Hotel Condotti ★, p. 76
Hotel L'Orologio ★★, p. 73
Hotel Mediterraneo ★★★, p. 77

Hotel San Francesco ★★, p. 78
La Lumière ★, p. 76
La Residenza ★, p. 76
Lancelot ★★★, p. 71
Mama Shelter Roma ★, p. 68
Parlamento ★★, p. 76
QuodLibet ★★★, p. 68
Residenza Cellini ★★, p. 78
Residenza in Farnese ★★, p. 74
Residenza Paolo VI ★★, p. 69
Santa Maria ★★, p. 79
Villa Laetitia ★★★, p. 69

INEXPENSIVE
Arco del Lauro ★★, p. 80
Beehive ★★★, p. 78
Mimosa ★★, p. 74
Panda ★, p. 76
Rome Armony Suites ★★★, p. 70
Seven Kings Relais ★★, p. 78

Around Vatican City & Prati

For many, this is a rather dull area to be based in. It's well removed from the ancient sites, and though Prati has some good restaurants, the area overall is not geared to nightlife. But if the main purpose of your visit centers on the Vatican, you'll be fine here, and you will be joined by thousands of other pilgrims, nuns, and priests (see map p. 99).

MODERATE

Mama Shelter Roma ★　The Rome installment of the trendy, affordable-ish design hotel chain is certainly the most interesting recent opening in this corner of the city—an otherwise nondescript residential area northwest of the Vatican Museums. Rooms are small, busy, and perhaps a little too self-consciously hip, but definitely on-brand. Buzzy perks include a roof deck, a restaurant, bar and pizzeria, and an indoor pool—the latter a real rarity in Rome.

Via Luigi Rizzo 20. mamashelter.com/roma. ✆ **06-94538900.** 217 units. 129€–289€ double. Metro: Cipro. **Amenities:** Bar; restaurant; pizzeria; roof terrace; indoor pool; fitness room; free Wi-Fi.

QuodLibet ★★★　The name is Latin for "what pleases," and we'll be frank: Everything pleases us here. This upscale B&B boasts spacious, colorful rooms, gorgeous artwork and furnishings, and generous breakfasts (served on the roof terrace, which offers evening bar service). All the rooms are set on the fourth floor of an elegant building (with elevator and A/C), so it's quieter than many places. It's located just a 10-minute walk from the Vatican Museums,

The trendy rooftop at Mama Shelter Roma.

and a block from the Metro. Charming, conscientious hosts possess a deep knowledge of Rome and what will interest visitors. A top pick!

Via Barletta 29. www.quodlibetroma.com. ℭ **06-1222642.** 10 units. 89€–250€ double. Breakfast included. Minimum stay rules may apply. Metro: Ottaviano. **Amenities:** Roof terrace; free Wi-Fi.

Residenza Paolo VI ★★   Literally across the street from Vatican City limits, Residenza Paolo can legitimately claim it's "steps from St. Peter's." Taking breakfast on the rooftop terrace is a special treat, as this narrow strip overlooks St. Peter's Square—if your timing's right, you'll see the Pope blessing crowds on Sunday. (There's bar service on the terrace from 4pm onward.) Old-world rooms feature tile or hardwood floors, heavy drapes, Oriental rugs, and quality beds, though standard guest rooms can be a bit "cozy."

Via Paolo VI 29. www.residenzapaolovi.com. ℭ **06-684870.** 35 units. 129€–229€ double. Breakfast included. Metro: Ottaviano (15-min walk). Bus: 64. **Amenities:** Bar; room service; free Wi-Fi.

Villa Laetitia ★★★   This elegant hotel overlooking the River Tiber is the work of Anna Fendi of the Roman fashion dynasty. Thanks to her design aesthetic, the rooms are anything but traditional, despite the 1911 villa setting surrounded by tranquil gardens. The decor features bold patterns on the beds and floors, and modern art on the walls. Splurge for the black-and-white Giulio Cesare suite, with its round leather bed and blissful garden views. Standard rooms are on the snug side, but most have kitchenettes. It's worth noting that the hotel is a 20-minute walk to centro and, thus perhaps not the best choice for first-time visitors to Rome. **Enoteca la Torre** is the villa's two Michelin-starred restaurant. *Tip:* Look for great last-minute rates on the hotel website.

Lungotevere delle Armi 22–23. www.villalaetitia.com. ℭ **06-3226776.** 20 units. 135€–400€ double. Breakfast included. Metro: Lepanto. **Amenities:** Restaurant; bar; babysitting; bike rentals; fitness room; room service; free Wi-Fi.

INEXPENSIVE

Rome Armony Suites ★★★ A warning: Rome Armony Suites is almost always booked up months in advance, so if you're interested, book early. Why so popular? The answer starts with service; owner Luca is a charming, sensitive host, especially helpful with first-time visitors to Rome. Rooms are big, clean, and modern, with private baths, minimalist decor, tea and coffee facilities, and a fridge in each unit. Final, major perk: free loaner smartphones loaded with maps and tourist info, to help guests get the most out of their visit; calls to the U.S. and Canada included, too.

Via Orazio 3. www.romearmonysuites. com. ⓒ **348-3305419.** 6 units. 95€–150€ double. Breakfast included (served at a nearby cafe). Metro: Lepanto. **Amenities:** Free Wi-Fi.

Anna Fendi's Villa Laetitia Hotel.

(see map p. 111)

Ancient Rome, Monti & Celio

There aren't many hotel rooms on earth with a view of a 2,000-year-old amphitheater, so there's a definite "only in Rome" feeling to lodging on the edge of the ancient city (see map p. 111). The negative to staying in this area—and it's a big minus—is that the streets adjacent to those ancient monuments have little life outside tourism. There's a lot more going on in **Monti,** Rome's oldest "suburb" (only 5 min. from the Forum), which is especially lively after dark. **Celio** has more of a neighborhood vibe, a local, gentrified life quite separate from tourism.

EXPENSIVE

The Inn at the Roman Forum ★★ This small hotel tucked down a medieval lane on the edge of Monti has the forums of several Roman emperors its neighbors. Rooms are tastefully decadent, with colorful silks, rich textures, and spacious bathrooms. The posh fifth-floor Master Garden Rooms have private patios surrounded by flowers and greenery, ochre walls, and busts of emperors, and a plush apartment with a kitchen sleeps up to six people. The hotel's small **roof lounge** has views of the Campidoglio, and for archaeology buffs there's an ancient Roman *cryptoporticus* behind the lobby.

Via degli Ibernesi 30. www.theinnattheromanforum.com. ⓒ **06-69190970.** 21 units. 180€–550€ double. Breakfast included. Metro: Cavour. **Amenities:** 2 bars; roof terrace; concierge; room service; free Wi-Fi.

MODERATE

Duca d'Alba ★★   Located on one of the main drags of hip Monti, with all the nightlife and authentic dining you'll need, Duca d'Alba strikes a fine balance between old-world gentility and 21st-century amenities. Rooms in the main building are snug and contemporary, with modern furniture and gadgetry and smallish bathrooms. If you want to spring for slightly higher rates, the spacious annex rooms next door have a *palazzo* character, with terracotta floors, oak and cherry furniture, and soundproofed street-facing rooms. Second-floor rooms are the brightest.

Via Leonina 14. www.hotelducadalba.com. ✆ **06-484471.** 27 units. 79€–230€ double. Some rates include breakfast. Metro: Cavour. **Amenities:** Bar; free Wi-Fi.

The Glam ★★   A decidedly modern vibe pervades at this superbly located, boutiquey hotel—right on Via Nazionale, within walking distance of Termini Station, the Colosseum and Forum, Trevi Fountain, and just about everything else you'll want to see in central Rome. Art-filled rooms are cool and functional, if a little impersonal, but a very friendly and welcoming staff more than compensates for this. A rooftop restaurant and glorious open-air bar and terrace are popular gathering spots for young Romans, and the bartender mixes a good cocktail.

Via Nazionale 82. www.theglamhotelroma.it. ✆ **06-99345430.** 59 units. 160€–305€ double. Some rates include breakfast. Metro: Repubblica or Cavour. **Amenities:** Bar; restaurant; roof terrace; free Wi-Fi.

Lancelot ★★★   Expect warmth and hospitality from the minute you walk in the door. The staff, all of whom have been here for years, are the heart and

The Lancelot overlooks ancient Rome.

soul of Lancelot, and the reason why the hotel has so many repeat guests. The room decor is simple, and most of the units are spacious, immaculately kept, and light-filled, thanks to large windows. Bathrooms are small but serviceable. Sixth-floor rooms have private terraces overlooking Ancient Rome—well worth springing for. The 1938 building retains vestiges of its Art Deco past, most felt in the genteel, chandelier-lit common areas for meeting other travelers, *Room With A View*–style. Unusual for Rome, Lancelot also has limited private parking, for which you'll need to book ahead.

Via Capo d'Africa 47. www.lancelothotel.com. ℂ **06-70450615.** 60 units. 130€– 205€ double. Breakfast included. Metro: Colosseo. Bus: 53, 75, 85, 87, 118. Tram: 3. **Amenities:** Restaurant; bar; free Wi-Fi.

The Centro Storico & Pantheon

There's nothing like an immersion in the atmosphere of Rome's lively Renaissance heart, though you'll pay dearly for *location, location, location.* Since many of Centro's characteristic streets are pedestrian only, expect to do a lot of walking, but that's a reason many visitors come here in the first place—to wander and discover the glory that was and is Rome. Many restaurants and cafes are an easy walk from the hotels here.

EXPENSIVE

Chapter Roma ★★   Stylish and irreverently hip, this design hotel is in step with the evolving character of the Rome Ghetto, where modern art galleries and concept stores are springing up next to traditional kosher restaurants. Rooms range from small to party-size, and all have wood floors, an industrial-chic vibe, original artworks, Marshall speakers, and bars stocked with booze and mixers. We appreciate the eco-friendly bath amenities and absence of tiny plastic bottles. The millennial vibe is strong in the lobby bar and adjacent **Market** cafe, which serves smoothies, wraps, and salads. A seasonal rooftop restaurant serves margaritas and Mexican food.

Via di S. Maria De' Calderari, 47. www.chapter-roma.com. ℂ **06-89935351.** 42 units. 206€–600€ double. Bus: 40, 64 (to Largo Torre di Argentina). Tram: 8. **Amenities:** Bar; cafe; 2 restaurants; free Wi-Fi.

Del Sole al Pantheon ★   For history and atmosphere, it's hard to beat a place that's been hosting wayfarers since 1467, with past guests including Jean-Paul Sartre and Simone de Beauvoir, as well as at least one Hapsburg king.

Updated rooms have lost some of their period charm but are still classic in feel, with lots of plush textures and soothing colors. Some feature million-dollar views of the Pantheon. Suites offer separate bedrooms and Jacuzzi tubs.

Piazza della Rotonda 63. www.hotelsolealpantheon.com. ℂ **06-6780441.** 25 units. 200€–450€ double. Breakfast included. Bus: 40, 64, 85 (to Largo Torre Argentina). **Amenities:** Bar; bike rentals; concierge; garden; free Wi-Fi.

Raphael ★★★   This ivy-covered palace just off Piazza Navona is an ideal choice for a special-occasion stay, with luxurious rooms, enthusiastic staff, and a roof terrace with spectacular views across Rome. It's a gorgeous hotel, highlighted by 20th-century artwork inside, including Picasso ceramics and paintings by Mirò, Morandi, and De Chirico scattered across the property. The standard rooms are all decorated in Victorian style, with antique furnishings and hardwood floors. Some prefer staying in the Richard Meier–designed executive suites, which blend modern and Asian design and feature oak paneling, contemporary art, and Carrara marble. The haute organic, vegetarian restaurant will leave even diehard carnivores sated.

Largo Febo 2, near Piazza Navona. www.raphaelhotel.com. ℂ **06-682831.** 51 units. 220€–680€ double. Breakfast included. Bus: 40, 64, 70. **Amenities:** Restaurant; bar; babysitting; concierge; room service; free Wi-Fi.

MODERATE

Coronari Palace ★★   Once a cozy 10-room guesthouse with classic décor, Coronari Palace now sings a modern tune. Its 16 rooms feature modular furnishings and wood laminate floors; three junior suites have terraces. While some bathrooms are on the snug side, they're sleek and well-designed, most with enough counter/sink space for a toiletry bag. The communal roof terrace invites guests to BYOB and enjoy a pleasant evening looking out on the terracotta rooftops of Rome. There are no surprises here, just clean, up-to-date facilities, good prices, and amiable staff.

Via dei Coronari 231. www.coronaripalace.com. ℂ **06-68309541.** 16 units. 198€–350€ double. Breakfast included. Bus: 40, 64. **Amenities:** Roof terrace; free Wi-Fi.

Damaso Hotel ★★   Consistently rated as one of the top hotels in Rome, this upscale 3-star in a 19th-century palazzo punches above its weight class. Well-thought-out rooms and sleek marble bathrooms make the most of their small dimensions, though rooms overlooking busy Corso Vittorio Emanuele II may be a touch noisy. A decent breakfast buffet is offered in a woody dining room that converts to a cocktail bar at night; the rooftop terrace brings the views.

Piazza della Cancelleria 62. www.hoteldamaso.it. ℂ **06-45503061.** 39 units. 120€–250€ double. Breakfast included. Bus: 42, 62, 64, 916. **Amenities:** Bar; roof terrace; lounge; free Wi-Fi.

Hotel Adriano ★★   Just 5 minutes from the Pantheon, this stylish retreat occupies an elegant 17th-century *palazzo*. Rooms boast a chic and modern vibe, though standard rooms can be a tad utilitarian. A few deluxe rooms and suites have terraces with views of the Roman rooftops. In a crowded hotel market, Adriano stands out for its plush, well-designed common areas, including **The Gin Corner,** a trendy cocktail bar specializing in…you guessed it. Rooms in the nearby "Domus Adriani" share a small kitchen and common area. *Tip:* Email the hotel directly for the lowest rates.

Via di Pallacorda 2. www.hoteladriano.com. ℂ **06-68802451.** 40 units. 200€–400€ double. Bus: 70, 85. **Amenities:** Bar; babysitting; bikes; concierge; gym; free Wi-Fi.

Hotel L'Orologio ★★   Despite only opening in 2022, this sleek 4-star feels like it's been here a long time—maybe because it occupies a historic palazzo just steps from the Largo Argentina archaeological site. The lovely mid-century modern lobby also lends a vintage air. Rooms are small and well-organized, if a little on the dark side, and showers have excellent water pressure. Two things stand out here: the extremely welcoming staff and a stunner of a rooftop terrace, where breakfast and evening *aperitivi* are served with a glorious view of the Rome skyline.

Corso Vittorio Emanuele II 110. www.hotelorologioroma.com. © **06-6865019.** 43 units. 175€–450€ double. Breakfast included. Bus: 46, 62, 64, 81, 916. **Amenities:** Rooftop terrace, bar; free Wi-Fi.

Residenza in Farnese ★★ This little gem is tucked away in a 15th-century mansion across the street from the Palazzo Farnese, within stumbling distance of Campo de' Fiori but still reasonably quiet. Rooms vary in size and are eclectic and artsy, with tiled floors and a vaguely Renaissance theme. Prices are usually on the low end of the range shown here, but a 2-night minimum may apply on weekends. The complimentary breakfast spread is downright generous. *Tip:* Last-minute rates are often much lower than those shown below.

Via del Mascherone 59. www.residenzafarneseroma.it. © **06-68210980.** 31 units. 140€–240€ double. Breakfast included. Bus: 40, 64. **Amenities:** Bar; roof terrace; concierge; room service; free Wi-Fi.

INEXPENSIVE

Mimosa ★★ This budget stalwart in the heart of the *centro storico* enjoys great word of mouth, so book early. Recently renovated rooms are colorful and bright, with private bathrooms and A/C—neither a given at this price point. Larger units are suitable for families with small children. A location this close to the Pantheon at these prices is hard to beat.

Via di Santa Chiara 61. www.hotelmimosa.net. © **06-68801753.** 11 units. 89€–150€ double. Breakfast included. Bus: 40, 64, 70 to Largo di Torre Argentina. **Amenities:** Free Wi-Fi.

Tridente, the Spanish Steps & Via Veneto

The heart of the city is a great place to stay if you're a serious shopper or enjoy the romantic, somewhat nostalgic locales of the Spanish Steps and Trevi Fountain. But expect to part with a lot of extra euro for the privilege. This is one of the most elegant areas in Rome (see map p. 133), but we've found you a few bargains (and some worthy splurges).

EXPENSIVE

Babuino 181 ★★ Leave Renaissance and baroque Italy far behind at this sleek, contemporary hotel, with relatively spacious rooms and apartment-size suites outfitted with Frette bathrobes and Nespresso machines. Bathrooms are roomy and well-laid out, and shuttered windows with hefty curtains provide a quiet and perfectly blacked-out environment for light sleepers. The onsite restaurant **EMME** offers a fine dining experience. A surcharged breakfast is served on the rooftop terrace, which doubles as a cocktail bar at night.

Via del Babuino 181. www.romeluxurysuites.com/babuino. © **06-32295295.** 24 units. 225€–470€ double. Metro: Flaminio or Spagna. **Amenities:** Bar; babysitting; concierge; restaurant; roof terrace; room service; free Wi-Fi.

The Inn at the Spanish Steps.

The Inn at the Spanish Steps ★★★   Set in one of Rome's most desirable locations on the famed Via dei Condotti shopping street, this hotel is the epitome of luxe. Rooms are fantasias of design and comfort, some with parquet floors and cherubim frescoes on the ceiling, others decked out with wispy fabrics draping canopied beds; upgraded units have swoon-worthy views of Piazza di Spagna. The rooftop garden provides beautiful views, to be enjoyed at breakfast—with its generous buffet spread—or for evening cocktails.

Via del Babuino 181. www.romeluxurysuites.com/babuino. ⓒ 06-32295295. 24 units. 225€–470€ double. Metro: Flaminio or Spagna. **Amenities:** Bar; babysitting; concierge; restaurant; roof terrace; room service; free Wi-Fi.

Villa Spalletti Trivelli ★★★   This really is an experience rather than a hotel, an early-20th-century neoclassical villa remodeled into an exclusive 14-room guesthouse, where lodgers mingle in the gardens or the great hall, as if invited by an Italian noble for the weekend. There is no key for the entrance door; ring a bell and a staff member will open it for you, often offering you a glass of prosecco as a welcome. Onsite is a sizeable and modern wellness oasis for those who want extra pampering, while rooms feature elegant antiques and embroidered bed linens, with sitting areas or separate lounges. And the minibar? All free, all day. A rooftop lounge boasts Jacuzzis, a complimentary bar, and light fare.

Via Piacenza 4. www.villaspalletti.it. ⓒ **06-48907934.** 14 units. 415€–750€ double. Breakfast included. Metro: Barberini. **Amenities:** Restaurant; bar; concierge; exercise room; roof terrace; room service; Jacuzzis; sauna; spa; free Wi-Fi.

MODERATE

Hotel Condotti ★   This cozy hotel can be a tremendously good deal depending on when you stay and how far out you book. For your money you'll get a clean, unpretentious room, though the common areas aim higher, with marble floors, antiques, tapestries, and a Venetian-glass chandelier. Standard rooms are tight; you'll get a bit more space and modernity in the nearby annex rooms. Budget-priced "petite" rooms measure less than 100 sq. ft. Overall it's worth considering for its proximity to the Spanish Steps.

Via Mario de' Fiori 37. www.hotelcondotti.com. © **06-6794661.** 16 units. 135€–290€. Metro: Spagna. **Amenities:** Bar; babysitting; free Wi-Fi.

La Lumière ★   You won't be checking in for chic design or innovation—this traditional hotel just off Via dei Condotti smacks of old-school comfort, from rooms with matchy-matchy color schemes, wood floors, and warm lighting to the glassed-in roof terrace or open-air patio where breakfast and evening *aperitivi* are served. For all but highest season and holidays, it's a winner on the price/location ratio.

Via Belsiana 72. www.lalumieredipiazzadispagna.com. © **06-69380806.** 10 units. 120€–350€ double. Breakfast included. Metro: Spagna. **Amenities:** Bar; roof terrace; free Wi-Fi.

La Residenza ★   Considering its location just off Via Veneto, this hotel—hosting guests since 1936—is a smart deal. Renovated, modern rooms retain a touch of Art Deco appeal, and are all relatively spacious, with a couple of easy chairs or a small couch in addition to a desk. Families with children are especially catered to, with quad rooms and junior suites on the top floor featuring a separate kids' alcove with two sofa beds, and an outdoor terrace with patio furniture. The excellent breakfast buffet includes quality charcuterie and cheeses, homemade breads, and pastries.

Via Emilia 22–24. www.hotel-la-residenza.com. © **06-4880789.** 27 units. 150€–350€ double. Breakfast included. Metro: Barberini. **Amenities:** Bar; babysitting; cafe; terrace; room service; free Wi-Fi.

Parlamento ★★   Set on the top floors of a 17th-century *palazzo*, this is one of the best moderately-priced deals in the area. Rooms are pleasantly fresh and modern, with wood floors and monochromatic color schemes. Breakfast is served on the rooftop terrace—you can also chill up there with a glass of wine in the evening. The Trevi Fountain, Spanish Steps, and Pantheon are all within a 5- to 10-minute walk.

Via delle Convertite 5 (at Via del Corso). www.hotelparlamento.it. © **06-69921000.** 19 units. 165€–250€ double. Breakfast included. Metro: Spagna. **Amenities:** Bar; concierge; room service; free Wi-Fi.

INEXPENSIVE

Panda ★   Panda has long been popular among budget travelers, so it books up quickly. Rooms are spare, but not without some old-fashioned charm, like characteristic Roman *cotto* (terracotta) floor tiles, and the odd frescoed ceiling or exposed beams—and they do have air-conditioning. Most rooms are a bit cramped, but for these prices in this neighborhood they remain a very, very good deal. Outside your doorstep are several great cafes and wine bars where you can start the day with espresso and end it with a nightcap. *Tip:* With its budget single rooms with shared baths, Panda is a good pick for solo travelers. A 5€ breakfast voucher is good for the bar a couple of doors down.

Via della Croce 35. www.hotelpanda.it. ✆ **06-6780179.** 28 units (8 with shared bath). 85€–130€ double with bath. Metro: Spagna. **Amenities:** Free Wi-Fi.

Around Termini

Known for its concentration of cheap hotels, the Termini area (see map p. 141) is about the only part of the center where you can score a high-season double for under 100€. Lately the area has more upscale hotels, particularly in the zone northwest of the station. Streets close to the train station are hardly picturesque, and parts of the neighborhood are a little sketchy. Still, it's very convenient to most of Rome's top sights, and a hub for Metro lines, buses, and trams. The following are some of our favorites near Termini.

EXPENSIVE

Anantara Palazzo Naiadi ★★★ We won't sugar-coat it—this is one pricey palace. But in exchange for lots of dearly departed euros, guests are treated to a regal experience from the moment they approach the porticoed neoclassical façade, which wraps in a crescent around a quarter of Piazza della Repubblica. Rooms and suites are studies in rich textures and subtle color, with plush carpeting and marble baths. The lofty lobby bar serves fancy drinks and snacks, while the adjacent **Tazio** restaurant/bar swims in the ambiance of Fellini-era Rome. The hotel's spa is top-notch, and the summertime rooftop pool is a stunner.

Piazza della Repubblica 47. www.nh-hotels.com/hotel/anantara-palazzo-naiadi-rome-hotel. ✆ **06-489381.** 238 units. 340€–700€ double. Metro: Repubblica. **Amenities:** 2 bars; 2 restaurants (1 summer-only); concierge; rooftop pool; spa; fitness room; free Wi-Fi.

MODERATE

Hotel Mediterraneo ★★★ Within sight of Termini station, this surprisingly upscale hotel offers vintage art deco style, along with a team of long-time employees who warmly evoke the spirit of a bygone era of class and service. Freshly renovated rooms are large and well-equipped, with bathrooms of grand proportions; suites are downright palatial, and 7 top-floor units have terraces with sweeping views. Read about the hotel's interesting WWII-era history as you linger over cocktails in its Wes Anderson-y bar. Sister properties **Atlantico** and **Massimo D'Azeglio**, located next door and across the street, respectively, offer lower room prices and share amenities with Mediterraneo. *Tip:* Check online for off-season or last-minute deals on those top-floor suites.

Via Cavour 15. www.romehotelmediterraneo.it. ✆ **06-4884051.** 245 units. 165€–250€ double. Most rates include breakfast. Metro: Termini. **Amenities:** Bar; concierge; gym; restaurant; roof terrace; room service; free Wi-Fi.

Residenza Cellini ★★   It's tradition all the way at Cellini, a modest, refined hotel around the corner from Piazza della Repubblica. Antique-styled rooms are proudly 19th century, with thick walls (so no noise from your neighbors), solid furnishings, and handsome parquet floors, yet also offer modern comforts like memory-foam mattresses and A/C. Bathrooms come with Jacuzzi tubs or jetted showers. Service is topnotch and wonderfully personal.

Via Modena 5. www.residenzacellini.it. ℓ **06-47825204.** 18 units. 99€–199€ double. Breakfast additional. Metro: Repubblica. **Amenities:** Concierge; room service; free Wi-Fi.

INEXPENSIVE

Beehive ★★★   Conceived as part hostel and part hotel, the Beehive is an utterly cheerful lodging experience, run by eco-minded American owners and offering rooms for a variety of budgets. Options range from fancy-for-the-price private rooms with ensuites and TVs to economical rooms with shared bathrooms, as well as both mixed and female-only dorms. All are decorated with flair, adorned with artwork or flea-market treasures and they smell heavenly (go sniff for yourself). A garden offers trees and secluded reading/relaxing space. A buzzy cafe offers breakfast a la carte, as well as occasional, budget-friendly vegan/vegetarian meals; there's also a concerted effort to maintain eco-conscious practices. Weekly pizza and pasta-making classes add to the fun.

Via Marghera 8. www.the-beehive.com. ℓ **06-44704553.** 20 units. 60€–100€ double; 20€–35€ dorm beds. Metro: Termini or Castro Pretorio. **Amenities:** Cafe; garden; lounge; free Wi-Fi.

Seven Kings Relais ★★   This unfussy hotel has a slightly retro feel, kitted out with dark wooden furniture, chocolate-brown bedspreads, and modern tiled floors. Despite its location right on one of Rome's busiest thoroughfares, street noise is minimal—an external courtyard and modern soundproofing see to that. "Breakfast" is a 24-hour self-service bar with tea, coffee, and packaged cookies, but the area has plenty of inexpensive dining options. Management has several other nearby properties as well, run through **Roma Termini Suites** (www.romaterminisuites.com).

Via XX Settembre 58A. www.sevenkingsrelais.com. ℓ **06-42917784.** 11 units. 86€–180€ double. Metro: Repubblica. **Amenities:** Free Wi-Fi.

Trastevere

This was once an "undiscovered" neighborhood—but no longer. Being based here does give some degree of escape from the busy *centro storico*, though Trastevere's narrow streets can be packed to the gills in the evenings, as this boho section of Rome (see map p. 143) has bars, shops, and restaurants galore. The preponderance of Airbnb-type rentals here has led to a less "local" feel in the neighborhood, but it still oozes atmosphere.

MODERATE

Hotel San Francesco ★★   Lying at the edge of Trastevere, close to the Porta Portese gate in an area that hasn't (yet) been gentrified, this hotel still

When you book a "charity room" at Hotel San Francesco, the hotel makes a 4€ donation to help Rome's shelter dogs.

has a local feel that has disappeared from much of the neighborhood. All rooms are bright, with color-washed walls and modern tiling. Doubles are fairly small, but the bathrooms are quite roomy. The grand piano in the lobby adds a touch of old-time charm; a top-floor garden with a cocktail bar overlooks terracotta rooftops and pealing church bell towers. A tasty cooked breakfast costs extra here. *Tip:* Book a "charity room," and the hotel will match your 2€ donation to help Rome's shelter dogs.

Via Jacopa de' Settesoli 7. www.hotelsanfrancesco.net. © **06-48300051.** 24 units. 130€–199€ double. Bus: H, 44 or 75. Tram: 3 or 8. **Amenities:** Bar; free Wi-Fi.

Santa Maria ★★　Hidden behind an ivy-covered wall, the lovely Santa Maria is built around a 16th-century cloister, now a relaxing courtyard fragrant with orange trees. Cheerful rooms, some with exposed brick walls and beamed ceilings, are mostly on the ground floor. Free breakfast and loaner bikes, a roof garden, and a cocktail bar all make this charmer a stand-out in hotel-deprived Trastevere. *Tip:* Several spacious, multi-bed rooms make this a fine option for families.

Vicolo del Piede 2. www.htlsantamaria.com. © **06-5894626.** 20 units. 106€–240€ double. Breakfast included. Tram: 8. Bus: 23, 280, H. **Amenities:** Bar; courtyard; loaner bikes; free Wi-Fi.

INEXPENSIVE

Arco del Lauro ★★   Hidden in Trastevere's snaking alleyways, this serene little B&B occupies the ground floor of a shuttered pink *palazzo*. Bright rooms have wood floors, plush beds, and simple decor, with a mix of modern and period furnishings. Rooms can't be defined as large, but they all feel spacious thanks to lofty wood ceilings. Breakfast is taken at a nearby cafe (with a 5€ surcharge); coffee and snacks are laid out around the clock. Minimum stay rules may apply in high season.

Via Arco de' Tolomei 29. www.arcodellauro.it. © **06-97840350.** 6 units. 85€–155€ double. Bus: 23, 280, H. Tram: 8. **Amenities:** Free Wi-Fi.

WHERE TO EAT

Rome remains a top destination for food lovers and today offers more dining diversity than ever. Though many of its *trattorie* haven't changed their menus in a quarter of a century (for better or worse), the city has an increasing number of creative spots with chefs willing to revisit tradition.

Restaurants generally serve lunch between 12:30 and 2:30pm, and dinner between 7:30 and 10:30pm. At all other times, most restaurants are closed—though a new generation is moving toward all-day dining, with a limited service at the "in-between" time of mid-afternoon.

If you have your heart set on any of these places below, we seriously recommend *reserving ahead of arrival.* Hot tables go quickly, especially on high-season weekends—often twice: once for the early-dining tourists, and then again for locals, who dine later, typically around 9pm.

A *servizio* (tip or service charge) is almost always added to your bill or included in the price. Sometimes it is marked on the menu as *coperto e servizio* or *pane e coperto* (bread, cover charge, and service). You can leave extra if you wish—a couple of euros as a token—but in general, big tipping is not the norm here. Contrary to advice on some travel blogs, Italian waitstaff will *not* be offended if you overtip. If you have any questions about an item on your bill, don't hesitate to ask for an explanation.

Restaurants by Cuisine

BAKERY

Antico Forno Roscioli ★★★, p. 88
Biscottificio Artigiano Innocenti, p. 91

CAFE

Antico Caffè Greco, p. 89
Babington's Tea Rooms, p. 89
La Bottega del Caffè ★★, p. 158

GELATO

Come il Latte, p. 85
Fatamorgana ★★★, p. 85
Fior di Luna ★★★, p. 85
Frigidarium, p. 85

Gelateria Alberto Pica ★★★, p. 85
Old Bridge Gelateria, p. 85

INTERNATIONAL

Imàgo ★★★, p. 90
Maharajah ★★, p. 83

JEWISH

Nonna Betta ★★, p. 87

MODERN ITALIAN/ROMAN

Antico Arco ★★★, p. 92
Glass Hostaria ★★, p. 92
Il Bacaro ★★, p. 87

La Barrique ★★, p. 83
Osteria degli Amici ★★, p. 96
Pipero Roma ★★, p. 85
Porto Fluviale ★, p. 96
Taverna Angelica ★★, p. 81
Trimani Il Wine Bar ★, p. 91

PIZZA
Bonci Pizzarium ★★★, p. 82
Da Baffetto ★★, p. 88
Da Remo ★★, p. 96
Dar Poeta ★, p. 94
Li Rioni ★★, p. 84
Pinsere ★★, p. 91
Pinsa 'm po! ★★, p. 81

PUB FARE
L'Elementare, p. 158

REGIONAL ITALIAN
Al Ceppo ★★, p. 89
Colline Emiliane ★★★, p. 90
Trattoria Monti ★★, p. 90

SALAD & SANDWICHES
Duecento Gradi ★★, p. 81
L'Insalata Ricca ★, p. 85
Pic Nic ★★ , p. 89

SEAFOOD
Osteria La Gensola ★★★, p. 94
Pierluigi ★★, p. 85
Taverna Angelica ★★, p. 81

TRADITIONAL ITALIAN/ ROMAN
Alfredo e Ada ★★, p. 88
Antica Hostaria Romanesca ★, p. 86
Armando al Pantheon ★★, p. 86
Canova Tadolini ★★, p. 86
Checchino dal 1887 ★★, p. 90
Da Enzo ★★, p. 95
Flavio al Velavevodetto ★, p. 93
InRoma al Campidoglio ★, p. 95
La Campana ★★, p. 83
Mercato Centrale Roma, p. 87
Nonna Betta ★★, p. 91
Osteria Cacio e Pepe ★, p. 87
Osteria La Gensola ★★★, p. 94
Retrobottega ★★, p. 87
Spirito DiVino ★★, p. 93

VEGETARIAN
Armando al Pantheon ★★, p. 86

Near Vatican City

For restaurant locations, see map p. 99. The path leading from the Vatican Museums to St. Peter's Basilica is something of a gauntlet of bad food—overpriced tourist traps preying on the dazed crowds that have just wandered out of the museum and need sustenance before tackling the basilica. Fortunately, a handful of very fine options for inexpensive fast food are right near the Vatican—and no, we don't mean McDonald's (though it's here, too). If you just want a quick, tasty sandwich before or after your Vatican safari, **Duecento Gradi ★★,** is a topnotch panino joint with lots of yummy choices, right across from the Vatican walls at Piazza Risorgimento 3 (www.duecentogradi.it; ✆ **06-39754239;** Sun–Thurs 10am–2am; Fri–Sat 11am–5am). Around the corner, in a friendly hole-in-the-wall at Via Dei Gracchi 7, **Pinsa 'm po! ★★** serves light and crispy "pinsa" pizzas with organic ingredients and gourmet toppings, most priced around 5€ (pinsampo.it; ✆ **06-88980716;** Mon–Sat 10:30am–9pm).

EXPENSIVE

Taverna Angelica ★★ MODERN ITALIAN/SEAFOOD In a sea of mediocre restaurants near St. Peter's, Angelica serves up surprisingly good and justly priced (though not cheap) fare. Specialties include salted cod-stuffed ravioli in spicy sauce, a divine risotto with blueberries and goat cheese,

Taverna Angelica, near St. Peter's, serves up modern Italian cuisine.

or baked turbot, roast pigeon, or a vegetarian Wellington. Save room for the delicious, non-run-of-the-mill dessert options. Reservations required.

Piazza A. Capponi 6. tavernaangelica.com. ℭ **06-6874514.** Entrees 17€–38€; tasting menus from 50€. Mon–Thurs and Sun noon–3:30pm, dinner daily 6pm–midnight. Closed 10 days in Aug. Metro: Ottaviano.

MODERATE

Bonci Pizzarium ★★★ PIZZA   Celebrity chef Gabriele Bonci has always had a cult following in the Eternal City. And since he's been featured on TV shows overseas and written up by influential bloggers, you can expect long lines at his pizzeria. No matter—it's worth waiting (and walking 10 minutes west of the Vatican Museums) for some of the best pizza you'll ever taste, sold by the slice or by weight. His ingredients are fresh and organic, the crust is perfect, and the toppings often experimental (try the mortadella and crumbled pistachio). There's also a good choice of Italian craft IPAs and wheat beers, and wines by the glass. Only a handful of stand-up tables are inside and benches outside for seating, and reservations aren't taken.

Via della Meloria 43. www.bonci.it. ℭ **06-39745416.** Pizza 12€–40€ per kilo, depending on toppings. Mon–Sat 11am–10pm. Metro: Cipro.

Ancient Rome, Monti & Celio

For restaurant locations, see map p. 111. For a cappuccino, a quick bite, or aperitivo snacking, head to the epicenter of Monti, **La Bottega del Caffè** ★★

(© **06-4741578**) on lively Piazza Madonna dei Monti, open from 8am to the wee hours. When we hanker for something other than Italian food, we head to **Maharajah ★★**, an elegant Northern Indian eatery at Via dei Serpenti 124 (www.maharajah.it; © **06-4747144**).

MODERATE

InRoma al Campidoglio ★ ITALIAN   Once a club for Rome's film industry, InRoma sits on a cobbled lane opposite the Palatine Hill. Though the place rests heavily on its cinematic laurels, it still serves up authentic Roman and regional cuisine. Meals might start with *caprese di bufala affumicata* (salad of tomatoes and smoked buffalo mozzarella) followed by classic pasta *carbonara*—they claim to do the best in Rome—or a main course of *saltimbocca* (veal cutlets wrapped with prosciutto and sage). Opt for a sidewalk table with a view to remember.

Via dei Fienili 56. www.inroma.eu. © **06-69191024**. Entrees 10€–20€. Daily 12:30–3:30pm and 7–11pm. Bus: H, 81, 83, 160, 170, 628.

La Barrique ★★ MODERN ROMAN   At this cozy, contemporary *enoteca* (wine bar with food), the kitchen knocks out fresh farm-to-table fare that complements the well-chosen wine list. The atmosphere is lively and informal, with rustic place settings and friendly service—as any proper *enoteca* should be. The menu offers classic comfort food, like meatballs in tomato sauce, and creative takes like a pumpkin tortino with gorgonzola and amaretti cookies. Vegetarians will find plenty of options.

Via del Boschetto 41B. labarriquevinoecucina.wordpress.com. © **06-47825953**. Entrees 11€–17€. Mon–Sat 12:45–2:30pm, 7–11pm, Sun 12:30–11pm. Metro: Cavour.

foodie FEAST: CULINARY TOURS & CLASSES

Nowhere is eating as important as it is in Italy. Numerous food tours and cooking classes offer a taste of Rome's culinary variety, from morning market tours, street food crawls, or daylong cooking classes that you leave with new recipes and skills to try out at home. In addition to all that eating, drinking, and cooking, all tours offer historical context and a more intimate look at Roman life as it relates to food. Here are two of our favorite ways to sample the vibrant, storied cuisine of the Eternal City:

Eating Europe (www.eatingeurope.com) offers in-depth small-group food and wine tours in Rome, particularly of Testaccio and Trastevere. Guides connect Rome's culinary culture to the city's history and traditions, and guests leave with their curiosity (and hunger) sated. Tours from 79€.

Run by a trio of food experts, including American **Eleonora Baldwin,** a TV foodie celebrity in Italy, **Casa Mia Tours** (www.casamiatours.com) offers private tours of Rome's markets and neighborhoods, with plenty of sampling along the way. They also do private cooking classes and dinners with locals. Prices range from 160€ per person for a cooking class to 390€ for a 3-hour private food tour for two.

GETTING YOUR FILL OF gelato

Don't leave town without trying one (or several) of Rome's outstanding **ice-cream parlors.** However, choose your gelato carefully: Don't buy close to the tourist-packed piazzas, and don't be dazzled by vats of brightly (and artificially) colored, air-pumped gelato. The best gelato is made only from natural ingredients, which impart a natural color—if the pistachio gelato is bright green, move on.

Grab a gelato to go for your wander around central Rome's landmarks.

INEXPENSIVE

Li Rioni ★★ PIZZA   This fab neighborhood pizzeria is close enough to the Colosseum to be convenient, but just distant enough to avoid the dreaded "touristy" label that applies to so much dining in this part of town. Roman-style pizzas baked in the wood-stoked oven are among the best in town, with perfect crisp crusts. There's also a bruschetta list (from around 4€) and a range of salads. Outside tables can be cramped, but there's plenty of room inside. If you want to eat late, booking is essential or you'll be fighting with hungry locals for a table. *Tip:* After visiting the Colosseum or the Basilica of San Clemente, stop for an aperitivo, then head here at 7 for an early (and cheap) pizza dinner.

Via SS. Quattro 24. www.lirioni.it. ✆ **06-70450605.** Pizzas 6€–9€. Wed–Mon 7pm–midnight. Closed 2 weeks in Aug. Metro: Colosseo. Bus: 51, 85, 87. Tram: 3 or 8.

Centro Storico & the Pantheon

For restaurant locations, see map p. 125. Vegetarians looking for massive salads (or anyone who just wants a break from meat and carbs) can find great

Take your cone (cono) or small cup (coppetta) and stroll as you eat—sitting down on the premises is usually more expensive. The recommended spots below are generally open mid-morning to late, sometimes after midnight on summer weekends. Cones and small cups cost between 2.50€ and 5€—at those prices you can eat it twice a day!

Near Campo de' Fiori, one of Rome's oldest artisan gelato makers, **Gelateria Alberto Pica** ★★★, Via della Seggiola 12 (✆ **06-6868405;** Bus H, 63 or 780; Tram 8) produces top-quality gelato churned with local ingredients, including wild strawberries grown on the family's country estate. In Monti, fabulous (and gluten-free) **Fatamorgana** ★★★, Piazza degli Zingari 5 (www.gelateria fatamorgana.com; ✆ **06-86391589;** Metro Cavour, plus other locations across Rome) is the place to try inventive flavors like delicate lavender and chamomile, or zingy avocado, lime, and white wine.

Two exceptions to the rule about avoiding gelato in touristy areas: venerable **Old Bridge Gelateria** ★, Viale Bastioni di Michelangelo (✆ **328-411-9478**; gelateriaoldbridge.com), which delights customers lined up for the Vatican Museums; and, near Piazza Navona, **Frigidarium** ★★★, Via del Governo Vecchio 112 (www.frigidarium-gelateria. com; ✆ **334-995-1184**), whose intense and creamy flavors will make you weep with joy. Have a copetta of mango and coconut for me.

In the Termini area, tiny but sleek **Come il Latte** ★★★, Via Silvio Spaventa 24 (www.comeillatte.it; ✆ **06-42903882;** Metro Repubblica or Castro Pretorio) turns out artisan gelatos in flavors ranging from salted caramel (yes please!), to mascarpone and crumbled cookies; fruit flavors change according to season.

Trastevere's best artisan gelato, **Fior di Luna** ★★★, Via della Lungaretta 96 (www.fiordiluna.com; ✆ **06-64561314;** Bus H or 780; Tram 8), is made with natural and Fair Trade produce. Star flavors are the incredibly rich chocolates, spiked with fig or orange, and an absolutely perfect pistachio.

food at the neighborhood branch of **L'Insalata Ricca,** Largo dei Chiavari 85 (www.linsalataricca.it; ✆ **06-68803656;** daily 11am–midnight).

EXPENSIVE

Pierluigi ★★ SEAFOOD   This hallowed seafood restaurant tucked near Piazza Farnese and in business since 1938 has a lot of pomp and circumstance. Fish that were swimming that morning and still-wiggling lobsters are brought tableside for inspection prior to being dispatched and impeccably prepared to order. There's also an extensive raw bar menu, as well as items for landlubbers. The wine list is encyclopedic, and service is discrete and flawless. This is event dining, and the ambiance—and prices—reflect it. *Tip:* Fresh fish is priced *per etto* (100 grams) and can add up fast.

Piazza de'Ricci 144. www.pierluigi.it. ✆ **06–6868717.** Entrees 32€–38€; fresh fish can go much higher. Daily noon–2:30pm and 7–11pm. Bus: 40, 64.

Pipero Roma ★★ MODERN ITALIAN   This Michelin-starred, long-established foodie haven occupies chic digs opposite the Chiesa Nuova, in a setting that's as sophisticated as the plates paraded forth from the kitchen.

Lamb chop at Pipero Roma.

While a la carte items are available, the focus here is on 3-, 6- or 8-course tasting menus, with options like tagliolini pasta with yellow peppers and miso, and an exquisite dessert of almonds, lychee fruit, and rosewater. Everything is expensive here and the small, precious servings will either dazzle you or drive you nuts with their pretention—it's better to make that decision beforehand.

Corso Vittorio Emanuele II 250. www.piperoroma.it. © **06-68139022.** Entrees 32€–45€, tasting menus 100€–160€. Tues–Fri 12–3pm and 7–11pm; Mon & Sat 7–11pm. Bus: 40, 46, 62, 64, 916.

MODERATE

Antica Hostaria Romanesca ★ ROMAN   It's very easy to eat badly on Campo de' Fiori, which makes this authentic spot with ringside seats on the piazza such a pleasant surprise. Romanesca does dependable, old-school Roman fare at fair prices, including a gloriously juicy *pollo e peperoni* (stewed chicken with peppers) and *abbacchio scottadito*, lamb chops hot off the grill. Locals snatch up the tables after 9pm, so a reservation is advised.

Campo de' Fiori 40 (east side of square). www.facebook.com/anticahostaria romanesca/. © **06-6864024.** Entrees 11€–16€. Daily noon–3pm and 7–11pm. Bus: 40, 64, 70. Tram: 8.

Armando al Pantheon ★★ ROMAN/VEGETARIAN   Despite a location just a few steps from the Pantheon, this family-run trattoria serves as many locals as tourists. Chef Armando Gargioli took over the place in 1961, and his progeny now run the business. Roman favorites to look for include *cacio e pepe*, marinated artichokes, and spaghetti alla Gricia. Despite the preponderance of offal on the menu, vegetarians will still find many suitable options. Advance reservations are a must, via a booking link on their website (no email).

Salita dei Crescenzi 31. www.armandoalpantheon.it. © **06-68803034.** Entrees 10€–25€. Mon–Sat 12:30–3pm and 7–11pm. Closed Sun, all of Aug. Bus: 40, 64, 70. Tram: 8.

Il Bacaro ★★ MODERN ITALIAN   Romantic and low-key, Il Bacaro's setting on a hidden backstreet near the Pantheon offers respite from the traffic and tourist crush. Delicious *primi* and *secondi* include white truffle tagliolini or a salted cod puttanesca. Desserts are of the creamy and fluffy variety, including the obligatory tiramisu. The wine list features well-priced varietals from all over Italy, including a couple dozen by the glass. Try to get a prized sidewalk table on a balmy summer evening.

Via degli Spagnoli 27 (near Piazza delle Coppelle). www.ilbacaroroma.com/en. © **06-6872554.** Entrees 24€–32€. Daily noon–midnight. Bus: 70, 71.

La Campana ★★ ROMAN/TRADITIONAL ITALIAN   Family atmosphere and a classic Roman elegance prevail in Rome's oldest restaurant (feeding guests since 1518!). The atmosphere is convivial yet refined, with a lovely mixture of regulars and locals. The broad selection of *antipasti* is displayed on a long table at the entrance, and the daily menu features authentic *cucina romana* that is heavy on offal—if you're not a fan, be sure to bring your Italian/English dictionary. You'll also find classics like *cacio e pepe,* plus myriad vegetarian choices. The wine list includes interesting local labels, and the staff and service are impeccable.

Vicolo della Campana 18. www.ristorantelacampana.com/en. © **06-6875273.** Main courses 12€–22€. Tues–Sun 12:30–3pm and 7:30–11pm. Metro: Spagna. Bus: 70.

Nonna Betta ★★ ROMAN/JEWISH   The history is palpable at Nonna Betta's, where photos of the Rome Ghetto of the 19th century line the walls. Traditional dishes include delicious *carciofi alla giudia:* deep-fried artichokes served with small morsels like battered cod filet, stuffed and fried zucchini flowers, carrot sticks, and whatever vegetable is in season. Don't forego the *baccalà* with onions and tomato or the zucchini carbonara. Middle Eastern standards such as falafel and hummus are on the menu, and all desserts are homemade, including a stellar cake with pine nuts. In keeping with kosher law, meat and dairy are on separate menus and never combined in recipes.

Via del Portico d'Ottavia 16. www.nonnabetta.it. © **06-68806263.** Entrees 12€–17€. Wed–Mon 12:15–3pm and 6:30–10pm. Bus: 40, 64, 170. Tram 8.

Retrobottega ★★ ROMAN   Fresh, modern, and progressive, the somewhat misnamed Retrobottega is a nice contrast to the well-worn streets of the touristy heart of town. This culinary laboratory, founded by four young, accomplished chefs, is an intimate but convivial choice. Most seats surround the open kitchen and customers interact directly with the chefs—there is no waitstaff. The day's offerings focus on local, seasonal, responsibly sourced ingredients and unexpected pairings, like risotto with malt and smoked ham, or pigeon with tamarind and artichokes. From the same owners, next-door **Pasta e Pane,** serves dine-in and takeaway pasta.

Via della Stelletta 4. www.retro-bottega.com. ℰ **06-68136310.** Entrees 20–28€, tasting menus 110€. Tues–Sun 1–2:30pm, 7:30pm–midnight. Adjacent pasta restaurant open Tues–Sun 12–4pm. Bus: 40, 70, 85.

INEXPENSIVE

Alfredo e Ada ★★ ROMAN   A daily chalkboard menu is the norm here, which speaks to the freshness and simplicity of this ultimate comfort food destination, now in its third generation of family ownership. Look for classic trattoria fare like eggplant parmigiana, artichoke lasagna, excellent carbonara, or tripe. The whole place oozes character, with shared tables, scribbled walls, and the house wine poured into carafes from a tap in the wall. Make a reservation or get here early—the restaurant only has five tables. This sort of place is becoming rare in Rome—enjoy it while you can.

Via dei Banchi Nuovi 14. ℰ **06-6878842.** Entrees 8€–12€. Tues–Sat noon–3pm and 7–10:30pm. Closed Aug. Bus: 40, 64.

Antico Forno Roscioli ★★★ BAKERY   The Rosciolis have been running this celebrated bakery for three generations since the 1970s, though bread has been made here since at least 1824. Today it's the home of the finest crusty sourdough in Rome, assorted cakes, and addictive pastries and biscotti, as well as exceptional Roman-style *pizza bianca* and *pizza rossa* sold by weight. This is largely a takeout joint, with limited seating—and the wider range of pizza toppings is only available from noon to 2:30pm. Around the corner is the wonderful **Roscioli restaurant and** *salumeria* **deli** at Via dei Giubbonari 21 and, at Piazza Benedetto Cairoli 16, **Roscioli Caffè,** the latest outpost of the family empire, which offers breakfast treats, cappuccini, and palate-pleasing panini.

Via dei Chiavari 34. www.anticofornoroscioli.it. ℰ **06-6864045.** Pizza from 5€ (sold by weight). Mon–Sat 7am–7:30pm, Sun 8am–6pm. Bus: 40, 85, 492. Tram: 8.

Da Baffetto ★★ PIZZA   You don't come to Baffetto for cheerful service or even for comfort—tables are cramped and you might wind up sharing one with strangers—but for the gloriously authentic Roman pizza. Crisp-crusted, oozing with toppings and dispatched quickly from the wood oven. This place is dirt-cheap and immensely popular with locals. If there's a line out the door, take heart: they shuffle people in and out of here pretty fast (and a lot of people are in line for take-away). After dinner, pop next door to Frigidarium (p. 85) for a gelato.

Via del Governo Vecchio 114. www.pizzeriabaffetto.it. ℰ **06–6861617.** Pizzas 6€–10€. Daily 12:30–3pm, 6:30pm–12:30am. Bus: 40, 64, 70, 492.

Tridente, the Spanish Steps & Via Veneto

For restaurant locations, see map p. 133. The historic cafes near the Spanish Steps are saturated with history but, sadly, tend to be overpriced tourist traps, where mediocre slices of cake or even a cup of coffee or tea will cost 5€. Nevertheless, you may want to pop inside the two most celebrated institutions: **Babington's Tea Rooms** (www.babingtons.com; ✆ **06-6786027;** Wed–Mon 12pm–10pm), established in 1893 at the foot of the Spanish Steps by a couple of English *signore,* and **Antico Caffè Greco,** Via dei Condotti 86 (anticocaffegreco.eu, ✆ **06-6791700;** daily 9am–9pm), Rome's oldest bar, which opened in 1760 and has hosted Keats, Ibsen, Goethe, and many other historical *cognoscenti.* In the heart of the Villa Borghese park, on Piazzale delle Canestre, **Pic Nic ★★** (✆ **06-855-7493**; daily 9am–7pm) is a great spot for lunch or a snack.

EXPENSIVE

Al Ceppo ★★ MARCHIGIANA/ROMAN   The setting of this Parioli neighborhood dining institution is an elegant 19th-century parlor, with dark wood furnishings, chandeliers, fresh flowers, family portraits on the walls, and an open kitchen with a wood-stoked hearth. The menu features regional dishes from the owners' home, the Le Marche region northeast of Rome: fish stews, fresh seafood, and grilled meats, all artfully prepared and presented, along with pastas both hearty and delicate. It's reason enough to head north to explore Parioli's many charms.

Via Panama 2 (near Piazza Ungheria). www.ristorantealceppo.com. ✆ **06-8419696.** Entrees 24€–32€. Tues–Sun 12:30–3pm and 7:30–11pm, Mon 7:30pm–11pm. Closed last 2 weeks Aug. Bus: 223, 360, 910. Tram: 3 or 19.

The delicate ravioli at Al Ceppo.

Imàgo ★★★ INTERNATIONAL   The views of Rome from this 6th-floor hotel restaurant are jaw-dropping, the old city laid out before you, glowing pink as the sun goes down. The food is equally special, as chef Andrea Antonini reinterprets Italian cuisine, borrowing heavily from international culinary traditions. His Michelin-starred menu changes seasonally but may include orecchiette pasta with sea urchin and turnip greens, deviled guinea fowl, or wild boar prepared with chocolate, cauliflower, and orange. Reservations are essential; jackets required for the gentlemen.

In Hotel Hassler, Piazza della Trinità dei Monti 6. www.imagorestaurant.com. © **06-69934726.** Tasting menus 170€–200€. Tues–Sat 7–10:30pm. Closed most of Jan. Metro: Spagna.

MODERATE

Canova Tadolini ★★ ROMAN   Few restaurants are as steeped in history as this place. Antonio Canova's sculpture studio was kept as a workshop by the descendants of his pupil Adamo Tadolini until 1967, and even today it's littered with tools and sculptures in bronze, plaster, and marble. The whole thing really does seem like a museum, with tables squeezed between models, casts, drapes, and bas-reliefs. Menus change from summer to winter, and always feature an interesting variety of traditional Roman pastas, plus meat, fish, and vegetarian dishes.

Via del Babuino 150A–B. www.canovatadolini.com. © **06-32110702.** Entrees 18€–30€. Daily noon–11pm (bar/cafe 8am–midnight). Metro: Spagna.

Colline Emiliane ★★★ EMILIANA-ROMAGNOLA   This family-owned restaurant tucked in an alley beside the Trevi Fountain has been serving traditional dishes from Emilia-Romagna since 1931. Service is excellent and so is the food: Classics include *tortelli di zucca* (pumpkin ravioli in butter sauce) and magnificent *tagliatelle alla Bolognese*, the mother of all Italian comfort foods. A menu of *secondi* is heavy on beef. Save room for the walnut-and-caramel cake or lemon meringue pie. Reservations are essential.

Via degli Avignonesi 22 (off Piazza Barberini). www.collineemiliane.com. © **06-4817538.** Entrees 15€–19€. Tues–Sun 12:45–2:45pm; Tues–Sat 7:30–10:45pm. Closed Aug. Metro: Barberini.

Around Termini

For restaurant locations, see map p. 141. Mostly catering to dazed travelers toting wheeled suitcases, restaurants around Termini don't have to be good to bring in business. The following are some of our favorite exceptions to that norm.

MODERATE

Trattoria Monti ★★ REGIONAL/MARCHE   Word is definitely out on this cozy, plain-Jane trattoria near Termini station. But that just means you need to reserve in advance to sample outstanding, hearty pastas and meat and game dishes from the Marche region. You will remember the *tortello al rosso d'uovo*—a large, delicate ravioli filled with spinach, ricotta, and egg yolk—for the rest of your life. You also may discover a few new favorites among the territory's underappreciated wines. Vegetarians take heart: There are always 4 or 5 non-meat entrees available.

Via di San Vito 13A (at Via Merulana). ℂ **06-4466573.** Main courses 12€–22€. Tues–Sat 1–2:45pm and 8–10:45pm; Sun lunch only. Metro: Cavour or Vittorio Emanuele. Bus: 360, 714. Tram: 5 or 14.

Trimani Il Wine Bar ★ MODERN ITALIAN   This small bistro and well-stocked wine bar (with a 20-page wine list!) attracts white collars and wine lovers in a modern, relaxed ambience, accompanied by smooth jazz. The refined entrees might include rabbit stuffed with asparagus or Luganega sausage with a zucchini puree. The wines-by-the-glass list changes daily. If you just want a snack to accompany your vino, cheese and salami platters range from 9€ to 14€. The selection at Trimani's vast wine shop next door boggles the oenophilic mind.

Via Cernaia 37B. www.trimani.com. ℂ **06-4469630.** Main courses 12€–24€. Mon–Sat 11:30am–3pm and 5:30pm–midnight. Closed 2 weeks in mid-Aug. Metro: Repubblica or Castro Pretorio.

INEXPENSIVE
Mercato Centrale Roma ★★ GOURMET MARKET   This ambitious, three-story gourmet dining hall and street food hub is the best place to dine in Termini Station, with top-notch purveyors of everything from gourmet pizza to chocolate to truffles, plus a wine bar and a high-end restaurant. The space is inviting, if a little chaotic. Even if you don't have a train to catch, it's worth having lunch or a quick snack here. *Tip:* Walk through the hall and check out all the offerings, then snag a table and have members of your party take turns going to order their food.

Via Giovanni Giolitti 36 (in Termini Station). www.mercatocentrale.it/roma. ℂ **06-46202900.** Daily 8am–midnight. Metro: Termini.

Pinsere ★★ PIZZA   *Pinsa* is an ancient Roman preparation: an oval focaccia made with a blend of four organic flours and olive oil that's left to rise for 2 to 3 days. The result is a crispy yet feather-light single-portion snack perfect for a light lunch. This friendly, small bakery always has an assortment of pies ready to pop in the oven. Favorites come with pureed pumpkin, smoked cheese, and pancetta; classic tomato, basil, and *mozzarella di bufala;* or the surprising combo of ricotta, fresh figs, raisins, pine nuts, and honey. Food to go only, or to eat standing up at one of the few small inside or outside counters. *Note:* Closed Saturday and Sunday.

Via Flavia 98. ℂ **06-42020924.** Pinsa 4€–6€. Mon–Fri 10am–4pm. Metro: Castro Pretorio. Bus: 38, 66, 90, 223.

Trastevere

For restaurant locations, see map p. 143. The popular craft-beer bar Bir and Fud has been reimagined as **L'Elementare** (see p. 158), but still serves hungry drinkers pizzas and traditional snacks like *supplì* (fried stuffed rice croquettes). Hearts and tastebuds soar at **Biscottificio Artigiano Innocenti ★★**,

Via della Luce 21 (© **06-5803926**), where Stefania and her family have been turning out delicate handmade cookies and cakes since the 1920s.

EXPENSIVE

Antico Arco ★★★ CREATIVE ITALIAN This well-known address for new Italian cuisine consistently delivers exquisite dishes made with the finest local and seasonal ingredients—like a beef fillet with buffalo mozzarella sauce and grilled eggplant, or amberjack with cauliflower, toasted hazelnuts, and lemon thyme, accompanied by excellent wine and topnotch service. A full meal here makes a special night out (reservations essential), but you can also just come to the restaurant's wine bar for *vino* and finger food—it pairs nicely with rapturous *centro storico* views from the nearby terraces of the Janiculum Hill. *Tip:* It's a 15-minute walk uphill from Trastevere, but the climb is gradual and pleasant.

Piazzale Aurelio 7 (at Via San Pancrazio). www.anticoarco.it. © **06-5815274.** Entrees 32€–35€. Wed–Mon noon–midnight. Bus: 75, or tram 3 or 8 then a 15-min walk.

Glass Hostaria ★★ CONTEMPORARY ROMAN In an industrial-chic setting of exposed brick, stark white walls, and polished floors, Michelin-starred chef Cristina Bowerman serves refined food using high-quality ingredients. The menu changes seasonally, but expect carefully prepared shellfish,

An exquisite dish at Antico Arco.

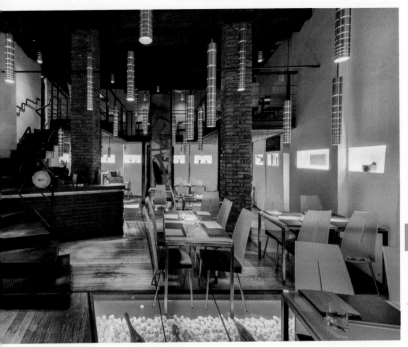

The very chic Glass Hostaria in Trastevere.

inventive pastas (such as linguine with pepper juice, cherries, mint, anchovies, and fish roe), and dishes like lamb with sumac, pecorino, and chicory). A vegetarian menu is available. Reservations are essential.

Vicolo del Cinque 58. glasshostaria.it. ℭ **06-58335903.** Entrees 38€–45€; tasting menu 125€. Wed–Sun 7:30–11pm; open for lunch Sat–Sun. Closed 2 weeks Jan., 2 weeks July. Bus: H, 75. Tram: 8.

Spirito DiVino ★★ ROMAN/SLOW FOOD   In a medieval synagogue on a 2nd-century street (which you can visit on a cellar tour), the Catalani family does exceptional modern cuisine using only organic ingredients. Dishes such as an appetizer of raw sheep's cheese with cinnamon-pear compote, as well as ancient Roman cuisine (like *maiale alla mazio,* a favorite pork dish of Julius Caesar's), are as warm and comforting as the ambience. Finish with almond and chocolate cake served with banana and chile pepper.

Via dei Genovesi 31 (at Vicolo dell'Atleta). www.ristorantespiritodivino.com. ℭ **6-5896689.** Entrees 14€–26€. Mon–Sat 7–11:30pm. Bus: H, 75. Tram: 8.

MODERATE
Da Enzo ★★ ROMAN   For traditional Roman cuisine, try this down-homey, non-touristy, family-run trattoria. *Cucina romana,* including classic carbonara, *amatriciana,* and *cacio e pepe,* win the gold, as do meat-heavy

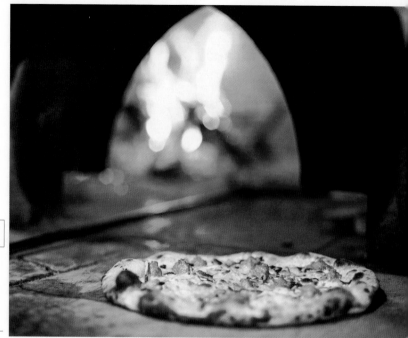

Wood-fired pizza at Dar Poeta.

secondi like stewed tripe, or meatballs braised in tomato sauce. Local wines can be ordered by the jug or glass, and desserts are worth the calories (try the mascarpone with wild strawberries). A few outdoor tables look out on some of Trastevere's characteristic alleyways.

Via dei Vascellari 29. www.daenzoal29.com. (② **06-5812260.** Entrees 12€–18€. Mon–Sat 12:15–3pm and 7–11:00pm. Bus: 75, 85, 170, H. Tram: 8.

Osteria Cacio e Pepe ★ ROMAN   This neighborhood stalwart is an ultra-traditional trattoria, complete with paper tablecloths, a TV showing the game, the owner chatting up the ladies, and a bustling crowd of patrons waiting to be seated. Start with cheapo plates of fried tidbits, from rice *suppli* to cod to vegetables, then move on to the namesake pasta *cacio e pepe* or other classic Roman pasta dishes—be ready for hearty portions. For *secondi*—if you have room left—consider *saltimbocca alla romana* (veal cutlets with sage and ham), or grilled meats, all reasonably priced. They even have pizza for the kids.

Vicolo del Cinque 15. (② **06-89572853.** Entrees 12€–22€. Daily 7:30pm–12:30am; Sat-Sun also noon–3pm. Bus: H. 75. Tram: 8.

Osteria La Gensola ★★★ SEAFOOD/ROMAN   Considered one of the best seafood destinations in Rome, this warm and welcoming family-run restaurant feels like a true Trastevere home; decor is cozy, with soft lighting and a life-size wood-carved tree in the middle of the main dining room. Fish-lovers come for heavenly spaghetti with fresh clams, *polpettine* (meatballs) made with tuna, and other traditional Roman cuisine with a marine twist. The grill churns out succulent beefsteaks, among non-fish dishes. Reservations are a must on weekends.

Piazza della Gensola 15. ℭ **06-58332758.** Main courses 15–20€. Daily 12:30–3pm and 7:30–11:30pm. Bus: 75, 85, 170, H. Tram: 8.

INEXPENSIVE

Dar Poeta ★ PIZZA   Ranking among the best pizzerias in Rome, "the poet" is a fine place to enjoy a classic Roman pizza margherita (tomato sauce, mozzarella, and fresh basil) or a more creative combo like the *patataccia* (potatoes, creamed zucchini, and *speck* [a smoked prosciutto]). The line is long for dining in, but you can also order takeout. The decadent dessert cal-zone is filled with fresh ricotta and Nutella.

Vicolo del Bologna 45. www.darpoeta.com. ℭ **06-5880516.** Pizzas 5€–9€. Daily noon–midnight. Bus: 75, H.

Testaccio

The slaughterhouses of Rome's old meatpacking district (see map p. 143) have been transformed into art venues, markets, and the museum **MACRO** (p. 137), but restaurants here still specialize in (though are not limited to) meats from the *quinto quarto* (the "fifth quarter")—the leftover parts of an animal after slaughter, typically offal like sweetbreads, tripe, tails, and other goodies you won't find on most American menus. This is an area to eat *cucina romana*—either in the restaurants below or from street-food stalls in the **Nuovo Mercato di Testaccio** (p. 153). Food-themed tours of Rome invariably end up here.

EXPENSIVE

Checchino dal 1887 ★★ ROMAN   Often mischaracterized as an offal-only joint, this establishment, opened in 1887 across from Rome's now-defunct abattoir, is a special-night-out type of place, serving wonderful *bucatini all'amatriciana* and veal saltimbocca—as well as hearty plates of sweet-breads, intestine, and liver. Checchino is a pricier choice than most restaurants in this area, but Romans from all over the city keep coming back when they want the real thing. Despite its meat-centric leanings, Checchino also has decent vegetarian options. They will also make gluten-free pasta.

Via di Monte Testaccio 30 (at Via Galvani). www.checchino-dal-1887.com. ℭ **06-5746316.** Entrees 12€–25€. Wed–Sun 12:30–3pm and 7:30–11pm. Closed Aug and part of Dec–Jan. Metro: Piramide.

MODERATE

Flavio al Velavevodetto ★ ROMAN   Flavio's plain dining room is burrowed out of the side of Rome's most unusual "hill": a large mound made from amphorae discarded during the Roman era (p. 30). Food-lovers, however, come here for classic Roman pastas like *cacio e pepe* and *amatriciana*, plus *quinto quarto* (nose-to-tail) entrees at fair prices. Hearty dishes like *polpette al sugo* (meatballs in red sauce), *coda alla vaccinara* (oxtail), and fried calamari and anchovies are good for sharing. Flavio is justly famous but may be coasting on its reputation just a wee bit.

Via di Monte Testaccio 97–99. www.ristorantevelavevodetto.it. ✆ **06-5744194.** Entrees 12€–16€. Daily 12–3pm and 7:30–11pm. Metro: Piramide.

Osteria degli Amici ★★ MODERN ROMAN   On the corner of night-club central and the hill of broken amphorae, this intimate and friendly *osteria* serves both traditional Roman classics and creative variations. Claudio and Alessandro base their menu on their combined experience in famous kitchens around the world, and presentations are more sophisticated than is typical for the 'hood. Signature musts include fish- and seafood-based pastas and mains, golden-fried mozzarella *in carrozza,* and a range of pastas from classic *carbonara* to *paccheri* tubes with squid, olives, and potatoes. Leave room for the apple tartlet with cinnamon gelato.

Via Nicola Zabaglia 25. www.osteriadegliamiciroma.it. ✆ **06-5781466.** Main courses 12€–20€. Wed–Mon 12:30–3pm and 8pm–midnight. Metro: Piramide.

Porto Fluviale ★ MODERN ITALIAN   This multifunctional restaurant—part trattoria, part street-food stall, part pizzeria—can accommodate pretty much whatever you fancy. The decor is vaguely industrial, with a daytime clientele of families and professionals on lunch break; the vibe gets younger after dark. From the various menus, best bets are the 30 or so *cicchetti,* small plates that allow you to taste the kitchen's range. Several pastas and main courses are available in half-portions. Both the locale and the menus are highly kid-friendly.

Via del Porto Fluviale 22. www.portofluviale.com. ✆ **06-5743199.** Cicchetti 3€–5€, entrees 11€–28€. Daily 10:30am–2am. Metro: Piramide.

INEXPENSIVE

Da Remo ★★ PIZZA   Mentioning "Testaccio" and "pizza" in the same sentence elicits one typical response from locals: Da Remo, a Roman institution. In the summer especially, come early or be prepared to wait for a table. Every crisp-crusted, perfectly foldable pizza is made for all to see behind open counters. The most basic ones (margherita and marinara) start at around 7€. If it's too crowded on a summer evening, order your pizza for takeout and eat it in the park across the street.

Piazza Santa Maria Liberatrice 44. ✆ **06-5746270.** Most pizzas 6€–8€. Daily 7pm–1am. Bus: 75. Tram: 3, 8.

EXPLORING ROME

Rome's ancient monuments are a constant reminder that one of Western civilization's greatest cities once prospered here. In the heyday of the Empire, all roads led to Rome, with good reason. Rome was one of the first cosmopolitan

Via dei Condotti, leading to Piazza di Spagna.

cities, importing food, textiles, slaves, gladiators, great art, and even citizens from the far corners of their world. Despite its brutality and corruption, Rome left a legacy of law, a heritage of art, architecture, and engineering, and an effective lesson in how to conquer enemies by absorbing their cultures.

But ancient Rome is only part of the spectacle. The Vatican has tremendous influence on making the city a tourism hub. Although Vatican architects stripped down much of the city's ancient glory during the Renaissance, looting ruins (the Forum especially) for their precious marble, they created more treasures and occasionally incorporated the old into the new—as Michelangelo did when turning Diocletian's Baths complex into a church. And in the years that followed, Bernini adorned the city with baroque wonders, especially his glorious fountains.

Bypassing the Lines

It used to be that going to Rome's three biggest attractions—the Colosseum, the Vatican Museums, and St. Peter's Basilica—meant waiting in long, long lines. Now thanks to advance ticket sales for timed entry, there's no reason to wait in excessively long lines for the Colosseum or the Vatican Museums. (See individual listings for more details.) St. Peter's, however, offers no skip-the-line perk. The only way to jump the line here is with the **Omnia Card** (see p. 54) or by booking a private or group tour (p. 99).

St. Peter's & the Vatican

VATICAN CITY

The world's smallest sovereign state, **Vatican City** is a truly tiny territory, comprising little more than St. Peter's Basilica, the Vatican Museums, and the walled headquarters of the Roman Catholic Church. There are no border controls, though the city-state's 800 inhabitants (essentially clergymen and Swiss Guards) have their own radio station, daily newspaper, tax-free pharmacy and petrol pumps, postal service, and head of state—the Pope. The Pope had always exercised a high degree of political independence from the rest of Italy, formalized by the 1929 Lateran Treaty between Pope Pius XI and the Italian government to create the Vatican. The city is still protected by the flamboyantly uniformed (allegedly designed by Michelangelo) Swiss Guards, a tradition dating from

St. Peter's Square, Vatican City.

Making the Most of a Day in Vatican City

Most Vatican visitors allot a day to see its two major sights, **St. Peter's Basilica** and the **Vatican Museums** (including the Sistine Chapel). We recommend starting with the museums. **Pre-order** tickets for the earliest time slot (from 9am) available the day you wish to visit. Plan to devote several hours to see the highlights of the museum collections (see p. 103).

Next, grab a quick late lunch, either in the museum cafeteria or at a nearby sandwich shop or pizza joint. Cheap eateries line the streets leading from the museum exit to St. Peter's Basilica—most are mediocre, but they'll do in a pinch. (See p. 81 for some notably good options.)

When you enter **St. Peter's Square,** head to the back of the line (always long, but it moves fairly quickly) to enter the basilica. From the time you enter the basilica, you'll need at least 1 hour for even the most cursory tour.

By now it'll be late afternoon, and you've got 2 options: Visit the **Vatican Grottoes,** burial place of dozens of popes, or climb the 551 steps (320 if you take the elevator) to the top of the **dome of St. Peter's.** Note that the dome and grottoes are open April to September until 6pm, and October to March until 5pm. If you've still got energy, head to nearby **Castel Sant'Angelo** (see p. 108)—the view of Rome from the castle's roof is a perfect way to cap off your marathon Vatican day.

Want more time at the Vatican Museums? Arrive at St. Peter's early in the morning to get in line before it opens at 7am; that way you can tour the basilica before the crowds show up. Then head to a late morning appointment at the museums and spend the rest of the day there.

Vatican City & Prati

14

ATTRACTIONS

Basilica di San Pietro
in Vaticano **8**

Castel Sant'Angelo **12**

Musei Vaticani &
the Sistine Chapel **7**

Piazza San Pietro **9**

RESTAURANTS

Bonci Pizzarium **2**

Duecento Gradi **5**

Old Bridge
Gelateria **4**

Pinsa 'm pò **6**

Taverna Angelica **11**

HOTELS

QuodLibet **3**

Mama Shelter **1**

Residenza Paolo VI **10**

Rome Armony Suites **13**

Villa Laetitia **14**

when the Swiss, known as brave soldiers, were often hired out as mercenaries
for foreign armies. Today the Vatican remains the center of the Roman Catholic world, the home of the Pope—and the resting place of St. Peter. **St. Peter's
Basilica** is obviously one of the highlights, but the only part of the Apostolic
Palace itself that you can visit independently is the **Vatican Museums,** the
world's biggest and richest museum complex.

On the left side of Piazza San Pietro, the **Vatican Tourist Office** (www.
vatican.va; ℂ **06-69882019;** Mon–Sat 8:30am–6:30pm) sells maps and guides
that will help you make sense of the treasures in the museums; it also accepts
reservations for tours of the Vatican Gardens. Adjacent to the information

office, the **Vatican Post Office** sells special Vatican postage stamps (open Mon–Sat 8:30am–6pm).

The only entrance to St. Peter's for tourists is through one of the glories of the Western world: Bernini's 17th-century **St. Peter's Square (Piazza San Pietro).** As you stand in the huge piazza, you are in the arms of an ellipse partly enclosed by a majestic **Doric-pillared colonnade.** Stand in the marked marble discs embedded in the pavement near the fountains to see all the columns lined up in a striking optical/geometrical play. Straight ahead is the facade of St. Peter's itself, and to the right, above the colonnade, are the dark brown buildings of the **papal apartments** and the Vatican Museums. In the center of the square stands a 4,000-year-old **Egyptian obelisk,** created in the ancient city of Heliopolis on the Nile delta and appropriated by the Romans under Emperor Augustus. Flanking the obelisk are two 17th-century **fountains.** The one on the right (facing the basilica), by Carlo Maderno, who designed the facade of St. Peter's, was placed here by Bernini himself; the other is by Carlo Fontana.

Basilica di San Pietro (St. Peter's Basilica) ★★★ CHURCH The Basilica di San Pietro, or simply **St. Peter's,** is the holiest shrine of the Catholic Church, built on the site of St. Peter's tomb by the greatest Italian artists of the 16th and 17th centuries. The line of the right side of the piazza funnels you into the basilica (from where you can access the underground grottoes), or the dome. Whichever you opt for first, you must be **properly dressed**—a rule that is very strictly enforced.

In Roman times, the Circus of Nero, where Peter is said to have been crucified, was just to the left of where the basilica is today. He was allegedly buried here in A.D. 64, and in A.D. 324 Emperor Constantine commissioned a church to be built over Peter's tomb. That structure stood for more than 1,000 years. The present basilica, mostly completed in the 1500s and 1600s, is predominantly High Renaissance and baroque. Inside, the massive scale is almost too much to absorb, showcasing some of Italy's greatest artists: Bramante, Raphael, and Michelangelo. In a church of such grandeur—overwhelming in its detail of gilt, marble, and mosaic—you can't expect much subtlety. It is meant to be overpowering.

Deep below St. Peter's Basilica is the Necropolis Vaticana.

Going straight into the basilica, the first thing you see on the right side of the nave—the longest nave in the world, as clearly marked in the floor along with other cathedral measurements—is the chapel containing Michelangelo's graceful **"Pietà" ★★★**. Created in the 1490s when the master was still in his 20s, it clearly shows his genius for capturing the human form. (The sculpture has been kept behind reinforced glass since an act of vandalism in the 1970s.) Note the lifelike folds of Mary's robes and her youthful features; although she would've been middle-aged at the time of the Crucifixion, Michelangelo portrayed her as a young woman to convey her purity. A few yards past the Pietà is a chapel housing the **tomb of Pope John Paul II.**

Further inside the nave, Michelangelo's dome is a mesmerizing space, rising high above the supposed site of St. Peter's tomb. With a diameter of 41.5m (136 ft.), the dome is Rome's largest, supported by four bulky piers decorated with reliefs depicting the basilica's key holy relics: St. Veronica's handkerchief (used to wipe the face of Christ); the lance of St. Longinus, which pierced Christ's side; and a piece of the True Cross. The fourth relic, St. Andrew's skull, is now in Patras, Greece.

Under the dome is the twisty-columned **baldacchino ★★**, by Bernini, sheltering the papal altar. The ornate 29m-high (96-ft.) canopy was created in part, so it is said, from bronze stripped from the Pantheon. Bernini sculpted the face of a woman on the base of each pillar; starting with the face on the left pillar (with your back to the entrance), circle the entire altar to see the progress of expressions from the agony of childbirth through to the fourth pillar, where the woman's face is replaced with that of her newborn baby.

Just before reaching the dome, on the right, the devout stop to kiss the foot of the 13th-century **bronze of St. Peter ★**, attributed to Arnolfo di Cambio. Elsewhere the church is decorated by more of Bernini's lavish sculptures, including his monument to Pope Alexander VII in the south transept, its winged skeleton writhing under the heavy marble drapes.

An entrance off the nave leads to the Sacristy and the **Historical Museum (Museo Storico)** or **treasury ★**, which is chock-full of richly jeweled chalices, reliquaries, and copes, as well as the late-15th-century bronze tomb of Pope Sixtus IV by Pollaiuolo.

An entrance to the left of the baldacchino leads down to the **Vatican grottoes ★★**, with their tombs of the popes, both ancient and modern. Behind a wall of glass is what is considered to be the tomb of St. Peter.

4

ROME

Exploring Rome

papal AUDIENCES

When the pope is in Rome, he gives a public audience every Wednesday beginning at 9:30am. If you want to get a good seat near the front, arrive early and prepare to wait—security begins to let people in between 7 and 7:30am but the line starts much earlier. Audiences take place in the Paul VI Hall of Audiences, although sometimes St. Peter's Basilica and St. Peter's Square are used to accommodate a large attendance in the summer. You can check on Pope Francis's appearances and the ceremonies he presides over, including celebrations of Mass, on the Vatican website (www.vatican.va). Anyone is welcome, but you must first obtain a **free ticket,** which you can order in advance or, subject to availability, pick up in person. To reserve in advance, visit www.vatican.va/various/prefettura/index_en.html to download a request form, which can be submitted via email or fax. Tickets can be picked up at the office just inside the Bronze Doors from 3 to 7pm on the preceding day or on the morning of the audience from 7am. Without a reservation, you can request tickets from the Swiss Guards posted at the Bronze Doors located just after security at St. Peter's (8am–8pm in summer and 8am–7pm in winter). You can pick up tickets here up to 3 days in advance, subject to availability.

If you prefer to reserve a place in advance, visit www.vatican.va/various/prefettura/index_en.html to download a request form, which must be submitted via fax (yes, really) to the **Prefecture of the Papal Household** at ✆ **06-69885863.** Tickets can be picked up at the office located just inside the Bronze Doors from 3 to 7pm on the preceding day or on the morning of the audience from 7am.

At noon on Sundays, the Pope speaks briefly from his study window and gives his blessing to the visitors and pilgrims gathered in St. Peter's Square (no tickets are required for this). From about mid-July to mid-September, the Angelus and blessing historically takes place at the Pope's summer residence at **Castel Gandolfo**, some 26km (16 miles) out of Rome. Under Pope Francis, the residence, gardens, and villas of the castle have been opened to visitors as a museum, accessible via Metro and bus as well as a new train service that leaves from the Roma San Pietro station. Visit biglietteriamusei.vatican.va for information on seeing Castel Gandolfo by train.

After you leave the grottoes, you find yourself in a courtyard and ticket line for the grandest sight in the basilica: the climb to **Michelangelo's dome ★★★**, about 114m (375 ft.) high. You can walk all the way up or take the elevator as far as it goes (this saves you 171 steps). At this first stop, you can walk on the roof of the basilica (where there's also a restroom, a snack bar, and a gift shop) and also around the interior of the drum of the dome, which offers a bird's eye view of the basilica below. After that, you *still* have 320 to go to reach the very top. Claustrophobes take note: the last part of the climb is up a very narrow spiral staircase.

After you've made it to the top, you'll have a scintillating view over the rooftops of Rome and even the Vatican Gardens and papal apartments. The elevator back down drops you back in the basilica interior, near the front entrance, or you can descend via a spiral ramp, the walls of which are lined with inscriptions recalling famous visitors to the dome.

Visits to the **Necropolis Vaticana** ★★ and St. Peter's tomb itself are restricted to 250 persons per day on guided tours (90 min.) You must send a fax or e-mail at least 3 weeks beforehand or apply in advance in person at the Ufficio Scavi (Ⓒ/fax **06-69873017**; e-mail: scavi@fsp.va; Mon–Fri 9am–6pm, Sat 9am–2pm), which is located through the arch to the left of the stairs up from the basilica. For details, check www.scavi.va/content/scavi/en/ufficio-scavi.html. Children 14 and under are not admitted to the Necropolis.

Piazza San Pietro. www.vatican.va. Ⓒ **06-69881662**. Basilica (including grottoes) free admission. Necropolis Vaticana (St. Peter's tomb) 13€. Stairs to the dome 8€; elevator (part-way) to the dome 10€; sacristy (with Historical Museum) 5€ adults, 3€ 12 and under. **Basilica** Oct–Mar daily 7am–6:30pm, Apr–Sep daily 7am–7pm. **Dome** Oct–Mar daily 7:30am–5pm, Apr–Sept daily 7:30am–6pm. **Note:** Basilica opening time may be delayed to 12 or 1pm on Wednesdays when the Pope holds an audience in the square. **Sacristry/museum** Apr–Sep 9am–6:15pm, Oct–Mar to 5:15pm. **Grottoes** Apr–Sep 7am–6pm, Oct–Mar to 5pm. Metro: Ottaviano/San Pietro, then a 10 min walk; or take bus 40, 46, or 62 to Piazza Pia/Traspontina, then about a 10 min walk.

Musei Vaticani & the Sistine Chapel ★★★ MUSEUM

Nothing else in Rome quite lives up to the awe-inspiring collections of the **Vatican Museums,** a 15-minute walk from St. Peter's out of the north side of Piazza San Pietro. It's a vast treasure trove of art from antiquity and the Renaissance gathered by the Roman Catholic Church through the centuries, filling a series of ornate Papal palaces, apartments, and galleries leading to one of the world's most beautiful interiors, the justly celebrated **Cappella Sistina (Sistine Chapel)**.

Note that the Vatican dress code also applies to its museums (no sleeveless blouses, no miniskirts, no shorts, no hats allowed), though it tends to be less rigorously enforced than at St. Peter's.

Obviously, one trip will not be enough to see everything here. Below are previews of the main highlights, showstoppers, and masterpieces on display (in alphabetical order).

APPARTAMENTO BORGIA (BORGIA APARTMENTS) ★

Created for Pope Alexander VI (the infamous Borgia pope) between 1492 and 1494, these rooms were frescoed with biblical and allegorical scenes by Umbrian painter Pinturicchio and his assistants. Look for what is thought to be the earliest European depiction of Native Americans, painted little more than a year after Columbus returned from the New World and Alexander had "divided" the globe between Spain and Portugal.

CAPPELLA SISTINA (SISTINE CHAPEL) ★★★

Michelangelo labored for 4 years (1508–1512) to paint the ceiling of the Sistine Chapel; it is said he spent the entire time on his feet, paint dripping into his eyes. Could he have imagined that more than 500 years later, his magnum opus would still be

The detailed and bright frescos by Pinturicchio in the Borgia Apartments.

considered one of the greatest accomplishments in Western art? Today, the world's most famous fresco is as vibrantly colorful and filled with roiling life as it was in 1512. And the chapel is still of central importance to the Catholic Church: This is where the Papal Conclave meets to elect new popes.

The "Creation of Adam," at the center of the ceiling, is one of the best known and most reproduced images in history, the outstretched hands of God and Adam—not quite touching—an iconic symbol of not just the Renaissance but the Enlightenment that followed. Nevertheless, it is somewhat ironic that this is Michelangelo's best-known work: The artist always regarded himself as a sculptor first and foremost.

Tip: The ceiling **frescoes** are obviously the main showstoppers, but staring up at them tends to take a heavy toll on the neck. To relieve your neck (and your tired feet), make your way to one of the benches that line both long sides of the gallery. As soon as someone gets up, grab a seat so you can gaze upward in relative comfort.

Commissioned by Pope Julius II in 1508 and completed in 1512, the ceiling frescoes primarily depict nine scenes from the Book of Genesis (including the famed "Creation of Adam"), from the "Separation of Light and Darkness" at the altar end to the "Great Flood" and "Drunkenness of Noah." Surrounding these main frescoes are paintings of 12 people who prophesied the coming of Christ, from Jonah and Isaiah to the Delphic Sibyl. After you have admired the ceiling, turn your attention to the altar wall. At the age of 60, Michelangelo was summoned to finish the chapel 23 years after he finished the ceiling work. Apparently saddened by leaving Florence and depressed by the morally bankrupt state of Rome at that time, he painted these dark moods in his "Last Judgment," where he included his own self-portrait on a sagging human hide held by St. Bartholomew (who was martyred by being flayed alive).

Yet the Sistine Chapel isn't all Michelangelo. The southern wall is covered by a series of astonishing paintings completed in the 1480s: "Moses Leaving to Egypt" by Perugino, the "Trials of Moses" by Botticelli, "The Crossing of the Red Sea" by Cosimo Rosselli (or Domenico Ghirlandaio), "Descent from Mount Sinai" by Cosimo Rosselli (or Piero di Cosimo), Botticelli's "Punishment of the Rebels," and Signorelli's "Testament and Death of Moses."

On the right-hand northern wall are Perugino's "The Baptism of Christ," Botticelli's "The Temptations of Christ," Ghirlandaio's "Vocation of the Apostles," Perugino's "Delivery of the Keys," and Cosimo Rosselli's "The Sermon on the Mount" and "Last Supper." On the eastern wall, originals by Ghirlandaio and Signorelli were painted over by Hendrik van den Broeck's "The Resurrection" and Matteo da Lecce's "Disputation over Moses" in the 1570s.

COLLEZIONE D'ARTE CONTEMPORANEA (COLLECTION OF MODERN RELIGIOUS ART) ★ Spanning 55 rooms of almost 800 works, these galleries contain the Vatican's concession to modern art. There are some

The Sistine Chapel.

big names here and the quality is high, and themes usually have a spiritual and religious component: Van Gogh's "Pietà, after Delacroix" is here, along with Francis Bacon's eerie "Study for a Pope II." You will also see works by Paul Klee ("City with Gothic Cathedral"), Siqueiros ("Mutilated Christ No. 467"), Otto dix ("Road to Calvary"), Gauguin ("Religious Panel"), Chagall ("Red Pietà"), and a whole room dedicated to Georges Rouault.

MUSEI DI ANTICHITÀ CLASSICHE (CLASSICAL ANTIQUITIES MUSEUMS) ★★★ The Vatican maintains four classical antiquities museums, the most important being the **Museo Pio Clementino** ★★★, crammed with Greek and Roman sculptures in the small Belvedere Palace of Innocent VIII. At the heart of the complex lies the Octagonal Court, where highlights include the sculpture of the Trojan priest **"Laocoön"** ★★★ and his two sons locked in a struggle with sea serpents, dating from around 40 B.C., and the exceptional **"Belvedere Apollo"** ★★★ (a 2nd-c. Roman reproduction of a Greek work from the 4th c. B.C.), the symbol of classic male beauty and a possible inspiration for Michelangelo's "David." Look out also for the impressive gilded bronze statue of **"Hercules"** in the Rotonda, from the late 2nd century A.D., and the **Hall of the Chariot,** containing a magnificent sculpture of a chariot combining Roman originals and 18th-century work by Antonio Franzoni.

The **Museo Chiaramonti** ★ occupies the long loggia that links the Belvedere Palace to the main Vatican palaces, jam-packed on both sides with more than 800 Greco-Roman works, including statues, reliefs, and sarcophagi. In the **Braccio Nuovo** ★ ("New Wing"), a handsome Neoclassical extension of the Chiaramonti sumptuously lined with colored marble, lies the colossal statue

---

Strategies for visiting the Vatican Museums

The sheer size of the collections and vast crowds mean that seeing one of the greatest museums of art in the world isn't a leisurely, or even pleasant, experience. Visitors tend to get herded through room after room of galleries as they make their way to the Sistine Chapel, and lack of descriptive labels means they often don't know what they're looking at. Here are some tips to make sense of it all:

o Book **timed-entry** tickets in advance through the Vatican Museums website and avoid the risk of finding either a long entrance line or the museum at capacity.

o Do some advance research and decide which collections you most want to see.

o Once you're in the museum, take a few minutes to review the galleries map and map out your visit.

o If your priority is to see the Sistine Chapel, follow signs for the "Percorso Breve" (short route) to the Cappella Sistina.

For a deeper experience, consider a breakfast or after hours visit (p 98), or springing for a private tour of the collections. These are a great way to get the most out of a visit, especially if you have limited time. They're also the only way to visit the **Vatican Gardens.** Booking online is mandatory; **visit https://biglietteriamusei.vatican.va/musei/tickets** for information. See Organized Tours (p 149) for info on private companies offering Vatican tours.

of the **"Nile"** ★, the ancient river portrayed as an old man with his 16 children, most likely a reproduction of a long-lost Alexandrian Greek original.

The **Museo Gregoriano Profano** ★★, built in 1970, houses more Greek sculptures looted by the Romans (some from the Parthenon), mostly funerary steles and votive reliefs, as well as some choice Roman pieces, notably the restored mosaics from the floors of the public libraries in the **Baths of Caracalla** (p. 110).

MUSEO ETNOLOGICO (ETHNOLOGICAL MUSEUM) ★★

Founded in 1926, this astounding assemblage of artifacts and artwork is from cultures around the world, from ancient Chinese coins and notes, to plaster sculptures of Native Americans and ceremonial art from Papua New Guinea.

MUSEO GREGORIANO EGIZIO ★★

Nine rooms are packed with plunder from Ancient Egypt, including sarcophagi, mummies, pharaonic statuary, votive bronzes, jewelry, cuneiform tablets from Mesopotamia, inscriptions from Assyrian palaces, and Egyptian hieroglyphics.

MUSEO GREGORIANO ETRUSCO ★★

The core of this collection is a cache of rare Etruscan art treasures dug up in the 19th century, dating from between the 9th and the 1st centuries B.C. The Romans learned a lot from the Etruscans, as the highly crafted ceramics, bronzes, silver, and gold on display attest. Don't miss the **Regolini-Galassi tomb** (7th c. B.C.), unearthed at Cerveteri. The museum is housed within the *palazzettos* of Innocent VIII (reigned 1484–92) and Pius IV (reigned 1559–65), the latter adorned with frescoes by Federico Barocci and Federico Zuccari.

PINACOTECA (ART GALLERY) ★★★

The great painting collections of the Popes are displayed in the Pinacoteca, including work from all the big names in Italian art, from Giotto and Fra' Angelico to Perugino, Raphael, Veronese, and Crespi. Early medieval work occupies Room 1, with the most intriguing piece a keyhole-shaped wood panel of the "Last Judgment" by Nicolò e Giovanni, dated to the late 12th century. **Giotto** takes center stage in Room 2, with the "Stefaneschi Triptych" (six panels) painted for the old St. Peter's Basilica between 1315 and 1320. **Fra' Angelico** dominates Room 3, his "Stories of St. Nicholas of Bari" and "Virgin with Child" justly praised (check out the Virgin's microscopic eyes in the latter piece). Carlo Crivelli features in Room 6, while decent works by Perugino and Pinturicchio grace Room 7, though most visitors press on to the **Raphael salon** ★★★ (Room 8), where you can view five paintings by the Renaissance master. The best are the "Coronation of the Virgin," the "Madonna of Foligno," and the vast "Transfiguration" (completed shortly before his death). Room 9 boasts Leonardo da Vinci's **"St. Jerome with the Lion"** ★★, as well as Giovanni Bellini's "Pietà." Room 10 is dedicated to Renaissance Venice, with Titian's "Madonna of St. Nicholas of the Frari" and Veronese's "Vision of St. Helen" being paramount. Don't skip the remaining galleries: Room 11 contains Barocci's "Annunciation," while Room 12 is really all about one of the masterpieces of the baroque, Caravaggio's **"Deposition from the Cross"** ★★.

STANZE DI RAFFAELLO (RAPHAEL ROOMS) ★★★ In the early 16th century, Pope Julius II hired the young Raphael and his workshop to decorate his personal apartments, on the second floor of the Pontifical Palace. Completed between 1508 and 1524, the **Raphael Rooms** now represent one of the great artistic spectacles inside the Vatican.

The **Stanza dell'Incendio** served as the Pope's high court room and later, under Leo X, a dining room. Most of its lavish frescoes have been attributed to Raphael's pupils. Leo X commissioned much of the work here, which explains the themes (past Popes with the name Leo). Note the intricate ceiling, painted by Umbrian maestro Perugino, who was Raphael's first teacher.

Raphael is the main focus in the **Stanza della Segnatura,** originally used as a Papal library and private office and home to the awe-inspiring **"School of Athens"** ★★★ fresco, depicting primarily Greek classical philosophers such as Aristotle, Plato, and Socrates. Many of the figures are thought to be based on portraits of Renaissance artists, including Bramante (on the right as Euclid, drawing on a chalkboard), Leonardo da Vinci (as Plato, the bearded man in the center), and even Raphael himself (in the lower-right corner with a black hat). On the wall opposite stands the equally magnificent "Disputa del Sacramento," where Raphael used a similar technique; Dante Alighieri stands behind the pontiff on the right, and Fra' Angelico poses as a monk (which in fact, he was) on the far left.

The **Stanza d'Eliodoro** was used for the private audiences of the Pope and was painted by Raphael immediately after he did the Segnatura. His aim here was to flatter his papal patron, Julius II: The depiction of the pope driving Attila from Rome was meant to symbolize the contemporary mission of Julius II to drive the French out of Italy. Finally, the **Sala di Costantino,** used for Papal receptions and official ceremonies, was completed by Raphael's students after the master's death, but based on his designs and drawings. It's a jaw-dropping space, commemorating four major episodes in the life of Emperor Constantine.

Vatican City, Viale Vaticano (walk around Vatican walls from St. Peter's Sq.). www.museivaticani.va. ⓒ **06-69884676.** Advance booking with timed entrance is strongly recommended. 17€ adults, 8€ ages 6–13, free for children 5 and under; 2-hr. tours of Vatican Gardens 34€ (no tours Wed or Sun). Advance tickets (reservation fee 5€) and guided tours (35€ per person) through biglietteriamusei.vatican.va. Mon–Sat 9am–6pm (ticket office closes 4pm), last Sun every month 9am–2pm (free admission). Closed Jan 1 and 6, Feb 11, Mar 19, Easter, May 1, June 29, Aug 15, Nov 1, Dec 8, and Dec 25–26. Metro: Ottaviano or Cipro–Musei Vaticani. Buses 23 and 492 to Bastioni di Michelangelo (3-min walk from entrance), or buses 590, 982, and 19 tram to Piazza del Risorgimento (10-min walk from entrance).

Castel Sant'Angelo ★★ CASTLE/PALACE Over the years, this bulky cylindrical fortress on the Vatican side of the Tiber has had many lives: As the mausoleum tomb of Emperor Hadrian in A.D. 138; as a papal residence in the 14th century; as a castle, where in 1527 Pope Clement VII hid from the looting troops of Charles V; and as a military prison from the 17th century on.

Vatican Museum visitors have an extraordinary opportunity to stroll through the galleries after closing time or before galleries open to the public, on guided tours that include the Raphael Rooms, the Sistine Chapel, and other areas. Morning visits begin or end with an American breakfast service, while evening visits conclude with happy hour, both served in the museum. The website has a long menu of tour options; be sure to read the tour descriptions to pick the right one. Prices for these special tours start at 40€ per person and include museum admission.

Consider renting an audio guide at the entrance to fully appreciate its various manifestations.

From the entrance a stone ramp *(rampa elicoidale)* winds to the upper terraces, where you can see amazing views of the city and enjoy a coffee at the cafe. The sixth floor features the **Terrazza dell'Angelo,** crowned by a florid 18th-century statue of the Archangel Michael. It's famous to opera fans—the last act of Puccini's "Tosca" is set here.

From here you can walk back down through five floors. On levels 3 to 5 you'll see the Renaissance apartments used by some of Rome's most infamous Popes, including Alexander VI, the Borgia pope. Below the apartments are the grisly dungeons **("Le Prigioni")** used as torture chambers in the medieval period (Cesare Borgia made great use of them). The castle is connected to St. Peter's Basilica by **Il Passetto di Borgo,** a walled passage built in 1277 by Pope Nicholas III, used by popes who needed to make a quick escape to the fortress in times of danger.

Lungotevere Castello 50. www.castelsantangelo.com. © **06-32810.** 15€. Daily 9am–7:30pm. Bus: 23, 40, 62, 280, 982 (to Piazza Pia).

The Colosseum, Forum & Ancient Rome

THE MAJOR SIGHTS OF ANCIENT ROME

Your sightseeing experience will be enhanced if you know a little about the history and rulers of Ancient Rome: See p. 28 for a brief rundown.

Arco di Costantino (Arch of Constantine) ★★ MONUMENT   The
photogenic triumphal arch next to the Colosseum was erected by the Senate in A.D. 315 to honor Constantine's defeat of the pagan Maxentius at the Battle of the Milvian Bridge (A.D. 312). Many of the reliefs have nothing whatsoever to do with Constantine or his works, but they tell of the victories of earlier Antonine rulers (lifted from other, long-forgotten memorials).

The arch marks a period of great change in the history of Rome. Converted to Christianity by a vision on the eve of battle, Constantine ended the centuries-long persecution of the Christians, during which many followers of the new religion had been put to death in a gruesome manner. Although Constantine didn't ban paganism (which survived officially for another half century or so),

The Arch of Constantine.

he espoused Christianity himself and began the process that ended in the conquest of Rome by the Christian religion.

Btw. Colosseum and Palatine Hill. Metro: Colosseo. Bus: 51, 85, 87, 118. Tram: 3.

Baths of Caracalla (Terme di Caracalla) ★★ RUINS   Named for Emperor Caracalla, a particularly unpleasant individual, the Baths of Caracalla were completed in A.D. 217 after his death. The richness of decoration has faded, but the massive brick ruins and the mosaic fragments that remain give modern visitors an idea of the complex's scale and grandeur. In their heyday, the baths sprawled over 11 hectares (27 acres) and included hot, cold, and tepid pools, as well as a *palestra* (gym) and changing rooms. A museum in the tunnels below the complex—built over an even more ancient *mithraem*, a worship site of an eastern cult—explores the hydraulic and heating systems (and slave power) needed to serve 8,000 or so Romans per day. Summer operatic performances here are an ethereal treat (see p. 156). For an extra 7€, **a virtual reality experience** ★ brings the baths vividly to life.

Via delle Terme di Caracalla 52. www.coopculture.it/en. ⓒ **06-39967702.** 8€ (10€ online). Virtual reality guide 7€. Tues–Sun 9am–dusk (as early as 4:30pm or as late as 7:15pm). Last entry 1 hr. before closing. Bus: 118 or 628.

Musei Capitolini ★★ MUSEUM   The Capitoline Museums' masterpieces are considered Rome's most valuable (recall that the Vatican Museums are *not* technically in Rome). They certainly were collected early: This is the oldest public museum *in the world.* Try and schedule adequate time, as there's much to see.

Ancient Rome, Monti & Celio

First stop is the courtyard of the **Palazzo dei Conservatori** (the building on the right of the piazza designed by Michelangelo, if you enter via the ramp from Piazza Venezia). It's scattered with gargantuan stone body parts—the remnants of a massive 12m (39-ft.) statue of the emperor Constantine, including his colossal head, hand, and foot. It's nearly impossible to resist posing for a photo next to the giant finger.

On the *palazzo*'s ground floor, the unmissable works are in the first series of rooms. These include "Lo Spinario" (Room 3), a lifelike bronze of a young boy digging a splinter out of his foot that was widely copied during the Renaissance; and the **"Lupa Capitolina"** (Room 4), a bronze statue of the famous she-wolf that suckled Romulus and Remus, the mythical founders of Rome. Scholars disagree on the date of the statue: long thought to be from around 500 B.C., recent analysis suggests it may be from the 1100s. What is certain is that the twins were not on the original statue but were added in the 15th century. Room 5 has Bernini's famously pained portrait of "Medusa," even more compelling when you see its writhing serpent hairdo in person.

Before heading upstairs, go toward the newer wing at the rear, which houses the original equestrian **statue of Marcus Aurelius ★★★**, dating to around A.D. 180—the piazza outside, where it stood from 1538 until 2005, now has a copy. There's a giant bronze head from a statue of Constantine (ca. A.D. 337) and the foundations of the original Temple of Jupiter that stood on the Capitoline Hill since its inauguration in 509 B.C.

The second-floor **picture gallery ★** is strong on Baroque oil paintings. Masterpieces include Caravaggio's "John the Baptist" and "The Fortune Teller" (1595) and Guido Reni's "St. Sebastian" (1615).

A tunnel takes you under the piazza to the other part of the Capitoline Museums, the **Palazzo Nuovo,** via the **Tabularium ★★**. Built in 78 B.C. to house ancient Rome's city records, it was later used as a salt mine and then as a prison. Here, the moody *galleria lapidaria* houses a well-executed exhibit of ancient portrait tombstones and sarcophagi, many of their poignant epitaphs translated into English, and provides access to one of the best balcony **views ★★★** in Rome: along the length of the Forum toward the Palatine Hill.

Much of the Palazzo Nuovo is dedicated to statues excavated from the forums below and brought in from outlying areas like Hadrian's Villa in Tivoli (p. 168). If you're running short on time, head straight for Room 3 and the 1st-century **"Capitoline Venus" ★★** modestly covering up after a bath, and, in Rooms 4 and 5, a chronologically arranged row of distinct, expressive busts of Roman emperors and their families. Another favorite is the beyond handsome **"Dying Gaul" ★★**, a Roman copy of a lost ancient Greek work. Lord Byron considered the statue so lifelike and moving that he mentioned it in "is poem "Childe Harold's Pilgrimage."

Piazza del Campidoglio 1. www.museicapitolini.org. ✆ **060608.** 11.50€ (more during special exhibits), 13.50€ for 7-day ticket that includes Centrale Montemartini. Daily 9:30am–7:30pm. Last entry 1 hr. before closing. Bus: 40, 44, 60, 63, 64, 70, 118, 160, 170, 628, 716 or any bus that stops at Piazza Venezia.

Circus Maximus (Circo Massimo) ★ HISTORIC SITE   Today mostly an oval-shaped field, the once-grand circus was plundered by medieval and Renaissance builders in search of marble and stone—it's a far cry from its *Ben-Hur*-esque heyday. What the Romans called a "circus" was a large arena ringed by tiers of seats and used for sports or spectacles. At one time, 300,000 Romans could assemble here, while the emperor observed the games from his box high on the Palatine Hill.

The last games were held in A.D. 549 on the orders of Totilla the Goth, who had seized Rome twice. Afterwards, the Circus Maximus was never used again, and the demand for building materials reduced it, like so much of Rome, to a great dusty field, now used mostly for big-name rock concerts. An archaeological area at its eastern end (closest to the Metro station) offers insights into how the space once functioned.

A 40-minute virtual reality tour (12€, including site admission) is available at various times during the year; see www.circomaximoexperience.it for info. *Tip:* If you're crunched for time, bypass the Circus Maximus and instead take in the emperor's-eye views of the arena from atop the Palatine Hill.

Btw. Via dei Cerchi and Via del Circo Massimo. www.sovraintendenzaroma.it (search "Circo Massimo" then translate). ✆ **060608.** Archaeological area 5€. Summer Tues–Sun 9:30am–7pm (last entrance 6pm); winter until 5pm. Metro: Circo Massimo. Bus: 81, 118, 160.

Colosseo (Colosseum) ★★★ ICON   No matter how many pictures you've seen, your first view of the Flavian Amphitheater (the Colosseum's original name) is likely to amaze you with its sheer size and ruined grandeur. While you're still outside its massive walls, take time to walk completely

Inside the Colosseum.

around its 500m (1,640-ft.) circumference. It doesn't matter where you start but do the circle. Look at the various stages of ruin; note the different column styles on each level. Mere photos could never convey its physical impact.

Vespasian ordered the construction of the elliptical bowl in A.D. 72; it was inaugurated by Titus in A.D. 80. Built for gladiator contests and wild animal fights, the stadium could hold as many as 87,000 spectators by some counts; seats were sectioned on three levels, dividing the people by social rank and gender. Some 80 entrances allowed the massive crowds to be seated and dispersed within a few minutes. When the Roman Empire fell, however, the abandoned arena was eventually overgrown. Much of the travertine that once sheathed its outside was used for palaces like the nearby **Palazzo Venezia** and **Palazzo Cancelleria.**

An ongoing conservation effort, funded in large part by the Italian design house Tod's, has scoured 2,000 years of soot from the monument's exterior and opened restored areas previously closed to the public, including the **Arena Floor and Underground,** which were formerly open only by guided or private tour. (The upper tier, called the **Belvedere,** is open periodically but is closed as of this writing.) The arena floor/underground area is ticketed separately from standard Colosseum admission and *not* included with the RomaPass. Ticket options are numerous, but the two relevant to most visitors are the Ordinary (also called Regular) and Full Experience tickets. Ordinary tickets (18€) are good for 24 hours from their first activation and include admission to the Colosseum, Roman Forum, and Palatine Hill. Full Experience tickets (24€, valid for 48 hours from first activation) add the Arena Floor and Underground (the latter visited only via a 40-minute guided tour), plus the S.U.P.E.R. sites of the Palatine. The Colosseum Underground tour includes explanations of the complex system of ramps, elevators, and trap doors that unleashed onto the arena floor the gladiators, wild animals, and array of theatrical effects that once thrilled and stunned audiences in the stands. These tours fill up very quickly. Though the pre-ticketing system has eliminated the long line to enter, you still must go through security screening, which can take up to an hour on busy days.

Piazzale del Colosseo. www.coopculture.it/en/colosseo-e-shop.cfm. (℃) **06-39967700.** 18€ pre-purchased online, includes Roman Forum & Palatine Hill. "Full Experience" ticket including Underground, Arena Floor and S.U.P.E.R. sites of the Palatine 24€. Daily 9:30am–dusk (as early as 4:30pm in winter, as late as 7:15pm Mar-Aug). Last entry 1 hr. before closing. Metro: Colosseo. Bus: 51, 75, 85, 87, 118. Tram: 3.

Fori Imperiali (Imperial Forums) ★ RUINS

Begun by Julius Caesar to relieve overcrowding in Rome's older forums, the Imperial Forums were, at the time of their construction, flashier, bolder, and more impressive than anything that had come before them in Rome. They conveyed the unquestioned authority of the emperors at the height of their absolute power.

Alas, Mussolini felt his regime was more important than the ancient one and issued the controversial orders to cut through centuries of debris and buildings to carve out Via dei Fori Imperiali, linking the Colosseum to the

19th-century monuments of Piazza Venezia. Excavations under his Fascist regime uncovered countless archaeological treasures. Most ruins more recent than imperial Rome were destroyed—*argh!*

The best view of the Forums is from the railings on the north side of Via dei Fori Imperiali; begin where Via Cavour joins the boulevard. Closest to the junction are the remains of the **Forum of Nerva,** built by the emperor whose 2-year reign (A.D. 96–98) followed the assassination of the paranoid Domitian. You'll be struck by how much the ground level has risen in 19 centuries. The only recognizable remnant is a wall of the Temple of Minerva with two fine Corinthian columns. The next along is the **Forum of Augustus ★★**, built to commemorate Emperor Augustus's victory over Julius Caesar's assassins, Cassius and Brutus, in the Battle of Philippi (42 B.C.). Continuing along the railing, you'll see the vast, multilevel semicircle of **Trajan's Markets ★★**, essentially an ancient shopping mall whose arcades were once stocked with merchandise from the far corners of the Roman world. You can visit the part that has been transformed into the **Museo dei Fori Imperiali & Mercati di Traiano** (see p. 119).

In front of the Markets, the **Forum of Trajan ★★** was built between A.D. 107 and 113, designed by Greek architect Apollodorus of Damascus (who also laid out the adjoining market building). Many statue fragments and pedestals bear still-legible inscriptions, but more interesting is the great Basilica Ulpia, whose gray marble columns rise roofless into the sky. This forum was once regarded as one of the architectural wonders of the world. Beyond the

THREE free views **TO SAVOR FOR A LIFETIME**

The Forum from the Campidoglio
Standing on Piazza del Campidoglio, outside the Musei Capitolini (p. 110), walk around the right or left side of the Palazzo Senatorio to terraces overlooking the best panoramas of the Roman Forum, with the Palatine Hill and Colosseum as a backdrop. At night, the ruins look even more haunting when the Forum is dramatically floodlit.

The Whole city from the Janiculum Hill
From many vantage points in the Eternal City, the views are panoramic. But one of the best spots for a memorable vista is the Janiculum Hill (Gianicolo), above Trastevere. Laid out before you are Rome's rooftops, peppered with domes ancient and modern. From up here, you will understand why Romans complain about the 19th-century Vittoriano (p. 123)—it's a gigantic white shock in a sea of rose- and

honey-colored stone. Walk 50 yards north of the famous balcony (favored by tour buses) for a slightly better angle, from the Belvedere 9 Febbraio 1849. Views from the 1612 Fontana dell'Acqua Paola are also splendid, especially at night.

The Aventine Hill & the Priori dei Cavalieri di Malta The mythical site of Remus's original settlement, the Aventine (Aventino) is now a leafy, upscale residential neighborhood—but also blessed with some magical views. From Via del Circo Massimo walk through the gardens along Via di Valle Murcia and keep walking in a straight line. Along your right side, the Giardino degli Aranci (Orange Tree Garden) offers views over the dome of St. Peter's. When you reach Piazza dei Cavalieri di Malta, look through the keyhole of the Priory gate (on the right) for a "secret" view of the Vatican.

Basilica Ulpia is **Trajan's Column ★★★**, in magnificent condition, with an intricate bas-relief sculpture depicting Trajan's victorious campaign in Dacia (modern Romania).

The **Forum of Julius Caesar ★★**, the first of the Imperial Forums to be built, lies on the opposite side of Via dei Fori Imperiali, adjacent to the Roman Forum. This was the site of the stock exchange as well as the Temple of Venus.

Along Via dei Fori Imperiali. Metro: Colosseo. Bus: 51, 75, 85, 87, 118.

Foro Romano (Roman Forum) & Palatino (Palatine Hill) ★★★

RUINS   Traversed by the **Via Sacra (Sacred Way) ★**, the main thoroughfare of ancient Rome, the Roman Forum flourished as the center of religious, social, and commercial life in the days of the Republic, before it gradually lost prestige (but never spiritual draw) to the Imperial Forums (see above).

You'll see ruins and fragments, some partially intact columns, and monumental arches, and you'll feel the rush of history here. That any semblance of the Forum remains today is miraculous: It was used for years as a quarry (as was the Colosseum) and eventually became a *campo vaccino* (cow pasture). Excavations in the 19th century and later in the 1930s began to bring to light one of the world's most historic spots.

You can spend at least a morning wandering the ruins of the Forum. Enter via the gate on Via dei Fori Imperiali, at Via della Salara Vecchia. (Note that an access point in front of the Colosseum is also open from time to time.) Turn right at the bottom of the entrance slope to walk west along the old Via Sacra toward the arch. Just before it on your right is the large brick **Curia ★★**, the main seat of the Roman Senate, built by Julius Caesar, rebuilt by Diocletian, and consecrated as a church in A.D. 630.

The triumphal **Arch of Septimius Severus ★★** (A.D. 203), is the next important sight, displaying time-bitten reliefs of the emperor's victories in what are now Iran and Iraq. During the Middle Ages, Rome became a provincial backwater, and frequent flooding of the Tiber helped bury (and thus preserve) most of the Forum. Some bits did still stick out aboveground, including the top half of this arch, which was used to shelter a barbershop!

Just to the left of the arch, you can make out the remains of a cylindrical lump of rock with some marble steps curving off it. That round stone was the **Umbilicus Urbis,** considered the center of Rome and of the entire Roman Empire; the curving steps are those of the **Imperial Rostra ★**, where great orators and legislators stood to speak and the people gathered to listen. Nearby, a much-photographed trio of fluted columns with Corinthian capitals supports a bit of architrave from the corner of the **Temple of Vespasian and Titus ★★**. (Emperors were routinely deified after death, with temples built in their honor.)

Start heading to your left toward the eight Ionic columns marking the front of the **Temple of Saturn ★★** (rebuilt in 42 B.C.), which housed the first treasury of Republican Rome. It was also the site of one of the Roman year's biggest annual blowout festivals, the December 17 feast of Saturnalia, which, after a bit of tweaking, Christians now celebrate as Christmas. Turn left to start

The Arch of Septimus Severus.

heading back east, past the worn steps and stumps of brick pillars outlining the enormous **Basilica Julia ★★**, built by Julius Caesar. Farther along, on the right, are the three Corinthian columns of the **Temple of the Dioscuri ★★★**, dedicated to the Gemini twins, Castor and Pollux. Forming one of the most photogenic sights of the Roman Forum, a trio of columns supports an architrave fragment. The founding of this temple dates from the 5th century B.C.

Ancient Rome, with Dramatic License

We're fans of the new Bardeum app (www.bardeum.com), whose step-by-step audio walking tours of the Colosseum, Forum, Palatine Hill, and Circus Maximus combine meticulously researched historical details with riveting, fictionalized accounts of the ancient Romans who once trod over these stones. The tours—each costing $4.99 and lasting between 20 and 75 minutes—are written by noted authors and engagingly narrated by professional actors.

Beyond the bit of curving wall that marks the site of the little round **Temple of Vesta** (rebuilt several times after fires started by the sacred flame within), you'll find the reconstructed **House of the Vestal Virgins** (A.D. 3rd–4th c.). The temple was the home of the consecrated young women who tended the sacred flame in the Temple of Vesta. Vestals were girls chosen from patrician families to serve a 30-year-long priesthood. During their tenure, they were among Rome's most venerated citizens, with unique powers such as the ability to pardon condemned criminals. The cult was quite serious about the "virgin" part of the job description—if one of Vesta's earthly servants was found to have "misplaced" her virginity, the miscreant Vestal was buried alive, because it was forbidden to shed a Vestal's blood. (Her amorous accomplice was merely flogged to death.) The overgrown rectangle of their gardens is lined with broken, heavily worn statues of senior Vestals on pedestals.

The path dovetails back to Via sacra. Turn right, walk past the so-called "Temple of Romulus," and then left to enter the massive brick remains of the 4th-century **Basilica of Constantine and Maxentius ★★** (Basilica di Massenzio). These were Rome's public law courts, and their architectural style was adopted by early Christians for their houses of worship (the reason so many ancient churches are called "basilicas").

Return to the path and continue toward the Colosseum. Veer right to the Forum's second great triumphal arch, the extensively rebuilt **Arch of Titus ★★** (A.D. 81), on which one relief depicts the carrying off of treasures from Jerusalem's temple. Look closely and you'll see a menorah among the booty. The war that this arch glorifies ended with the expulsion of Jews from the colonized Judea, signaling the beginning of the Jewish Diaspora throughout Europe. You can exit behind the Arch to continue on to the Colosseum, or head up to the Palatine Hill.

Access the **Palatine Hill ★★** (Palatino)—where Romulus, after eliminating his twin brother Remus, founded Rome around 753 B.C. Later, emperors and other ancient bigwigs built their palaces and private entertainment facilities up here. After climbing to the top of the hill, visitors are presented with a sprawling, mostly crowd-free archaeological garden, with some shady spots for cooling off in summer.

The Palatine was where the first settlers built their huts under the direction of Romulus. In later years, the hill became a patrician residential district that attracted such citizens as Cicero. In time, however, the area was gobbled up by imperial palaces and drew an infamous roster of tenants, such as Livia (some of the frescoes in the House of Livia are in miraculous condition), Tiberius, Caligula (murdered here by members of his Praetorian Guard), Nero, and Domitian. A museum houses some of the most important finds from hill excavations. The elaborately decorated **houses of Livia and Augustus ★★** are open to those who purchase the Full Experience ticket, which also includes other sites not normally open to the public.

> ### Famine in the Forum
>
> While the Palatine and the Forum have a few water fountains, they do not have any places to eat—not even so much as a vending machine. If you're making a day of it, pack some snacks.

Only the ruins of the Palatine's grandeur remain today, but it's worth the climb for the panoramic views of both the Roman and the Imperial Forums,

NERO'S golden HOUSE

After the Great Fire of 64 A.D., charismatic, despotic Emperor Nero staged a land grab to facilitate construction of his *Domus Aurea*, or Golden House, a massive, gilded villa complex covering all or parts of the Palatine, Esquiline, and Caelian hills and displaying a level of ostentation and excessiveness unheard of even among past emperors. After his death by noble suicide in 68 A.D., a campaign to erase all traces of Nero from the imperial city ensured that the palace was stripped of its gold, marble, jewels, mosaics, and statuary, then intentionally buried under millions of tons of rubble. It remained buried until the Renaissance, when young artists, including Raphael, descended into its "grottos" (actually the vaulted ceilings) to study the fanciful frescoes—the term grotesque (*grottoesque*) was coined here. Later excavations, both haphazard and scientific, revealed the scale and richness of the villa, but also subjected it to catastrophic moisture damage. The Domus Aurea is open for tours—but only if you time your trip well and plan ahead. Guided tours (16€; www.coopculture.it/en) of the scaffolded underground site (hardhats required) are currently offered on **Fridays, Saturdays, and Sundays only,** and with advance reservations. The tour includes a spectacular **virtual reality experience ★★★** that in itself is worth the visit. https://parcocolosseo.it/en/area/the-domus-aurea/

as well as the Capitoline Hill, the Colosseum, and Circus Maximus. You can also enter from here and do the entire tour in reverse.

Note: In recent years, archaeological areas of the Palatine and Forum, called S.U.P.E.R. sites and normally closed to visitors, are accessible via the Full Experience ticket.

Forum entrance on Via dei Fori Imperiali at Via della Salara Vecchia. Palatine Hill entrance at Via di San Gregorio 30 (south of the Colosseum). www.coopculture.it/en. ℂ **06-39967700.** 18€ pre-purchased online (includes Colosseum), Full Experience ticket 24€. Daily 9:30am–dusk (in winter as early as 4:30pm and Mar-Aug as late as 7:15pm). Last entry 1 hr. before closing. Metro: Colosseo. Bus: 51, 75, 85, 87, 118. Tram: 3, 8.

Museo dei Fori Imperiali & Mercati di Traiano (Museum of the Imperial Forums & Trajan's Markets) ★★ RUINS/MUSEUM

Built on three levels, Emperor Trajan's Market housed 150 shops and commercial offices—think of it as the world's first shopping mall. Grooves still evident in the thresholds allowed merchants to slide doors shut and lock up for the night. You're likely to have the covered, tunnel-like market halls mostly to yourself—making the ancient past feel all the more present in this overlooked site. The Museum of the Imperial Forums occupies a converted section of the market and has excellent visual displays that help you imagine what these grand public squares and temples used to look like. All in all, it's home to 172 marble fragments from the Fori Imperiali; here are also original remnants from the Forum of Augustus and Forum of Nerva.

Via IV Novembre 94. www.mercatiditraiano.it. ℂ **060608.** 11.50€ (more during special exhibits). Daily 9:30am–7:30pm. Last admission 1 hr. before closing. Bus: 40, 60, 64, 70, 170.

Even though they're all included in the same admission fee, the ruins of the Colosseum, Roman Forum, and Palatine Hill are quite a lot to take in on a single day, particularly in the heat of Roman summer. But if a day is all you have budgeted, buy your tickets well in advance so you can choose the earliest morning entry to the Colosseum. Then you'll have the rest of the day free for the Forum and Palatine Hill. If you've got a little more time (and interest), buy the 2-day Full Experience ticket (24€), which also gets you access to the S.U.P.E.R. sites. These are archaeological sites which normally have limited hours or are closed to the public entirely. The S.U.P.E.R. sites include the Houses of Livia and Augustus, the Neronion Crytpoporticus, the Domus Transitoria, the Palatine Museum, the Temple of Romulus, the Loggia Mattei (part of a Renaissance Palace) and, at the foot of the Palatine, the paleochristian church of Santa Maria Antiqua.

OTHER ATTRACTIONS NEAR ANCIENT ROME

Basilica di San Clemente ★★ CHURCH   A perfect example of how layers of history overlap in Rome, this 12th-century Norman church, full of beautiful Byzantine mosaics, hides much more. Down in its eerie grottos (which you explore on your own) you'll find frescoes and mosaic floors from its previous incarnations as a 4th-century Christian church and a temple dedicated to the pagan deity Mithras—and below that, the foundations of a Roman house from the 1st century A.D., where early Christians worshipped in secret. Access to the underground area is limited to 30 minutes.

Via San Giovanni in Laterano (at Piazza San Clemente). www.basilicasanclemente.com. ✆ **06-7740021.** Basilica free admission; excavations 10€ (also bookable online). Mon–Sat 10am–12:30pm and 3–5:30pm; Sun 12–5:30pm. Last entry 30 min before closing. Metro: Colosseo. Bus: 51, 85, 87, 117. Tram: 3.

Basilica di San Giovanni in Laterano ★★ CHURCH   This church, not St. Peter's, is officially the cathedral of the diocese of Rome; the Pope celebrates Mass here on certain holidays. Though it was built in A.D. 314 by Constantine, only parts of the original baptistery remain; what you see today is an 18-century I by Alessandro Galilei (note signs of damage from a 1993 terrorist bomb) and an interior by Borromini, built for Pope Innocent X. In a misguided redecoration long ago, frescoes by Giotto were apparently destroyed; remains attributed to Giotto, discovered in 1952, are displayed against the first inner column on the right.

Across the street is the **Santuario della Scala Santa (Palace of the Holy Steps),** Piazza San Giovanni in Laterano 14 (✆ **06-7726641**), a set of 28 marble steps supposedly brought from Jerusalem by Constantine's mother, Helen. Though some historians say the stairs might date only from the 4th century, legend claims these were the stairs Christ climbed at Pontius Pilate's villa the day he was sentenced to death. Today pilgrims from the world over come here to climb the steps on their knees.

Piazza San Giovanni in Laterano 4. ℘ **06-69886433.** Free admission. Daily 7am–6:30pm. Metro: San Giovanni.

Case Romane del Celio ★ RUINS Beneath the 5th-century Basilica of SS. Giovanni e Paolo lies a fascinating archaeological site: A complex of Roman houses of different periods—a wealthy family's townhouse from the 2nd century A.D. and a 3rd-century-A.D. apartment building for artisans. According to tradition, the latter was the home of two Roman officers, John and Paul (not the Apostles), who were beheaded during the reign of Julian the Apostate (361–63) for refusing to serve in a military campaign. They were later made saints, and their bones were said to have been buried here. The two-story construction also contains a small museum with finds from the site and fragmented 12th-century frescoes.

Piazza Santi Giovanni e Paolo 13 (entrance on Clivo di Scauro). www.coopculture.it/en. ℘ **06-70454544.** 10€ adults. Fri–Mon; Wed 10am–4pm. Metro: Colosseo or Circo Massimo. Bus: 75, 81, 118. Tram: 3.

Domus Romane di Palazzo Valentini ★★★ RUINS/EXHIBIT All too often in Italy, archaeological sites are presented with little context, and it's difficult for untrained eyes to really understand what they're seeing. Not so at Palazzo Valentini, possibly Rome's best-presented ancient site. Visitors descend underneath a Renaissance palazzo and peer through a glass floor into the remains of several upscale Roman homes. With innovative use of 3-D projections, the walls, ceilings, floors, and fountains of these once-grand houses spring to life, offering a captivating look at lifestyles of the ancient rich and possibly famous.

Via Foro Traiano 85 (near Trajan's Column). www.palazzovalentini.it. ℘ **06-22761280.** 13.50€. Wed–Mon 10am–7pm timed entrance, with guided tours in English several times daily; reservations suggested. Metro: Colosseo. Bus: 40, 63, 70, 81, 83, 87, or any bus to Piazza Venezia. Tram: 8.

Museo Nazionale del Palazzo di Venezia ★ MUSEUM Best remembered today as Mussolini's Fascist headquarters in Rome, the palace was built in the 1450s as the Rome outpost of the Republic of Venice—hence the name. Today, several of its rooms house an eclectic mix of European paintings and decorative and religious objects spanning the centuries; highlights include Giorgione's enigmatic "Double Portrait" and some early Tuscan altarpieces.

Via del Plebiscito 118. www.museopalazzovenezia.beniculturali.it. ℘ **06-6780131.** 12€. Daily 9:30am–6:30pm, with guided entry admission at the bottom of every hour (English guides at 10:30 and 4:30). Bus: 30, 40, 46, 62, 64, 70, 87, or any bus to Piazza Venezia. Tram: 8.

San Pietro in Vincoli (St. Peter in Chains) ★ CHURCH Founded in the 5th century to house the chains that supposedly bound St. Peter in

Jerusalem (preserved under glass below the main altar), this lovely church is mainly worth visiting to see one of the world's most famous sculptures: **Michelangelo's "Moses"** ★★, carved for the tomb of Pope Julius II. Michelangelo never completed the 44 magnificent figures planned for the tomb, but this "minor" figure he did complete is now considered among his masterpieces.

Piazza San Pietro in Vincoli no. 4. ℂ **06-97844952.** Free admission. Daily 8am–12:30pm and 3–7pm. Metro: Colosseo or Cavour. Bus: 75, 117.

"Moses", a Michelangelo masterpiece in San Pietro in Vincoli.

Santa Maria in Aracoeli ★★

CHURCH   This plain-on-the-outside church is worth the climb for its splendid interior. According to legend, Augustus ordered a temple erected on this spot on the Capitoline Hill, where a sibyl foretold the coming of Christ. The current church, built for the Franciscans in the 13th century, boasts a coffered Renaissance ceiling and the tomb of Giovanni Crivelli carved by the great Renaissance sculptor Donatello. The **Cappella Bufalini ★** (first chapel on the right) was frescoed by Pinturicchio with scenes of the life and death of St. Bernardino of Siena. A chapel behind the altar contains the **Santo Bambino,** a wooden figure of the Baby Jesus, which is venerated annually on Christmas Eve. The long flight of stairs leading up to the church was built in 1348 to celebrate the end of the Black Plague.

Scala dell'Arcicapitolina 12. ℂ **06-69763838.** Free admission. Daily 7am–7pm. Bus: 30, 40, 46, 62, 64, 70, 87, or any bus to Piazza Venezia.

Santa Maria in Cosmedin ★ CHURCH

People line up outside this ancient church (of Meklite Greek denomination) not for great art treasures (though it's worth a peek inside), but for the **"Mouth of Truth,"** a large disk on the wall of the portico. As Gregory Peck demonstrated to Audrey Hepburn in the film *Roman Holiday*, the mouth is supposed to chomp down on the hands of liars. It may have been an ancient drain cover, though one hypothesis says it was a so-called "talking statue," where anonymous notes were left to betray wrongdoers. Our take? Save this hokey photo op until you've seen everything else you want to see in Rome.

Piazza della Bocca della Verità 18. ℂ **06-6787759.** Free admission. Daily 9:30am–6pm (5pm winter). Bus: 30, 44, 81, 83, 85, 87, 118, 160, 628, 715.

Love it or loathe it, the massive Vittoriano monument at Piazza Venezia is a helpful landmark for visitors to get their bearings, and almost every bus line convenient to tourists stops here. Streets fanning out from the piazza lead to Termini Station, the Colosseum, the Trevi Fountain, and across the Tiber to the Vatican and Trastevere.

Vittoriano (Altare della Patria) ★ MONUMENT   It's impossible to miss the white marble Vittorio Emanuele monument dominating Piazza Venezia. Built in the late 1800s to honor the first king of a united Italy, this flamboyant (and widely disliked) landmark has been compared to everything from a wedding cake to a Victorian typewriter, its harsh white color glaring in a city of honey-gold tones. An eternal flame burns at the Tomb of the Unknown Soldier. For a panoramic city view, take a glass elevator to the **Terrazza delle Quadrighe (Terrace of the Chariots)** ★.

Piazza Venezia. vittoriano.beniculturali.it/en. © **06-6780664.** Free admission. Elevator to panoramic terrace 15€ (includes admission to Palazzo Venezia; see p. 114). Daily 9:30am–7:30pm (last entry 6:45pm). Bus: 30, 40, 46, 62, 64, 70, 87, or any bus to Piazza Venezia.

4

The ambitious Vittorio Emanuele Monument on Piazza Venezia.

Centro Storico & the Pantheon

CENTRO STORICO

Just across the Tiber from the Vatican and Castel Sant'Angelo lies the true heart of Rome, the **Centro Storico,** or "historic center," the triangular wedge of land that bulges into a bend of the river. Although the area lay outside the Roman city, it came into its own during the Renaissance, and today its streets and alleys are crammed with piazzas, elegant churches, and lavish fountains, all buzzing with scooters and people. It's a wonderful area in which to wander and get lost.

PIAZZA NAVONA & NEARBY ATTRACTIONS

Rome's most famous square, **Piazza Navona ★★★**, is a gorgeous Baroque gem, lined with cafes and restaurants and often full of tourists, street artists, and pigeons. Its long, oval shape follows the contours of the old ruined Roman Stadium of Domitian, where chariot races once took place, made over in the 17th century by Pope Innocent X. The twin-towered facade of 17th-century **Sant'Agnese in Agone** lies on the piazza's western side, while the **Fontana dei Quattro Fiumi (Fountain of the Four Rivers) ★★★** opposite is one of three great fountains in the square, this one a typically exuberant creation by Bernini, topped with an Egyptian obelisk. The four stone personifications

Lively Piazza Navona.

Centro Storico

ATTRACTIONS

Campo de' Fiori **26**
Fontana delle Tartarughe **33**
Galleria Doria Pamphilj **18**
Museo Ebraico di Roma
 & Tempio Maggiore **35**
Palazzo Altemps **5**
Palazzo Farnese **27**
Palazzo Spada **29**
Pantheon **15**
Piazza Navona **11**
San Luigi dei Francesi **10**
Sant'Agnese in Agone **12**
Santa Maria della Pace **2**
Santa Maria sopra Minerva **17**

HOTELS

Chapter Roma **32**
Coronari Palace **4**
Damaso Hotel **23**
Del Sole al Pantheon **14**
Hotel Adriano **7**
Hotel L'Orologio **24**
Mimosa **16**
Raphael **3**
Residenza in Farnese **28**

RESTAURANTS

Alfredo e Ada **1**
Antica Hostaria
 Romanesca **25**
Antico Forno
 Roscioli **30**
Armando al
 Pantheon **13**
Da Baffetto **20**

Frigidarium **21**
Gelateria Alberto
 Pica **31**
Il Bacaro **9**
La Campana **6**
Nonna Betta **34**
Pierluigi **22**
Pipero Roma **19**
Retrobottega **8**

125

below symbolize the world's greatest rivers: the Ganges, Danube, de la Plata, and Nile. It's fun to try to figure out which is which. (*Hint:* The figure with the shroud on its head is the Nile, so represented because the river's source was unknown at the time.) At the south end is Bernini's **Fontana del Moro (Fountain of the Moor)** and the 19th-century **Fontana di Nettuno (Fountain of Neptune)**.

Art lovers should make the short walk from the piazza to **Santa Maria della Pace** ★★ on Arco della Pace, a 15th-century church given the usual baroque makeover by Pietro da Cortona in the 1660s. The real gems are inside, beginning with Raphael's **"Four Sibyls"** ★★ fresco, above the arch of the Capella Chigi, and the **Chiostro del Bramante (Bramante cloister)** ★, built between 1500 and 1504 and the Renaissance master's first work in the city. The church is normally open daily from 9:30am to 6:30pm, while the cloister opens daily 10am to 8pm (Sat and Sun to 9pm). Admission to the church and cloister is free (www.chiostrodelbramante.it).

Tip: Waiters from Piazza Navona's many overpriced restaurants lie in wait, hoping to woo passing tourists. While the setting is unmatchable, you'll have a far better meal on any of the side streets off the piazza.

Palazzo Altemps ★★ MUSEUM   Inside this 15th-century *palazzo*, today a branch of the National Museum of Rome, is one of Rome's most charming museums housing some of the city's most famous private and public art collections. Much of it was once part of the famed **Boncompagni Ludovisi Collection,** created by Cardinal Ludovico Ludovisi (1595–1632) and sold at auction in 1901.

Among the highlights is the **"Ludovisi Ares"** ★★, a handsome 2nd-century copy of an earlier Greek statue of Mars (Ares to the Greeks). Equally renowned is the **"Ludovisi Gaul"** ★, a marble depiction of a Gaulish warrior plunging a sword into his chest (rather than become a slave of Rome), looking backwards defiantly as he supports a dying woman with his left arm. Also worth a look is the **"Ludovisi Throne,"** a sculpted block of white marble, thought to date from the 5th century B.C., depicting Aphrodite rising from the sea.

Piazza d' Sant'Apollinare 46. www.museonazionaleromano.beniculturali.it. (✆**06-39967700.** 12€ for single museum, or 16€, valid for 1 week and includes Palazzo Massimo and Baths of Diocletian; free for children 17 and under. Tues–Sun 11am–6pm. Last entry 1 hr. before closing. Bus: 70, 81, 87, 492, 628.

San Luigi dei Francesi ★★ CHURCH   For a painter of such stratospheric standards as Caravaggio, it is impossible to name just one of his works as his "masterpiece." However, the **"Calling of St. Matthew"** ★★, in the far-left chapel of Rome's French church, must be a candidate. Done in Caravaggio's distinct *chiaroscuro* (extreme light and shade) style, the panel dramatizes the moment Jesus and Peter "called" Matthew, a customs officer, to join them. Around the same time (1599–1602) Caravaggio also painted the other two St. Matthew panels in the Capella Contarelli, including one depicting the saint's martyrdom. Other church highlights include Domenichino's masterful

"Histories of Saint Cecilia" fresco cycle. Scan the QR code at the entrance for a free audioguide in English.

Via di Santa Giovanna d'Arco 5. www.saintlouis-rome.net. ☎ **06-688271.** Free admission. Mon–Fri 9:30am–12:45pm; Sat 9:30am–12:15pm; Sun 11:30–12:45pm, plus daily 2:30–6:30pm. Bus: 30, 70, 81, 87, 492, 628.

THE PANTHEON & NEARBY ATTRACTIONS

The Pantheon stands on **Piazza della Rotonda,** a lively square with outdoor cafes, vendors, and great people-watching.

The Pantheon ★★★ HISTORIC SITE Stumbling onto Piazza della Rotunda from the dark warren of streets surrounding it will likely leave you agape, marveling at one of ancient Rome's great buildings—the only one that remains intact. The Pantheon ("Temple to All the Gods") was originally built in 27 B.C. by Marcus Agrippa but was entirely reconstructed by Hadrian in the early 2nd century A.D. This remarkable building, 43m (142 ft.) wide and 43m (142 ft.) high (a perfect sphere resting in a cylinder) is among the architectural wonders of the world, even today. Hadrian himself is credited with the basic plan. There are no visible arches or vaults holding up the dome; instead they're sunk into the concrete of the building's walls. The ribbed dome outside is a series of cantilevered bricks.

Animals were once sacrificed and burned in the center, with the smoke escaping through the only means of light, the oculus, an opening at the top

Pantheon interior.

5.5m (18 ft.) in diameter. The interior was richly decorated, with white marble statues ringing the central space in its niches. Nowadays, apart from the jaw-dropping size of the space, the main items of interest are the tombs of two Italian kings (Vittorio Emanuele II and his successor, Umberto I) and artist **Raphael** (fans still bring him flowers), with its poignant epitaph. Since the 7th century, the Pantheon has been used as a Catholic church, the **Santa Maria ad Martyres,** informally known as "Santa Maria della Rotonda."

> ### Weekends at the Pantheon
>
> At press time, weekend and holiday entrance to the Pantheon is by reservation only (not required on weekdays). Entry is still "free"—technically, but reservations are only bundled with audio and guided tours, which cost 8.50€ and up. See what they just did there? The situation is in flux, so check the Pantheon website (www.pantheonroma.com/en) for the latest updates.

Piazza della Rotonda. www.pantheon roma.com/en. © **06-68300230.** Free admission. Daily 9am–7pm. Bus: 30, 40, 62, 64, 81, 87 or 492 to Largo di Torre Argentina.

Santa Maria sopra Minerva ★★★ CHURCH   Just one block behind the Pantheon, Santa Maria sopra Minerva is Rome's most significant Dominican church and the only major Gothic church downtown. The façade is in Renaissance style (the church was begun in 1280 but worked on until 1725), but inside, the arched vaulting is pure Gothic. The main art treasures here are the "Statua del Redentore" (1521), a statue of Christ by **Michelangelo** (just to the left of the altar), and a wonderful fresco cycle in the **Cappella Carafa** (on the right before the altar), created by Filippino Lippi between 1488 and 1493 to honor St. Thomas Aquinas. Devout Catholics flock to the tomb of **Saint Catherine of Siena** under the high altar—the room where she died in 1380 was reconstructed by Antonio Barberini in 1637 (far left corner of the church). **Fra' Angelico,** the Dominican friar and painter, also rests here, in the **Cappella Frangipane e Maddaleni-Capiferro.** A delightful elephant statue by **Bernini** holds up a small obelisk in the piazza in front of the church.

Piazza della Minerva 42. www.santamariasopraminerva.it/en. © **06-69920384.** Free admission. Daily 9am–12pm, 4–7pm.

Galleria Doria Pamphilj ★★ ART MUSEUM   One of the city's finest rococo palaces, the Palazzo Doria Pamphilj is still privately owned by the aristocratic Doria Pamphilj family, but their stupendous art collection is open to the public. The *galleria* winds through the old apartments, their paintings displayed floor-to-ceiling among antique furniture and richly decorated walls. The strong Dutch and Flemish collection includes Pieter Brueghel the Elder's "Battle in the Port of Naples," and his son Jan Brueghel the Elder's "Earthly Paradise with Original Sin." Among the best Italian works are two Caravaggio paintings, the moving "Repentant Magdalene" and his wonderful "Rest on the Flight into Egypt," hanging near Titian's "Salome with the Head of St. John." There's also Raphael's "Double Portrait," an "Annunciation" by Filippo Lippi, and a "Deposition from the Cross" by Vasari. The gallery's real treasures occupy a special room: Bernini's bust of the Pamphilj **"Pope Innocent X"** ★, and **Velázquez's enigmatic painting** ★★ of the same man. Make sure you grab a free audio guide at the entrance—it's colorfully narrated by Prince Jonathan Doria Pamphilj himself, who recalls roller-skating in the palazzo as a child.

Via del Corso 305 (just N of Piazza Venezia). www.doriapamphilj.it. © **06-6797323.** 15€ adults, 1€ 12 and under. Mon–Thurs 9am–7pm, Fri–Sun 10am–8pm, last entry 1 hr. before closing. Closed 3rd Wed every month. Bus: 64 or any to Piazza Venezia.

CAMPO DE' FIORI

The southern section of the Centro Storico, **Campo de' Fiori** is another neighborhood of narrow streets, small piazzas, and ancient churches. Its main focus remains the piazza of **Campo de' Fiori** ★★ itself, where a touristy but delightful open-air market runs daily (with fewer vendors on Sunday) from early in the morning until midday, selling a dizzyingly colorful array of fruits, vegetables, and spices as well as cheap T-shirts and handbags. (Keep an eye on your valuables here.) From the center of the piazza rises a statue of the severelooking monk **Giordano Bruno,** a reminder that heretics were occasionally burned at the stake here: Bruno was executed by the Inquisition in 1600. Curiously this is the only piazza in Rome that doesn't have a church in its perimeter.

Built from 1514 to 1589, the **Palazzo Farnese** ★, on Piazza Farnese just to the south of the Campo, was designed by Sangallo and Michelangelo, among others, and was an astronomically expensive project for the time. Its famous residents have included 16th-century member of the Farnese family, plus Pope Paul III, Cardinal Richelieu, and the former Queen Christina of Sweden, who moved to Rome after abdicating. During the 1630s, when the heirs couldn't afford to maintain the *palazzo,* it was inherited by the Bourbon kings of Naples and was purchased by the French government in 1874; the French Embassy is still located here, so the building is mostly closed to the general public. Tours are offered in English on Monday, Wednesday, and Friday afternoons and cost 12€. Reservations are mandatory (visite-palazzofarnese.it/).

Palazzo Spada/Galleria Spada ★ MUSEUM   Built around 1540 for Cardinal Gerolamo Capo di Ferro, Palazzo Spada was purchased by the eponymous Cardinal Spada in 1632, who then hired Borromini to restore it—most of what you see today dates from that period. Its richly I facade, covered in high-relief stucco decorations in the Mannerist style, is the finest of any building from 16th-century Rome. The State Rooms are closed (the Italian Council of State still meets here), but the richly decorated courtyard and corridor, Borromini's masterful illusion of perspective *(la prospettiva di Borromini* ★★), and the four rooms of the **Galleria Spada** are open to the public. Inside you will find some absorbing paintings, such as the "Portrait of Cardinale Bernardino Spada" by Guido Reni, and Titian's "Portrait of a Violinist," plus minor works from Parmigianino, Pietro Testa, and Giambattista Gaulli.

Piazza Capo di Ferro 13. www.galleriaspada.beniculturali.it. © **06-6874893.** 5€. Wed–Mon 8:30am–7:30pm. Bus: 23, 280, or any bus to Largo di Torre Argentina; Tram: 8.

THE JEWISH GHETTO

Across Via Arenula, Campo de' Fiori merges into the old **Jewish Ghetto ★★**, established near the River Tiber by a Papal Bull in 1555, which required that all the Jews in Rome live in one area. Walled in, overcrowded, prone to floods and epidemics, and on some of the worst land in the city, it was an extremely grim place to live. After the Ghetto was abolished in 1882, its walls were finally torn down and the area largely reconstructed. Rome's Jewish population continued living in this neighborhood up to World War II. In the waning years of WWII, Nazis raided the Ghetto and sent more than 1,000 Roman Jews to concentration camps; only a handful returned.

Today, the **Via Portico d'Ottavia** forms the heart of a flourishing Jewish Quarter, with Romans and tourists flocking here to sample the **Roman-Jewish and Middle Eastern food** for which the area is known. Head north on winding Via di S. Ambrogio to toss a coin in the **Fontana delle Tartarughe ★**, a beloved Renaissance fountain. The turtles, added in the 1600s, are thought to be by Bernini.

Museo Ebraico di Roma (Jewish Museum of Rome) & Great Synagogue ★★ MUSEUM   On the premises of the Great Synagogue of Rome, this museum chronicles the history of not only Roman Jews but Jews from all over Italy. Displays include works of 7th- and 18th-century Roman silversmiths, precious textiles from all over Europe, and several parchments

Kosher restaurant in the Jewish Ghetto.

and marble carvings that were saved when the Ghetto's original synagogues were demolished. Admission to the museum includes a guided English-language tour of the **Great Synagogue of Rome** (Tempio Maggiore), built from 1901 to 1904 in an eclectic style evoking Babylonian and Persian temples. Attacked by terrorists in 1982, the synagogue is now heavily guarded by *carabinieri*, a division of the Italian police armed with machine guns.

Via Catalana. www.museoebraico.roma.it/en. 𝄄 **06-6840061.** 11€ adults, 5€ students, free for children 10 and under. Apr–Sept Sun–Thurs 10am–6pm and Fri 10am–4pm; Jan 21–Mar, Oct Sun–Thurs 10am–5pm and Fri 9am–2pm (Nov 1–Jan 20 closes 4 or 4:30pm Mon–Thurs; last entry 3:15pm). Closed on Jewish holidays.

The Tridente & the Spanish Steps

The northern half of central Rome is known as the **Tridente,** thanks to the trident shape formed by three roads—Via di Ripetta, Via del Corso, and Via del Babuino—leading down from **Piazza del Popolo.** The area around **Piazza di Spagna** and the **Spanish Steps** was once the artistic quarter of the city, attracting English poets Keats and Shelley, German author Goethe, and film director Federico Fellini (who lived on Via Margutta). Institutions such as **Antico Caffè Greco** and **Babington's Tea Rooms** are still here (see p. 89), but between the high rents and the throngs of tourists and shoppers, you're unlikely to see many artists left.

PIAZZA DEL POPOLO

Elegant **Piazza del Popolo ★★** is haunted with memories. Legend has it that the ashes of Nero were enshrined he, until 11th-century residents began complaining to the pope about his imperial ghost. The **Egyptian obelisk** date from the 13th century B.C.; it was removed from Heliopolis to Rome during Augustus's reign (it once stood at the Circus Maximus).

The current piazza was designed in the early 19th century by Valadier, Napoleon's architect. Standing astride the three roads that form the "trident" are almost-twin baroque churches, **Santa Maria dei Miracoli** (1681) and **Santa Maria di Montesanto** (1679). The stand-out church, however, is at the piazza's northern curve: the 15th-century **Santa Maria del Popolo ★★**, with its splendid baroque façade modified by Bernini between 1655 and 1660. Inside, look for Raphael's mosaic series the "Creation of the World" adorning the interior dome of the **Capella Chigi** (the second chapel on the left). Pinturicchio decorated the main choir vault with frescoes such as the "Coronation of the Virgin." The **Capella Cerasi** (to the left of the high altar) contains gorgeous examples of baroque art: an altarpiece painting of "The Assumption of Mary" by Carracci, and on either side two great works by Caravaggio, "Conversion on the Road to Damascus" and "The Crucifixion of Saint Peter."

MAXXI (National Museum of the XXI Century Arts) ★ MUSEUM

Ten minutes north of Piazza del Popolo by tram, leave the Renaissance far behind at MAXXI, a masterpiece of contemporary architecture with bending and overlapping oblong tubes designed by the late, great Zaha Hadid. The museum is divided into two sections, MAXXI art and MAXXI architecture, primarily serving as a venue for temporary exhibitions of contemporary work in both fields (although it does have a small permanent collection). The building is worth a visit in its own right.

Via Guido Reni 4a. www.maxxi.art/en. ℗ **06-3201954.** 12€ adults, 9€ youth 25 and under, free for children 13 and under. Tues–Sun 11am–7pm. Metro: Flaminio, then Tram 2.

Museo dell'Ara Pacis ★★ MUSEUM   Set in a stunning ultra-modern building designed by American architect Richard Meier (long before his #MeToo contrition), the temple-like marble "Altar of Peace" was erected in 9 B.C. to honor soon-to-be-Emperor Augustus's success in subduing tribes north of the Alps. For centuries the monument was lost to memory; signs of its existence surfaced in the 16th century, but it wasn't until the 1930s that it was fully excavated, and even so it lay virtually abandoned after World War II, until a true restoration began in the 1980s. The exhibit complex provides context, with interactive displays in English.

Lungotevere in Augusta. www.arapacis.it/en. ℗ **06-060608.** 10.50€. Daily 9:30am–7:30pm (last entry 6:30pm). Metro: Spagna. Bus: 30, 70, 81, 87, 119, 280, 492, 628, 913.

PIAZZA DI SPAGNA

The undoubted highlight of Tridente is **Piazza di Spagna,** which attracts hordes of tourists to admire its celebrated **Spanish Steps (Scalinata della Trinità dei Monti)** ★★, the widest stairway in Europe. The Steps are especially enchanting in early spring, when they are framed by thousands of

The ever-romantic Spanish Steps.

The Tridente to Via Veneto

ATTRACTIONS

Fontana di Trevi 31
Galleria Borghese 22
Galleria Nazionale d'Arte Antica 28
Galleria Nazionale d'Arte Moderna 20
Keats-Shelley House 15
MACRO Via Nizza 24
Mausoleo di Augusto (Piazza Augusto Imperatore) 7
MAXXI (Museo Nazionale delle Arti del XXI Secolo) 1
Museo dell'Ara Pacis 6
Museo e Cripta dei Frati Cappuccini 26
Museo Nazionale Etrusco di Villa Giulia 19
Palazzo del Quirinale 34
Palazzo Barberini 27
Piazza del Popolo 3
Santa Maria del Popolo 2
Spanish Steps 14
SS. Vincenzo e Anastasio 32
Trinità dei Monti 16

Vicus Caprarius 33
Villa Borghese 18

RESTAURANTS

Al Ceppo 23
Antico Caffè Greco 12
Babington's Tea Rooms 13
Canova Tadolini 5
Colline Emiliane 29
Imàgo 17
Pic Nic 21

HOTELS

Babuino 181 4
Hotel Condotti 10
The Inn at the Spanish Steps 11
La Lumière 8
La Residenza 25
Panda 9
Parlamento 30
Villa Spalletti Trivelli 35

No swimming, sitting or picnicking allowed

In an effort to keep tourists from littering the city's monuments, or soaking their feet and even swimming (yes, it's happened) in its famous fountains, visitors are no longer permitted to picnic (or even sit) on the Spanish Steps, or sit on the edge of the Trevi and other landmark fountains. You can stop long enough for a photo or coin toss, but don't plan on getting comfortable (or taking a dip).

---

blooming azaleas. At their foot lies "Fontana della Barcaccia," a fountain shaped like an old boat, the work of Pietro Bernini, father of sculptor and fountain-master Gian Lorenzo Bernini.

Built from 1723 to 1725, the monumental stairway of 135 steps and the square take their names from the Spanish Embassy (it used to be headquartered here), but were actually funded almost entirely by the French. That's because the **Trinità dei Monti** church at the top was under the patronage of the Bourbon kings of France at the time. The facade of the 16th-century Trinità dei Monti is perched photogenically at the top of the Steps, behind yet another Roman obelisk, the "Obelisco Sallustiano." It's worth climbing up just for the views.

Keats-Shelley House ★ MUSEUM   At the foot of the Spanish Steps is the 18th-century house where the Romantic English poet John Keats died of consumption on February 23, 1821, at age 25. Since 1909, it has been a working library established in honor of Keats and fellow Romantic Percy Bysshe Shelley, who drowned off the coast of Viareggio with a copy of Keats' works in his pocket. Mementos range from kitsch to extremely moving. The apartment where Keats spent his last months, tended by his close friend Joseph Severn, shelters a death mask of Keats as well as the "deadly sweat" drawing by Severn. Both Keats and Shelley are buried in their beloved Rome, at the Protestant cemetery near the Pyramid of Cestius, in Testaccio (p. 144).

Piazza di Spagna 26. www.keats-shelley-house.org. ☏ **06-6784235.** 6€. Mon–Sat 10am–1pm and 2–6pm. Metro: Spagna.

Palazzo del Quirinale ★★ HISTORIC SITE   One the palace of popes and the king of Italy, since 1946 the Quirinale has been the official residence of the President of Italy, but parts of it are open to the public.

Although it can't compare to Rome's major artistic showstoppers (the rooms have very little art or furniture), the palace's baroque and neoclassical

---

Art in the Pope's Stables

Across from the Palazzo del Quirinale, the **Scuderie del Quirinale** or **Scuderie Papali,** Via XXIV Maggio 16 (www.scuderiequirinale.it; ☏ **06-399670**), originally 18th-century stables for the pope's horses, now function as remarkably atmospheric art galleries hosting temporary exhibitions, including the occasional blockbuster. The galleries are open daily from 10am to 8pm. Admission is 15€.

---

walls and ceilings are quite a spectacle. Few rooms anywhere are as impressive as the richly decorated 17th-century **Salone dei Corazzieri,** the **Sala d'Ercole** (once the apartments of Umberto I but completely rebuilt in 1940), and the tapestry-covered 17th-century **Sala dello Zodiaco.** Despite its Renaissance origins, this *palazzo* is rich in associations with ancient emperors and deities. The colossal statues of the "Dioscuri," Castor and Pollux, which now form part of the fountain in the piazza, were found in the nearby Baths of Constantine; in 1793 Pius VI had an ancient Egyptian obelisk moved here from the Mausoleum of Augustus. The sweeping view of the city from the piazza, which crowns the highest of the seven ancient hills of Rome, is itself worth the trip.

Piazza del Quirinale. palazzo.quirinale.it/palazzo.html. (*) **06-39967557.** 1.50€ for an 80-minute tour following one of 3 themed itineraries. Reservations must be made at least 5 days prior to visit. Tues–Wed and Fri–Sun 9:30am–4pm. Closed Aug. Metro: Barberini. Bus: 53, 60, 62-63, 70, 71, 80, 83, 85, 492.

Trevi Fountain (Fontana di Trevi) ★★ MONUMENT

As you elbow your way through the summertime crowds around the **Trevi Fountain,** it's hard to believe that this little piazza was nearly always deserted before 1950, when it began "starring" in films. The first was *Three Coins in the Fountain*, and later it was the setting for an iconic scene in Fellini's 1960 masterpiece *La Dolce Vita*. It was also where Audrey Hepburn gets her signature haircut in *Roman Holiday*. To this day, visitors toss thousands of euros worth of coins into the fountain daily. The area is always jam-packed with selfie stick-wielding tourists and the people who profit off of them, so keep your eye (and your hands) on your belongings.

> #### Coin Toss: A Guaranteed Return to Rome?
>
> The custom of tossing a coin into the Trevi Fountain to ensure your return to Rome apparently only works if you use correct form: With your back to the fountain, toss a coin with your right hand over your left shoulder. Works for me every time!

Completed in 1762, this glorious baroque fountain centers on the triumphant figure of Neptune, standing on a shell chariot drawn by winged steeds and led by a pair of tritons. Two allegorical figures in the side niches represent good health and fertility.

On the southwestern corner of the piazza is an unimpressive church, **SS. Vincenzo e Anastasio,** with a strange claim to fame. Within it are the relics (hearts and intestines) of several popes. In an alley nearby, **Vicus Caprarius— the City of Water ★** (www.vicuscaprarius.com. (*) **339-7786192;** 4€; reservations suggested) is a privately run archaeological area comprised of several underground levels of ancient development, including an upscale home and part of the Acquedotto Vergine, the aqueduct that still feeds the Trevi.

Piazza di Trevi. Metro: Barberini. Bus: 52, 62-63, 80, 83, 85, 160, 492.

Villa Borghese & Parioli

Villa Borghese ★★, just northeast of the Tridente, is not actually a villa but a large park, 6km (3¾ miles) in circumference. Cardinal Scipione Borghese created the park in the 1600s; Umberto I, king of Italy, acquired it in 1902 and presented it to the city of Rome. Roads crisscross this greenbelt, but you can escape from the traffic and seek a shaded area under a tree to enjoy its landscaped vistas. On a sunny weekend, it's a pleasure to stroll here and see Romans at play, relaxing or inline skating. The park has a few casual cafes and food vendors (Pic Nic is a solid choice; Piazzale delle Canestre; ✆ **06-855-7493**; daily 9am–7pm); you can also rent bikes or Segways here. In the northeast part of the park, you'll find a **zoo** and the **Galleria Borghese** (see below).

Galleria Borghese ★★★ ART MUSEUM   On the far northeastern edge of the Villa Borghese, the Galleria Borghese occupies the former Villa Bor-

ghese Pinciana, built between 1609 and 1613 for Cardinal Scipione Borghese, an early patron of Bernini and an astute collector of work by Caravaggio. Today the gallery displays much of his collection and a lot more besides, making this one of Rome's great art treasures. It's also one of Rome's most pleasant sights to tour, thanks to the curators' mandate that only a limited number of people be allowed in at a time.

The ground floor is a **sculpture gallery** par extraordinaire, housing Canova's famously risqué statue of Paolina Borghese, sister of Napoleon and wife of the reigning Prince Camillo Borghese (when asked if she was uncomfortable posing nude, she reportedly replied, "No, the studio was heated."). The genius of Bernini reigns supreme in the following rooms, with his "David" (the face is thought to be a self-portrait) and **"Apollo and**

A rotunda in the Villa Borghese gardens.

Daphne" ★★ both seminal works of baroque sculpture. Look also for Bernini's Mannerist sculpture next door, "The Rape of Persephone." Caravaggio is represented by the "Madonna of the Grooms," the shadowy "St. Jerome," and the frightening **"David Holding the Head of Goliath" ★★**.

Upstairs lies a rich collection of paintings, including Raphael's graceful "Deposition" and his sinuous "Lady with a Unicorn." Also here is a series of self-portraits by Bernini, and his lifelike busts of Cardinal Scipione and Pope Paul V. One of Titian's best, **"Sacred and Profane Love"** ★, lies in one of the final rooms.

Note: No more than 360 visitors at a time are allowed on the ground floor, and no more than 90 are allowed on the upper floor, during set 2-hour windows. **Reservations are essential** and can be made through the museum website. Roma Pass holders need to reserve an entry time by calling ✆ **06-32810** (Mon–Fri 9am–6pm; Sat 9am–1pm). English labeling in the museum is minimal. Guided tours of the galleries in English cost an extra 6.50€, or you can opt for an audio guide.

Piazzale del Museo Borghese 5 (off Via Pinciana). www.galleriaborghese.it. ✆ **06-32810.** 15€; 18 and under 2€. Audio guides 5€. Tues–Sun 9am–7pm. Bus: 52, 53, 61, 89, 160, 490, 495, 590, 910. Tram: 3 or 19.

MACRO Via Nizza ★ MUSEUM Rome's contemporary art museum occupies an entire block of early-1900s industrial buildings, formerly the Peroni beer factory, located near the Porta Pia gate of the Aurelian walls. The museum hosts contemporary art exhibits with edgy installations, visuals, and multimedia events. Another branch of the museum is in a converted slaughterhouse in Testaccio (p. 144).

Via Nizza 138. www.museomacro.org. ✆ **06-696271.** Free admission (special exhibits may be ticketed). Tues–Fri, Sat–Sun 10am–7pm. Bus: 38, 66, 90, 223. Tram: 3, 19.

Museo Nazionale Etrusco di Villa Giulia (National Etruscan Museum) ★★★ MUSEUM The great Etruscan civilization was one of Italy's most advanced, although it remains relatively mysterious, in part because of its centuries-long rivalry with Rome. Rome definitively conquered the Etruscans by the 3rd century B.C., and though they adopted certain aspects of Etruscan culture, including religious practices, engineering innovations, and gladiatorial combat, gradual Romanization eclipsed virtually all the Etruscans' achievements.

This museum, housed in the handsome Renaissance Villa Giulia, built by Pope Julius III between 1550 and 1555, is the best place in Italy to learn about the Etruscans, thanks to a cache of precious artifacts, sculptures, vases, monuments, tools, weapons, and jewels, the vast majority of it from tombs. Fans of ancient history could spend several hours here, but for those with less time, the most striking attraction is the stunning **Sarcofago degli Sposi (Sarcophagus of the Spous)** ★★, a late 6th-century-B.C. terracotta funerary monument featuring a life-size bride and groom lounging at a banquet in the afterlife (Paris's Louvre has a similar monument). Equally fascinating are the **Pyrgi Tablets,** gold-leaf inscriptions in both Etruscan and Phoenician from the 5th century B.C., and the **Apollo of Veii,** a huge painted terracotta statue of Apollo dating to the 6th century B.C.

Piazzale di Villa Giulia 9. www.museoetru.it. ✆ **06-3226571.** 10€. Tues–Sun 8:30am–7:30pm, last entry 6:30pm. Bus: 982. Tram: 2, 19.

National Gallery of Modern Art (Galleria Nazionale d'Arte Moderna) ★ ART MUSEUM   Housed in the monumental Bazzani Building constructed in 1911, this "modern" art collection ranges from unfashionable neoclassical and Romantic paintings and sculpture to better 20th-century works. Quality varies, but fans should seek out van Gogh's "Gardener" and "Portrait of Madame Ginoux" in Room 15, the handful of Impressionists in Room 14 (Cézanne, Degas, Monet, and Rodin), and Klimt's harrowing "Three Ages" in Room 16. Surrealist and Expressionist works by Miró, Kandinsky, and Mondrian appear in Room 22, and Pollock's "Undulating Paths" and Calder's "Mobile" hold court in Room 27. One of Warhol's "Hammer and Sickle" series is tucked away in Room 30.

Viale delle Belle Arti 131. Lagallerianazionale.com/en. ℰ **06-322981.** 10€, 5€ for MAXXI ticketholders, free for children 17 and under. Mon–Fri 9am–7pm. Metro: Flaminio. Bus: 61, 89, 160, 490, 495. Tram: 3 or 19.

Via Veneto & Piazza Barberini

Piazza Barberini lies at the foot of several streets, among them Via Barberini, Via Sistina, and Via Vittorio Veneto. It would be a far more pleasant spot were it not for the traffic swarming around its principal feature, Bernini's **Fountain of the Triton (Fontana del Tritone)** ★★. For almost 4 centuries, the figure sitting in a vast open clam has been blowing water from his triton. To one side

Piazza Barberini and its nearly-400-year-old fountain.

of the piazza is the aristocratic façade of the **Palazzo Barberini,** named for one of Rome's powerful families; inside is the **Galleria Nazionale d'Arte Antica** (see p. 138). The Barberini reached their peak when a son was elected pope as Urban VIII; he encouraged Bernini and gave him patronage.

As you walk up **Via Vittorio Veneto,** look for the small fountain on the right corner of Piazza Barberini—it's another Bernini, the **Fountain of the Bees (Fontana delle Api)** ★. At first they look more like flies, but they're the bees of the Barberini, the crest of that powerful family complete with the crossed keys of St. Peter above them. (Keys were always added to a family crest when a son was elected pope.)

Museo e Cripta dei Frati Cappuccini (Museum and Crypt of the Capuchin Friars) ★★ RELIGIOUS SITE/MUSEUM

One of the most mesmerizingly macabre sights in all Christendom, this otherwise restrained museum dedicated to the Capuchin order ends with a series of six chapels in the crypt, adorned with the skulls and bones of more than 3,700 Capuchin brothers, woven into mosaic works of art. Some of the skeletons are intact, draped with Franciscan habits; others form lamps and ceiling friezes. The tradition of the friars dates to a period when Christians had a richly creative cult of the dead and great spiritual masters meditated and preached with a skull in hand. Whatever you believe, the experience is a mix of spooky and meditative. The entrance is halfway up the first staircase on the right of the church of the Convento dei Frati Cappuccini, completed in 1630 and rebuilt in the early 1930s.

Note: Because this site is located within a church, it maintains a strict dress code: no short pants or skirts and no bare arms—and no photos. We don't recommend this experience for kids under 10 or so.

Via Vittorio Veneto 27. www.cappucciniviaveneto.it. © **06-88803695.** 8.50€, 5€ ages 17 and under. Daily 10am–7pm, last entry 6:30pm. Metro: Barberini. Bus: 52, 53, 61, 63, 80, 83, 160, 590.

National Gallery of Ancient Art (Galleria Nazionale d'Arte Antica) ART MUSEUM

On the southern side of Piazza Barberini, the grand **Palazzo Barberini** houses the Galleria Nazionale d'Arte Antica, which despite the "ancient" in its title is a trove of Italian art mostly from the early Renaissance to late baroque periods. Some of the art on display is wonderful, but the building itself is the main attraction, a baroque masterpiece begun by Carlo Maderno in 1627 and completed in 1633 by Bernini, with additional work by Borromini (notably a whimsical spiral staircase). The **Salone di Pietro da Cortona** in the center is the most captivating space, with a trompe l'oeil ceiling frescoed by da Cortona, a depiction of "The Triumph of Divine Providence."

The museum has intriguing works, including Raphael's "La Fornarina," a baker's daughter thought to have been the artist's lover (look for Raphael's name on her bracelet); paintings by Tintoretto and Titian (Room 15); a portrait of English King Henry VIII by Holbein (Room 16); and a couple of typically

Palazzo Barberini and the Galleria Nazionale d'Arte Antica.

unsettling El Grecos in Room 17. Caravaggio dominates room 20 with the justly celebrated **"Judith and Holofernes"** ★★★ and **"Narcissus"** ★★.

Via delle Quattro Fontane 13. www.barberinicorsini.org. ℰ **06-4814591.** 12€, valid for 20 days, also includes Palazzo Corsini; free for children 17 and under. Tues–Sun 10am– 7pm, last entry 6pm. Metro: Barberini. Bus: 52, 53, 61–63, 80, 81, 83, 160, 492, 590.

Around Stazione Termini

Palazzo Massimo alle Terme ★★ MUSEUM   A third of Rome's assortment of ancient art can be found at this branch of the Museo Nazionale Romano; among its treasures are a major coin collection, extensive maps of trade routes (with audio and visual exhibits on the network of traders over the centuries), and a vast sculpture collection that includes portrait busts of emperors and their families, as well as mythical figures like the Minotaur and Athena. But the real draw is on the second floor, where you can see some of the oldest of Rome's **frescoes** ★★; they depict an entire garden, complete with plants and birds, from the Villa di Livia a Prima Porta. (Livia was the wife of Emperor Augustus and was deified after her death in A.D. 29.)

Largo di Villa Peretti. www.museonazionaleromano.beniculturali.it. ℰ **06-39967700.** 10€ for single museum, or 15€, valid for 1 week; also includes Palazzo Altemps and the Baths of Diocletian; free for children 17 and under. Tues–Sun 11am–6pm, last entry 1 hr. before closing. Metro: Termini or Repubblica. Bus: 40, 64, or any bus that stops at Termini.

Metro A — Ⓜ —
Metro B — Ⓜ —

Around Termini

Piazza Sallustio

Via Quintino Sella
Via Silvio Spaventa
Via Giosuè Carducci
Via Sallustiana
Via Aureliana
Via XX Settembre
Via Flavia
Via Piave
Via Montebello
Via Palestro
Via Castelfidardo
Via Cernaia
Via Goito
Via San Martino della Battaglia
Castro Pretorio Ⓜ
Viale Castro Pretorio
Viale Pretoriano

Ministero dell'Economia e delle Finanze

Via Leonida Bissolati
Salita di S. Nicola da Tolentino
Largo di S. Susanna
Piazza San Bernardo
Via Vittorio Emanuele Orlando
Via P. Barberi

National Roman Museum

Piazza Indipendenza
Via Volturno
Via Gaeta
Via Solferino
Via Vicenza
Via dei Mille
Via Marghera
Via Varese
Via Milazzo
Via Palestro
Viale Enrico de Nicola
Via Magenta

Repubblica Ⓜ
Piazza della Repubblica
Via Nazionale
Via Modena
Via Firenze
Via delle Quattro Fontane
Via Napoli
Via Agostino Depretis
Piazza del Viminale
Palazzo del Viminale
Teatro dell'Opera
Via del Viminale
Via Giovanni Giolitti
Piazza Cinquecento
Termini Ⓜ
Via d'Azeglio
Via Torino
Via Balbo
Via Cavour
Via Amendola
Via Daniele Manin
Via Filippo Turati

Termini Station

Via Marsala
Via del Castro Pretorio

Piazza dell'Esquilino
Santa Maria Maggiore
Piazza dell'Esquilino
Via Farini
Via Gioberti
Via Cavour
Via Napoleone III
Piazza Manfredo Fanti
Casa dell' Architettura
Via Carlo Alberto

MONTI
Via Panisperna
Via Urbana
Via Cesare

ESQUILINO

Via di San Martino ai Monti
Via Giovanni Lanza
Largo Brancaccio
Via di San Martino
Via di San Vito
Vittorio Emanuele Ⓜ
Piazza Vittorio Emanuele II

ATTRACTIONS
Palazzo Massimo alle Terme **9**
Santa Maria della Vittoria **1**
Santa Maria Maggiore **13**
Terme di Diocleziano **6**

RESTAURANTS
Come il Latte **2**
Mercato Centrale Roma **12**
Pinsere **3**
Trattoria Monti **14**
Trimani Il Wine Bar **5**

HOTELS
Anantara Palazzo Naiadi **8**
Beehive **10**
Hotel Mediterraneo **11**
Residenza Cellini **7**
Seven Kings Relais **4**

0   200 y
0   200 m

Santa Maria della Vittoria ★★ CHURCH   A visit to this pretty little baroque church is all about one artwork: Gian Lorenzo Bernini's **"Ecstasy of St. Teresa"** ★★★. Crafted from marble between 1644 and 1647, it shows the Spanish saint at the moment of her ecstatic encounter with an angel (the so-called "Transverberation"), who gleefully pierces her with a spear. Bernini's depiction is deliciously erotic. Look for the Cornaro family, who sponsored the chapel's construction, watching the saint's ecstasy from their voyeuristic perch on the right.

Via XX Settembre 17 (at Largo S. Susanna). ☎ **06-42740571.** Free admission. Mon–Sat 9am–noon and 3:30–6pm; Sun 3:30–6pm. Metro: Repubblica. Bus: 61, 62, 85, 492, 590.

Santa Maria Maggiore (St. Mary Major) ★★ CHURCH   This imposing church, one of Rome's four papal basilicas, was founded by Pope Liberius
in A.D. 358 and rebuilt on the orders of Pope Sixtus III from 432 to 440. Its
14th-century **campanile** is the city's loftiest. Don't be put off by the overdone
18th-century façade—the treasures within include the 5th-century Roman
mosaics in its nave, and its coffered ceiling, said to have been gilded with gold
brought from the New World. The church also contains the **tomb of Bernini,**
Italy's most important baroque sculptor–architect. The man who changed the
face of Rome is buried in a tomb so simple that it takes a sleuth to track it
down (to the right, near the altar).

Piazza di Santa Maria Maggiore. © **06-69886800.** Free admission. Daily 7am–6:45pm.
Metro: Termini or Cavour. Bus: 16, 70, 71, 75, 360, 590, 649, 714.

Terme di Diocleziano (Baths of Diocletian) ★★ MUSEUM/RUINS
Originally this spot held the largest of Rome's baths (dating back to A.D. 298
and the reign of Emperor Diocletian). The vast baths once accommodated
3,000 at a time and were abandoned in the 6th century after the Goth invasions. During the Renaissance a church, cloister, and convent were built
around the ruins—much of it designed by Michelangelo, no less. Today the
entire hodgepodge is part of the Museo Nazionale Romano; it's a compelling
museum stop that's usually quieter than the city's blockbusters. Exhibits
include statuary and a large collection of inscriptions and other stone carvings
from the Roman and pre-Roman eras. Since 2022, the new **Museo dell'Arte
Salvata (Museum for Rescued Art)** ★★ occupies one hall of the baths and
mounts changing exhibits that reveal the massive scale and history of art and
artifact looting, dubious museum acquisitions, and items recovered by Italy's
highly effective Carabinieri Unit for the Protection of Cultural Heritage.

Viale E. di Nicola 78. www.museonazionaleromano.beniculturali.it. © **06-39967700.**
10€ for single museum, or 15€, valid for 1 week; also includes Palazzo Massimo & Palazzo Altemps; free for children 17 and under. Tues–Sun 11am–6pm, last entry 1 hr. before
closing. Metro: Termini or Repubblica. Bus: 66, 82, 85, 590, 910 or any bus to Termini.

Trastevere

Galleria Nazionale d'Arte Antica in Palazzo Corsini ★ PALACE/
ART MUSEUM   Palazzo Corsini first found fame—or more accurately,
notoriety—as the home of Queen Christina of Sweden, a Catholic convert
who moved to Rome after abdicating the Swedish throne. (She was famously
described as "Queen without a realm, Christian without a faith, and a woman
without shame," referring to her open bisexuality.) Several other big names
stayed in this beautiful palace, from Michelangelo to Napoleon's mother, Letizia.
Today one wing houses a moderately interesting museum, with a lot of the runoff
from Italy's national art collection. Worth a look is Caravaggio's "St. John the
Baptist" (1606) and panels by Luca Giordano, Fra' Angelico, and Poussin;
otherwise, the palace history is more interesting than the museum itself.

Via della Lungara 10. www.barberinicorsini.org. © **06-68802323.** 12€, valid for 20 days,
also includes Palazzo Barberini; free for children 17 and under. Tues–Sun 10am–7pm;
last entry 6pm. Bus: 23 or 280.

Trastevere & Testaccio

Metro B

A TRIO OF churches IN TRASTEVERE

Before Trastevere became bohemian and cool, it was a working-class neighborhood, separated by the Tiber from Rome's bustle. Step into the shadowy calm of any of these neighborhood churches to get a glimpse of the old Trastevere. Admission is always free, and they're open daily, though they may close at lunchtime.

On Piazza Santa Maria, the heart of Trastevere, ornate **Santa Maria in Trastevere** ★★ is one of Rome's oldest churches, founded around A.D. 350. The pride of the neighborhood, it's spectacular inside and out, with a Romanesque brick bell tower, colorful frescoes, mosaics, and loads of recycled ancient marbles. Look for Cavallini's 1293 mosaics of the "Life of the Virgin Mary" in the apse.

From there, Via di San Francisco a Ripa angles southeast to the church of **San Francesco d'Assisi a Ripa** ★ (www.sanfrancescoinripa.com), so named because it's built over a convent where St. Francis stayed in 1219 when he came to Rome to see the pope (his simple cell is preserved inside). A Bernini treasure is tucked into the last chapel on the left: the "Tomb of Beata Ludovica Albertoni" (1675), commemorating a noblewoman who dedicated her life to the city's poor.

Next, follow Via Anicia northeast to **Santa Cecilia in Trastevere** ★★ (Piazza Santa Cecilia; www.benedettinesanta cecilia.it), a still-functioning convent with a peaceful courtyard garden. Tradition holds that the saint herself once lived on this site; the church's altar has an exquisite marble sculpture of her (ca. 1600) carved by Stefano Maderno. The basilica and Roman-era ruins underneath can be visited Monday to Saturday from 10am to 12:30pm and from 4 to 6pm (from 11:30am on Sun). The partial remains of a "Last Judgment," by Pietro Cavallini (ca. 1293), a masterpiece of Roman medieval painting can be visited only in the morning.

Villa Farnesina ★ HISTORIC HOME Originally built for Sienese banker Agostino Chigi in 1511, this elegant villa was acquired by the Farnese family in 1579. With two such wealthy Renaissance patrons, it's hardly surprising that the interior decor is top drawer. Architect Baldassare Peruzzi began the decoration, with frescoes and motifs rich in myth and symbolism. He was later assisted by Sebastiano del Piombo, Sodoma, and, most notably, Raphael. Raphael's **"Loggia of Cupid and Psyche"** ★★ was frescoed to mark Chigi's marriage to Francesca Ordeaschi—though his assistants did much of the work. The ornamental and perfumed gardens are colorful in the spring and summer.

Via della Lungara 230. www.villafarnesina.it. ✆ **06-68077268.** 10€. Mon–Sat 9am–2pm; 2nd Sun of month 9am–5pm. Bus: 23, 280.

Testaccio & Southern Rome

Centrale Montemartini ★★ MUSEUM The renovated boiler rooms of Rome's first thermoelectric plant now house a grand collection of Roman and Greek statues, creating a unique juxtaposition of classic and industrial archaeology. The 19th-century powerhouse was the first public plant to produce electricity for the city. Striking installation spaces include the vast boiler hall, a 1,000-square-meter (10,764-sq.-ft.) room where classical statues share space with a complex web of pipes, masonry, and metal walkways. Equally striking is the Hall of Machines, where two towering turbines stand opposite the reconstructed pediment of the **Temple of Apollo Sosiano ★★**, which illustrates a famous Greek battle.

Unless you run across a school group, this place is never crowded, and it provides an intimate look at the ancient world, despite the cavernous setting.

Via Ostiense 106. www.centralemontemartini.org/en. ℭ **060608.** 7.50€ (higher during special exhibitions), 13.50€ for 7-day ticket that includes Musei Capitolini. Tues–Sun 9am–7pm. Last entry 1 hr. before closing. Metro: Garbatella. Bus: 23 or 769.

MACRO Testaccio/Mattatoio ★ MUSEUM

The Testaccio outpost of Rome's contemporary art museum and performance space is housed—appropriately for this former meatpacking neighborhood—in a converted slaughterhouse (*mattatoio* in Italian). Its edgy exhibits are a mix of installations, visuals, events, and special viewings. It's only open when there's something on. Make an early evening visit before going on to dinner in Testaccio.

Piazza Orazio Giustiniani 4. www.mattatoioroma.it. ℭ **06-671070400.** 8€. Tues–Sun 11–8pm, last entry 1 hr. before closing. Metro: Piramide. Bus: 23, 75, 83, 170, 280, 716. Tram: 3, 8.

San Paolo Fuori le Mura (St. Paul Outside the Walls) ★★ CHURCH

The giant Basilica of St. Paul, whose origins date from the time of Constantine, is Rome's fourth great patriarchal church. It was erected over the tomb of St. Paul and is the second-largest church in Rome after St. Peter's. The basilica fell victim to fire in 1823 and was subsequently rebuilt—hence the relatively modern look. Inside, translucent alabaster windows illuminate a forest of single-file columns and mosaic medallions (portraits of the various popes). Its most important treasure is a 12th-century marble candelabrum by Vassalletto, who's also responsible for the remarkable cloisters containing twisted pairs of columns enclosing a rose garden. Miraculously, the baldacchino by Arnolfo di Cambio (1285) wasn't damaged in the fire; it now shelters the tomb of St. Paul the Apostle.

Via Ostiense 190 (at Piazzale San Paolo). www.basilicasanpaolo.org. ℭ **06-69880800.** Basilica free admission; cloisters 4€. Basilica daily 7am–6:30pm; cloisters 9am–5:30pm. Metro: Basilica di San Paolo. Bus: 23, 769, 792.

Mussolini's City of the Future

South of the city center, the outlying **EUR suburb ★** (the acronym stands for *Esposizione Universale Romana*) was designed and purpose-built by Mussolini in the Fascist era to stage the planned World Fair of 1942—canceled, thanks to World War II. Today, EUR's mix of rationalist and classical-inspired elements will enthuse anyone with a serious interest in architecture. Perfect symmetry and sleek marble-lined avenues house a number of museums, corporate headquarters, and office agglomerates, easily connected to the *centro* by Metro (Line B). We keep hoping that the **Museum of Roman Civilization** (www.museociviltaromana.it), closed indefinitely for renovation and known for its huge scale model of Rome at the time of Emperor Constantine, will reopen one of these days.

Via Appia Antica (Appian Way) & the Catacombs

Of all the roads that led to Rome, **Via Appia Antica** (begun in 312 B.C.) was the most famous. It stretched all the way to the seaport of Brindisi, which received trade with Greece and the East. (According to Christian tradition, it was along the Appian Way that an escaping Peter encountered the vision of Christ, causing him to go back into the city to face martyrdom.) The road's initial stretch in Rome is lined with the monuments and ancient tombs of patrician Roman families—burials were forbidden within the city walls as early as the 5th century B.C.—and, below ground, miles of tunnels hewn out of the soft tufa stone that hardens on exposure to the air.

Riding bikes along the Appian Way.

These tunnels, or catacombs, were where early Christians buried their dead. A few are open to the public, so you can wander through tunnels whose walls are gouged out with tens of thousands of now mostly empty burial niches, including small niches made for children. Early Christians referred to each chamber as a *dormitorio*—they believed the bodies were only sleeping, awaiting resurrection (which is why they could not observe the traditional Roman practice of cremation). In some you can still discover the remains of early Christian art. The obligatory guided tours feature occasionally biased history, plus a dash of sermonizing, but the guides are very knowledgeable.

The Appia Antica park is a popular Sunday picnic site for Roman families, following the half-forgotten pagan tradition of dining in the presence of one's ancestors on holy days. On Sundays, Via Appia Antica closes to cars and is left for the picnickers, walkers, and bicyclists. See **www.parcoappiaantica.it** for more, including downloadable maps.

To reach the catacombs area, take bus no. 218 from the San Giovanni Metro stop or the 118 from Colosseo or Circus Maximus. *Tip:* The 118 runs more frequently than the 218 and deposits you closer to the catacombs but runs less frequently on Sundays. If you are in a hurry to accommodate your visit to the catacombs, take a taxi (p. 63).

Catacombe di San Callisto (Catacombs of St. Callixtus) ★★

RELIGIOUS SITE/TOUR   "The most venerable and most renowned of Rome," said Pope John XXIII of these funerary tunnels. These catacombs are

A Noble Survivor

Of all the monuments on the Appian Way itself, the most impressive is the **Tomb of Cecilia Metella ★**, within walking distance of the catacombs. The cylindrical tomb, clad in travertine and topped with a marble frieze, honors the wife of one of Julius Caesar's military commanders from the republican era. Why such an elaborate tomb for a figure of relatively minor historical importance? Other mausoleums may have been even more elaborate, but Cecilia Metella's earned enduring fame simply because her tomb has remained while the others have decayed. Part of the reason is its symbiotic relationship with the early-14th-century **Castle Caetani** attached to the rear. For centuries, the tomb survived being plundered for building materials because of the castle, which was built to guard the road and collect tolls; in later eras, the castle was spared because it was attached to the romantic ruin of the tomb. Admission to the tomb (10€) includes access to other sites in the archaeological park. See www.parcoarcheologicoappiaantica.it for more info (Italian only).

often packed with tour-bus groups, but the tunnels are phenomenal. They're the first cemetery of Christian Rome, burial place of 16 popes in the 3rd century. They bear the name of the deacon St. Callixtus, who served as pope from A.D. 217–22. The network of galleries is on four levels and reaches a depth of about 20m (65 ft.), the deepest in the area. There are many sepulchral chambers and almost half a million tombs of early Christians.

Entering the catacombs, you see the most important crypt, that of nine popes. Some of the original marble tablets of their tombs are preserved. Also

Artistic detail among the Catacombs of Saint Callixtus.

commemorated is St. Cecilia, patron of sacred music (her relics were moved to her church in Trastevere during the 9th century; see p. 144). Farther on are the Cubicles of the Sacraments, with 3rd-century frescoes.

Via Appia Antica 110–26. www.catacombe.roma.it. ☎ **06-5130151.** 10€ adults, 7€ ages 7–15. Thurs–Tues 9am–noon and 2–5pm. Closed mid-Jan–mid-Feb. Bus 118, 218.

Catacombe di Domitilla ★★★ RELIGIOUS SITE/TOUR   The oldest of the catacombs is the hands-down winner for most enjoyable experience. Groups are relatively small (in part because the site is not directly on the Appian Way), and guides are entertaining and personable. The catacombs—Rome's longest at 17km (11 miles)—were built below land donated by Domitilla, a noblewoman of the Flavian dynasty who was exiled from Rome for practicing Christianity. They were rediscovered in 1593, after a church abandoned in the 9th century collapsed. The visit begins in the sunken church founded in A.D. 380, the year Christianity became Rome's state religion.

There are fewer "sights" here than in the other catacombs, but this is the only catacomb where you'll still see bones; the rest have emptied their tombs to rebury the remains in inaccessible lower levels. Elsewhere in the tunnels, 4th-century frescoes contain some of the earliest representations of Saints Peter and Paul. Notice the absence of crosses: It was only later that Christians replaced the traditional fish symbol with the cross. During this period, Christ's crucifixion was a source of shame to the community. He had been killed like a common criminal.

Via delle Sette Chiese 282. www.domitilla.info. ☎ **06-5110342.** 10€ adults, 7€ children 6–14. Wed–Mon 9am–noon and 2–5pm. Closed mid-Dec–mid-Jan. Bus: 30, 160, 714 (to Piazza dei Navigatori) or 218.

Catacombe di San Sebastiano (Catacombs of St. Sebastian) ★
RELIGIOUS SITE/TOUR   Today the tomb and relics of St. Sebastian are in the ground-level basilica, but his original resting place was in the catacombs beneath it. Sebastian was a senior Milanese soldier in the Roman army who converted to Christianity and was martyred during Emperor Diocletian's persecutions, which were especially brutal in the first decade of the 4th century. From the reign of Valerian to that of Constantine, the bodies of Saints Peter and Paul were also hidden in the catacombs, which were dug from the soft volcanic rock (tufa). The church was built in the 4th century and remodeled in the 17th century.

In the tunnels and mausoleums are mosaics and graffiti, along with many other pagan and Christian objects, as well as four Roman tombs with their frescoes and stucco fairly intact, found in 1922 after being buried for almost 2,000 years.

Via Appia Antica 136. www.catacombe.org. ☎ **06-7850350.** 10€ adults, 7€ ages 6–15. Daily 10am–5pm. Closed Dec. Bus: 118, 218.

Especially for Kids

There's a real Jekyll and Hyde quality to exploring Rome with kids. On the one hand, it's a capital city, big, busy, and hot. On the other, the very best parts

ORGANIZED TOURS

Forget the flag-waving guides leading a herd of dazed travelers around monuments. A better class of professionally guided tours delivers insider expertise, focused themes, and personal attention, plus perks such as skipping entry lines and visiting after hours. For **food tours and cooking classes** in Rome, see p. 106.

One of the leading tour operators in Rome, **Context Travel** ★ (www.contexttravel.com; ℂ **800/691-6036** in the U.S., or 06-96727371) uses historians, art historians and archaeologists to lead small-group walking tours around Rome's monuments, museums, and piazzas, as well as culinary walks and excellent family programs. Tour prices are high, beginning at about 100€ per person for 2 hours, but most participants consider them a highlight of their trip.

The affable team at **The Roman Guy** (www.theromanguy.com, ℂ **06-342-8761859**) provides knowledgeable guides who explain thousands of years of history in an engaging, informal way. They offer small-group (most about 15 people) tours of the Colosseum, Vatican Museums, Catacombs, and food tours of Trastevere, among other options. Prices run from 60€ per person to much more for exclusive VIP access and/or private excursions.

Walks of Italy (www.walksofitaly.com; ℂ **06-95583331**) also runs excellent guided tours of Rome starting from 39€;

more in-depth explorations of the Colosseum, Vatican Museums, and Forum go for 60€ to 125€.

Enjoy Rome (www.enjoyrome.com; ℂ **06-4451843**), offers a number of "greatest hits" walking tours, plus an early-evening tour of the Jewish Ghetto and Trastevere; their bus excursion to the catacombs and Appian Way visits an ancient aqueduct that most Romans, let alone tourists, never see. Tours start at 45€ per person; entrance fees are included with some, but not all tours.

The team at **Through Eternity** (www.througheternity.com; ℂ **06-7009336**) are art historians and architects; what sets them apart is their theatrical delivery, helped along by the dramatic scripts that many of the guides follow. It can be a lot of fun, but it's not for everyone. A 3.5-hour tour of the Vatican is 69€; most other tours range from 39€ to 129€.

Tour broker **Get Your Guide** (www.getyourguide.com) offers a raft of options in Rome, including the usual ancient Roman suspects, as well as guided tours of Galleria Borghese and day trips to Pompeii, Tivoli.

For something completely different, artist Kelly Medford runs **Sketching Rome Tours** (www.sketchingrometours.com), 2.5-hour small group drawing and painting lessons in some of Rome's prettiest corners. Supplies are provided and no artistic talent is required (75€ per person).

of the city for kids—Roman ruins, subterranean worlds, and *gelato*—are aspects you'd want to explore anyway. Seeing Rome with kids doesn't demand an itinerary redesign. And despite what you have heard about its famous seven hills, much of the center is mercifully flat, and pedestrian- (if not always stroller) friendly.

Food is pretty easy too: Roman **pizzas** are some of the best in the world—see "Where to Eat" (p. 80) for our favorites. Ditto the ice cream, or *gelato* (p. 84). Restaurants in any price category will be happy to serve up a simple *pasta al pomodoro* (pasta with tomato sauce), and kids are welcomed virtually everywhere, including late in the evening.

Kids can let off steam in the Villa Borghese park.

The city is shorter on green spaces than many European cities, but the land-scaped gardens of the **Villa Borghese** have plenty of space for kids to let off steam. Pack a picnic or rent some bikes (p. 136). The **Parco Appia Antica** (www.parcoappiaantica.it) is another favorite, especially on a Sunday or holi-day when the old, cobbled road closes to traffic. The park's **catacombs** (p. 146) are eerie enough to satisfy young minds, but also fascinating Chris-tian and historical sites in their own right.

Museums, of course, are trickier. My then-8-year-old was enthralled by a small museum exhibit of gory Renaissance paintings depicting biblical mur-ders and sacrifices but could not get out of the crowded Vatican Museums fast enough—it's not much fun when you can't see over the backs of all those adults. You can probably get kids fired up more easily for the really ancient stuff. Make the bookshop at the **Colosseum** (p. 113) an early stop; it has a good selection of guides aimed at under-12s, gladiator-themed and featuring funny or cartoonish material. The **Musei Capitolini** (p. 110) invites kids to hunt down the collection's treasures highlighted on a free leaflet—it'll buy you a couple of hours to admire the exhibits and perhaps see them from a new and unexpected angle, too. The multiple levels below **San Clemente** (p. 120) and the **Case Romane del Celio** (p. 121) are another draw for small visitors.

Aspiring young gladiators may want to spend 2 hours at the **Scuola Gladi-atori Roma (Rome Gladiator School,** (www.romegladiatorschool.com; 120€ per person), where they can prepare for a duel in a reasonably authentic way.

Kids will also likely enjoy some of the cheesier city sights—at the very least these will make some good family photos to share on social media. Build in some time to throw a coin in the **Trevi Fountain** (p. 135), and to enjoy watching the feral cats relaxing amid the ruins of **Largo di Torre Argentina.** A cat sanctuary here provides basic healthcare to Rome's many strays.

Several of the tour operators listed on p. 149 offer family-oriented tours with special activities and perks for younger travelers.

SHOPPING

Of all the sectors of the Rome economy affected by the pandemic, traditional retail appears to have taken the hardest hit. Even businesses that had been around for decades weren't spared, and many now stand vacant or have been replaced by fast fashion outlets or cheap souvenir stores. We expect that the retail scene will eventually bounce back, but it might take longer than anyone would like.

That said, Rome is still a magnet for high-end shoppers, foodies, and lovers of antiques. In our limited space below we've summarized streets and areas known for their shops. Keep in mind that the monthly rent on the famous streets is very high, and those costs are passed on to you. Note that **sales** usually run twice a year, starting in January and July.

The Top Shopping Streets & Areas

AROUND PIAZZA DI SPAGNA   Most of Rome's haute couture and seriously upscale shopping fans out from the bottom of the Spanish Steps. **Via Condotti** is probably Rome's poshest shopping street, where you'll find Prada, Gucci, Bulgari, and the like. A few more down-to-earth stores have opened, but it's still largely a playground for the super-rich. Neighboring **Via Borgognona** is another street where the merchandise is chic and ultra-expensive, but thanks to its pedestrian-only access and handsome baroque and neoclassical

Campo de' Fiori market.

facades, it offers a nicer window-browsing experience. Shops are more densely concentrated on **Via Frattina,** the third member of this trio of upscale streets. Chic boutiques for adults and kids rub shoulders with ready-to-wear fashions, high-end chains, and a few tourist tat vendors. It's usually crowded with shoppers who appreciate the lack of motor traffic.

VIA COLA DI RIENZO   The commercial heart of the Prati neighborhood, this long, straight street runs from the Tiber to Piazza Risorgimento and is known for stores selling a variety of merchandise at reasonable prices—from jewelry to fashionable clothing, bags, and shoes. Among the most prestigious is the historic Roman perfume store (with products for men and women), **Bertozzini Profumeria dal 1913,** at no. 192 (www.bertozzinidal1913.it). The department store **Coin** is at no. 173 (with a large supermarket in the basement) and the largest branch of venerable gourmet food store **Castroni** at no. 196 (www.castronicoladirienzo.com).

VIA DEL CORSO   With less of a glamour quotient (and less stratospheric prices) than Via Condotti or Via Borgognona, Via del Corso boasts affordable styles aimed at younger consumers. Occasional gems are scattered amid international shops selling jeans and sportswear. The most interesting stores are toward the Piazza del Popolo end of the street (**Via del Babuino** here has a similar profile). Or turn at Largo Chigi towards Via del Tritone, and run a retail gauntlet that includes **Altariva Shoes**, for high-quality, Made-in-Italy

The gourmet heaven of Castroni.

footwear (www.altarivashoes.it); **Rinascente**, a high-end department store; **Hugo BOSS**; and **Sephora.** The farther south you walk (towards the Vittoriano monument), the narrower the sidewalks—and generally, the more tacky the stores. *Tip:* If you are shopping with young children, it's useful to know that the upper part of Via del Corso (from Piazza Colonna to Piazza del Popolo) is largely car-free, save for taxis and the occasional bus.

VIA DEI CORONARI An antique-lover's souk. If you're shopping, or just window-shopping for antiques, art or vintage-style souvenir prints, then spend an hour walking the length of this pretty, pedestrian-only street.

CAMPO DE' FIORI Though the campo itself is now chockablock with restaurants, the streets leading up to it, notably **Via dei Giubbonari** and **Via Dei Baullari,** offer edgy and often one-of-a-kind fashions. Boutiques go in and out of business with dizzying frequency, but something interesting is always popping up.

VIA DEL GOVERNO VECCHIO It's Vintage Valhalla on this pretty street that winds parallel to Corso Vittorio Emanuele II. Lined with tiny resale shops stuffed to the gills with merchandise, Via del Governo Vecchio also has great places to eat and drink, particularly on the end closest to Piazza di San Pantaleo. Poke into vintage treasure trove **Omero e Cecilia** (at no. 110) or **Cinzia** (no. 45; https://cinziavestitiusati.wordpress.com/) before taking a restorative gelato break at **Frigidarium** (p. 85).

VIA MARGUTTA This beautiful, tranquil street is home to numerous art stalls and artists' studios—Federico Fellini used to live here—though a lot of stores these days tend to offer the same sort of antiques and mediocre paintings. You have to shop hard to find real quality. A definite highlight is **Bottega del Marmoraro** at no. 53b, the whimsical studio of master stone carver Sandro Fiorentini.

MONTI Rome's most fashion-conscious central neighborhood has a pleasing mix of artisan retailers, vintage boutiques, and honest, everyday stores frequented by locals, with not a brand name in sight. Roam the length of **Via del Boschetto** for one-off fashions, designer ateliers, and unique homewares. In fact, you can roam in every direction from the spot where Via del Boschetto meets **Via Panisperna.** Turn on nearby **Via Urbana** or **Via Leonina,** where boutiques jostle for space with cafes that are ideal for a break or light lunch.

Rome's Best Markets

Campo de' Fiori ★ Central Rome's food market has been running since at least the 1800s. It's no longer the place to find a produce bargain (though the fruit and veg displays are dazzling and colorful) and it tends to attract more tourists than locals, but it's still a genuine slice of Roman life in one of its most attractive squares. The market runs daily 7am to 1 or 2pm, with fewer produce vendors on Sunday. Campo de' Fiori. No phone. Bus: 40, 64, 170. Tram: 8.

Nuovo Mercato di Testaccio (New Testaccio Market) ★★★ Traditional food and produce stalls meet street food central in this modernist,

THE ETERNAL drinking water CITY

There's no excuse for being dehydrated in Rome.

At the height of the Roman Empire, 11 aqueducts brought the city 25 million gallons of water a day for its baths, ornamental fountains, and basic utilities. That tradition of hydroabundance continues in modern Rome: Not only are there monumental fountains everywhere you look, but one of the city's most generous gifts to tourists and citizens alike is its free, perfectly drinkable spring water, in the form of *nasoni*.

In almost every piazza in town, on countless side streets, and in archaeological sites, you'll see these cast-iron hydrants marked "spqr," whose curved pipes emit a continuous stream of water into a drain below. These hydrants are properly called *fontanelle* ("little fountains") but in Roman slang, they're **nasoni** ("big noses"), for the shape of the spigots.

One method for drinking from a Roman nasone.

Naturally, many newcomers' first question is: Is it really safe to drink this water? The answer is an emphatic yes. *Fontanelle* draw on spring water in the hills outside the city—the same sources the ancients tapped for their aqueducts, minus the lead pipes—that tastes better and is cleaner than Rome's tap water, which is also potable. (Only a handful of fountains around town, mostly in the parks, are not potable, in which case they're clearly marked *acqua non potabile*.) What's more, the water issuing from the *fontanelle* is always ice-cold, even in the height of summer.

You can refill your water bottle at *nasoni* all over town—for free. If you don't have a bottle handy, here's how the pros do it: Simply block up the bottom of the spigot with your finger, and the stream of water will come out a small hole in the top of the curved pipe, like a drinking fountain. Be careful with this method, though, as some *nasoni* are quite powerful and will shoot water all over you if you completely block up the bottom of the pipe. Of course, in July or August, this might feel very refreshing.

When you master drinking from a *nasone*, it's time to move onto the big, ornamental fountains of Rome. No, we're not recommending you drink from their dirty basins, but from the side jets of water that feed fountains such as the Trevi and the Barcaccia at Piazza di Spagna. These jets are the same as *nasone* water, fresh and clean. Tradition even holds that the water supply for the Barcaccia guarantees eternal youth for all who drink it.

sustainably powered market building. It's not just the best place to go produce shopping, but a terrific stop for a lunch of *suppli* (fried rice balls) and craft beer (at **Food Box** ★★, Box 66), meat and sauce-stuffed panini (at **Mordi e Vai** ★★, Box 15, www.mordievai.it), or an espresso and something sweet from **Chicchi e Lettere** ★ (Box 43). There are also clothes and kitchenware stalls, but the food is the star. The market runs Monday through Saturday 7am to 3:30pm. Btw. Via Luigi Galvani and Via Aldo Manuzio (at Via Benjamin Franklin). www.mercatoditestaccio.it. No phone. Metro: Piramide.

Porta Portese ★   Trastevere's vast weekly flea market stretches all the way from the Porta Portese gate along Via di Porta Portese to Viale di Trastevere. You have to wade through a lot of junk (and a sea of humanity—hold tight to your belongings), but there are good stalls for vintage housewares, clothing, and collectibles. It runs Sundays from dawn until midafternoon. Via di Porta Portese. No phone. Tram: 8.

ENTERTAINMENT & NIGHTLIFE

Several English-language outlets offer current information about nightlife and cultural events in the Eternal City. *Wanted in Rome* (www.wantedinrome. com) has listings of opera, rock, English-language cinema showings, and such and gives an insider look at expat Rome. *Romeing* (www.romeing.it) is worth consulting, especially for contemporary arts and culture.

Unless you're dead set on making the Roman nightclub circuit, try what might be a far livelier and less expensive option—sitting late into the evening on **Piazza della Rotonda** (the Pantheon), **Piazza del Popolo,** or one of Rome's other piazzas, all for the (admittedly inflated) cost of an espresso or a Campari and soda. If you're a clubber who likes it loud and late, jump in a cab to **Monte Testaccio** or **Via del Pigneto** and barhop wherever your fancy takes

The Pantheon and its piazza glow at night.

Rome, Illuminated

When the sun goes down, Rome's palaces, ruins, fountains, and monuments are bathed in a theatrical white light. During your stay in Rome, be sure to make time for a memorable evening stroll past the solemn pillars of old temples or the cascading torrents of Renaissance fountains glowing under the blue-black sky.

The **Fountain of the Naiads** ("Fontana delle Naiadi") on Piazza della Repubblica, the **Fountain of the Tortoises** ("Fontana della Tartarughe") on Piazza Mattei, the **Fountain of Acqua Paola** ("Fontanone") at the top of the Janiculum Hill, and the **Trevi Fountain** (p. 134) are particularly beautiful at night. The **Capitoline Hill** (or Campidoglio) is magnificently lit after dark, with its Renaissance facades glowing like jewel boxes. The view of the Roman Forum seen from the rear of Piazza del Campidoglio is perhaps the grandest in Rome (see "Three Free Views to Savor for a Lifetime" box, p. 115). If you're across the Tiber, the Vatican's **Piazza San Pietro** (p. 100) is impressive at night without the crowds. The combination of illuminated architecture, baroque fountains, and sidewalk shows makes **Piazza Navona** (p. 124) even more delightful after dark.

you. In Trastevere, there's always a bit of life on **Via del Politeama** where it meets **Piazza Trilussa.** In the *centro storico,* a nice *aperitivo-cena* scene unfolds along **Via del Governo Vecchio.**

Performing Arts & Live Music

Rome's music scene doesn't have the same vibrancy as Florence's (p. 242), nor the high-quality opera of **La Fenice** in Venice (p. 313). Still, classical music fans have plenty to enjoy here. In addition to the major venues featured below, be on the lookout for concerts and one-off events in churches and salons around the city. Check **www.operainroma.com** for a calendar of opera and ballet staged by the Opera in Roma association at enchanting venues across the city. The **Pontificio Instituto di Musica Sacra** regularly runs classical music and operatic evenings.

Alexanderplatz Jazz Club ★★ Alexanderplatz has been the home of Rome's jazz scene since the early 1980s. If there's a good act in the city, you will find it here. Live music 7 nights a week. Via Ostia 9. www.alexanderplatzjazz. com. ✆ **06-39742171.** Cover usually 10€. Metro: Ottaviano.

Auditorium–Parco della Musica ★★ This exciting multipurpose center for the arts, designed by Renzo Piano, brings a refreshing breath of modernity to Rome. The schedule features lots of aging rockers and eclectic singer-songwriter acts, as well as traditional orchestras. Great cafes and a bookstore are on-site, too. Viale Pietro de Coubertin 30. www.auditorium.com. ✆ **06-80241281.** Metro: Flaminio, then Tram 2. Bus: 910.

Teatro dell'Opera di Roma ★★ Here you'll find marquee operas such as *La Traviata, Carmen,* and *Tosca;* classical concerts from top-rank orchestras; and such ballets as *Giselle, Swan Lake,* and *The Nutcracker.* In summer, the action moves outdoors for unforgettable open-air operatic performances at the ruined **Baths of Caracalla** (p. 110). Piazza Beniamino Gigli 1 (at Via del Viminale). www.operaroma.it. ✆ **06-4817003** (box office). Tickets 25€–150€. Metro: Repubblica.

Cafes

Remember: In Rome and everywhere else in Italy, if you just want to drink a quick coffee and bolt, walk up to *il banco* (the bar), order *"un caffè, per favore"* or *"un cappuccino,"* and stay at the bar. They will make it for you to drink on the spot. It will usually cost more (at least double) to sit down to drink it (if you're in high-traffic, touristy areas—which you'll most likely be!), and outdoor table service is the most expensive way to go. Even in the heart of the city center, a short coffee *al banco* should cost about 1€; add around .30€ for a *cappuccino*. Expect to pay up to five times that price if you sit outdoors on a marquee piazza. Most cafes in the city serve a decent cup of coffee, but here's a small selection of places worth hunting down.

With its shabby-chic interior and namesake fig tree backdrop to charming outdoor seating, **Bar del Fico ★**, Piazza del Fico 26 (www.bardelfico.com; ✆ **06-68808413**) is one of Rome's most beloved aperitivo spots and a coveted see-and-be-seen nightlife destination. **Sant'Eustachio il Caffè ★★**, Piazza Sant'Eustachio 82 (www.santeustachioilcaffe.it; ✆ **06-68802048**) roasts its own Fair Trade Arabica beans and draws a friendly crowd a few deep at the bar. (Unless you ask, the coffee comes with sugar.) Debate still rages among Romans as to whether the city's best cup of coffee is served at Sant'Eustachio or **Tazza d'Oro ★**, near the Pantheon (Via degli Orfani 84; www.tazzadoro coffeeshop.com; ✆ **06-6789792**). Jacketed baristas work at 100mph at **Spinelli ★**, Via dei Mille 60 (✆ **06-31055552**), a no-nonsense locals' cafe near Termini station.

Beer, Wine & Cocktail Bars

The mass social phenomenon of the *aperitivo* (happy hour) provides great insight into the particular ways of real Romans. It started in hard-working northern cities like Milan, where you'd go to a bar after leaving the office and, for the price of one drink, you'll be served one or more plates of high-quality food—often with cheese, cured meats, bruschetta, and pasta salad. Luckily for Rome, the custom trickled down here, and now the city is filled with casual little places to drop in for a drink (from 6 or 7pm onward) and eat to your heart's content. Aperitivo spreads vary in quantity and quality, but generally you'll anywhere from 8€ to 12€ per person for a drink and buffet. All the places listed here are fine for families, too—Italian kids love *aperitivo* (minus the alcohol)! Look for signs in the window and follow your nose. The **Monti** neighborhood is a good place to begin.

Ai Tre Scalini ★ This little *bottiglieria* (wine bar) is the soul of Monti. The menu is traditional and the wine list is sourced from across Italy. Arrive early or call for a table: This place is usually jammed. Via Panisperna 251. www. aitrescalini.org. ✆ **06-48907495.** Metro: Cavour.

Cavour 313 ★★   As traditional and genuine as you will find this close to the ancient ruins, this wine bar serves over 30 wines by the glass (from 3.50€) as well as cold cuts, cheese, and vegetable platters, or excellent carpaccio. Closed Aug. Via Cavour 313. www.cavour313.it. ⓒ **06-6785496.** Metro: Colosseo and Cavour.

Ex Circus ★   This convivial hub for digital nomads, hungry tourists on a budget, and aperitivo drinkers seeking an ample spread is just a few blocks from Piazza Navona. They also do a great salads, smoothies, and Sunday brunch. Via della Vetrina 15. ex-circus.business.site. ⓒ **06-97619258.** Bus: 40, 64, 70.

Freni e Frizioni ★★   Trastevere's "Brakes and Clutches" is a former mechanics' garage turned nighttime hot spot, with an ethnic-inflected *aperitivo* spread (think curried risotto). On the adjacent square, an effervescent crowd lounges against stone walls and parked *motorini*. Via del Politeama 4–6 (near Piazza Trilussa). www.freniefrizioni.com. ⓒ **06-45497499.** Bus: H. Tram: 8.

La Bottega del Caffè ★   Beers, wine, cocktails, *aperitivo*—there's a little of everything at one of Monti's busiest neighborhood bars. Piazza Madonna dei Monti 5. www.facebook.com/labottegadelcaffemonti/. ⓒ **06-64741578.** Metro: Cavour.

L'Elementare ★   Formerly called Bir and Fud, this Trastevere craft beer watering hole has taken on a new name and devoted more attention to pizza and other snacky foods. But the beers are still there—most of them Italian craft brews, some as strong as 9%. It's 6€ for a small draft beer. Via Benedetta 23. pizzerialelementare.it. ⓒ **06-5894016.** Bus: H. Tram: 8.

Open Baladin ★★   If anyone ever tells you that Italians don't do good beer, send them to this bar near the Ghetto. Forty taps line the bar, with beers from their own Piedmont brewery and across Italy. Via degli Specchi 5–6. www.baladin.it/en/open-baladin-roma. ⓒ **06-6838989.** Bus: 40, 64, 70. Tram: 8.

Salotto42 ★★   It's all fancy cocktails and well-chosen wines at this über-hip bookbar opposite the columned facade of 2nd-century Hadrian's Temple (near the Pantheon). A classy after-dinner stop, it also does shared plates, fresh juices, smoothies, and infused teas. Piazza di Pietra 42 (off Via del Corso). www.salotto42.it. ⓒ **06-6785804**. Bus: 64, 85, 492.

The very classy Salotto42.

4

Entertainment & Nightlife

ROME

Stravinskij Bar in Hotel de Russie

Stravinskij Bar ★ An evening at this award-winning cocktail bar inside one of Rome's most famous grand hotels is always a regal affair. Mixology, ingredients, and canapés are all topnotch. Inside Hotel de Russie, Via del Babuino 9. www.roccofortehotels.com/hotels-and-resorts/hotel-de-russie/. ✆ **06-32888874.** Metro: Spagna.

Vale la Pena Pub ★★ This way-casual, tongue-in-cheek beerpub, part of a non-profit that works to reduce recidivism, offers beer from its own microbrewery, made by inmates from Rome's Rebibbia prison. It fits like a glove in the working-class Tuscolano district. Via Eurialo 22. www.facebook.com/PubShopValeLaPena/. ✆ **06-87606875.** Metro: Furio Camillo.

DAY TRIPS FROM ROME

By Elizabeth Heath

You could easily spend a week in Rome and still not see everything there is to see. But if you want a break from the city, the countryside outside Rome has its fair share of important ancient ruins, old towns, and historic villas. A few hours south of Rome, the archaeological site of Pompeii is on many a traveler's bucket list and can be visited on a long day trip. If you can't get to Pompeii, the ruins of Ostia Antica are an excellent substitute.

POMPEII ★★★

240km (150 miles) SE of Rome

Completely destroyed by Vesuvius on August 24, A.D. 79, the Roman city of Pompeii was one of Italy's most important commercial centers. For almost 2,000 years, the city lay frozen in time under a thick layer of solidified ash. Today, the excavated ruins provide an unparalleled insight into the everyday life of Roman Italy, especially that of its ordinary citizens and, notoriously, the erotic art that decorated its homes and villas. It is estimated that only 2,000 people actually died in the disaster, with most of the population of 20,000 escaped before the full eruption. Those who stayed perished horribly: asphyxiated by toxic gases and buried in several feet of volcanic ash. Pliny the Elder, the celebrated Roman naturalist, was one of the registered casualties. Although parts of the city were rediscovered in 1599, full excavations only began in 1748, starting a process that has never really ended, with new finds still being made.

By making a long day of it, you can visit the famous ruins from Rome without having to spend the night near Pompeii, where the modern city has little appeal. It's 3½ hours from the capital by car, and even less by train. Count on spending at least 4 or 5 hours wandering the site to do it justice. Remember also to take plenty of water with you as well as **sunscreen,** because the ruins don't have much shade, and you'll be doing a lot of walking: Wear sturdy, comfortable shoes and a hat and/or sunglasses to shield your face/eyes/top of head from Pompeii's typically penetrating sun. Uneven stone streets make for difficult walking—consider a cane or walking stick if you're the least bit unsteady on your feet.

Essentials

GETTING THERE   The best option is to take the Trenitalia (www.tren italia.com) "Frecciarossa" high-speed **train** from Termini to Naples (1 hr. 10 min.; from 35€ one-way), though InterCity trains are cheaper (around 27€) and take just over 2 hours—still doable if you start early. The first Frecciarossa departs at 7am. Italo (www.italotreno.it/en) also offers frequent, fast service from Termini to Naples, with the first train departing at 6am and rates starting at 30€. Whatever way you get to Napoli Centrale (Naples Central Station), once there, follow the signs to Napoli Piazza Garibaldi station **downstairs**, where you transfer to the **Circumvesuviana Railway** (www.eavsrl.it; website in Italian only; ℭ **800/211-388** toll-free in Italy). Note that this railway is separate from Trenitalia, so you won't be able to buy a through ticket to Pompeii from Rome; just get a return to Naples and buy the Pompeii portion on arrival in Naples. Trains depart to Pompeii every half-hour from Piazza Garibaldi, but make sure you get on the train headed toward Sorrento and get off at Pompei Scavi/Villa Dei Misteri (*scavi* means "archaeological dig"). If you get on the "Pompei" train (toward Poggiomarino), you'll end up in the

Mt. Vesuvius looms over the ruins of Pompeii.

town of Pompei—which is in a totally different place—and will have to double back to get to the ruins. A ticket costs about 4€ one-way; trip time is 35 minutes.

To reach Pompeii by **car** from Rome, take the A1 *autostrada* toward Naples, then the A3 all the way to the signposted turnoff for the ruins just after the tollbooth—a straightforward and usually hassle-free drive.

In High Season, a Better Way to Pompeii

The Circumvesuviana train will get you to Pompeii, but not in style—and possibly not even in comfort. Travelers frequently complain about crowds, stifling heat, and—even worse—pickpockets on board the commuter train. From spring to fall, EAV (www.eavsrl.it, which runs the Cir-cumvesuviana) also offers the **Campania Express** train, which runs from Naples to Sorrento but only stops at tourist destinations. Trains run four times a day in each direction and tickets are about 8€ one way for Naples to Pompeii—a small price to pay for a fast, clean, air-conditioned ride with guaranteed seating.

TOURS Consider letting someone else take care of the driving and logistics of a Pompeii trip. Scores of tour operators, including many of those listed on p. 149 as well as Dark Rome (www.darkrome.com), run guided day tours of Pompeii from Rome, and may include brief stops in Naples, Sorrento, or along the Amalfi Coast. Get Your Guide (www.getyourguide.com) has the option of a narrated shuttle bus from Rome to Pompeii, where you're free to wander the ruins at your own pace for several hours before catching the same bus back to Rome. Rates start at 77€.

VISITOR INFORMATION Official infopoints (pompeiisites.org/en; 081-8575347) can be found at the Porta Marina and Piazza Esedra, and Piazza Anfiteatro entrances. The ruins are open April to October daily from 9am to 7pm and November to March 9am to 5pm. Last admission is 90 minutes before closing. Admission is 18€. The site can be crowded in the mornings, especially when tours arrive in force in July and August. Crowds thin out by early afternoon.

PARKING There is no official parking lot at Pompeii, though there are several private paid lots just outside the park. Expect to pay about 2€ per hour. *Tip:* Do not leave valuables in your rental car and if you have luggage aboard, keep it out of sight.

Exploring Pompeii

Pompeii covers a large area with a lot to see, so try to be selective. Note that many of the streets run through little more than stone foundations, and although wandering the site is a magical experience, ruin-fatigue can set in by the end of a frenetic day of sightseeing. Also keep in mind that even some of the best-known buildings might be temporarily closed off to the public without notice or explanation.

Entering through the **Porta Marina,** the **Forum (Foro)** ★ is a long, narrow, open space surrounded by the ruins of the **basilica** (the city's largest single structure), the **Temple of Apollo (Tempio di Apollo)** ★★, the **Temple of Jupiter (Tempio di Giove)** ★★, and a little farther west, the **Terme Stabian**

Fresco in Villa dei Misteri, Pompeii.

(Baths) ★★, where some plaster casts of Vesuvius's victims have been preserved.

Walk north along the Via di Mercurio to see some of Pompeii's most famous villas: The **Casa del Poeta Tragico (House of the Tragic Poet)** ★ contains some eye-catching mosaics, notably the CAVE CANEM ("Beware of the Dog") design by the main entrance. The vast **Casa del Fauno (House of the Faun)** ★★ features an amicable *"Ave"* ("welcome") mosaic and the copy of a tiny, bronze faun (the original is in Naples's Archaeological Museum). Nearby, the recently restored **Casa dei Vettii** ★★★ is in excellent shape, arranged around a pretty, central courtyard and containing celebrated murals, notably an image of Priapus (the fertility god), resting his ludicrously over-sized phallus on a pair of scales.

Keep walking beyond the old city walls to the northwest for the **Villa dei Misteri** ★★★, Pompeii's best-preserved insula, a 3rd-century B.C. mansion containing a series of stunning depictions of the Dionysiac initiation rites. The paintings are remarkably clear, bright, and richly colored after all these years.

Walking to the eastern side of Pompeii from the Porta Marina, you'll pass the 5th-century B.C. **Teatro Grande** ★, well-preserved and still used for performances today. Continue west on the Via dell'Abbondanza, passing the **Fullonica Stephanus** (a laundry where, typical of the time, clients' clothes were washed in human urine); and the **Casa della Venere in Conchiglia (House of the Venus in a Shell)** ★★, named after the curious painting on its

Pompeii's amphitheater.

back wall. At the far western end of the town lies the **Anfiteatro ★★**, Italy's oldest amphitheater, dating from 80 B.C.

Where to Eat

To dine really well around Pompeii, you have to go into (and stay overnight in) Naples or Sorrento. If you're doing Pompeii as a day trip, pack a picnic before you set off from Rome and skip the so-so restaurants around Pompeii itself. Of course, if you're in a bind and need a quick bite, a sizeable food service bar within the ruins serves basic pastas and panini.

OSTIA ANTICA ★★

24km (15 miles) SW of Rome

The ruins of Rome's ancient port are a must-see for anyone who can't make it to Pompeii. It's an easier day trip than Pompeii, on a similar theme: the chance to wander around the preserved ruins of an ancient Roman settlement that has been barely touched since its abandonment.

Ostia, at the mouth of the Tiber, was the port of Rome, serving as the gateway for riches from the far corners of the Empire. Founded in the 4th century B.C., it became a major port and naval base under two later emperors, Claudius and Trajan. A prosperous city developed, full of temples, baths, theaters, and patrician homes.

Ostia flourished between the 1st and 3rd centuries, and survived until around the 9th century before it was abandoned. Gradually it became little more than a malaria bed, a buried ghost city that faded into history. A papal-sponsored commission launched a series of digs in the 19th century; however, the major work of unearthing was carried out under Mussolini's orders from 1938 to 1942. The city is only partially dug out today, but it's believed that all the chief monuments have been uncovered. There are quite a few impressive ruins, and the site is extensive. Archaeology enthusiasts, especially those with their own car, might want to visit some of the other sites in the area, including the remains of the Imperial Harbors and the vast Necropolis of Porto.

A word to the wise: Ostia is a mostly flat site, but the Roman streets underfoot are all clad in giant basalt cobblestones—wear comfortable walking shoes.

Essentials

GETTING THERE Take the Metro to Piramide, changing lines there for the Lido train to Ostia Antica. (From the platform, take the exit for "Air Terminal" and turn right at the top of the steps, where the station name changes to Porta San Paolo.) Departures to Ostia via Roma Lido trains are at minimum every half-hour; the trip takes 25 minutes and is included in the price of a Metro single-journey ticket or Roma Pass (see p. 54). It's just a 5-minute walk to the excavations from the train station: Exit the station, walk ahead and over the footbridge, and then continue straight ahead until you reach the car park. The ticket booth is to the left.

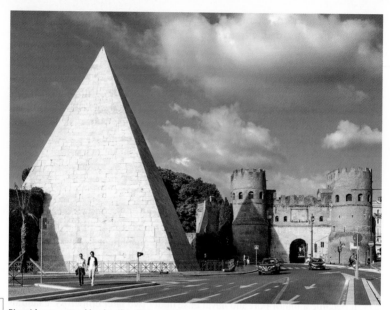

Piramide, an unusual landmark in Testaccio, Rome.

VISITOR INFORMATION   The site opens Tuesday to Sunday at 8:30am. Closing time is at dusk, so changes seasonally, ranging from 7pm in spring/ summer (Apr–Aug) to 4:30pm in fall and winter (Nov–Feb 15); check at **www.ostiaantica.beniculturali.it** or call © **06-56350215.** The ticket office closes 1 hour before the ruins close. Admission costs 12€ (14€ if pre- purchased online) and is free for ages 17 and under and 65 and over. The inexpensive map on sale at the ticket booth is a wise investment.

PARKING   The car park, on Viale dei Romagnoli, costs a few euro per day, but it is fairly small. Limited street parking is also available. Arrive early if you're driving.

Exploring Ostia Antica

The principal monuments are all labeled. On arrival, visitors first pass the *necropoli* (burial grounds, always outside the city gates in Roman towns and cities). The main route follows the giant cobblestones of the **Decumanus ★** (the main street) into the heart of Ostia. The **Piazzale delle Corporazioni ★★** is like an early version of Wall Street: This square contained nearly 75 corpo- rations, the nature of their businesses identified by the patterns of preserved mosaics. Nearby, Greek dramas were performed at the **Teatro,** built in the early days of the Empire. The theater as it looks today is the result of much rebuilding. Every town the size of Ostia had a **Forum ★**, and the layout is still intact: A well-preserved **Capitolium** (once the largest temple in Ostia) faces the remains of the 1st-century A.D. **Temple of Roma and Augustus.**

Ostia Antica's Piazzale delle Corporazioni.

Elsewhere in the grid of streets are the ruins of the **Thermopolium ★★**, which was a bar; its name means "sale of hot drinks." Of the *insula* (a Roman block of apartments), **Casa Diana ★** remains, with its rooms arranged around an inner courtyard. The **Terme di Nettuno ★** was a vast baths complex; climb the building at its entrance for an aerial view of its well-preserved mosaics. In the enclave is a **museum** displaying Roman statuary along with fragmentary frescoes.

Mosaic floors at the Baths of Neptune, Ostia Antica.

Where to Eat

There is no real need to eat by the ruins—a half-day here should suffice, and Ostia is within easy reach of the abundant restaurants of Rome's city center. The obvious alternative is a picnic; the well-stocked foodie magnet **Eataly,** Piazzale XII Ottobre 1492, is only a couple of minutes from the Lido platform at Piramide Metro station, making it easy to grab provisions when you make the Metro interchange. The site has perfect picnic spots beside fallen columns or old temple walls. If you crave a sit-down meal, trattoria **Allo Sbarco di Enea,** Viale dei Romagnoli 675 (allosbarcodienea.com; ✆ **06-5650034**) is right outside the archaeological park. A snack and coffee bar are also at the site.

TIVOLI & THE VILLAS ★★

32km (20 miles) E of Rome

Perched high on a hill east of Rome, Tivoli is an ancient town that has always been something of a retreat from the city. In Roman times it was known as Tibur, a retirement town for the wealthy; later during the Renaissance, it again became the playground of the rich, who built their country villas out here. You need a full day to do justice to the gardens and villas that remain—especially if Villa Adriana is on your list, as indeed it should be—so set out early.

Essentials

GETTING THERE Tivoli is 32km (20 miles) east of Rome on Via Tiburtina, about an hour's drive with traffic (the Rome–L'Aquila *autostrada*, A24, is usually faster). If you don't have a car, you can take one of several daily trains from Termini or Tiburtina to Tivoli station. Villa d'Este is in Tivoli itself, close to the train station; to get to Villa Adriana you need to catch a regional bus from town. Or take the Cotral bus that runs on Via Prenestina; this stops a short walk from the Villa Adriana entrance.

Another option is to take Metro Line B to Ponte Mammolo. After exiting the station, transfer to a Cotral bus for Tivoli (www.cotralspa.it). Cotral buses depart every 15 to 30 minutes during the day, and the trip will take less than an hour.

Exploring Tivoli and the Villas

Villa Adriana (Hadrian's Villa) ★★★ HISTORIC SITE/RUINS   The globe-trotting Emperor Hadrian spent the last 3 years of his life in the grandest style. Less than 6km (3¾ miles) from Tivoli, between 118 and 134 A.D. he built one of the greatest estates ever conceived, and he filled acre after acre with some of the architectural wonders he'd seen on his many travels. Hadrian erected theaters, baths, temples, fountains, gardens, and canals bordered with statuary, filling the palaces and temples with sculpture, some of which now rest in the museums of Rome. In later centuries, barbarians, popes, and cardinals,

Hadrian's Villa.

as well as anyone who needed a slab of marble, carted off much that made the villa so spectacular. But enough of the fragmented ruins remain to inspire a real sense of awe. For a glimpse of what the villa used to be, see the plastic reconstruction at the entrance.

The most outstanding remnant is the **Canopo ★★★**, a recreation of the Egyptian town of Canopus with its famous Temple of the Serapis. The ruins of a rectangular area, **Piazza d'Oro**, are still surrounded by a double portico. Likewise, the **Edificio con Pilastri Dorici (Doric Pillared Hall)** remains, with its pilasters with bases and capitals holding up a Doric architrave. The apse and the ruins of some magnificent vaulting are found at the **Grandi Terme (Great Baths)**, while only the north wall remains of the **Pecile ★**, otherwise known as the *Stoà Poikile di Atene* or "Painted Porch," which Hadrian discovered in Athens and had reproduced here. The best is saved for last—the **Teatro Marittimo ★★★**, a circular maritime theater in ruins, with its central building enveloped by a canal spanned by small swing bridges.

For a closer look at some of the items excavated, you can visit the museum on the premises and a visitor center near the villa parking area.

Largo Marguerite Yourcenar 1, Tivoli. www.levillae.com/en. ℂ **0774-312070.** 12€. Daily 8:15am–sunset. Bus: 4 from Tivoli.

Villa d'Este ★★ PARK/GARDEN

Like Hadrian centuries before, Cardinal Ippolito d'Este of Ferrara ordered this villa built in the mid-16th century on a Tivoli hillside. The dank Renaissance structure, with its second-rate paintings, is not that interesting; the big draw for visitors is the **spectacular gardens ★★★**, designed by Pirro Ligorio.

As you descend the cypress-studded garden slope you're rewarded with everything from lilies to gargoyles spouting water, torrential streams, and waterfalls. The loveliest fountain is the **Fontana dell Ovato ★★**, by Ligorio. But nearby is the most spectacular engineering achievement: the **Fontana dell'Organo Idraulico (Fountain of the Hydraulic Organ) ★★**, dazzling with its music and water jets in front of a baroque chapel, with four maidens who look tipsy (the fountain "plays" every 2 hours from 10:30am).

A fountain in Villa d'Este.

The moss-covered **Fontana dei Draghi (Fountain of the Dragons)**, also by Ligorio, and the so-called **Fontana di Vetro (Fountain of Glass)**, by Bernini, are also worth seeking out, as is the main promenade, lined with 100 spraying fountains. The garden is worth hours of exploration, but it involves a lot of walking, with some steep climbs.

Piazza Trento 5, Tivoli. www.levillae.com/en. ☎ **0774-312070.** 10€. Tue–Sun 8:15am to 1 hr. before sunset; Mon from 2pm. Bus: Cotral service from Ponte Mammolo (Roma–Tivoli); bus stops near the entrance.

Villa Gregoriana ★ PARK/GARDEN

Villa d'Este dazzles with artificial glamour, but the Villa Gregoriana relies more on nature. Originally laid out by Pope Gregory XVI in the 1830s, its main highlight is the panoramic waterfall of Aniene, with the trek to the bottom studded with grottoes and balconies that open onto the chasm. The only problem is that if you do make the full descent, you might need a helicopter to pull you up again (the climb back up is fierce). From one of the belvederes, there's a view of the **Temple of Vesta** on the hill.

Largo Sant'Angelo, Tivoli. www.fondoambiente.it/luoghi/parco-villa-gregoriana/visita. ☎ **0774-332650.** 8€. Late Apr–mid-Dec daily 10am–dusk (from 9am in summer); closed mid-Dec–late Apr. Bus: Cotral service from Ponte Mammolo (Roma–Tivoli); the bus stops near the entrance.

Where to Eat

Tivoli's gardens make for a pleasant picnic place, but if you crave an upscale meal with a view, **Ristorante Sibilla**, Via della Sibilla 42 (www.ristorante sibilla.com; © 0774-335281; closed Mon) sits in the shadow of the Temple of Vesta and is a 10-minute walk from the station. In the center of town, **La Fornarina** at Piazza Palatina 8 (www.pizzerialafornarina.it; © 0774-312786) is a casual choice for pizza, pasta, and Roman specialties.

6

FLORENCE

By Donald Strachan

Florence may be small, but over the centuries it has exercised major influence over European history and society. Its historic center—which you can easily cross on foot—still evokes this illustrious past, packed as it is with monuments from the city's golden age. In the 15th and 16th centuries, Florence's achievements in art, architecture, science, literature, and even banking were unmatched—and the rest of Europe knew it.

This was the center of the Renaissance movement and the hometown of its leading figures, Michelangelo, Brunelleschi, Leonardo da Vinci, Galileo, and others. Florence built up a store of riches that still dazzles today: the **Uffizi Gallery** heaving with masterpieces, the ingenious domed Cathedral, Michelangelo's **"David,"** and any number of decorated palaces and chapels. These treasures are still representative of one of the highest points human history. And because of this, Florence remains a must-visit destination for every first-time traveler to Italy, and a must-return destination for anyone who cares about art and architecture.

Florence is also well located for exploring the Tuscany region. For the best day trips from Florence, see chapter 7.

STRATEGIES FOR SEEING FLORENCE

You want to make the most of your time in Florence, but also get the most for your money, know the best ways to get around, and avoid hassles like long lines. The following essential strategies and hard-working tips will help you enrich your time and travels in Florence.

o **Avoid the lines.** If I was to give one single piece of advice to a friend visiting Florence, it would be this: **Book tickets for the Uffizi, Accademia, and Brunelleschi's dome as far in advance as you can.** Reserving a timed entrance slot is relatively easy (see box p. 174) and often compulsory. And tickets to climb the cathedral dome are strictly limited: fail to plan ahead, and you'll have to settle for a street-level view.

Florence rests along the River Arno and is hemmed in by the Tuscan hillside.

- **Save on unnecessary booking fees.** Conversely, apart from the Uffizi, Accademia, dome, and Brancacci Chapel, you won't usually need a timed admission slot anywhere else. Save the booking fee.
- **Discount tickets.** Do you need one? The answer, unfortunately, is "it depends." To decide whether the 85€ **Firenzecard** is for you, turn to p. 205.
- **Walk.** Florence's tortuous one-way road system makes taxis expensive, and the city has no metro. Pack comfortable shoes and hit the streets on foot. *Note:* The hill up to Piazzale Michelangelo is fairly steep: If this sounds daunting, buses 12 and 13 go there.
- **Mondays.** Italian state museums are traditionally closed on Mondays, which means no Uffizi, no Pitti Palace, and no "David." Monday, then, is a good time to visit Florence's other sights, like the Palazzo Vecchio, Santa Maria Novella, and churches including the Duomo complex—all of which are open as usual. One caveat: With the big-hitters closed, other sights are busier, so Mondays also make a perfect day-trip day; see chapter 7 for our recommended short trips from the city.
- **Eat lunch and *aperitivo;* skip dinner.** Unless you have a huge appetite, you won't need three big meals a day. To save money, eat a full, late lunch, which is usually cheaper, and exchange dinner for an *aperitivo*. These are often generous and appear around 6:30pm at bars all over the city. Buy one

As soon as you set a date for your visit Florence, consider making advance reservations for the **Uffizi** and **Accademia** museums—as well as Brunelleschi's cathedral dome, if you wish to climb it (see p. 209). As elsewhere in Italy, walk-ups are either no longer allowed or strongly discouraged at many major museums. (Buying a cumulative ticket—see "Discount Tickets for Florence," p. 205—is your other smart strategy.) Book via **Firenze Musei** at **www.uffizi. it**. This is the **only official ticketing agent for state museums:** Do not buy from elsewhere. There's a 4€ fee; you can pay by credit card. Reservations are also possible for the Galleria Palatina in the Pitti Palace, the Bargello, and several others. If you arrive in Florence without reservations, you can also reserve in person at a kiosk in the facade of Orsanmichele, on Via dei Calzaiuoli (Mon–Sat); from the bookshop **Libreria My Accademia,** Via Ricasoli 105R, almost opposite the Accademia (Tues–Sun); or at **Opera Your Preview,** Via Por Santa Maria 13R (www.opera yourpreview.com). For prebooking timed-admission slots at city-run museums such as the Palazzo Vecchio or Cappella Brancacci, visit a separate ticketing hub at **ticketsmuseums.comune.fi.it.** These are less urgent, however.

drink and you can nosh as much as you like. Florentines even have a name for this: *apericena* (*cena* means "dinner").

o **First Sundays.** Like elsewhere in Italy, the first Sunday of every month is #domenicalmuseo, meaning admission to state-owned museums is free (*note:* this is not the same as *city*-owned). So, you can enter the Uffizi, Bargello, Medici Chapels, Pitti Palace, Boboli Garden, and more without paying a cent. The downside? Queues and crowds, of course—mostly Italians taking advantage of the promotion. Forget the Uffizi, which will be packed, and try your luck at others. The **tourist office** (see p. 177) has a full list. And obviously, if you're here for one day only and it's a First Sunday, do not buy a Firenzecard.

ESSENTIALS

Arriving

BY PLANE Most international travelers will reach Florence via the airports in Rome (see p. 52) or Milan, proceeding on to Florence via train (see below). There are also direct international flights into Pisa's **Galileo Galilei Airport** (see p. 254), 97km (60 miles) west of Florence; several budget airlines fly here from European cities. Around four to eight daily **Sky Bus Lines** (www. skybuslines.it; ✆ 366/126-0651) buses connect Florence with Pisa Airport in just over 1 hour (15€ adults; 7€ children 2–11). Florence drop-off/pick-up is at the Guidoni tram stop near Florence Airport (T2 line; see below), except during the night, when the bus runs to/from Florence's main rail station. Enter your phone number during booking to confirm a seat booking via WhatsApp.

The Ponte Vecchio, seen from the banks of the River Arno.

A growing number of European airlines, including British Airways, KLM, Lufthansa, and Vueling, also serve **Florence Airport (FLR)** (sometimes called **Peretola;** www.aeroporto.firenze.it/en; ☎ **055/306-15**), just 5km (3 miles) northwest of downtown. A modern **tram line (T2)** is the most cost-efficient way to reach the center from there (1.50€ each way). Trams depart every 4 to 9 minutes from 5am to midnight. Journey time to Florence's rail station is 20 minutes. **Taxis** line up outside the arrivals terminal: Exit and turn immediately to the right to find the rank. Taxis charge a regulated flat rate of 22€ for the 15-minute journey to the city center (24€ on holidays, 25.30€ after 10pm; additional 1€ per bag).

BY TRAIN   Most travelers arrive in Florence by train. This is the Tuscany region's rail hub, with regular connections to all Italy's major cities. To get here from Rome or Milan, take a high-speed **Frecciarossa** or **Frecciargento** train (1½ hr.; www.trenitalia.com) or rival high-speed trains operated by **Italo** (www.italotreno.it). High-speed trains run from Venice (2 hr.) via Padua and Bologna; and also direct from Rome's Fiumicino Airport. On high-speed trains, you must sit in your reserved seat.

Most Florence-bound trains roll into **Stazione Santa Maria Novella,** Piazza della Stazione, which you'll see abbreviated as **S.M.N.** The station is an architectural masterpiece, albeit one dating to Italy's Fascist period, rather than the Renaissance. It lies on the northwestern edge of the city's compact historic center, a 10-minute walk from the Duomo and a brisk 15-minute walk from Piazza della Signoria and the Uffizi.

BY CAR   The **A1 autostrada** runs north from Rome past Arezzo to Florence and continues to Bologna. Unnumbered superhighways run to and from Siena (the *SI-FI raccordo*) and Pisa (the so-called *FI-PI-LI*). To reach Florence from Venice, take the A13 southbound, then switch to the A1 at Bologna.

Driving *to* Florence is easy; the problems begin once you arrive. Almost all cars are banned from the historic center for much of the time; only residents or merchants with special permits are allowed into this clearly marked, camera-patrolled *zona a traffico limitato* (ZTL). You can enter the ZTL to drop off baggage at your hotel or go direct to a prebooked parking garage (either can organize a temporary ZTL permit when provided with your license plate number). Usual ZTL hours are Monday to Friday 7:30am to 7:30pm, Saturday 7:30am to 6pm. All summer this ZTL also operates Thursday through Saturday evenings until 3am the following morning. It's a real hassle, so **only rent a car if you're leaving town to visit somewhere off the rail network.**

If you do drive here, your best bet for overnight or longer-term parking is one of the city-run garages. The best deal—better than most hotels' garage rates—is at the **Parterre parking lot** under Piazza Libertà at Via del Ponte Rosso 4 (© **055/5030-2209**). Open around the clock, it costs 2€ per hour, 15€ per day. Find more info on parking at **www.fipark.com**.

This drone's-eye view gives a sense of the density of Florence's key landmarks and piazzas.

The address system in Florence has a split personality. Private homes, some offices, and hotels are numbered in black (or blue), but businesses, shops, and restaurants are numbered independently in red. (That's the theory anyway. In reality, the division between black and red numbers isn't so clear-cut.) The result is that 1, 2, 3 (black) addresses march up the block numerically oblivious to their 1R, 2R, 3R (red) neighbors. You might find doorways on one side of a street numbered 1R, 2R, 3R, 1, 4R, 2, 3, 5R. The color codes occur only in the *centro storico* and other old sections of town. Outlying districts didn't bother with this confusing system.

Don't park your car overnight on the streets in Florence without local knowledge. If you're ticketed and towed, the fine is hefty and the headaches to retrieve your car are beyond description—and a near-impossible task on weekends. If this happens to you, start by calling the vehicle removal department (**Recupero Veicoli Rimossi**) at ☏ **055/422-4142.** One more reason **you should not drive around Florence.**

Visitor Information

TOURIST OFFICES The most convenient tourist office is opposite Florence's main rail terminus at Piazza della Stazione 4. With your back to the tracks, take the left exit and then bear right; it's across the tram tracks and road junction ahead. This office is usually open Monday through Saturday 9am to 7pm and Sunday 9am to 2pm, and provides useful free street maps. Another office, close to Santa Croce church at Borgo Santa Croce 29R, is open the same hours. A third central office at Via Cavour 1R, two blocks north of the Duomo, is open only Monday through Friday 9am to 1pm. Florence airport also has an information kiosk in the Arrivals Hall, open daily 9am to 7pm. One central **phone number covers all tourist assistance:** ☏ **055/000** (Mon–Sat 9am–7pm, Sun 9am–2pm).

WEBSITES Florence's official tourism website, **www.feelflorence.it**, contains up-to-date information, including on local events. In the "Organize Your Trip" section of the site, you can download a PDF with opening hours for city sights; the document is updated and uploaded daily. The **Feel Florence app** is available for Android and Apple mobile devices. For one-off exhibitions and culture, **Art Trav** (www.arttrav.com) is an essential blog, written in English. For more Florence info, go to **www.frommers.com/destinations/florence**.

City Layout

Florence is a smallish city, sitting on the Arno River and petering out rather quickly to olive-planted hills to the north and south, but extending farther west and east along the Arno valley with suburbs and light industry. Its compact center is best negotiated on foot. No two major sights are more than a

25-minute walk apart, and most hotels and restaurants in this chapter are in a relatively small **centro storico** (historic center), a compact tangle of medieval streets and *piazze* (squares) where visitors spend most of their time. The bulk of Florence, including most of the tourist sights, lies north of the river, with the **Oltrarno,** an old working artisans' neighborhood, hemmed in between the Arno and hills on the south side.

Florence Neighborhoods in Brief

The Duomo The area surrounding Florence's gargantuan cathedral is as central as you can get. The Duomo itself is halfway between the churches of Santa Maria Novella and Santa Croce, as well as at the midpoint between the Uffizi Gallery to the south and the Accademia (home of Michelangelo's "David") to the north. A medieval tangle of streets south of the Duomo head toward Piazza della Signoria (see below). Southwest of the Duomo, Piazza della Repubblica lies in an even older part of town, still laid out in its Roman-era grid, though the square itself was "modernized" in the 19th century. It's also a bit of a tourist trap. The Duomo neighborhood is one of the most hotel-heavy parts of town, offering everything from luxury inns to student dives. But beware: Many hotels and restaurants here rely on location, rather than quality, for their success.

Piazza della Signoria The city's civic heart is prime territory for museum hounds: The Uffizi Gallery, Palazzo Vecchio, Bargello sculpture collection, and Ponte Vecchio are all nearby. A few blocks just north of the Ponte Vecchio have good shopping but unappealing modern buildings, thanks to post–World War II reconstruction. The neighborhood is crowded in peak season, but in rare moments when it's empty of tour groups, its narrow lanes remain the romantic heart of medieval Florence. As in the Duomo neighborhood, be very choosy when picking a restaurant (or even an ice cream shop!) around here.

San Lorenzo & the Mercato Centrale Centered on the Medici family church of San Lorenzo, this wedge of streets between the train station and the Duomo is market territory, with the vast indoor Mercato Centrale food hall and the San Lorenzo street market. It's a colorful and rarely quiet area,

with many budget hotels and some very good, affordable dining.

Piazza Santa Trínita This piazza is just north of the river at the south end of Florence's high-end shopping mecca, Via de' Tornabuoni. It's a quaint, well-to-do, and still medieval neighborhood—and if you're a shopping fiend, there's no better place to be.

Santa Maria Novella Bounding the western edge of the *centro storico*, this neighborhood has two characters: a bland, busy zone around the train station and a nicer area south of it. The noisy rail-station area lacks atmosphere, but it does have more budget hotel options than any other quarter, especially around Via Faenza. Try to avoid staying on heavily trafficked Via Nazionale. The situation improves dramatically as you head south, where Piazza Santa Maria Novella and its tributary streets have several stylish hotels, including some which are very affordable.

San Marco & Santissima Annunziata On the northern edge of the *centro storico*, you'll find Piazza San Marco, a busy transport hub; and Piazza Santissima Annunziata, the city's most architecturally unified square. The neighborhood is home to Florence's university, the Accademia, the San Marco paintings of Fra Angelico, and quiet streets with some hotel gems. It's just far enough from the action to escape most crowds.

Santa Croce Few tourists roam east beyond Piazza Santa Croce, so if you want to feel like a Florentine, head here. Streets around the Mercato di Sant'Ambrogio get lively after dark, especially Via Pietrapiana and the northern end of Via de' Macci. Some of the city's best restaurants and bars are here; aperitivo time is vibrant along Via de' Benci. There are fewer hotels over here: Affordable apartment rentals are everywhere.

The Oltrarno, San Niccolò & San Frediano "Across the Arno" is the artisans' neighborhood, and still dotted with workshops. It began as a working-class neighborhood to catch overflow from the medieval city, and later became a chic area for aristocrats to build palaces with country views. The largest of these, the Pitti Palace, today houses a set of paintings second only to the Uffizi. The Oltrarno's tree-shaded center, Piazza Santo Spirito, is surrounded with great restaurants and nightlife. West of here, the neighborhood of San Frediano is ever more fashionable, and San Niccolò at the foot of Florence's southern hills has popular bars. Oltrarno's hotel range isn't great, but you can eat and drink better here than in the *centro storico*, an easy walk away.

Getting Around Florence

Florence is a **walking** city. You can stroll between the two top sights, Piazza del Duomo and the Uffizi, in 5 minutes or so. The hike from the most northerly major sights, San Marco and the Accademia, to the most southerly, the Pitti Palace across the Arno, will take no more than 25 minutes for most. From Santa Maria Novella eastward to Santa Croce is a flat 20- to 30-minute walk. But beware: **Flagstones,** some of them uneven, are everywhere. Wear sensible shoes with good padding and foot support.

BY BUS & TRAM You'll rarely need Florence's efficient **AT Bus** network (www.at-bus.it; ⓒ **800/142424** in Italy) since the city is so compact. Bus tickets cost 1.50€ (2.50€ on board) and are good for 90 minutes, irrespective of how many changes you make (even if you switch to a tram). Tickets are sold

at *tabacchi* (tobacconists), automatic machines, some bars, and most newsstands. *Note:* Once on board, validate a paper ticket in the box to avoid a steep fine. Since traffic is restricted in most of the center, buses make runs on principal streets only, except for four tiny electric bus lines (*bussini* services C1–4) that trundle about the *centro storico.* The most useful routes to outlying areas are no. 7 (for Fiesole) and nos. 12 and 13 (for Piazzale Michelangelo). Buses run from 6am until 9:30 or 10pm daily, with a limited night service on a few routes.

Tram lines (www.gestramvia.com) run from 5am until after midnight (Fri–Sat till 2am). Route T1 connects Careggi and the Fortezza via Santa Maria Novella station to the Opera di Firenze, Cascine Park, and Florence's southwestern suburbs. Line T2 heads northward from the station to Peretola airport.

The only public transport in Florence's historic center is the electric Microbus.

179

BY TAXI Taxis are not cheap, and with the city so small and the one-way system forcing drivers on convoluted routes, they aren't an economical way to get about the old center. They are most useful to get you and your bags between the train station and a hotel. It's 3.30€ to start the meter (which rises to 5.30€ on Sun, or to 6.60€ 10pm–6am), plus 1€ per bag or for a fourth passenger in the cab. Taxi stands are outside the train station, on Borgo San Jacopo, and in Piazza Santa Croce; otherwise, call **Radio Taxi SOCOTA** at ℭ **055/4242** (hail a cab by WhatsApp on ℭ **334/662-2550**), or **Radio Taxi COTAFI** at ℭ **055/4390.**

BY BICYCLE & SCOOTER Florence had already begun expanding its network of marked cycle lanes before the pandemic, and the project has accelerated since. The app-powered, dockless **bike-sharing** scheme **Movi by Mobike** (www.ridemovi.com) operates in Florence. When you've downloaded the app and registered, you're free to rent: Simply scan the QR code and ride. All payments are handled inside the app, which also displays prices for longer rentals (from 1€ per 20 min.). The Movi fleet includes standard city bikes and e-bikes.

Fully electric, Italian-made scooters can also be rented by the minute, hour, or full day using a similar dockless sharing scheme. You can register for **Helbiz** (www.helbiz.com) at the website or by using the app.

The area around Piazza Santa Croce has a genuine neighborhood feel.

The surviving private bike-rental specialists are mostly located around San Lorenzo and San Marco, including **Florence by Bike** ★, Via San Zanobi 54R (www.florencebybike.it; © **055/488-992**), which rents city bikes and kids bikes (15€ for the first day, then 10€ per day), as well as touring bikes (33€/25€) and e-bikes (39€/35€). Advanced reservations are essential—and sometimes discounted. They also provide detailed route maps for rides into the hills north and south of the center. Make sure to use the lock provided: Bike theft is depressingly common.

BY CAR Trying to drive in the *centro storico* is a frustrating, useless exercise, and moreover, for most of the time unauthorized cars will be fined if they enter the restricted traffic zone (ZTL). You need a permit to do anything beyond dropping off and picking up bags at your hotel. Park your vehicle in one of the underground lots on the center's periphery and pound the sidewalk. (See "By Car" under "Arriving," p. 176.)

[Fast FACTS] FLORENCE

Business Hours Hours mainly follow the Italian norm (see p. 360), although many larger and/or central shops stay open through the midday *riposo* (note the sign *orario nonstop*).

Doctors & Dentists Tourist-oriented **Medical Service Firenze,** at Via Roma 4 (www.medical service.firenze.it; © **055/ 475-411**), is usually open Monday to Friday 11am to noon, 1 to 3pm, and 5 to 6pm; Saturday 11am to noon and 1 to 3pm. **All visits should be arranged in advance by phone;** call in the morning. A similar rule operates at **Dr. Stephen Kerr,** Piazza Mercato Nuovo 1 (www.dr-kerr.com; © **335/836-1682**), open Monday to Friday 10am to 12:20pm and 2 to 4:40pm. His consultation fee is 87€, or 55€ if you show student ID.

Hospitals The most central hospital is **Santa**

Maria Nuova, a block northeast of the Duomo on Piazza Santa Maria Nuova (www.uslcentro.toscana.it; © **055/54-5454**), with an emergency room (*pronto soccorso*) open 24 hours.

Left Luggage At Santa Maria Novella Station, platform 16, you can leave luggage at **KiPoint** (www. kibag.it), open daily 7am to 9pm; the cost is 10€ per bag per day. Even cheaper (1€/hr.; 5€/day) is **Left Luggage Florence,** Via de' Boni 5R (www.leftluggage florence.com).

Mail Florence's **main post office** is at Via Pellicceria 3, off the southwest corner of Piazza della Repubblica. It's open Monday to Friday 8:20am to 7:05pm and Saturday 8:20am to 12:35pm.

Pharmacies There is a 24-hour pharmacy (also open Sun and state holidays) in **Stazione Santa Maria Novella** (© **055/ 216-761;** ring the bell

across from the taxi rank 11pm–7am). On holidays and at night, look for the sign in any pharmacy window telling you which ones are open locally or check www.feelflorence.it/en/farmacieh24.

Police To report a crime or a lost passport, call the *questura* (police headquarters) at © **055/49-771.** General lost property might find its way to the *Ufficio oggetti ritrovati*: © **055/334-802.**

Safety As in any city, pickpockets are a risk in Florence, often light-fingered youngsters hanging around the train station. Otherwise, it's a fairly safe city, but steer clear of the Cascine Park after dark, and in the wee hours when nightlife is finished, avoid the area around Piazza Santo Spirito and the back-streets behind Santa Croce.

181

WHERE TO STAY

Even before Covid-19, a fast-growing stock of hotel beds had kept lodging prices stable in recent years. But it remains difficult to find a high-season double you'd want to sleep in for much less than 100€. Once-irresistible August deals have mostly dried up: Florence no longer seems to get much quieter in its hottest month. Rooms almost everywhere are smaller than North American travelers are used to.

Florence's city tax adds an extra 3€ to 5€ **per person per night,** depending on the hotel's official star rating, for the first 7 nights of any stay. This is payable on departure and is not usually included in quoted rates. Children below age 12 are exempt from the tax. Airbnb and other holiday rentals are **not** exempt.

Peak hotel season is Easter through early July, September through late October, and Christmas through January 6. May, June, and September are very popular; January and February are the months to grab a bargain—never be shy to haggle if you're coming then. A room at 220€ in June could be as low as 75€ in February, especially if you stay multiple nights. **Booking direct** via phone, e-mail, or the hotel's own website is often key to unlocking the lowest rates or complimentary extras.

To help you decide in which area you'd like to base yourself, consult "Florence Neighborhoods in Brief," p. 178. For first-time visitors, there's no good reason to base yourself outside the center or Oltrarno. Note that many hotels offer babysitting services, but almost always "on request." At least a couple of days' notice is advisable. Enhanced cleaning protocols remain in place at all reputable accommodations; check individual booking websites for details.

Apartment Rentals & Alternative Accommodations

Global players in apartment rental have overwhelmed most of the local specialists in Florence. **Vrbo.com**, TripAdvisor–owned **HolidayLettings.co.uk**, **Airbnb**, **Booking.com**, and others are well stocked.

Tip: For basic grocery shopping in the center, try PAM Local, Via Cavour 66R, or any central branch of Carrefour Express or Conad City. Both the Mercato Centrale and Mercato di Sant'Ambrogio sell an abundance of fresh produce (see "Florence's Best Markets," p. 239).

A genuine budget accommodation option, offering a unique perspective, is to stay in a **religious house ★★.** A few monasteries and convents in the center offer simple guest rooms at unbeatable rates. Our favorites are the **Suore di Santa Elisabetta,** Viale Michelangiolo 46 (near Piazza Ferrucci; ℓ **055/681-1884**), in a colonial villa just south of the Ponte San Niccolò; and close to Santa Croce, the **Istituto Oblate dell'Assunzione,** Borgo Pinti 15 (www.oblate.it; ℓ **055/2346-291**), which has peaceful rooms in a Medici-era building ranged around a courtyard garden. The easiest way to build a monastery and convent itinerary in Florence and beyond is via the specialist agent

MonasteryStays.com. This option is less attractive for night owls: Most religious houses have a curfew, generally 11pm or midnight.

Hotels by Price

EXPENSIVE
Continentale ★★★, p. 187
Grand Hotel Minerva ★★★, p. 189
Palazzo Tolomei ★★★, p. 187
Residence Hilda ★★, p. 190

MODERATE
Alessandra ★★, p. 188
Antica Dimora Johlea ★★, p. 190
Davanzati ★★, p. 188
Garibaldi Blu ★★, p. 189
Il Guelfo Bianco ★★, p. 187
La Casa di Morfeo ★★, p. 191

La Dimora degli Angeli ★★, p. 183
Loggiato dei Serviti ★★, p. 191
L'Orologio ★★, p. 190
Morandi alla Crocetta ★★, p. 191
Palazzo dal Borgo ★★, p. 190
Palazzo Galletti ★★, p. 183
Residenza della Signoria ★★, p. 183
Riva Lofts ★★★, p. 192

INEXPENSIVE
Alloro ★★, p. 187
Soggiorno Battistero ★★, p. 186

Near the Duomo

MODERATE

La Dimora degli Angeli ★★   This B&B occupies two levels of a grand apartment building in one of the city's busiest shopping districts. Rooms on the original floor are for romantics; bright wallpaper contrasts pleasingly with iron-framed beds and classic furniture. (Beatrice is the largest, with a view of Brunelleschi's dome—just.) The floor below is totally different, with sharp lines and leather or wooden headboards throughout. Breakfast is served at a local cafe. On peak season weekends, the minimum stay is 2 or even 3 nights.

Via Brunelleschi 4. www.dimoredeicherubini.it. ℹ️ **055/288-478.** 12 units. 90€–185€ double. Breakfast (at cafe) 12€. Bus: C2. **Amenities:** Free Wi-Fi.

Palazzo Galletti ★★   Not many hotels within a sensible budget give you the chance to live like a Florentine noble. Rooms here have towering ceilings and an uncluttered arrangement of carefully chosen antiques. Most have frescoed or painted-wood showpiece ceilings. Bathrooms, in contrast, have a contemporary design, decked out in travertine and marble. Aside from two street-facing suites, every room has a small balcony, ideal for a pre-dinner glass of wine. If you're here for a once-in-a-lifetime trip, spring for the large suites "Giove" or (especially) "Cerere"; the latter has walls covered in frescoes from the 1800s.

Via Sant'Egidio 12. www.palazzogalletti.it. ℹ️ **055/390-5750.** 11 units. 80€–199€ double. Breakfast included. Parking 30€–35€. Bus: C1, C2, 14, 23. **Amenities:** Free Wi-Fi.

Residenza della Signoria ★★   Location and value take center-stage at this small inn on an upper floor of an old palace. It's right on Florence's main drag, but thanks to modern soundproofing you'd never know. Rooms are spacious with antique-styled furnishings and ceilings, parquet flooring, luscious drapes, and king-size beds with firm mattresses. Only the junior suites have a

184

Florence Hotels

Guestroom at Residenza della Signoria.

proper panorama of Brunelleschi's cathedral dome, but for a smaller outlay, room 6 has a view from its bathroom window. A simple but tasty Continental breakfast is served next door at one of our favorite cafe-bars, **Cantinetta dei Verrazzano** (p. 243).

Via dei Tavolini 8. www.residenzadellasignoria.com. ℂ **055/493-3301.** 7 units. 99€–299€ double. Some rates include breakfast (otherwise 10€). Parking 35€–45€. Bus: C2. **Amenities:** Free Wi-Fi.

INEXPENSIVE

Soggiorno Battistero ★★   The Baptistery is almost close enough to touch when you take a room with a view at this super-central B&B—a modest investment you'll remember forever. Location and value are hard to beat: You lodge mere paces from the Duomo steps. Rooms are simple, gently modernized, and spacious (although some bathrooms are a squeeze), with traditional decor of terracotta tiling and antique armoires. The square below can be noisy at night, but soundproofing keeps the racket out. Note the early checkout time: 10:30am.

Piazza San Giovanni 1. www.fortehospitality.it. ℂ **349/552-5398.** 6 units. 101€–295€ double. Breakfast included. Bus: C2. **Amenities:** Free Wi-Fi.

Near San Lorenzo & the Mercato Centrale

EXPENSIVE

Palazzo Tolomei ★★★ In its heyday, this palace was at the heart of Medici power. In 1505 it even welcomed the painter Raphael as a guest (probably in two rooms at the front, now Barocco 1 and 2). Guest rooms are all large, with Renaissance wooden ceilings, terracotta floors, and Nespresso coffee makers. Modern fittings—leather sofas, soft mattresses, and florid crystal chandeliers—chime perfectly with a 17th-century baroque redecoration, complete with ceiling frescoes by Alessandro Gherardini. The lower floor is given over to opulent public rooms, just like when it was the *piano nobile* of the family palazzo. These days you'll find a music room, art books, a welcoming host, and probably an open bottle of Tuscan red wine. Book direct for deals—perhaps free late checkout or a discounted room rate.

Via de' Ginori 19. www.palazzotolomei.it. ⓒ **055/292-887.** 8 units. 159€–339€ double. Breakfast included (in nearby cafe). Bus: C1. **Amenities:** Concierge; free Wi-Fi.

MODERATE

Il Guelfo Bianco ★★ Decor in this former noble home retains its authentic palazzo feel, although there's full hotel service and a thorough renovation of guestrooms and common areas was completed in 2023. No two units are the same—stone walls this thick cannot be knocked through—and several have antiques integrated into their individual schemes. Grand rooms at the front have Renaissance coffered ceilings and extra space. Sleep at the back and you'll wake to an unusual sound in Florence: birdsong.

Via Cavour 29. ilguelfobianco.it. ⓒ **055/288-330.** 40 units. 70€–310€ double. Breakfast included. Parking 31€–39€. Bus: C1, 14, 23. **Amenities:** Restaurant; bar; babysitting; free Wi-Fi.

INEXPENSIVE

Alloro ★★ Officially a "bed-and-breakfast," this feels more like a small hotel, whose modern rooms inside a Renaissance palace overlook a silent inner courtyard—neatly soundproofing them in a noisy neighborhood. Rooms offer an excellent value for the price and location, with high ceilings, color-washed walls, and air-conditioning. Breakfast is a traditional spread of fresh fruit and pastries. A friendly ghost from the Renaissance era reputedly roams part of the palace; you're unlikely to get a discount if you spot him, but there's no harm in asking.

Via del Giglio 8. www.allorobb.it. ⓒ **055/211-685.** 5 units. 100€–195€ double. Breakfast included. Bus: C1. **Amenities:** Free Wi-Fi.

Near the Ponte Vecchio

EXPENSIVE

Continentale ★★★ Everything about the Continentale is cool, and the effect is achieved without even a hint of frostiness. Rooms are uncompromisingly modern, decorated in bright white and bathed in natural light. Deluxe units, which are built into a medieval riverside tower, have mighty walls and medieval-size windows (that is, small). Standard rooms are large (for Florence),

Some rooms at the Alessandra have river views.

and there's a retro-1950s feel to the overall styling. Communal areas are a major hit, too: A relaxation room has a glass wall facing the Ponte Vecchio.

Vicolo dell'Oro 6R. www.lungarnocollection.com. ⓒ **055/27-262.** 43 units. 292€–750€ double. Parking 39€. Bus: C3 or C4. **Amenities:** Bar; concierge; spa; free Wi-Fi.

MODERATE

Alessandra ★★   This typical Florentine *pensione* transports you back to the age of the gentleman and lady traveler. Decor has grown organically since it opened as a hotel in 1950; Alessandra is a place for evolution, not revolution. A pleasing mix of styles is the result: some rooms have carved headboards, gilt frames, and gold damask; others eclectic postwar furniture, like a mid-century period movie set. A couple have views of the Arno, while frontside rooms overlook Borgo SS. Apostoli, one of the center's most atmospheric streets. Five additional rooms with all-out contemporary decor—including, across the street, two mezzanine mini-apartments with kitchenettes—have a separate website, www.residenzaalessandra.com.

Borgo SS. Apostoli 17. www.hotelalessandra.com. ⓒ **055/283-438.** 27 units. 100€– 189€ double. Breakfast included. Parking 25€. Bus: C3, C4, 6, 11, 36, 37. Closed a few days around Christmas. **Amenities:** Free Wi-Fi.

Davanzati ★★   Although installed inside a historic building, the Davanzati never rests on its medieval laurels: There is an iPad with cellular data in every room for free guest use, and movies to stream to your TV. Rooms are simply decorated in the Tuscan style, with color-washed walls, cool tiled floors, and half-canopies over the beds. Room 100 is one of the best family hotel rooms in Florence, full of nooks, crannies, and split-levels that give adults and the kids some private space. A free daily afternoon team and *aperitivo* from 6:30pm is part of the Davanzati's welcome for guests.

Via Porta Rossa 5 (on Piazza Davanzati). www.hoteldavanzati.it. © **055/286-666.** 27 units. 99€–303€ double. Breakfast included. Parking 26€. Bus: C2. **Amenities:** Bar; babysitting; concierge; use of nearby gym; free Wi-Fi.

Near Santa Maria Novella

EXPENSIVE

Grand Hotel Minerva ★★★ American poet Henry Wadsworth Longfellow stayed in lodgings on the site of this hotel, on what is now one of Florence's most prestigious squares. I doubt the service he experienced was anywhere near the international standards now set here. Art-filled public spaces give way to quietly stylish rooms with soothing cream tones, natural wood, tan leather, and travertine bathrooms. Each one is well soundproofed against neighbors and outdoor noise. A major bonus from April to October: a rooftop pool with panoramic sundeck, cocktail bar, and evening *aperitivo* service.

Piazza Santa Maria Novella 16. www.grandhotelminerva.com. © **055/27-230.** 97 units. 260€–995€ double. Breakfast included. Parking 35€–45€. Bus: C2, 6, 11, or 22. **Amenities:** Restaurant; 2 bars; concierge; gym; outdoor pool; free Wi-Fi.

MODERATE

Garibaldi Blu ★★ The hotels of Piazza Santa Maria Novella are frequented by fashion models, rock stars, and blue-chip business folk. You can get a taste of that, for a fraction of the price, at this boutique hotel with attitude. Each of the mostly midsized rooms has a "warm denim" palette, with retro 1970s furniture, parquet floors, and marble bathrooms. It's well worth paying 30€ extra for a deluxe room at the front: These have much more space and a view over

The Grand Hotel Minerva presides over Piazza Santa Maria Novella.

Florence's prettiest church facade, Santa Maria Novella. Dotted around the hotel, life-sized models of superheroes like Captain America add a fun surreal touch.

Piazza Santa Maria Novella 21. www.hotelgaribaldiblu.com. ℂ **055/277-3001.** 21 units. 130€–350€ double. Breakfast included. Parking 35€–48€. Bus: C2, 6, 11, 22. **Amenities:** Bar; babysitting (prebooking essential); concierge; free Wi-Fi.

L'Orologio ★★ As the name suggests, this hotel is an homage to the clock, with historic timepiece designs scattered artfully about. The color palette is rich, with mahogany wood and natural leather everywhere. The cheapest rooms ("superior") are not large, but their marble bathrooms are, and library-like wood-paneled common areas are spacious and comfortable. Staff is superb. L'Orologio is atmospheric and close to the train station; the view from its top-floor breakfast room is a showstopper.

Piazza Santa Maria Novella 24. www.hotelorologioflorence.com. ℂ **055/277-380.** 55 units. 180€–400€ double. Breakfast included. Parking 35€–48€. Bus: C2, 6, 11, 22. **Amenities:** Bar; babysitting; concierge; gym; sauna; free Wi-Fi.

Palazzo dal Borgo ★★ High ceilings and spacious rooms—especially second-floor Superior units—are typical of a Florentine noble palace. Built in the 1500s, Palazzo dal Borgo was converted into a hotel in the early 1900s, leaving many original ceiling frescoes and architectural features intact. For an extra-silent night, request a room overlooking its interior courtyard or Santa Maria Novella, which is out back. A breakfast buffet is served in a quaint bar or outside among the citrus trees. The hotel's location is super-convenient for the rail station and airport tram.

Via della Scala 6. www.hotelpalazzodalborgo.it. ℂ **055/216-237.** 34 units. 99€–299€ double. Breakfast included. Parking 30€–35€. Bus: 6 or 11. **Amenities:** Bar; concierge; free Wi-Fi.

Near San Marco & Santissima Annunziata
EXPENSIVE
Residence Hilda ★★ With no hint of the Renaissance, these spacious, luxe mini-apartments are all bright-white decor and designer furnishings, with natural wood flooring, hypoallergenic mattresses, Starck chairs, and modern gadgetry. Each is spacious, cool in summer, and soundproofed against Florence's perma-noise. Every unit has a mini-kitchen equipped for preparing a simple meal—ideal if you have kids in tow. *Bonus:* Unusual for apartments, all units are bookable by the single night—some guests stay for a year.

Via dei Servi 40. www.residencehilda.com. ℂ **055/288-021.** 12 units. 90€–400€ for 2- to 4-person apartment. Parking 31€. Bus: C1. **Amenities:** Airport transfer; babysitting; concierge; room service; free Wi-Fi.

MODERATE
Antica Dimora Johlea ★★ There's a real neighborhood feel to the streets around this *dimora* (traditional Florentine home) guesthouse, which means evenings are lively and Sundays are quiet (although it's less than a 10-min. walk to San Lorenzo). Standard-size rooms are snug; upgrade to an

Executive if you need more space, but there is no difference in the standard of decor, a mix of Florentine and earthy boho. A snug roof terrace has knockout views over the terracotta rooftops to the center and hills beyond. Dusk is pure magic as the scent of lavender drifts by on the evening breeze. Breakfast is a la carte.

Via San Gallo 80. www.antichedimorefiorentine.it. © **055/463-3292.** 6 units. 100€–250€ double. Breakfast included. Parking 25€. Bus: C1, 1, 6, 11, 14, 17, 23. **Amenities:** Bar; free Wi-Fi.

Loggiato dei Serviti ★★ This city icon reopened in 2023, restyled under the new ownership of Rome's Del Sole at Pantheon (p. 72). As it always did, a stay here evokes Florence as experienced by the noble travelers of the Grand Tour. For starters, the building is a genuine Renaissance landmark, built by Sangallo the Elder in the 1520s. A sense of grandeur and unconventional luxury pairs well with high-class vintage ambience throughout the common areas and guestrooms. Every unit is a comfortable size. However, go up a grade from standard to enjoy a room with a view, of either Brunelleschi's dome or the perfect piazza outside.

Piazza Santissima Annunziata 3. www.loggiatodeiservitihotel.it. © **055/289-592.** 37 units. 180€–350€ double. Breakfast included. Bus: C1, 6, 14, 19, 23, 31, 32. **Amenities:** Concierge; free Wi-Fi.

Morandi alla Crocetta ★★ Like many Florence inns, Morandi alla Crocetta was built in the shell of a former convent, and it has retained the original convent layout, meaning some rooms are snug. But what you lose in size, you more than gain in character: Every single one oozes *tipico fiorentino*—even the "new" breakfast room feels like you're on the Grand Tour. Rooms have parquet floors, throw rugs, and antique wood furniture. Original 1744 Zocchi prints of Florence are scattered around the place. Superior rooms have more space and either a private courtyard terrace or, in one, original frescoes decorating an entrance to the former convent chapel (the chapel itself is sealed off). The hotel is set on a quiet street.

Via Laura 50. www.hotelmorandi.it. © **055/234-4747.** 12 units. 80€–220€ double. Parking 27€. Bus: 6, 19, 31, 32. **Amenities:** Bar; babysitting; concierge; free Wi-Fi.

Near Santa Croce
MODERATE

La Casa di Morfeo ★★ For a cheery, affordable room in the lively eastern part of the center, look no further than this small hotel on the second floor of a grand, shuttered palace. There is no huge difference in quality among the guest rooms: All are midsized, with modern gadgetry, and painted in bright, contemporary colors, each individual scheme corresponding to a flower after which the room is named. Our favorite is Mimosa, painted in light mustard, with a ceiling fresco and a view over Via Ghibellina. Colored lighting adds a sense of fun.

Via Ghibellina 51. www.lacasadimorfeo.it. © **055/241-193.** 9 units. 101€–263€ double. Breakfast included. Parking 25€. Bus: C2 or C3. **Amenities:** Concierge; free Wi-Fi.

West of the Center
MODERATE

Riva Lofts ★★★ The traditional Florentine alarm call—a morning mix of traffic and tourism—is replaced by birdsong when you awake in one of these stylish rooms on the banks of the River Arno. A former artisan workshop, Riva had a refit to earn its "loft" label. Mellow colors predominate, with laminate flooring, floating staircases, marble bathrooms with rainfall showers, and clever integration of natural materials such as original wooden workshop ceilings. The center is a 30-minute walk, or hop on one of Riva's vintage-style bikes and cycle along the river to the Uffizi. Further standout features are a shaded

The plunge pool at Riva Lofts.

garden—where you can often dine on summer evenings—and an outdoor plunge pool. Staff also organize Tuscan cookery classes with a pro chef.

Via Baccio Bandinelli 98. www.rivalofts.com. ✆ **055/713-0272.** 12 units. 120€–400€ double. Breakfast included. Parking 15€. Tram: T1 (3 stops from central station). **Amenities:** Restaurant (Tues–Fri evenings); bar; babysitting (on request); free bike rental; outdoor pool; free Wi-Fi.

WHERE TO EAT

Florence is well supplied with restaurants, although in the most touristy areas (around the Duomo, Piazza della Signoria, Piazza della Repubblica, and the Ponte Vecchio), you must choose carefully—many eateries are of below-average quality or charge high prices, sometimes both. The highest concentrations of excellent *ristoranti* and *trattorie* are east of Santa Croce around **Piazza Ghiberti,** and across the river in the **Oltrarno** and **San Frediano.** There's much improved dining around **San Lorenzo** since the reopening of the Mercato Centrale top floor (see p. 199) with a wealth of street-food counters. The city has also become much more

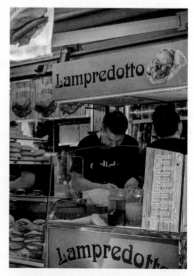

Lampredotto (tripe) is a Florentine specialty.

gluten-savvy. If you have a food intolerance, just ask. **Vegan** food is widely available.

Reservations are strongly recommended if you have your heart set on somewhere in particular, especially at dinner on weekends. Bear in mind that restaurant menus can change weekly or even daily. *Tip:* You can book at many Florence restaurants, including several of our favorites below, via **The Fork** (www.thefork.it) or **Quandoo** (www.quandoo.it).

FLORENTINE CUISINE   Florentine cuisine is increasingly cosmopolitan, but flavors are often Tuscan at heart. Even in fine restaurants, meals may kick off with country concoctions like *ribollita* (seasonal vegetable stew) before moving on to the chargrilled delights of a *bistecca alla fiorentina* (Florentine beefsteak on the bone), washed down with a robust **Chianti Classico.** A plate of cold cuts and Pecorino cheese makes a classic light lunch, or for the adventurous, *lampredotto alla fiorentina,* a sandwich of cow's stomach stewed in tomatoes and garlic. Popular global dishes like burgers, sushi, pizza, and ramen are widely available.

Restaurants by Cuisine

CAFES
Cantinetta dei Verrazzano ★★, p. 243
Ditta Artigianale ★★, p. 243
La Menagère ★, p. 244
Procacci ★★, p. 244
Rivoire ★, p. 244
Tosca & Nino ★, p. 244

FLORENTINE
Bondi ★★, p. 198
Da Rocco ★★, p. 201
Il Magazzino ★★, p. 202
La Gratella ★★, p. 198
Mario ★★, p. 199

GELATO
Gelateria della Passera ★★, p. 204
Gelateria de' Neri ★★, p. 204
La Carraia ★★, p. 204

GRILL
La Gratella ★★, p. 198
Il Nutino ★★, p. 198

JAPANESE
Koto ★★, p. 200

LIGHT FARE/SANDWICHES
Bondi ★★, p. 198
I Due Fratellini ★★, p. 197
Pugi ★, p. 200

SandwiChic ★★★, p. 199
SchiacciaMatta ★, p. 200

MODERN ITALIAN
Il Santo Bevitore ★★, p. 202
Mercato Centrale ★★, p. 199

MODERN TUSCAN
iO: Osteria Personale ★★★, p. 201
Osteria dell'Enoteca ★★★, p. 203
Osteria di Giovanni ★★★, p. 197

PIZZA
Mercato Centrale ★★, p. 199

RAW FOOD
Fishing Lab Alle Murate ★★, p. 197

SEAFOOD
Fishing Lab Alle Murate ★★, p. 197

TRADITIONAL TUSCAN
Coquinarius ★★, p. 196
Da Tito ★★★, p. 200
Il Nutino ★★, p. 198
Osteria del Porcellino ★, p. 197

VEGETARIAN/VEGAN
Brac ★★, p. 200

Florence
Restaurants

Giardino
dei Semplici

Giardino
della
Gherardesca

Piazza
Donatello

33

San Marco

Piazza
San Marco

Santissima
Annunziata

31

32

Galleria dell'
Accademia

Piazza
della
SS. Annunziata

Ospedale
degli
Innocenti

Museo
Archeologico

30

Palazzo
Medici-Riccardi

Palazzo
Pucci

Piazza
Brunelleschi

Santa Maria
Maddalena
dei Pazzi

Piazza
d'Azeglio

Duomo

Ospedale
S. Maria Nuova

Teatro d.
Pergola

Sinagoga
(Museo
Ebraico)

Piazza del Duomo

Piazza
S. M. Nuova

Via dell'Oriuolo

24

Via del Corso

Borgo degli Albizi

Via Pietrapiana

Piazza
Sant'
Ambrogio

29
28

Piazza
Cesare
Beccaria

23

22

Via Dante
Alighieri

25

Via de' Pandolfini

27

Piazza
L. Ghiberti

Badia

Bargello

Teatro
Verdi

Casa di
Buonarroti

Carceri delle
Murate

Archivio
di Stato

Piazza della
Signoria

Palazzo
Vecchio

Borgo de' Greci

Piazza
S. Croce

Via di San Giuseppe

Uffizi

21

20

Santa
Croce

SANTA
CROCE

Piazza
Mentana

19

Biblioteca
Nazionale

Piazza dei
Cavalleggeri

Piazza
Piave

Lung. Gen. Diaz

Lungarno delle Grazie

Via Tripoli

Lung. della Zecca Vecchia

Lung. P. Giraldi

Fiume Arno

Lungarno Torrigiani

Lungarno Serristori

Via dei Renai

Piazza
G. Poggi

Lungarno B. Cellini

Piazza
F. Ferrucci

SAN
NICCOLÒ

Via di S. Niccolo

Viale G. Poggi

Piazzale
Michelangiolo

Viale Michelangiolo

New York has the hot dog. London has pie and mash. Florence has...cow's intestine in a sandwich. The city's traditional street food, *lampredotto* (the cow's fourth stomach), stewed with tomatoes, has made a big comeback, including in some fine-dining establishments. The most affordable places to sample it are the city's *trippai*, tripe vendors who sell from food trucks around the center. The most convenient are in **Piazza de' Cimatori** and on **Via de' Macci** at Piazza Sant'Ambrogio. A hearty, nutritious lunch should come in around 5€. Most are open Monday through Saturday but close in August, when Florentines flee the city.

Near the Duomo
MODERATE

Coquinarius ★★ TUSCAN   There is a regular menu here, offering pasta, main courses (such as stuffed rabbit with creamed carrot), and traditional desserts. But it's equally pleasurable just tucking into a couple of sharing plates and quaffing from the excellent wine list. Go for a swordfish carpaccio, and maybe pair a *selezione di salumi e formaggi* (mixed Tuscan salami and cheeses) with a full-bodied red wine, to cut through the strong flavors of the deliciously fatty, salty pork and Tuscan sheep's milk cheese, pecorino.

Via delle Oche 11R. www.coquinarius.it. ☎ **055/230-2153.** Entrees 16€–24€. Mon–Sat noon–3pm and 7pm–midnight. Bus: C1 or C2.

A plate of mixed appetizers at Coquinarius.

Fishing Lab Alle Murate ★★ SEAFOOD   This contemporary-styled temple to seafood serves fish any way you like (almost) at fair prices. Shrimp, tuna, bream, bass, and salmon dominate; fish are carefully sourced and preparation is modern. The raw bar has a selection of tartare and carpaccio, both super-fresh and dressed delicately with citrus. Hot main courses include grilled filets, fishy pastas, and the ubiquitous poke bowl. Both clientele and staff are young and lively, matching the decor of urban furniture amid frescoes. Service is brisk. Reservations highly recommended.

Via del Proconsolo 16R. www.fishinglab.it. ✆ **055/240-618.** Entrees 12€–16€. Wed–Mon noon–11pm. Bus: C1 or C2.

INEXPENSIVE
I Due Fratellini ★★ PANINI/LIGHT FARE   This hole-in-the-wall has been serving sandwiches to go since 1875 (and fed Conan O'Brien on his Italian gastronomic tour). The drill is simple: Choose a filling, pick a drink, then eat your fast-filled roll on the curb opposite or find a nearby piazza to perch. There are around 30 combos to choose from, including the usual Tuscan meats and cheeses—porchetta, pecorino, prosciutto—and more flamboyant options such as fennel-spiked salami with cream cheese or *bresaola* (air-dried beef) and arugula. A glass of wine to wash it down costs from 2€. Lunchtime lines can be long.

Via dei Cimatori 38R (at corner of Via Calzaiuoli). ✆ **055/239-6096.** Sandwiches 5€. Daily 10am–7pm. Bus: C2.

Near the Ponte Vecchio
MODERATE
Osteria del Porcellino ★ TUSCAN   So many characterful restaurants of "old Florence" have dropped standards in the age of mass tourism, but not this place. Traditional Tuscan is what they do best, and pasta dishes such as *pappardelle* with wild boar sauce are always tasty. Follow that with a *tagliata* (sliced steak) with arugula and Parmigiano to savor the city's carnivorous traditions. Lighter options include sublime "flan"—a potato cake with cured ham, Vin Santo wine, and *stracchino* cheese sauce—and house salads. On weekends, all-day dining means you (or the kids) can eat when you choose.

Via Val di Lamona 7R. www.osteriadelporcellino.com. ✆ **055/264-148.** Entrees 20€–25€. Mon–Fri noon–3pm and 7–11pm, Sat–Sun noon–11pm. Closed 2 weeks in Feb. Bus: C2.

Near Santa Trínita
MODERATE
Osteria di Giovanni ★★★ MODERN TUSCAN   If only every Tuscan restaurant in town was this good. Family-run Osteria di Giovanni is a standout in its category and therefore always buzzing: You should reserve even in low season. Meat is a specialty, both traditional (the *bistecca alla fiorentina* is legendary) and modern interpretations like *faraona all'arancia* (guinea hen

stewed in slightly sweet orange). Portions are large, so only the very brave should attempt a *primo/secondo/dolce* route. A steep cover charge (4€) is actually a good deal, because it includes a couple of tasty snacks and all the mineral water you can drink.

Via del Moro 22. www.osteriadigiovanni.com. © **055/284-897.** Entrees 24€–28€. Daily 7–10:30pm; Sat–Sun also 12:30–2:30pm. Bus: 6, 11.

Near San Lorenzo & the Mercato Centrale
MODERATE
Il Nutino ★★ TUSCAN/GRILL   This tiny, traditional joint has been in business since the 1950s. It's become our go-to for *bistecca alla fiorentina,* in both classic and marbled styles. Whichever you choose, your meat spends a short time over the flames and is best served simply with roasted potatoes and *fagioli al fiasco* (beans stewed in olive oil). There's also a full Tuscan menu of fresh pasta, *crostini,* soups, and the like—but the grill is the star. Service is attentive and knowledgeable, especially when it comes to selecting a wine to wash down the red meat (Chianti Rufina Nipozzano is our choice). The location is one of Florence's most heavily touristed areas, but with over 7 decades behind it, Il Nutino is doing things the right way.

Borgo San Lorenzo 39R. © **349/453-6035.** Entrees 17€–26€. Daily 8am–11pm. Bus: C1.

La Gratella ★★ FLORENTINE/GRILL   It doesn't look like much—a workers' canteen on a nondescript side street—but looks don't matter much when you can source and cook meat like they do here. With Florence's main market nearby, the unsurprising star of the show is the *fiorentina* steak. This large T-bone-like cut is grilled on the bone and brought to the table over coals. It is sold by weight and made for sharing; expect to pay about 70€ for enough to feed two or three. Pair this or any meat on the menu with simple Tuscan sides like *fagioli all'uccelletto* (beans stewed with tomato). They cater to gluten-free diets and offer child portions, too.

Via Guelfa 81R. www.lagratella.it. © **055/211-292.** Entrees 12€–24€. Daily noon–3pm and 7–11pm. Bus: 1, 6, 11, 14, 17, 23.

INEXPENSIVE
Bondi ★★ LIGHT FARE   To label this place opposite the Mercato Centrale a mere sandwich shop is like describing the Super Bowl as a football game. Bondi is an institution, specializing in *piadine* (flatbread sandwiches) in the Florentine style. Choose from a long list of traditional and unusual sandwiches, toasted or not, then order at the counter and take a seat on rustic wooden benches to await its arrival. Filling combos include anchovies with mozzarella, capers, and tomatoes or eggplant Parmigiana. Wash it down with a glass of Chianti at 2€ a pop. No credit cards.

Via dell'Ariento 85. © **055/287-390.** Sandwiches 3.50€–4.50€. Tues–Sun 11am–11pm. Bus: C1.

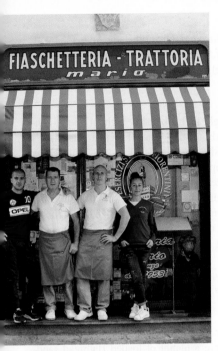

Mario ★★ FLORENTINE There is no doubt this market workers' trattoria is firmly on the tourist trail. But Mario's is as authentic Florentine as you'll find: They even changed their brand of pasta when it started sponsoring soccer rivals, Juventus. Food here clings to the traditions and ethos Mario adopted when the burners first fired up 60 years ago. Food is simple, hearty, and traditionally served at communal tables. If you don't reserve ahead, arrive early, "check in" and you will be offered seats together wherever they come free. A typical meal may be *passato di fagioli* (bean puree soup) followed by traditional Tuscan beef pot roast or *maialino al forno* (roast piglet).

Via Rosina 2R (north corner of Piazza Mercato Centrale). www.trattoriamario.com. ℭ **055/218-550.** Entrees 7.50€–20€. Mon–Sat noon–3pm, Thurs–Fri also 7–10pm. Closed Aug. Bus: C1.

Mario's is a family run Florentine institution since the 1950s.

Mercato Centrale ★★ MODERN ITALIAN The upper floor of Florence's produce market is a bustling shrine to modern street food. Counters offer dishes from all over Italy: authentic Neapolitan pizza, vegetarian and vegan fare, pasta, meats, and cheeses, fresh fish, Chianina burgers or a mixed grill from the butchers' counter, Florentine boiled beef dripping in its own juices, and much more. It's a perfect choice for families who can't agree on a dinner choice. Or just stop by for a drink and soak up the buzz: There's a beer bar and a superb enoteca where you can sip by the glass or bottle.

Piazza Mercato Centrale. www.mercatocentrale.it/firenze. ℭ **055/239-9798.** Dishes 5€–20€. Daily 9am–11pm. Bus: C1.

SandwiChic ★★★ LIGHT FARE Perhaps Florence's best sandwich bar, SandwiChic succeeds because it keeps things simple, with freshly baked bread and expertly sourced ingredients including Tuscan cured meats, preserved vegetables, and savory condiments. Try combinations like *finocchiona* (salami spiked with fennel), pecorino cheese, and *crema di porri* (a creamy leek relish). The inside of this former haberdashery store is a tight squeeze: Go for takeout.

Via San Gallo 3R. www.instagram.com/sandwichic_firenze. ℭ **055/281-157.** Sandwiches 4€–5.50€. Sun–Fri 11am–6pm. Bus: C1.

Near San Marco

San Marco is the place to head for *schiacciata,* olive-oil flatbread loaded with savory toppings. You will find some of the best at **Pugi ★,** Piazza San Marco 9B (www.fornopugi.it; ℰ **055/280-981**), open Monday to Saturday 7:30am to 7:10pm, but closed most of August.

MODERATE

Da Tito ★★★ TUSCAN   Every night feels like party night at one of central Florence's rare genuine neighborhood trattorias. (For that reason, it's usually packed—book ahead.) The dishes are classic Florentine, with a few modern Italian curveballs: Start, perhaps, with a seasonal treat like raw artichokes with shaved Grana Padano cheese or, in summer, *risotto con piselli e guanciale* (rice with fresh peas and cured pork cheek) before going on to a traditional grill such as *lombatina di vitella* (veal chop steak). The neighborhood location, a 10-minute walk north of San Lorenzo, and a mixed clientele keep quality very consistent: We visit again and again, and have yet to be disappointed.

Via San Gallo 112R. https://trattoriadatito.business.site. ℰ **055/472-475.** Entrees 12€–18€. Daily 12:30–3pm and 7–11pm. Bus: C1, 1, 7, 20, 25.

Near Santa Croce

For a fast, informal lunch on the move, squeeze into **SchiacciaMatta ★,** Borgo La Croce 68R (ℰ **055/493-7714**), where a platter of loaded flatbread sandwiches or cold cuts like cured ham and *finocchiona* (fennel-spiked) salami, washed down with a glass of wine, costs around 10€. They also do takeout.

MODERATE

Brac ★★ VEGETARIAN/VEGAN   An artsy cafe-bookshop for most of the day, this place is also one of Florence's best spots for vegetarian and vegan food. A *piatto unico* works out best for hungry diners: one combo plate loaded with three different dishes from the menu, perhaps avocado carpaccio; *agnolotti* (pasta parcels) with red onion, plum, and pine nut cream; plus a *pane carasau* (Sardinian flatbread) with egg and datterini tomatoes. The courtyard atmosphere is intimate and romantic, yet singletons won't feel out of place eating at the counter out front. Reservations are a must at dinner or for Brac's popular Sunday brunch.

Via dei Vagellai 18R. www.libreriabrac.net. ℰ **055/094-4877.** Entrees 10€–18€. Daily noon–midnight. Bus: C1, C3, 23.

Koto ★★ JAPANESE/PACIFIC   Ramen's march to world domination continues, in a city whose culinary traditions could hardly be further from Japan. The cooking here is authentic, however, with each item on the short menu floating in a deep, rich broth that's made in-house (as are the noodles). The *tantan* ramen, with chopped pork, sesame pesto, and Japanese hot pepper, is a spicy treat. Sides are also traditional, including edamame, filled *gyoza,*

Vegans, vegetarians, and booklovers unite at Brac.

and *kara-age* (fried marinated chicken thighs). There's also a strong sake list and a build-your-own poke bowl menu.

Via Verdi 42R. www.kotoramen.it. ℰ **055/0030-154.** Entrees 13€–17€. Daily 12:30–3pm and 7–10:30pm. Closed Aug. Bus: C3.

INEXPENSIVE

Da Rocco ★★ FLORENTINE   This tiny trattoria inside Sant'Ambrogio Market is our favorite place for a bargain full lunch. Behind a takeout counter is an enclosed seating area with snug booths. Hearty dishes of lasagne, roast meats like *coniglio* (rabbit), and *peposo* (spicy beef stew) are plenty filling, especially if you pair one with a side of seasonal vegetables. The house wine is farmhouse Chianti; a bottle is left on the table and you pay for whatever you drink. Get here before 1pm if you want a table. Service is friendly but brisk; lingering is gently discouraged.

Mercato di Sant'Ambrogio. No phone. Entrees 8€. Mon–Sat noon–2:45pm. Bus: C2, C3, or 14.

In the Oltrarno, San Niccolò & San Frediano
EXPENSIVE

iO: Osteria Personale ★★★ MODERN TUSCAN   There's a "grownup hipster" atmosphere here, with the whitewashed brick and young, enthusiastic

The stylish dining room of iO: Osteria Personale.

staff. But a fine dining ethos is ingrained, too. Ingredients are familiar to Tuscan cooking but combined in a fresh way. The menu is short, so iO is a better choice for adventurous rather than fussy eaters. There are always seafood, meat, and vegetarian options: perhaps guinea hen ravioli with roasted pumpkin and laurel followed by pork belly and roasted red pepper with a light tamarind and garam masala sauce. Reservations are advised: This place's reputation has only grown in more than a decade since we first championed it.

Borgo San Frediano 167R. www.io-osteriapersonale.it. ⓒ **055/933-1341.** Entrees 24€–28€; tasting menus 45€–63€. Mon–Sat 7:30–10pm. Closed 10 days Jan and all of Aug. Bus: D or 6.

MODERATE

Il Magazzino ★★ FLORENTINE   A traditional, value *osteria* that specializes in the flavors of old Florence, especially offal. It looks the part, too, with a terracotta tiled floor and barrel vault, chunky wooden furniture, and hanging lamps. If you dare, this is a place to try tripe or *lampredotto* (intestines), the traditional food of working Florentines, prepared expertly in ravioli or meatballs, boiled, or *alla fiorentina* (stewed with tomatoes and garlic). The rest of the menu is carnivore-friendly too: Follow *pici al ragù bianco* (thick spaghetti coated in a "white" veal sauce made with a little milk instead of tomatoes) with *guancia di vitello in agrodolce* (veal cheek stewed with baby onions in a sticky-sweet sauce).

Piazza della Passera 3. ⓒ **055/215-969.** Entrees 12€–20€. Daily noon–3pm and 7:30–11pm. Bus: C3 or C4.

Il Santo Bevitore ★★ MODERN ITALIAN   Sure, this place has lost its original in-the-know, local buzz. But the commitment to top produce served simply, and a trademark take on Tuscan ingredients, is unwavering—and reservations are still a must. Carefully sourced cold cuts make an ideal sharing antipasto: *prosciutto crudo* from the Casentino forests, *pecorino* cheese from Pienza in southern Tuscany. Main courses are eclectic, seasonal, and come in all appetite sizes, from a whole *burrata* (fresh cheese) served with crispy spinach to duck breast with red radicchio and orange. There is a long, expert wine list, with about 10 offered by the glass, plus craft beers.

Via Santo Spirito 66R (at Piazza N. Sauro). www.ilsantobevitore.com. © **055/211-264.** Entrees 15€–25€. Daily 12:30–2:30pm and 7:30–11pm. Closed 10 days mid-Aug. Bus: C3, C4, 6, 11, 36, or 37.

Osteria dell'Enoteca ★★★ MODERN TUSCAN Opened in 2017 by experienced wine bar owners, this place majors in reasonably priced, elegant dining. Traditional flavors dominate, although combinations are just as often modern, in such dishes as a poached egg yolk "*affogato*," floating in a pecorino cheese cream with wild mushrooms, or roast pigeon with Swiss chard. Portions are not large, so cut loose and order three courses. There's also no wine list; an English-speaking waiter leads you to a chiller stocked with boutique labels—strong on Tuscan as well as Langhe/Piedmont reds. The dining room itself is refined, with slate floors, stripped brick, and soft jazz: This is the place for a romantic meal that won't bust your budget. Reservations recommended.

Via Romana 70R. www.osteriadellenoteca.com. © **055/228-6018.** Entrees 14€–24€. Wed–Mon 7–10:30pm; also Fri–Sun noon–2:30pm. Closed Feb. Bus: 11, 36, 37.

Gelato

Having a fair claim to being the birthplace of gelato, Florence has some of the world's best *gelaterie*—but many, many poor imitations, too. Steer clear of spots around the major attractions, where air-fluffed mountains of ice cream are so full of artificial colors and flavors they practically glow in the dark. If you can see the Ponte Vecchio or Piazza della Signoria from the front door of the gelateria, you may want to move on. You might only have to walk a block, or duck down a side street, to find a genuine gelato artisan in the kitchen. Trust us, you'll taste the difference. Opening hours tend to be discretionary: On warm evenings, many places stay open beyond 11pm.

The only way to know which gelato flavor if your favorite is to try them all.

Gelateria della Passera ★★ Milk-free water ices here are intensely flavored, and with a sweetness that doesn't overpower the flavor. Try the likes of pink grapefruit or jasmine tea gelato. Via Toscanella 15R (at Piazza della Passera). www.gelateriadellapassera.it. © **055/291-882.** Cone from 2€. Bus: C3 or C4.

Gelateria de' Neri ★ There's a large range of fruit, white, and chocolate flavors here, but nothing overly elaborate. If the seasonal ricotta and fig flavor is offered, you are in luck. There's also a restroom. Via dei Neri 9R. www.gelateria deineri.it. © **055/210-034.** Cone from 2€. Closed Mon. Bus: C1, C3, 23.

La Carraia ★★ It's packed with locals late into the evening on summer weekends—for good reason. The range is vast, the quality high. Piazza N. Sauro 25R. www.gelaterialacarraia.it. © **055/280-695.** Cone from 2€. Bus: C3, C4, 6, 11, 36, 37. Closed Jan. Also at: Via de' Benci 24R.

EXPLORING FLORENCE

Many major museums now require advance reservations. Check individual museum websites and see "Essential: Reservations for the Uffizi, Accademia & More," p. 204, for details.

Precise opening times can change without notice, especially at city churches. Tourist offices distribute a list of opening hours, updated daily and also free to download from **www.feelflorence.it**. We **strongly advise** down-loading this PDF or collecting it from any tourist office (p. 177) on arrival. In the listings below are the opening times that *usually* apply. You should, alas, treat these as somewhat provisional. Last admission everywhere is usually between 30 and 45 minutes before the official closing time.

Piazza del Duomo

The cathedral square is always lively—filled with tourists and carica-ture artists during the day, strolling pedestrians in the early evening, and students strumming guitars on the Duomo's steps at night. The piazza's vivacity amid the glittering facades of the cathedral and the Baptistery doors makes this an eternal Florentine sight.

Battistero (Baptistery) ★★★ CHURCH In choosing a date to mark the beginning of the Renais-sance, art historians often seize on

The East Doors of the Baptistery.

discount TICKETS FOR FLORENCE

It may seem odd to label the **Firenzecard** (www.firenzecard.it) a "discount" ticket, since it costs a substantial 85€. Is it a good buy? For a busy, museum-packed visit, a Firenzecard is a good value. If you only expect to see a few highlights, skip it.

The details: This card (valid for 72 hr.) allows one-time entrance to 60-plus sites, including the Uffizi, Accademia, Cappella Brancacci, Palazzo Pitti, San Marco, and more. In fact, almost everything we recommend in this chapter *except the Duomo complex* is included with the card, even sites in Fiesole (see chapter 7). A Firenzecard gets you into "fast track" lines everywhere, and it includes prebooking fees—a saving of 3€ to 4€ for museums like the Uffizi and Accademia. However, many museums (including those two) **require Firenzecard holders to prebook** timed admission. The "Museums" section at www.firenzecard.it/en has an easy-to-follow traffic light system for tracking which places require prebooking.

Don't buy a Firenzecard for kids: With a full-priced card you can take family members ages 17 and under for free. Companions under 18 join the express queue with you and pay only the "reservation fee" at state-owned museums (4€ at the Uffizi, for example). Those under 18 also earn free admission to civic museums (such as the Palazzo Vecchio). Private museums and sights have their own payment rules, but this will not add up to 85€ per child. Not even close.

The Firenzecard **excludes** iconic sites on Piazza del Duomo. The **Brunelleschi Pass** gets you into everything here—including climbing the dome—and costs 30€ (12€ for ages 7–14), valid for 3 days. However, to ease crowding, only 1,800 of these comprehensive tickets are sold per day. If your heart is set on climbing the dome, **reserve a time slot as early as you can.** It is **obligatory** when you buy this pass. The cheaper **Giotto Pass** covers everything except the dome (Baptistery, Campanile, and revamped Museo dell'Opera; 20€/7€). The **Ghiberti Pass** excludes the Campanile (15€/5€). The cathedral is always free to visit. See **www.duomo.firenze.it/en** for details. In Florence, you can also buy from the ticket office opposite the cathedral's southern flank, at Piazza del Duomo 14, or inside the Museo dell'Opera. In peak season, it's unlikely any of the 1,800 slots to climb the dome will be left: Plan ahead. **Do not buy "skip the line" or other tickets for Brunelleschi's dome on the street.** These are not valid and you will be turned away.

Another value option for art-lovers is the **PassePartout 5 Days** ticket. It covers the Uffizi (including time slot), Pitti Palace, Boboli Garden, and Museo Archeologico (Mar–Oct 38€, Nov–Feb 18€). The Uffizi must be your first stop, after which you have 5 days to visit the others. You can combine this with a Piazza del Duomo ticket, above, for a shorter, yet still culture-packed visit at lower cost than a Firenzecard.

1401, the year Florence's powerful wool merchants' guild held a contest for the commission to design the **North Doors** ★★ of the Baptistery to match its Gothic **South Doors,** cast 65 years earlier by Andrea Pisano. The era's foremost Tuscan sculptors each cast a bas-relief bronze panel depicting their vision of the "Sacrifice of Isaac." Twenty-two-year-old Lorenzo Ghiberti, competing against Donatello, Jacopo della Quercia, and Filippo Brunelleschi, won. He spent the next 21 years casting 28 bronze panels and building his doors. The restored originals are inside the **Museo dell'Opera del Duomo** (see p. 211).

Florence Attractions

The result so impressed the merchants' guild—not to mention the public and Ghiberti's fellow artists—that they asked him in 1425 to do the **East Doors ★★★,** facing the Duomo, this time giving him artistic freedom to realize his Renaissance ambitions. Twenty-seven years later, just before his death, Ghiberti finished 10 dramatic Old Testament scenes in gilded bronze, each a masterpiece of Renaissance sculpture and some of the finest examples of low-relief perspective in Italian art. Each illustrates episodes in the stories of Noah (second down on left), Moses (second up on left), Solomon (bottom right), and others. The panels mounted here are also copies, created using historically accurate techniques, with the originals displayed in the Museo dell'Opera del Duomo. Years later, Michelangelo was standing before these doors, and someone asked his opinion. His response sums up Ghiberti's accomplishment as no art historian could: "They are so beautiful that they would grace the entrance to Paradise." They've been nicknamed the Gates of Paradise ever since.

The octagonal building itself is ancient, first mentioned in city records in the 9th century but perhaps already 300 years old by then. Its exterior is clad in gleaming white Carrara and green Prato marble; even the roof is marble, making this the world's only building completely covered in marble.

The interior is ringed with columns pilfered from ancient Roman buildings, with a riot of mosaic-work above and below. The floor was inlaid in 1209, and between 1225 and the early 1300s the ceiling was covered with **mosaics ★★** , most of approximately 10 *million* tiles crafted by Venetian or Byzantine-style workshops working off designs by the era's best artists. Coppo di Marcovaldo drew sketches for a 7.8m-high (26-ft.) "Christ in Judgment" and a "Last Judgment" that fills over a third of the ceiling. Four separate, concentric registers tell stories from the Old and New Testaments. Until the 1700s, this was the only place in Florence you could be legally baptized.

Tip: In 2023, a 6-year restoration project of the Baptistery ceiling began, which means its mosaics will not be fully visible from ground level. However, you now have a **once in a lifetime opportunity**—literally—to ascend the scaffolding and see these incredible artworks up close. You get near enough to see mosaic fish and octopus swimming in the waters at Jesus' Baptism. That close. Groups are 10 people maximum; 65€ per person (usually Fri–Sat only). Ages 14 and over only.

Piazza San Giovanni. www.duomo.firenze.it. ℰ **055/264-5789.** For admission prices, see "Discount Tickets for Florence", above. Daily 9am–7:30pm. Bus: C2.

Campanile di Giotto (Giotto's Bell Tower) ★★ ARCHITECTURE
In 1334, Giotto started the cathedral bell tower but completed only the first two levels before his death in 1337. A painter by trade, he was out of his league with the engineering aspects of architecture, and the tower was saved from falling by Andrea Pisano, who doubled the thickness of the walls. Pisano also changed the design to add statue niches—he even carved a few of the statues himself—before quitting the project in 1348. Francesco Talenti finished the job between 1350 and 1359. The **reliefs** and **statues** in the lower levels—by Andrea Pisano, Donatello, Luca della Robbia, and others—are all copies; the weatherworn

originals are housed in the Museo dell'Opera (p. 211). If you're physically fit, we suggest climbing the 414 steps to the top; the **view** ★★ is memorable as you ascend and offers one of the city's best close-ups of Brunelleschi's dome. If cupola tickets are sold out, the Campanile is a worthy substitute.

Piazza del Duomo. www.duomo.firenze.it. ⓒ **055/264-5789.** For admission prices, see "Discount Tickets for Florence" p. 205. Daily 8:15am–7pm. Bus: C2, 14, 23.

Duomo (Cattedrale di Santa Maria del Fiore) ★★★ CATHEDRAL

By the late 13th century, Florence was feeling peevish: Archrivals Siena and Pisa had flamboyant new cathedrals while it was saddled with a tiny 5th- or 6th-century cathedral dedicated to Santa Reparata. So, in 1296, the city hired Arnolfo di Cambio to design a new Duomo, and he raised the facade and the first few bays before his death (around 1310). Work continued under the auspices of the Wool Guild and architects Giotto di Bondone (who concentrated on the bell tower) and Francesco Talenti (who expanded the planned size and finished up to the drum of the dome). Over the centuries, many designs for the unfinished facade were offered and rejected. For one lavish Medici wedding the family even commissioned a temporary facade in papier-mâché. The permanent one is a neo-Gothic design by Emilio de Fabris, built from 1871 to 1887.

The Duomo's most distinctive feature is its enormous **dome** ★★★ (or *cupola*), which dominates the skyline and has become the symbol of Florence itself. The raising of this dome, the largest in the world in its time, was no

mean architectural feat, tackled by Filippo Brunelleschi between 1420 and 1436 (see "A Man & His Dome," p. 210). You can climb up between its two shells for one of the classic panoramas across the city—something that is not recommended for claustrophobes or anyone with no head for heights. Booking a time slot to climb the dome is **compulsory.** Book as far ahead as you can in peak seasons: Only 1,800 people are allowed up each day.

The cathedral interior is quite spartan, but one of the most dramatic episodes in the history of Florence played out here: The attempted assassination of the Medici brothers on Easter Sunday, 1478. The so-called Pazzi Conspiracy failed. Giuliano de'Medici was murdered, but a wounded Lorenzo barricaded himself into a sacristy (no one is certain which of the two) and escaped. Revenge was exacted in

Brunelleschi's dome, seen from the top of Giotto's bell tower.

A MAN & HIS dome

Filippo Brunelleschi, a diminutive man whose ego was as big as his talent, managed in his arrogant, quixotic, and brilliant way to invent Renaissance architecture. Having been beaten by Lorenzo Ghiberti in the contest to cast the **Baptistery** doors (see p. 186), Brunelleschi decided he would rather be Florence's top architect than its second-best sculptor and took off for Rome to study its ancient buildings. On returning to his home city, he combined subdued gray *pietra serena* stone quarried close to Fiesole with smooth white plaster to create airy arches, vaults, and arcades of perfect classical proportions, in his own variant on the ancient Roman orders of architecture. He designed **Santo Spirito** (p. 235), the elegant **Spedale degli Innocenti** (p. 230), a chapel at **Santa Croce** (p. 230), and a new sacristy for **San Lorenzo** (p. 222), but his greatest achievement was erecting the dome over Florence's cathedral.

The Duomo—at that time, the world's largest church—had already been built, but nobody had figured out how to cover the daunting octagonal space over its crossing. No one was even sure they could create a dome which would hold up under its own weight. Brunelleschi insisted he knew how, and once granted the commission, delivered on his ingenious plan, probably inspired by close study of Rome's **Pantheon** (p. 127). He never revealed his method in full, but certainly built the dome in two shells, the inner one thicker than the outer, both shells thinning as they near the top, thus leaving the center hollow and removing much weight. He also planned to construct the dome from giant vaults with ribs crossing them, and dovetailed the bricks making up the dome's fabric in a herringbone pattern. In this way his dome supported itself as it grew, with little need for scaffolding. In the process of building, Brunelleschi found himself as much an inventor as an architect, constantly designing winches and hoists to carry the materials (plus food and drink) faster and more efficiently up to the level of the construction work. Reputedly, only one person died during the build—a drunken worker who fell.

His finished work speaks for itself: This is still the world's largest brick-and-mortar dome, 45m (148 ft.) wide at the base, 90m (295 ft.) high, and built with an estimated 4 million bricks. The marble lantern—which Brunelleschi did not live to see dropped into place in 1446—serves as the structure's keystone. For his achievement, Brunelleschi was accorded the honor of a burial inside Florence's cathedral. Unfortunately, many construction secrets lie there with him. Academics still debate his techniques.

grisly fashion. Plotters including the powerful Pazzi family and the Archbishop of Pisa were found and hanged from the windows of the Palazzo Vecchio.

Restored in 2022, two optical-illusion **equestrian "statues"** ★ decorate the interior's north wall—of English soldier Sir John Hawkwood, painted in 1436 by Paolo Uccello, beside Niccolò da Tolentino by Andrea Del Castagno—elevate these two mercenaries to a status they perhaps did not deserve. The remains and mosaic floors of old **Santa Reparata** ★ are in the crypt. English Mass is Saturdays at 5pm.

Piazza del Duomo. duomo.firenze.it. (✆ **055/264-5789.** Church free admission; for dome admission, see "Discount Tickets for Florence" above. Church Mon–Sat 10:15am–4:30pm; Cupola Mon–Fri 8:15am–6:45pm; Sat 8:15am–4:30pm; Sun 12:45–4:30pm. Bus: C1 or C2.

Sacred sculpture and statuary at the Museo dell'Opera del Duomo.

Museo dell'Opera del Duomo (Cathedral Museum) ★★★

MUSEUM Florence's Cathedral Museum has a major overhaul in 2015, doubling and modernizing the space to show off Italy's second-largest collection of devotional art after the Vatican (p. 103). But at its heart, this is an homage to two Florentine geniuses: Lorenzo Ghiberti and Filippo Brunelleschi.

The location is significant: It was once the workshop where Michelangelo sculpted his statue of "David." Today the museum's prize exhibits are the original **Gates of Paradise ★★★** cast by Lorenzo Ghiberti in the early 1400s (see "Baptistery," p. 186), displayed as the centerpiece of an extraordinary, life-sized re-creation of the early 1400s piazza, complete with a re-imagined version of what the cathedral's Gothic-era facade looked like. Ghiberti's Baptistery **North Doors ★★** have also been moved inside, scrubbed to reveal rose gold below years of soot and dirt. In 2020, Pisano's restored **South Doors ★★** joined them to complete an unparalleled set of bronze relief sculpture. Also on the ground floor, freshly restored in 2021, is Michelangelo's **"Bandini Pietà" ★★** that nearly wasn't. Early in the process he had told students that he wanted this "Pietà" to stand at his tomb, but when he found an imperfection in the marble, he began attacking it with a hammer (look at Christ's left arm). The master never returned to the work, but his students later repaired the damage. The figure of Nicodemus was untouched—legend has it because it was a self-portrait of the artist—a Michelangelo myth that, for once, is probably true.

In a **multimedia section** ★★ dedicated to Brunelleschi, films, displays, and models explain the engineering process behind his dome. Exhibits include some of the original equipment and machines he invented or used. A **roof terrace** ★ provides a photo op and a close-up of his extraordinary achievement.

Elsewhere are works by Donatello—including a restored **"Magdalen"** ★ —as well as Andrea del Verrocchio, Luca della Robbia, and a restored early Giotto **"Madonna"** ★ damaged by the 1993 Uffizi car bomb.

Piazza del Duomo 9 (behind cathedral). www.duomo.firenze.it. © **055/264-5789.** For admission prices, see "Discount Tickets for Florence", above. Daily 9am–7:30pm. Closed 1st Tues of month. Bus: C1.

Around Piazza della Signoria & Santa Trínita

Galleria degli Uffizi (Uffizi Gallery) ★★★ ART MUSEUM   There is no collection of Renaissance art on the planet to match the Uffizi. Period. For this reason, **you must reserve a timed admission slot** as soon as you can. Despite all its crowds and other inconveniences, the Uffizi remains a must-see. And what will you see? Some 60-plus rooms and marble corridors—built in the 16th century as the Medici's private offices, or *uffici*—all packed with famous paintings, among them Botticelli's "Birth of Venus," Leonardo da Vinci's "Annunciation," Michelangelo's "Holy Family," and many, many more.

Initially, rooms are arranged chronologically. **Room A2** begins the pre-Renaissance, Gothic style of painting born in the Middle Ages. Compare

Galleria degli Uffizi, interior.

Cimabue's "Santa Trínita Maestà," painted around 1280, with his student Giotto's **"Ognissanti Madonna" ★★★,** done in 1310. Both paintings have a similar subject and setting but Giotto transformed Cimabue's icon-like Byzantine style into something more human. Giotto's Madonna looks like she's sitting on a throne, her clothes emphasizing the curves of her body, whereas Cimabue's Madonna and angels float in space, like portraits on coins, with stiff positioning. A third great Madonna, Duccio's **"Rucellai Madonna" ★** (1285), was a founding, ethereal work for the Sienese School of painters.

Room A3 showcases the Sienese School at its peak, with Simone Martini's dazzling **"Annunciation" ★★** (1333) slathered in gold ground and Ambrogio Lorenzetti's "Presentation at the Temple" (1342). Tragically, the Black Death of 1348 wiped out this entire generation of Sienese painters (and most of Siena's population along with them). **Rooms A5–A6** show Florentine painting at its most decorative, in a style now termed International Gothic. The iconic work, Gentile da Fabriano's **"Procession of the Magi" ★★★** (1423), depicts the line to see newborn Jesus as full of decorative and comic elements. It is even longer than the line waiting outside the Uffizi.

The unflattering profiles of the Duke Federico da Montefeltro of Urbino and his duchess, painted by **Piero della Francesca ★★★** around 1473, are the centerpiece of **Room A8.** Using newfangled oils rather than the standard tempera (a mix of egg yolk and pigment) enabled Piero to portray his subjects in a starkly realistic way—the duke exposes his warts and his crooked nose, which was broken in a tournament. A focus on earthly, rather than Christian, elements recalls the secular teachings of Greek and Roman times and is made more vivid by a depiction (on the back) of the couple riding chariots driven by the humanistic virtues of faith, charity, hope, and modesty (for her) and prudence, temperance, fortitude, and justice (for him). The same room displays works by **Filippo Lippi** from the mid–15th century. The best backstory belongs to his **"Madonna and Child with Two Angels" ★★,** from around 1465. The work was a celebrity scandal: The woman who modeled for Mary was said to be Filippo's lover—would-be nun Lucrezia Buti, whom he spirited away from a convent before she took vows—and the child looking toward the viewer the product of their union. (That son, Filippino Lippi, would also become a painter of note.) Note the background, with distant mountains on one side and water on the other framing the portrait of a woman's face; Leonardo da Vinci stole the idea 40 years later for his "Mona Lisa." Also here is Paolo Uccello's **"Battle of San Romano"** (1435), essentially an experiment in how to paint perspective—with crazy results.

Rooms A10 to A14 (two linked spaces, despite the numbering) are devoted to the works of Filippo Lippi's student (and later Filippino's teacher) Sandro Filipepi, better known by his nickname "Little Barrels," or Botticelli, one of the most famous artists of the 15th century. Botticelli's 1485 **"Birth of Venus" ★★** hangs like a billboard you have seen a thousand times. Venus's pose is taken from classical statues, while the winds Zephyr and Aura blowing her to shore, and the muse welcoming her, are based on tales from Ovid's

"Metamorphosis." Botticelli's 1478 **"Primavera"** ★★★, its dark, bold colors a stark contrast to filmy, pastel "Venus," defies definitive interpretation. But again it features Venus (center), alongside Mercury, with the winged boots, the Three Graces, and the goddess Flora—as well as staggering botanical detail.

Next, the **Tribuna** ★★ is an architectural oddity, an ornate octagonal room local architect Buontalenti built on the orders of Grand Duke Francesco I. Its centerpiece is the **"Medici Venus"** ★★, a Greek marble crafted in the 1st century B.C. Botticelli copied her pose for his famous Venus (as have many others over the centuries).

To cross to the Uffizi's west wing, you pass picture windows with views of the Arno River to one side and the perfect Renaissance perspective of the Uffizi piazza to the other—plus an often-overlooked Roman sculpture gallery most museums would kill for.

The Uffizi's west wing houses two true Renaissance heavyweights. **Room A35** displays Leonardo da Vinci's magnificent, unfinished **"Adoration of the Magi"** ★★★—much of the master's line drawing is still visible— beside his **"Annunciation"** ★★. In the latter, completed in the early 1470s while Leonardo was still a student in Verrocchio's workshop, his ability to orchestrate the viewer's focus is masterful: The line down the middle of the brick corner of the house draws your glance to Mary's delicate fingers, which themselves point along the top of a stone wall to the angel's two raised fingers. Those, in

"The Birth of Venus" by Botticelli in the Uffizi Gallery.

turn, draw attention to the mountain between the two parallel trees dividing Mary from the angel, representing the gulf between the worldly and the spiritual. Its apparently warped perspective was in fact painted intentionally, to be viewed from the lower right.

Room A38 is dedicated to the other two Italian masters of the High Renaissance. In Michelangelo's 1505–08 **"Holy Family"** ★, the twisting shapes of Mary, Joseph, and Jesus recall those in the Sistine Chapel for their sculpted form and bright colors. Among several Uffizi Raphaels, his enchanting **"Madonna of the Goldfinch"** ★★ has a background landscape in the style of Leonardo and Botticelli.

The torsion and tensions of Michelangelo's painting and sculpture inspired the next generation of Florentine painters, known as the **Mannerists** ★★. Andrea Del Sarto (**Room D2**), Rosso Fiorentino, and Pontormo (**Room D4**) are the focus of a suite of rooms downstairs, inaugurated in 2021 and dedicated to the **Cinquecento** (1500s). **Room D22** shows off Titian's reclining nude **"Venus of Urbino"** ★★. It's no coincidence that the edge of the curtain, the angle of her hand and leg, and the line splitting floor and bed all intersect at the forbidden part of her body. It's the highlight of a large collection of Venetian Renaissance art, which also includes Tintoretto and Giorgione.

The final big-hitters are in the **Sale Seicento (1600s Rooms):** paintings by Caravaggio, notably his crazed **"Medusa"** ★ self-portrait and an enigmatic **"Bacchus"** ★. These rooms also explore the 17th-century artists who aped his *chiaroscuro* (bright light and dark shadows) style. Greatest among them was Artemisia Gentileschi, a rare female painter from this period. Her **"Judith Slaying Holofernes"** ★ (ca. 1612), is one of the bloodiest paintings in the gallery.

If you find yourself flagging at any point (it happens to us all), a **coffee shop** is at the far end of the upper floor's west wing. Prices are in line with the piazza below, plus you get a great close-up of the Palazzo Vecchio's facade from the terrace. Fully refreshed, you can return to discover works by the many great artists we haven't space to cover here: Cranach, Rembrandt, and Dürer; Velazquez, El Greco, and Goya; Bellini, and Mantegna; and Masaccio, Bronzino, Parmigianino, and Veronese. In short, there is nowhere like the Uffizi—in Italy or anywhere else in the world.

Piazzale degli Uffizi 6 (off Piazza della Signoria). www.uffizi.it. (Reserve tickets at www.firenzemusei.it or ☏ **055/294-883.**) Admission Mar–Oct 25€ (19€ before 9am); Nov–Feb 12€; free for children 17 and under (booking fee still applies). Tues–Sun 8:15am–6:30pm; prebooking compulsory. Bus: C1 or C2.

Museo Nazionale del Bargello (Bargello Museum) ★★ MUSEUM

This is the most important museum anywhere for Renaissance **sculpture**—yet it's often quieter than other museums in the city. Originally the city's prison, torture chamber, and execution site, the Bargello now stands as a three-story art museum containing some of the best of Michelangelo, Donatello, and Ghiberti, as well as of their most successful Mannerist successor, Giambologna.

The Bargello Museum is a treasure trove of Renaissance sculpture and art.

In the ground-level Michelangelo room, you can scope out the variety of his craft, from a whimsical 1497 **"Bacchus"** ★★ to a severe, unfinished "Brutus" of 1539. "Bacchus," created when Michelangelo was just 22, genuinely looks drunk, leaning back a little too far, his head off kilter, with a cupid about to bump him over. Nearby is Giambologna's twisting **"Mercury"** ★ taking flight, propelled by the breath of Zephyr. Cellini's bronze "Cosimo I" casts the Florentine Grand Duke in the role of Roman imperial general. It was created around the same time as his "Perseus" (see below).

Upstairs a vaulted hall is filled with some of Donatello's most accomplished sculptures, including his original "Marzocco" (once outside the Palazzo Vecchio; p. 218), and **"St. George"** ★, from an exterior niche on Orsanmichele (p. 217). Notable among them is his bronze **"David"** ★★ (which some think might actually be the god Mercury), done around 1440, Italy's first freestanding nude sculpture after Roman times. The classical detail of these sculptures, as well as their naturalistic poses and reflective mood, is the essence of the Renaissance style.

Side by side on the back wall are the contest entries submitted by Ghiberti and Brunelleschi for the commission to do the Baptistery doors in 1401. With the "Sacrifice of Isaac" as their Biblical theme, both displayed innovative use of perspective. Ghiberti won the contest, perhaps because his scene is more thematically unified. Brunelleschi could have ended up a footnote in art history, but instead he gave up the chisel and turned his attention to architecture instead (see "A Man & His Dome," p. 210).

Faded 1330s frescoes by Giotto's workshop decorate the **Cappella della Maddalena,** the room where prisoners would wait before execution. Further extensive sections are dedicated to Italian majolica and Islamic art (carpets and ceramics).

Via del Proconsolo 4. www.bargellomusei.beniculturali.it. ℂ **055/064-9440.** Admission 9€. Wed–Fri and Sun–Mon 8:45am–1:30pm; Sat 8:15am–6:30pm. Closed 2nd and 4th Sun of each month. Bus: C1 or C2.

Orsanmichele ★★ CHURCH   This bulky structure halfway down Via dei Calzaiuoli looks less like a church than a Gothic warehouse—which is exactly what it was, built as a granary and grain market in 1337. After a miraculous image of the Madonna appeared on a column inside, its lower level was turned into a shrine and chapel. The city's merchant guilds each decorated a Gothic tabernacle around the outside with a statue of their guild's patron saint. Masters such as Ghiberti, Donatello, Verrocchio, and Giambologna all cast or carved masterpieces to set here (those remaining are mostly copies, including Donatello's "St. George"). Reopened after a 2023 restoration, the dark interior has an elaborate Gothic stone **Tabernacle** ★ (1349–59) by Andrea Orcagna which protects a luminous 1348 "Madonna and Child" painted by Giotto's student Bernardo Daddi, to which miracles were ascribed during the Black Death of 1348–50.

Upstairs, the airy rooms of the **Museo di Orsanmichele** ★ house many original sculptures which once adorned the exterior niches. Among its treasures are a trio of bronzes: Ghiberti's "St. John the Baptist" (1412–16), the first life-size bronze of the Renaissance; Verrocchio's "Incredulity of St. Thomas" (1483); and Giambologna's "St. Luke" (1602). Climb up one more floor, to the top, for an unforgettable **360° panorama** ★★ of the city.

Via Arte della Lana 1. www.bargellomusei.beniculturali.it. ℂ **055/238-8610.** Admission 4€. Hours vary during restoration; check website. Bus: C2.

Palazzo Davanzati ★★ HISTORIC HOME   Reopened after a 2022 restoration, one of the best-preserved 14th-century palaces in the city offers a glimpse of domestic life during the medieval and Renaissance period. It was originally built for the Davizzi family in the mid-1300s, then bought by the Davanzati clan in 1558; the latter's family tree, dating back to the 1100s, is emblazoned on the ground-floor courtyard walls. Painted wooden ceilings and murals have aged well (even surviving World War II damage). However, the emphasis here is not on façade, but on insights into the medieval life of a noble Florentine family: feasts and festivities in the **Sala Madornale;** a private internal well to secure water supply when things in Florence got sticky; and magnificent 14th-century bedchamber frescoes that recount, comic-strip style, "The Chatelaine of Vergy," a medieval morality tale. Interesting footnote: In 1916, a New York auction of furnishings from this palace launched a "Florentine style" trend in U.S. interior design circles, and 2 years later, the

When the medieval Guelph party came out on top after a long political struggle with the Ghibellines, they razed part of Florence's old city center to build a new palace for civic government. It's reputed that Guelphs ordered architect Arnolfo di Cambio to build what we now call the **Palazzo Vecchio** ★★ (p. 218) in the corner of this space to make sure not an inch would sit on Ghibelline land. (This odd legend was probably fabricated to explain Arnolfo's off-center architecture.) At any rate, the L-shaped space around the *palazzo* became the new civic center of town, **Piazza della Signoria** ★★, named after the medieval city's oligarchic ruling body (the "Signoria"). Today, it's an outdoor sculpture gallery, teeming with tourists and horse-and-buggies, and ringed by outdoor cafes. If you want to catch the square at its serene best, arrive by 8am and have it to yourself.

The statuary on the piazza is particularly beautiful, starting on the far left (as you face the Palazzo Vecchio) with Giambologna's 1594 equestrian statue of Grand Duke Cosimo I. To its right is one of Florence's favorite sculptures to hate, the **Fontana del Nettuno** (Neptune Fountain; 1560–75), created by Bartolomeo Ammannati as a tribute to Cosimo I's naval ambitions. "Il Biancone" ("Big Whitey") is whiter than ever and spurting water enthusiastically, after a restoration funded by the Ferragamo fashion house. A **porphyry plaque** in the ground in front of the fountain marks the site where puritanical monk Savonarola held the Bonfire of the Vanities: With fiery apocalyptic preaching, he whipped Florentines into a frenzy. Hundreds filed into this piazza, arms loaded with their "decadent" possessions to throw it all on the flames.

To the right of Neptune, a raised platform fronting the Palazzo Vecchio was known as the *arringheria*, from which soapbox speakers would lecture to crowds (from where we get our word "harangue"). On its far-left is a copy (original in the Bargello, p. 215) of Donatello's "Marzocco," symbol of the city, a Florentine lion resting his raised paw on a shield emblazoned with the *giglio* (lily). To its right is another Donatello replica, "Judith Beheading Holofernes." Farther down is a man who needs little introduction, Michelangelo's **"David,"** a 19th-century copy of the original now in the Accademia (p. 227). Near enough to David to look truly ugly in comparison is Baccio Bandinelli's lumpy "Hercules and Cacus" (1534).

At the piazza's south end, the **Loggia dei Lanzi** ★★ (1376–82) is named after the Swiss guard of lancers (*lanzi*) whom Cosimo de' Medici stationed here. (It's

set for the Met Opera premiere of Puccini's "Gianni Schicchi" was based on Palazzo Davanzati interiors.

Via Porta Rossa 13. www.bargellomusei.beniculturali.it. ⓒ **055/064-9460.** Admission 6€. Fri–Sun 1:15–6:50pm; Tues–Thurs 8:15am–1:50pm. Closed 1st, 3rd, and 5th Sun of each month. Bus: C2.

Palazzo Vecchio ★★ PALACE/MUSEUM   The core of this fortress-like town hall was built from 1299 to 1302 to the designs of Arnolfo di Cambio, master builder of Gothic-era Florence. Home to centuries of Florentine government, the palace is still city hall. When Duke Cosimo I and his Medici family moved to the *palazzo* in 1540, they redecorated: Michelozzo's 1453 **courtyard** ★ was left architecturally intact but frescoed by Vasari with scenes of Austrian cities, to celebrate the 1565 marriage of Francesco I de' Medici and also called the Loggia della Signoria or the Loggia di Orcagna, after its designer Andrea Orcagna.) At front left stands Benvenuto Cellini's masterpiece in bronze, **"Perseus" ★★★** (1545), holding up the severed head of Medusa. On the far right is Giambologna's **"Rape of the Sabines" ★★,** one of the most successful Mannerist sculptures in existence. You must walk all the way around to appreciate it, catching the action and artistry of its spiral design from different angles. Talk continues about moving it indoors, safe from the elements, and a copy has been commissioned...but for now, it's still here.

The controversial Fountain of Neptune in Piazza della Signoria.

Joanna of Austria. A grand staircase leads up to the **Sala dei Cinquecento ★,** named for a 500-man assembly that met here in the pre-Medici days of the Florentine Republic. It's also the site of the greatest fresco cycle that ever wasn't: Leonardo da Vinci was commissioned in 1503–05 to paint one long wall with a scene celebrating Florence's victory at the 1440 Battle of Anghiari. Always trying new methods and materials, he decided to mix wax into his pigments. Leonardo had finished painting part of the wall, but it wasn't drying fast enough, so he brought in braziers stoked with hot coals to hurry the process. As onlookers watched in horror, the wax in the fresco melted under the heat and colors ran to a puddle on the floor. The search for what remains of his work continues; some hope emerged in 2012 with the uncovering of pigments similar to those used by Leonardo in a cavity behind the current wall.

Vasari's Corridor

The enclosed passageway that runs along the top of the Ponte Vecchio is part of the **Corridoio Vasariano (Vasari Corridor)** ★, a private elevated link between the Palazzo Vecchio and Palazzo Pitti. Duke Cosimo I found the idea of mixing with the hoi polloi on his way to work distressing—and assassination was a real risk—so he commissioned Vasari to design his V.I.P. route in 1565. His former secret commuter passageway is now hung with the world's best collection of artists' self-portraits. The corridor has been closed since 2016, but is scheduled to open for public access by 2024. Inquire at the tourist office or check **www.uffizi.it/corridoio-vasariano** for updates.

Michelangelo was also supposed to paint a fresco on the opposite wall, but he never got past preparatory drawings before Pope Julius II called him to Rome to paint the Sistine Chapel. Vasari and his assistants covered the bare walls from 1563 to 1565, with subservient frescoes exalting Cosimo I and the military victories of his regime, against Pisa (on the near wall) and Siena (far wall). Opposite the door you enter, Michelangelo's statue of **"Victory"** ★ originally carved from 1533 to 1534 for Pope Julius II's tomb, was later donated to the Medici.

The first series of rooms on the upper floor façades the **Quartiere degli Elementi,** frescoed with allegories and mythological characters, again by Vasari. Crossing the balcony overlooking the Sala dei Cinquecento, you enter the **Apartments of Eleonora di Toledo** ★, decorated for Cosimo's Spanish wife. Her **private chapel ★★★** is a masterpiece of mid–16th-century fresco painting by Bronzino. Under the coffered ceiling of the **Sala dei Gigli** is Ghirlandaio's fresco of "St. Zenobius Enthroned," with figures from Republican and Imperial Rome, and Donatello's original **"Judith and Holofernes"** ★ bronze (1455), one of his last works. In the palace basement the **Scavi del Teatro Romano** ★ are remnants of the Roman Florentia theater, upon which the medieval palace was built, with walls and an intact paved street.

Visitors can also climb the **Torre di Arnolfo** ★★, the palace's crenelated tower. If you can bear small spaces and 218 steps, the views from the top of this medieval skyscraper are sublime. The 95m (312-ft.) Torre is closed in bad weather; the minimum age to climb up is 6, and children ages 17 and under must be accompanied by an adult.

Piazza della Signoria. ticketsmuseums.comune.fi.it. ℂ **055/276-8325.** Palazzo 12.50€; Torre 12.50€; free for children 17 and under. Palazzo: Fri–Wed 9am–7pm, Thurs 9am–2pm; Torre: Mon–Wed and Fri 9am–5pm, Thurs 9am–2pm. Bus: C1 or C2.

Ponte Vecchio ★ ARCHITECTURE   The oldest and most famous bridge across the Arno, the Ponte Vecchio was built in 1345–50 by Taddeo Gaddi to replace an earlier version. Overhanging shops have lined a bridge here since at least the 12th century. In the 16th century, it was home to butchers, until Duke Ferdinand I moved into the Palazzo Pitti across the river. He couldn't

Ponte Vecchio seen from the Vasari Corridor.

stand the stench, so he evicted the meat cutters and moved in goldsmiths, silversmiths, and jewelers, who occupy it to this day.

In 1944 the Ponte Vecchio's fame saved it from the Nazis, who had orders to blow up all the bridges before retreating as Allied forces advanced. They couldn't bring themselves to reduce this span to rubble, so instead they blew up the ancient buildings on either end to block it off. Less discriminating was the **Great Arno Flood** of 1966, which severely damaged the shops. A private night watchman saw waters rising alarmingly and called many of the goldsmiths at home. They rushed to remove valuable stock before it was washed away. *Tip:* The Ponte Vecchio is a busy bottleneck for people crossing the river. If you are not comfortable in crowds, we recommend you take another bridge, any of which will be much quieter.

Via Por Santa Maria/Via Guicciardini. Bus: C3 or C4.

Santa Trínita ★★ CHURCH   Behind Bernardo Buontalenti's late-16th-century facade lies a dark church, rebuilt in the 14th century but founded by the Vallombrosan order before 1177. The third chapel on the right has remains of 14th-century frescoes of the "Madonna Enthroned" by Spinello Aretino, found beneath Lorenzo Monaco's 1424 "Scenes from the Life of the Virgin" frescoes in the next chapel along. The chapel's iron gate is contemporaneous (1420). In the right transept, Ghirlandaio frescoed the **Cappella Sassetti ★** in

Catch an Exhibition at the Strozzi

The Renaissance **Palazzo Strozzi ★★,** Piazza Strozzi (www.palazzostrozzi.org; ℭ **055/264-5155**), is Florence's major space for temporary and contemporary art shows, and has been experiencing a 21st-century rebirth of its own. Hit shows in recent years include Bill Viola's "Electronic Renaissance" in 2017 and Olafur Eliasson in 2023. There's usually plenty going on around each show, including talks, late openings (usually Thurs), and downloadable activity kits for kids. Check the website. Admission to headline exhibitions is usually around 15€.

1485 with a cycle on the "Life of St. Francis," setting all the scenes against Florentine backdrops peopled with portraits of contemporary notables. His "Francis Receiving the Order from Pope Honorius" (in the lunette) takes place under an arcade on the north side of Piazza della Signoria; you'll recognize the Loggia dei Lanzi in the middle, and on the left, the Palazzo Vecchio (the Uffizi hadn't yet been built). Take a 2€ coin for the chapel lights. *Tip:* The south end of the piazza leads to the **Ponte Santa Trínita ★★,** Florence's most graceful bridge. In 1567, Ammannati built this span, set with four 16th-century statues of the seasons, for the wedding of Cosimo II. After the Nazis blew up the bridge in 1944, it was rebuilt and everything was set in place save the head on the statue of "Spring," which remained lost until a team dredging the river in 1961 found it by accident. If you want to photograph the Ponte Vecchio, head here at dusk.

Piazza Santa Trínita. ℭ **055/216-912.** Free admission. Mon–Sat 8am–noon and 4–6:15pm; Sun 8:15–10:45am and 4–6:15pm. Bus: C3, C4, 6, 11.

Around San Lorenzo & the Mercato Centrale

The church of San Lorenzo was once lost behind the leather and souvenir stalls of Florence's **San Lorenzo Street Market** (see p. 239), until a decade ago, when carts were moved into adjacent streets. A bustle of commerce characterizes this whole neighborhood, centered on both the tourist market and the nearby **Mercato Centrale,** whose upper floor is a showcase for Italian street food (see p. 239).

Cappelle Medicee (Medici Chapels) ★ MONUMENT/MUSEUM When Michelangelo built San Lorenzo's New Sacristy between 1520 and 1533 (finished by Vasari in 1556), it was to be a tasteful monument to Lorenzo the Magnificent and his generation of relatively enlightened Medici. When work got underway in 1604 on the adjacent **Cappella dei Principi** (Chapel of the Princes), it was to become one of Italy's most arrogant memorials, dedicated to the grand dukes, whose ranks include some of Florence's most decrepit tyrants. The Cappella dei Principi is a mountain of cut marbles and semiprecious stones—jasper, alabaster, mother-of-pearl, agate, and the like—slathered on walls and ceiling with no regard for composition and still less for chromatic unity. The pouring of ducal funds into this monstrosity lasted until

The Chapel of the Princes of the Medici Chapels.

Gian Gastone de' Medici drank himself to death in 1737, without an heir. Teams kept doggedly at the thing and were still finishing the floor in 1962. It was once again restored in 2019; judge for yourself.

Michelangelo's **Sagrestia Nuova (New Sacristy)** ★★, built to jibe with Brunelleschi's Old Sacristy in San Lorenzo proper (see p. 224), is much calmer. (An architectural tidbit: The windows in the dome taper as they get near the top to fool you into thinking the dome is higher.) Michelangelo was supposed to produce three tombs here (perhaps four) but ironically got only the two less important ones done. So, Lorenzo de' Medici ("the Magnificent")—wise ruler of his city, poet of note, grand patron of the arts, moneybags behind much of the Renaissance, and subject of his own Netflix miniseries—ended up with a mere inscription of his name next to his brother Giuliano's on a plain marble slab against the entrance wall. They did get one Michelangelo sculpture to decorate their slab, an unfinished **"Madonna and Child"** ★. On the left wall of the sacristy, Michelangelo's **"Tomb of Lorenzo"** ★ commemorates the duke of Urbino (Lorenzo the Magnificent's grandson), whose seated statue symbolizes the contemplative life. Below him on the curves of the tomb stretch a pair of sculptures, "Dawn" (female) and "Dusk" (male). Observing them, one wonders if Michelangelo perhaps hadn't seen many naked women.

Piazza Madonna degli Aldobrandini (where Via Faenza and Via del Giglio meet). ℂ **055/238-8602.** Admission 9€; free for children 17 and under. Mon and Wed–Sat 8:15am–6:50pm; Sun 8:15–1:45pm. Bus: C1, C2, 22.

Palazzo Medici-Riccardi ★ HISTORIC HOME   Built by Michelozzo in 1444 for Medici "Godfather" Cosimo il Vecchio, this is the prototype Florentine *palazzo,* on which the more overbearing Strozzi and Pitti palaces were later modeled. It remained the Medici private home until Cosimo I (not the same guy) officially declared his power as duke by moving to the Palazzo Vecchio, the city's civic nerve center. A door off the grandiose courtyard designed by Michelozzo leads up a staircase to the **Cappella dei Magi,** the oldest chapel to survive inside a private Florentine palace; its walls are covered with dense and colorful Benozzo Gozzoli **frescoes** ★★ (1459–63), classics of the International Gothic style. The walls depict an extended "Journey of the Magi" to see the Christ child, who's being adored by Mary in the altarpiece.

Via Cavour 3. www.palazzomediciriccardi.it. ⓒ **055/276-0552.** Admission 7€ (10€ during temporary exhibitions); free for children 17 and under; free admission to courtyard and citrus garden. Thurs–Tues 9am–7pm. Bus: C1, 14, 23.

San Lorenzo ★★ CHURCH   A rough brick anti-facade fronts what is most likely the oldest church in Florence, founded in A.D. 393. It was later the Medici family's parish church, and Cosimo il Vecchio, whose wise behind-the-scenes rule made him popular with Florentines, is buried in front of the high altar. A plaque marking the spot is inscribed PATER PATRIAE, "Father of the Homeland." Off the left transept, the **Sagrestia Vecchia (Old Sacristy)** ★ is one of Brunelleschi's purest pieces of early Renaissance architecture. The focal sarcophagus contains Cosimo il Vecchio's parents, Giovanni di Bicci de' Medici and his wife, Piccarda Bueri. A side chapel is decorated with a star map showing the night sky above the city in the 1440s—a scene that also features, precisely, in Brunelleschi's Pazzi Chapel in Santa Croce; see p. 230. On the wall of the main church's left aisle is Bronzino's huge fresco of the **"Martyrdom of San Lorenzo"** ★ (1568), showing the poor saint being roasted on a grill in Rome. Round the corner in the transept is another highlight: Filippo Lippi's **"Annunciation"** ★ (1447), heavily influenced by Flemish art. Two **bronze nave pulpits** ★★, depicting the "Passion" and "Resurrection," are thought to be Donatello's final completed works.

Piazza San Lorenzo. www.sanlorenzofirenze.it. ⓒ **055/214-042.** Admission 9€; free for children 11 and under. Mon–Sat 10am–4pm. Bus: C1.

Near Piazza Santa Maria Novella

The two squat obelisks in **Piazza Santa Maria Novella** ★, resting on tortoises by Giambologna, once served as turning posts for "chariot" races held here from the 16th to the mid–19th century. Down-at-heel just a couple of decades ago, this neighborhood now has some of Florence's priciest hotels.

Museo Marino Marini & Cappella Rucellai ★ MUSEUM   One of Florence's quirkiest museums showcases the work of sculptor Marino Marini (1901–80). A native of nearby Pistoia, Marini worked mostly in bronze, with "horse and rider" a recurring theme in his semi-abstract work. The open spaces, minimal crowds, monumental sculptures, and fun themes in Marini's

The geometric perfection of Santa Maria Novella.

work make this museum a good bet if kids are weary of the Renaissance. They won't escape it entirely, however: Tagged onto the side of the museum is the **Cappella Rucellai,** a Renaissance chapel housing the **Tempietto ★★,** a polychrome marble tomb completed by L. B. Alberti for Giovanni de' Rucellai in 1467. Decorated with symbols of both the Rucellai and Medici families, and frescoed on the inside, the tomb was supposedly based on drawings of the Holy Sepulcher in Jerusalem.

Piazza San Pancrazio. museomarinomarini.it. ⓒ **055/219-432.** Admission 10€. Sat–Mon 10am–7pm. Bus: C3, 6, 11.

Museo Novecento ★★ MUSEUM   This 21st-century museum covers 20th-century Italian art in a multitude of media. Crowds are often sparse—let's face it, you're in Florence to experience the 1400s, not the 1900s. This is no reflection on the collection's quality, which spans 100 years of visual arts. Exhibits include works by major names such as De Chirico and Futurist Gino Severini; examinations of Florence's major role in fashion; and Italy's relationship with European avant-garde art. In a tiny top-floor room, a 20-minute movie-clip montage shows Florence through the lens of the century's filmmakers, from Arnaldo Ginna's 1916 "Vita Futurista" to more recent hits like "Room with a View" and "Tea with Mussolini."

Piazza Santa Maria Novella 10. www.museonovecento.it/en. ⓒ **055/276-8224.** Admission 9.50€; free for children 17 and under. Fri–Wed 11am–8pm. Bus: 6 or 11.

Ognissanti ★★ CHURCH   The Biblical Last Supper (*Cenacolo* in Italian) was a favorite commission for wealthy Renaissance monasteries and convents, usually for their refectory (dining hall). Florence has several, including in the old refectory at **San Marco** (p. 228). Ghirlandaio's 1480 version here is set in a vaulted loggia beside a citrus grove with abundant bird life, all painted precisely in fresco. (Viewing hours are unfortunately limited.)

The church facade itself has a baroque facade, a common sight in Rome but unusual for Florence. It also has long links to the Vespucci family, whose most famous son—Amerigo—made his name as a seafaring explorer. Painted shortly before he did his Last Supper, Ghirlandaio's **"Madonna della Misericordia"** ★ on the aisle wall is basically a Vespucci family portrait. Amerigo is in the top-left. Among other art treasures is a Giotto **Crucifix** (ca. 1320) in the left transept.

Borgo Ognissanti 42. ℂ **055/239-8700.** Free admission. Cenacolo: hours vary. Church: Mon and Wed–Sat 9am–1pm and 3:30–7:30pm (Sat closes 6pm); Sun 3:30–7:30pm. Bus: C4.

Santa Maria Novella ★★★ CHURCH   Of all Florence's major churches, the home of the Dominicans is the only one with a contemporaneous **facade** ★★. The lower Romanesque half was started in the 1300s by architect Fra Jacopo Talenti. Renaissance architect Leon Battista Alberti finished it, adding a classically inspired top that not only chimed seamlessly with the lower half but also created a Cartesian plane of perfect geometry. Inside, Masaccio's **"Trinità"** ★★★ (ca. 1425) was the first painting ever to use linear mathematical perspective. Florentine citizens and artists flooded in to see the fresco's unveiling, many in awe that it seemed to punch a hole into space, creating a chapel out of a flat wall. Frescoes by Filippino Lippi and others fill the **transept.** The **Sanctuary** ★ behind the main altar was painted after 1485 by Ghirlandaio with the help of apprentices, probably including a young Michelangelo. The left wall is covered with a cycle on the "Life of the Virgin," and the right has a "Life of St. John the Baptist," works that are also snapshots of the era's fashions, stuffed with portraits of the Tornabuoni family who commissioned them.

The church and convent cloisters are now accessible on one admission ticket. The **Chiostro Verde (Green Cloister)** ★★ was partly frescoed between 1431 and 1446 by Paolo Uccello, a Florentine painter who became increasingly obsessed with the mathematics behind perspective. His Old Testament scenes include a "Universal Deluge," which ironically was badly damaged by the Great Arno Flood of 1966. Off the cloister, the **Spanish Chapel** ★ is a complex piece of Dominican propaganda, frescoed in the 1360s by Andrea di Bonaiuto. The **Chiostro dei Morti (Cloister of the Dead)** ★, one of the oldest parts, was also badly damaged in 1966. Its low-slung vaults were decorated by Andrea Orcagna and others. Visitors can also access the **Chiostro Grande** (Florence's largest cloister) and papal apartments frescoed by Florentine Mannerist painter Pontormo. Allow at least 90 minutes to explore this complex fully.

Tip: Take home some of the divinely scented soaps and skincare products of Florence's famed herbal pharmacy **Officina Profumo-Farmaceutica di Santa Maria Novella,** next door at Via della Scala 16. It traces its roots to 13th-century Dominican friars who founded the Santa Maria Novella convent (see "Shopping in Florence," p. 238).

Piazza Santa Maria Novella/Piazza della Stazione 4. www.smn.it. ⓒ **055/219-257.** Admission 7.50€ (10€ during exhibition). Mon–Sat 9:30am–5pm (Fri from 11am); Sun noon–5pm. Bus: C2, 6, 11, 22.

Near San Marco & Santissima Annunziata

Cenacolo di Sant'Apollonia ★ CONVENT/MUSEUM   Andrea del Castagno (1421–57) learned his trade painting portraits of condemned men in city prisons, and the influence of this apprenticeship is apparent on the faces of the disciples in his version of **"The Last Supper,"** the first of many painted in Florence during the Renaissance. This giant fresco, completed around 1447, covers an entire wall at one end of the former convent refectory. Judas is banished to the far side of a communal table. Castagno's "Crucifixion," "Deposition," and "Entombment" complete the sequence.

Via XXVII Aprile 1. ⓒ **055/238-8608.** Free admission. Daily 8:15am–1:50pm. Closed 1st, 3rd, and 5th Sat and Sun of each month. Bus: 1, 6, 11, 14, 17, 23.

Galleria dell'Accademia ★★ ART MUSEUM   The Accademia's star exhibit, **"David"** ★★★—"Il Gigante"—is much larger than you imagine, looming 4.8m (16 ft.) on top of a 1.8m (6-ft.) pedestal. He hasn't faded with time, either; the marble still gleams as if it were unveiling day in 1504. Viewing the statue is a pleasure in the bright and spacious room custom-designed for him after his move to the Accademia in 1873, following 300 years of pigeons perching on his head in Piazza della Signoria. (Replicas now take the abuse there, and at Piazzale Michelangelo; the spot high on the northern flank of the Duomo, for which he was originally commissioned, stands empty.) But the Accademia is not only about "David"; you will be delighted to discover he is surrounded by an entire museum of Renaissance works. Michelangelo's unfinished **"Prisoners"** ★★ statues are a contrast to "David," their rough forms struggling to emerge from the raw stone. Michelangelo famously said he tried to free the sculpture from within every block, and you can appreciate this technique here.

New **Renaissance rooms** showcase devotional paintings by Perugino, Filippino Lippi, and Paolo Uccello, as well as a preparatory model for the **"Rape of the Sabines"** ★ from the Loggia dei Lanzi (p. 218)—one of the world's oldest 1:1 scale models. Medieval rooms which extend upstairs showcase medieval Florentine art from 1370 onward, including Giotto and Andrea Orcagna. Also reopened after a 2-year restoration project, the **Plaster Cast Gallery (Gipsoteca)** ★★ displays more than 400 casts in a fresh, "studio" style, many by 19th-century sculptor Lorenzo Bartolini.

Via Ricasoli 60. www.galleriaaccademiafirenze.it. ⓒ **055/294-883.** Admission 12€; free for children 17 and under (prebooking compulsory). Tues–Sun 8:15am–6:50pm. Bus: C1, 1, 6, 14, 19, 23, 31, 32.

MAF Museo Archeologico Nazionale (Archaeological Museum) ★

MUSEUM   If you can force yourselves away from the Renaissance, rewind a millennium or two at one of the most important archaeological collections in central Italy. It has a particular emphasis on the Etruscan period. You'll need a little patience, however: The collection inside 17th-century Palazzo della Crocetta is not easy to navigate, though you will easily find the **"Arezzo Chimera"** ★★, a bronze figure of a mythical lion–goat–serpent dating to the 4th century B.C., perhaps the most important bronze sculpture to survive from the Etruscan era. It's displayed alongside the "Arringatore," a life-size bronze of an orator dating to the 1st century, just as Etruscan culture was being subsumed by Ancient Rome. On the top floor is the **"Idolino"** ★, an exquisite and slightly mysterious, lithe bronze. The collection is strong on Etruscan-era *bucchero* pottery and funerary urns, and Egyptian relics including several sarcophagi displayed in a series of eerie galleries. In 2018, the museum inaugurated a section dedicated to the vast collection of gems, cameos, and intaglio gathered by generations of Medici and Lorraine dukes. Some pieces date back many centuries B.C. With other travelers so focused on medieval and Renaissance sights in the city, you may have this museum almost to yourself.

Piazza Santissima Annunziata 9b. ☎ **055/23-575.** Admission 8€ (free with Uffizi ticket). Mon, Wed, Fri, and Sat 8:30am–2pm; Tues and Thurs 8:30am–7pm; open 1st Sun of each month 8:30am–2pm. Bus: 6, 19, 31, 32.

San Marco ★★★   CHURCH Showcasing the work of Fra Angelico, Dominican monk and Florentine painter in the International Gothic style, this is the most important collection in the world of his altarpieces and painted panels, residing in a deconsecrated 13th-century convent this multitasking artist-monk once called home. Seeing it all in one place—around a courtyard and upstairs library designed by Michelozzo— helps you to appreciate how his decorative impulses and the sinuous lines of his figures place his work right on the cusp of the Renaissance. The most moving and unusual is his **"Annunciation"** ★★★, a postcard favorite, but a close second are intimate frescoes of the life of Jesus—painted not on one giant wall, but scene by scene in small monks' cells which honeycomb the upper floor. The idea was for these scenes, painted by both Fra

At San Marco, masterpieces by Fra Angelico are painted simply right onto the convent walls.

Angelico and his assistants, to aid in prayer and contemplation. The final cell on the left corridor belonged to firebrand preacher Savonarola, who briefly incited the people of the most art-filled city in the world to burn their "decadent" paintings, illuminated manuscripts, and anything else he felt was a worldly betrayal of Jesus's ideals. You'll see his rosary, chair, and what's left of the clothes he wore in his cell, as well as an anonymous panel painted to show the day in 1498 when—having fallen out with everyone, including the pope—he was burned at the stake in Piazza della Signoria. There's much more Fra Angelico secreted around the cloisters, including a **"Crucifixion"** ★ in the Chapter House. The former Pilgrims' Hospice is now a gallery dedicated to Fra Angelico and his contemporaries; look especially for his **"Tabernacolo dei Linaioli"** ★★, painted for the linen workers' guild in the 1430s, and a seemingly weightless **"Deposition"** ★★.

Piazza San Marco 3. ℭ **055/238-8608.** Admission 8€; free for children 17 and under. Daily 8:15am–1:50pm. Closed 1st, 3rd, and 5th Sun and Mon after 2nd and 4th Sun of month. Bus: C1, 1, 6, 7, 10, 11, 14, 17, 19, 20, 23, 25, 31, 32.

Santissima Annunziata ★★ CHURCH This church's story begins humbly, in 1233, when seven Florentine nobles had a spiritual crisis, gave away their possessions, and retired to the forest to contemplate divinity. In 1250, they returned to what were then fields outside the city walls and founded a small oratory, proclaiming themselves Servants of Mary (the "Servite Order"). Over the years, thanks to a miraculous painting (more on that later), the oratory grew into a grand basilica, enlarged by Michelozzo (1444–81) and later redecorated in unrestrained baroque style.

Visitors enter through the **Chiostro dei Voti (Votive Cloister),** which is today the church's main art draw, decorated with some of the city's finest **Mannerist frescoes** ★★ (1465–1515), once again vibrant after a 5-year restoration. Rosso Fiorentino provided an "Assumption" (1513) and Pontormo the "Visitation" (1515) just to the right of the door. Their master, Andrea del Sarto, contributed a "Birth of the Virgin" (1513), in the far-right corner, one of his finest works. To the right of the door into the church is a damaged but still fascinating "Procession of the Magi" (1514) by del Sarto, who included a giraffe and a self-portrait (at the front-right, looking out from under a blue hat).

The church's interior is a flamboyant affair, smothered in multicolored marble and topped with a gilded coffered ceiling. In a side chapel to the left of the entrance, an ornate tabernacle houses a small 14th-century painting of the "Annunciation." Why such a grandiose setting? According to legend, the friar who was painting the picture became vexed that he couldn't paint the Madonna's face as beautifully as she should be, and went to take a nap. When he awoke, he found an angel had completed the face for him. This miraculous painting became an object of cult worship, and a once-humble church was changed forever.

On **Piazza Santissima Annunziata** ★★ outside, flanked by elegant Brunelleschi porticos, an equestrian statue of Grand Duke Ferdinand I was Giambologna's last work, cast in 1608 after his death by his student Pietro

Tacca, who also did the two fountains of fantastical mermonkey-monsters. *Tip:* You can stay right on this spectacular piazza, at one of our favorite Florence hotels, the **Loggiato dei Serviti ★★** (p. 191).

Piazza Santissima Annunziata. ℂ **055/266-181.** Free admission. Cloister: daily 7am–12:45pm and 4–5pm. Church: daily 4–5pm. Bus: 6, 19, 31, 32.

Spedale degli Innocenti ★★ MUSEUM/ARCHITECTURE   Originally funded by the silkworkers' guild, the "Nocenti" opened in 1419, and ever since has been one of the world's most famous childcare institutions. (The Institute still works with UNICEF.) Brunelleschi himself designed their landmark building with elegant Renaissance loggias on the facade and surrounding its interior "Women's" and "Men's" **courtyards.** Inside, a three-floor museum has multimedia exhibits tracing the history of the place and the personal stories of many who benefited from its care. The Institute also has a fine **art collection,** including Renaissance works by Botticelli and Ghirlandaio displayed in a top-floor gallery, alongside original painted ceramic roundels by Della Robbia, which elegantly completed Brunelleschi's facade. As you leave, notice the little grated window on the north wall of the main loggia, where for centuries babies were brought anonymously to the orphanage's care.

Piazza Santissima Annunziata 13. www.museodeglinnocenti.it. ℂ **055/203-7122.** Admission 8€. Daily 9am–7pm. Bus: 6, 19, 31, 32.

Around Piazza Santa Croce

Piazza Santa Croce is like any grand Florentine square: an open space ringed with souvenir and leather shops and thronged with tourists. Once a year (during late June), it's covered with dirt for a violent, Renaissance-style football tournament known as **Calcio Storico Fiorentino.** In December, you'll also find Florence's main **Christmas market**—a fun, if boilerplate German-style affair.

Santa Croce ★★ CHURCH   The center of Florence's Franciscan universe was begun in 1294 by Gothic master Arnolfo di Cambio to rival the church of Santa Maria Novella being raised by the Dominicans across the city. The church wasn't consecrated until 1442, and even then, it remained faceless until a neo-Gothic **facade** was added in 1857. This art-stuffed complex demands a couple hours of your time to see properly.

Inside Santa Croce.

The Gothic **interior** is vast and populated with the tombs of famous Florentines. Starting from the front door, immediately on the right is the tomb of the most venerated Renaissance master, **Michelangelo Buonarroti,** who died in Rome in 1564 at the ripe age of 89. The pope wanted him buried in the Eternal City, but Florentines snuck his body home. Two berths along from Michelangelo's monument is a pompous 19th-century cenotaph to **Dante Alighieri,** one of history's great poets, whose "Divine Comedy" laid the basis for the modern Italian language. (Exiled from Florence, Dante is buried in Ravenna.) Elsewhere are monuments to philosopher **Niccolò Machiavelli,** composer **Gioacchino Rossini,** sculptor **Lorenzo Ghiberti,** and scientist **Galileo Galilei.**

The church's right transept is richly decorated with **frescoes.** The **Cappella Castellani** was painted with stories of saints' lives by Agnolo Gaddi. His father, Taddeo Gaddi—one of Giotto's closest followers—decorated the **Cappella Baroncelli ★★** (1328–30) at the transept's end. The frescoes depict scenes from the "Life of the Virgin," and include an "Annunciation to the Shepherds," the first night scene in Italian fresco. Giotto himself painted the two chapels to the right of the high altar. Whitewashed over in the 17th century, they were uncovered in the 1800s and inexpertly restored. The more famous **Cappella Bardi ★★★** appeared in the movie "A Room with a View"; key panels, featuring episodes in the life of St. Francis, include the "Trial by Fire Before the Sultan of Egypt" on the right wall; and one of Giotto's best-known works, the "Death of St. Francis," in which monks weep and wail with convincing pathos. Ongoing restoration work will keep these artworks covered until 2025.

Outside in the cloister is the **Cappella Pazzi ★★★,** one of Filippo Brunelleschi's architectural masterpieces, faithfully finished after his death in 1446, more than 30 years before every Pazzi would become *persona non grata* after a failed coup against the Medici (see p. 40). Giuliano da Maiano probably designed the chapel's porch, set with glazed terracottas by Luca della Robbia. The chapel is one of Brunelleschi's signature pieces, decorated with his trademark *pietra serena* gray stone. It's a defining example of early Renaissance architecture. Curiously, the ceiling of the smaller dome depicts the same night sky as his Old Sacristy in San Lorenzo (p. 224). It is unclear why this was done.

Piazza Santa Croce. www.santacroceopera.it. ✆ **055/246-6105.** Admission 8€; free for children 17 and under. Mon–Sat 9:30am–5:30pm; Sun 1–5:30pm. Bus: C1, C2, C3.

The Oltrarno, San Niccolò & San Frediano

Giardino Bardini (Bardini Garden) ★ PARK/GARDEN   Hemmed in on the north by the city's medieval wall, the handsome Bardini Garden is less famous—and therefore less hectic—than its neighbor down the hill, the Boboli (see below). From a loftier perch over the Oltrarno, it beats the Boboli hands down for views and new angles on the city. The side view of Santa Croce—with the synagogue's copper dome rising in the background—shows how the church's 19th-century facade was bolted onto a building dating to the 1200s.

Costa San Giorgio 2. www.villabardini.it. ✆ **055/294-883.** Combined ticket with Boboli Garden 6€. Daily 10am–4pm. Closed 1st and last Mon of each month. Bus: C3 or C4.

Giardino di Boboli (Boboli Garden) ★★ PARK/GARDEN The statue-filled park behind the Pitti Palace is one of the earliest and finest Renaissance gardens, laid out mostly between 1549 and 1656 with box hedges in geometric patterns, groves of ilex (holm oak), dozens of statues, and rows of cypress. Just above the entrance through the courtyard of the Palazzo Pitti is an oblong **amphitheater** modeled on Roman circuses, with a **granite basin** from Rome's Baths of Caracalla and an **Egyptian obelisk** of Ramses II. In 1589 this was the setting for the wedding reception of Ferdinand de' Medici and Christine of Lorraine. For the occasion, the family commissioned entertainment from Jacopo Peri and Ottavio Rinuccini, who decided to set a classical story entirely to music and called it "Dafne"—the world's first opera. (Their follow-up hit, "Erudice," performed here in 1600, is the earliest opera whose score survives.) At the south end of the park, the **Isolotto** ★ is a dreamy island in a pond full of huge goldfish, with Giambologna's "L'Oceano" sculptural composition at its center. At the north end, around the end of the Pitti Palace, are fake caverns filled with statuary, attempting to invoke a classical sacred grotto. The most famous, the **Grotta Grande,** was designed by Giorgio Vasari, Bartolomeo Ammannati, and Bernardo Buontalenti between 1557 and 1593. Dripping with phony stalactites, it's set with replicas of Michelangelo's unfinished "Prisoners" statues. You can usually get inside on the hour (but not every hour) for 15 minutes.

Entrance via Palazzo Pitti. www.uffizi.it/en/boboli-garden. ✆ **055/238-8791.** Admission Mar–Oct 10€, Nov–Feb 6€; includes Giardino Bardini. Nov–Feb daily 8:15am–4:30pm; Mar daily 8:15am–5:30pm; Apr–May and Sept–Oct daily to 6:30pm; June–Aug daily to 7pm. Closed 1st and last Mon of month. Bus: C3, C4, 11, 36, 37.

Palazzo Pitti (Pitti Palace) ★★ MUSEUM/PALACE Although built by and named after a rival of the Medici—the merchant Luca Pitti—in the 1450s, this gigantic *palazzo* soon came into Medici hands. It was the Medici family's principal home from the 1540s and continued to house Florence's rulers until 1919. The Pitti contains five museums, including one of the world's best collections of canvases by Raphael. Out back are elegant Renaissance gardens, the **Boboli** (see above).

In the art-crammed rooms of the Pitti's **Galleria Palatina** ★★, paintings are displayed like cars in a parking garage, stacked on walls above each other following the Enlightenment method of exhibition. Rooms are alternately dimly lit, or garishly bright; this is how many of the world's great art treasures were once seen and enjoyed. For the casual browser, it can be a frustrating experience; but for art lovers, gems abound. One room here would be enough to build a museum around in many other cities, including some of the best efforts of Titian, Raphael, and Rubens. Filippo Lippi's **"Madonna and Child"** ★ (1452) is one key work in the **Sala di Prometeo** (Prometheus Room). It looks suspiciously like another portrait of nun-turned-lover, Lucrezia Buti (see Uffizi, p. 212). Two giant canvases of the "Assumption of the Virgin," both by Mannerist painter Andrea del Sarto, dominate the **Sala dell'Iliade** (Iliad Room). Here you will also find another Biblical woman

The walls of the Pitti Palace's Galleria Palatina are crammed with art.

painted by Artemisia Gentileschi, "Judith", and panels by Annibale Carracci and Rosso Fiorentino. The **Sala di Saturno** (Saturn Room) ★ overflows with Raphaels; in the **Sala di Giove** (Jupiter Room) is his sublime, naturalistic portrait of **"La Velata" ★★,** as well as **"The Three Ages of Man" ★.** The current attribution of the latter painting is awarded to Venetian Giorgione, although this has been disputed. Keep digging to unearth Allori, Bronzino, and more.

At the **Appartamenti Reali** (Royal Apartments) you get a feeling for the conspicuous consumption of the Medici Grand Dukes and their Austrian and Belgian Lorraine successors—and see some notable paintings in their original, ostentatious setting. Italy's first king lived here for several years during the 19th-century unification process—when Florence was the second national capital, after Turin, between 1865 and 1871—until Rome was finally conquered and the court moved there. Much of the gilded stucco, fabrics, and general decoration is in thunderously poor taste.

The Pitti's "modern" gallery, the **Galleria d'Arte Moderna ★,** has a good collection of 19th-century Italian paintings with a focus on Romanticism, Neoclassical works, and the **Macchiaioli,** a school of Italian painters who worked in an "impressionistic style" chronologically before the French Impressionists. Highlights hunters with limited time should head straight for major works of the latter, in Sala 18 through 20, where landscapes by

Giovanni Fattori ★ (1825–1908) and Telemaco Signorini (1835–1901) hang. The Pitti's two lesser museums—the **Galleria del Costume** (Costume Gallery) and **Museo degli Argenti** (Museum of Silverware)—combine to show that wealth and taste do not always go hand in hand. One thing you will notice in the Costume Gallery: how much smaller locals were a few centuries ago. In 2022, another Medici private collection was opened to the public as the **Museum of Russian Icons ★**, the oldest such collection in the Western world.

Piazza Pitti. www.uffizi.it. Admission Mar–Oct 16€, Nov–Feb 10€; free for children 17 and under. Tues–Sun 8:15am–6:50pm. Bus: C3, C4, 11, 36, 37.

Piazzale Michelangiolo ★★ SQUARE   This pedestrianized, panoramic piazza is on the itinerary of every tour bus. The balustraded terrace was laid out in 1869 to give a sweeping **vista ★★** of the Renaissance city, spread out in the valley below and backed by the hills of Fiesole beyond. You will get the classic photo of Florence's skyline from here. Nearby, a bronze replica of "David" points directly at his original home, the Palazzo Vecchio.

Viale Michelangiolo. Bus: 12 or 13.

San Miniato al Monte ★★ CHURCH   High atop a hill, its gleaming white-and-green marble facade visible from the city below, San Miniato is one of few truly ancient churches of Florence to survive the centuries virtually intact. The current building took shape in 1013, under the auspices of the powerful Arte di Calimala guild, whose symbol, a bronze eagle clutching a bale of wool, perches on the **facade ★★**. Above the central window is a 13th-century mosaic of "Christ Between the Madonna and St. Minias" (a theme repeated in the apse). The interior has a few Renaissance additions, but they blend well with the overall medieval aspect—an airy, stony space with a raised choir at one end, painted wooden trusses on the ceiling, and tombs interspersed with inlaid marble symbols of the zodiac paving the floor. Below the choir is an 11th-century **Crypt ★** with remains of frescoes by Taddeo Gaddi. Off to the right of the raised choir is the sacristy, which Spinello Aretino covered in 1387 with elaborate frescoes depicting the **"Life of St. Benedict" ★**. Off the left of the nave is the 15th-century **Cappella del Cardinale del Portogallo ★★,** a collaborative effort by Renaissance artists to honor a Portuguese humanist, Cardinal Jacopo di Lusitania. It's worth timing your visit to come here when the Benedictine monks are celebrating mass in Gregorian chant (usually 5:30pm). Around the back of the church is San Miniato's monumental **Cemetery ★**, its paths lined with tombs and mausoleums built in elaborate pastiches of every generation of Florentine architecture. It's a peaceful, often deserted spot, soundtracked only by birdsong and the occasional toll of a church bell.

Via Monte alle Croci/Viale Galileo Galilei (behind Piazzale Michelangelo). ✆ **055/234-2731.** Free admission. Mon–Sat 9:30am–12:30pm and 3–6pm; Sun 3–5:30pm. Bus: 12 or 13.

Santa Felicita ★ CHURCH   Greek sailors who lived in this neighborhood in the 2nd century brought Christianity to Florence, and this little church was probably the second to be established in the city, its first iteration rising in the late 4th century. The current church was remodeled in the 1730s. The star works are in the first chapel on the right, Brunelleschi-designed **Cappella Barbadori-Capponi** ★★, with paintings by the Mannerist master Pontormo (1525–27). Pontormo's **"Deposition"** ★★ and frescoed "Annunciation" are rife with his garish color palette of oranges, pinks, golds, lime greens, and sky blues, and exhibit his trademark surreal sense of figure.

Piazza Santa Felicita (on left off Via Guicciardini across the Ponte Vecchio). © **055/213-018.** Free admission (1€ to illuminate chapel lights). Mon–Sat 9:30am–12:30pm and 3:30–5:30pm. Bus: C3 or C4.

Santa Maria del Carmine ★★★ CHURCH   Following a 1771 fire that destroyed everything but the transept chapels and sacristy, this Carmelite church was almost entirely reconstructed in high baroque style. To see the much older **Cappella Brancacci** ★★★, in the right transept, you have to enter through the cloisters and pay admission. The frescoes here were commissioned by an enemy of the Medici, Felice Brancacci, who in 1424 hired Masolino and his student Masaccio to decorate it with the "Life of St. Peter." Masolino probably worked out the cycle's scheme and painted a few scenes along with his pupil before taking off for 3 years to serve as court painter in Budapest. Masaccio kept painting, quietly creating the early Renaissance's greatest frescoes. Masaccio eventually left for Rome in 1428, where he died at age 27; the cycle was completed between 1480 and 1485 by Filippino Lippi. Masolino painted "St. Peter Preaching," the upper panel to the left of the altar, and the two top scenes on the right wall, which shows his fastidious, decorative style in a long panel of "St. Peter Healing the Cripple" and "Raising Tabitha," and his "Adam and Eve." Contrast this first man and woman, about to take the bait offered by the snake, with Masaccio's **"Expulsion from the Garden"** ★★★, opposite. Masolino's figures are highly posed, expressionless models, while Masaccio's Adam and Eve burst with intense emotion. The top scene on the left wall, Masaccio's **"Tribute Money"** ★★, showcases his use of linear perspective. The scenes to the right of the altar are Masaccio's as well; **"Baptism of the Neophytes"** ★★ is another among his masterpieces. Prebooking a timed entrance slot one day ahead is **essential**.

Piazza del Carmine. Ticketsmuseums.comune.fi.it. © **055/276-8224.** Admission 10€; free for children 17 and under. Mon and Fri–Sat 10am–5pm; Sun 1–5pm. Bus: C4.

Santo Spirito ★ CHURCH   One of Filippo Brunelleschi's masterpieces of architecture, this 15th-century church doesn't look much from the outside (no proper facade was ever built). But the **interior** ★ is a marvelous High Renaissance space—an expansive landscape of proportion and mathematics in classic Brunelleschi style, with coffered ceiling, lean columns with Corinthian capitals, and the stacked perspective of arched arcading. Late Renaissance and baroque paintings are scattered throughout, but the best stuff lies in

The simple facade of Santo Spirito masks High Renaissance interior.

the transepts, especially the **Cappella Nerli** ★, with a panel by Filippino Lippi (right transept). The church's extravagant baroque altar has a ciborium inlaid in *pietre dure* around 1607—and frankly, looks a bit silly against the restrained elegance of Brunelleschi's architecture. A separate entrance admits you to the **Sacristy** to see a wooden "Crucifix" that has, controversially, been attributed to Michelangelo, as well as Santo Spirito's 17th-century cloister and refectory. *Tip:* Tree-shaded **Piazza Santo Spirito** ★ is one of the focal points of the Oltrarno, lined with cafes and outdoor tables. Sometimes a few farmers sell fresh produce on the square.

Piazza Santo Spirito. www.basilicasantospirito.it. ℂ **055/210-030.** Church free admission; 2€ sacristy and cloister. Mon–Tues and Thurs–Sat 10am–1pm and 3–6pm; Sun 11:30am–1:30pm and 3–6pm. Bus: C3, C4, 11, 36, 37.

Organized Tours

Insightful culture tours with **Context Travel** ★★ (www.contexttravel.com/cities/florence) are led by academics and other experts in their field on a variety of themes, from the gastronomic to the archaeological and artistic. Tours are limited to six people and generally cost around $150 per person including relevant museum admission fees. The quality of Context's walks is unmatched, and well worth their above-average cost. To book a private tour of between 2½ and 3½ hours is around $350 to $500.

Food tours are booming. A few hours in city markets, or in the company of street vendors or a pro chef, gives you an insight into traditions and trends in Florentine cooking. The glass-fronted Arclinea kitchens upstairs at the Mercato Centrale host the **Lorenzo de' Medici Cooking School** ★ (cucinaldm. com; ✆ 334/304-0551), where 2-hour small-group courses (85€–140€) teach the skills needed to create authentic staples such as stuffed fresh pasta as well as seasonal Italian sides, meat, or fish. The minimum age for children to participate is 14. **Eating Europe** (www.eatingeurope.com/florence) offers themed small-group tours (65€–85€) covering gelato-making, Oltrarno foodie haunts, and more. They can also customize a Florence food experience for you. **Curious Appetite Travel** ★ (curiousappetitetravel.com) runs offbeat small-group street-food market walks, a four-stop "dinner crawl," and artisan beer tastings. Prices range from $130 to $185 per person, which includes food and drink. **I Just Drive** ★★ (www.ijustdrive.us; ✆ 055/093-5928) offers fully equipped cars (Wi-Fi, complimentary bottle of Prosecco) plus an English-speaking driver for various themed visits. For example, you can book a ride in a luxury Bentley or Mercedes up to San Miniato al Monte at dusk (1½ hr.; 129€). They also operate full-day and half-day food and wine tours into the Chianti hills—by day or night—visits to the Ferrari factory, and even trips to the Cinque Terre.

Especially for Kids

You have to put in a bit of work (and reserve ahead) to reach some of Florence's best views. The climbs, up claustrophobic medieval staircases, are a favorite with many kids. The cupola of the **Duomo** (p. 209), the **Palazzo Vecchio**'s (p. 218) Torre di Arnolfo, and the **Campanile di Giotto** (p. 208) are perfect for any youngster who has a head for heights.

The best family activities with an educational component are run by **Mus.e** ★★ (www.musefirenze.it; ✆ 055/276-8224), including child's-eye tours in English around the Palazzo Vecchio led by guides in period costumes. Lively, affordable activities focus on life at the ducal court, including "The Turtle and the Snail," pitched at children ages 4 to 7. Programs cost 5€ per person; book online or at the desk next to the Palazzo Vecchio ticket booth.

When youngsters need a crowd-free timeout space, head for the ground floor of the **Biblioteca delle Oblate,** Via dell'Oriuolo 24 (www.biblioteche. comune.fi.it; ✆ 055/261-6526), a public library with a children's section for little ones (including in English), as well as space to spread out, color, or draw, and air-conditioning. It's free and open 9am to 6:45pm, except for Monday morning and all day Sunday (closed 1 week mid-Aug). *Tip:* The Oblate's **cafeteria** ★ is an excellent place to kick back, with fair prices and a view of Brunelleschi's dome that few visitors see.

Cycling is a pleasure in the riverside Parco delle Cascine: See p. 180 for bike rental advice. And remember: You are in the **gelato** capital of the world. At least one multi-scoop gelato per day is the minimum recommended dose; see p. 203.

SHOPPING IN FLORENCE

After Milan, Florence is **Italy's top shopping city**—beating even Rome. Here's what to buy: leather, designer fashion, shoes, marbleized paper and other stationery, hand-embroidered linens, Tuscan wines, handmade jewelry, *pietre dure* (known also as "Florentine mosaic," inlaid semiprecious stones), and antiques. *Note:* It is illegal to knowingly buy fake goods anywhere in the city (and yes, a "Louis Vuitton" bag at 10€ counts as *knowingly*). You may be served a hefty on-the-spot fine if caught.

Traditionally, Florentine **shopping hours** are Monday through Saturday from 9:30am to noon or 1pm and 3 or 3:30 to 7:30pm. Increasingly, larger shops and those in tourist areas stay open on Sunday and through the midafternoon *riposo,* or "nap." Some small or family-run places close Monday mornings instead of Sundays.

The Top Shopping Streets & Areas

AROUND SANTA TRÍNITA The cream of the crop lines both sides of elegant **Via de' Tornabuoni,** with an extension along **Via della Vigna Nuova** and other surrounding streets. Here you'll find the big Florentine fashion names like **Gucci ★**, at no. 73R (www.gucci.com; ✆ **055/264-011**), **Pucci ★**, at no. 22R (www.emiliopucci.com; ✆ **055/265-8082**), and **Ferragamo ★★**, at no. 5R (www.ferragamo.com; ✆ **055/292-123**), ensconced in old palaces or

Florence is known for its leather goods.

minimalist boutiques. Couture meets streetwear at concept sneaker store **SOTF ★**, at no. 17R (www.sotf.com; *℗* **055/588-302**). Florence-headquartered leather specialist **Benheart ★★**, Via della Vigna Nuova 97R (www.benheart. it; *℗* **055/239-9483;** also at Via dei Calzaiuoli 78R) sells up-to-the-minute leather clothing, footwear, and accessories. You can even create a personalized belt with your choice of leather and buckles. Benheart isn't cheap, but quality is first rate—which isn't always true for leather sold in the city. In 2022, a Florence branch of quality thrift store **Humana Vintage ★**, Via delle Belle Donne 4R (humanavintage.it) added another dimension to the neighborhood.

AROUND VIA ROMA & VIA DEI CALZAIUOLI These are some of Florence's busiest streets, lined with mostly mainstream storefronts. Here you'll find major department store **La Rinascente,** Piazza della Repubblica (www.rinascente.it; *℗* **055/219-113**), alongside quality clothing brands such as Geox, Patrizia Pepe, and Zara. **La Feltrinelli RED,** Piazza delle Repubblica 26 (www.lafeltrinelli.it; *℗* **199/151-173**), is the center's best bookstore. Online couture sales sensation **Luisa Via Roma ★** (www.luisaviaroma.com) also has its flagship physical store here, at Via Roma 21R.

AROUND SANTA CROCE The eastern part of the center has seen a flourishing of one-of-a-kind stores, with an emphasis on young, independent fashions. **Borgo degli Albizi** and its tributary streets are worth roaming— **Sabatini ★**, at no. 75R (*℗* **055/234-0240**) is an established go-to for affordable casual footwear. Across the street, **Marzotto ★**, at 86R (cartafiorentinafirenze. com; *℗* **055-234-0726**), is a fabulous old treasure cave of affordable Florentine stationery. They've been in business there since 1890.

Florence's Best Markets

Mercato Centrale ★★ The center's main market stocks the usual fresh produce, but you can also browse (and taste) cheeses, salamis and cured hams, sweets, oil and vinegar, Tuscan wines, takeout food, and more. This is a picnicker's nirvana; they'll also vacuum pack items for taking home. It runs Monday to Saturday until 2pm (until 5pm Sat for most of the year). Upstairs is street-food heaven, all day, every day; see p. 199. Btw. Piazza del Mercato Centrale and Via dell'Ariento. No phone. Bus: C1.

Mercato di San Lorenzo ★ The city's tourist street market is a fun place to pick up T-shirts, marbleized paper, a bound notebook, or another city souvenir. Leather wallets, purses, bags, and jackets are popular with international visitors—be sure to assess the workmanship, which can be variable, and haggle shamelessly. This busy market runs daily; watch for pickpockets. Via dell'Ariento and Via Rosina. No phone. Bus: C1.

Mercato di Sant'Ambrogio ★ A proper slice of Florentine life, six mornings a week (closed Sun). The piazza outside has fruit, vegetables, costume jewelry, preserves, and end-of-line discount clothing. Go inside the market building for meat, cheeses, olive oil, or a budget lunch at **Da Rocco** (p. 201). Piazza Ghiberti. No phone. Bus: C2 or C3.

Mercato Centrale.

Crafts & Artisanal Goods

Florence has a longstanding reputation for its craftsmanship. Although display windows along touristed streets are often stuffed with cheap imports and mass-produced goods, if you know where to look, you will find top-quality handmade items.

Aqua Flor ★★   Another Florentine shrine to all things scented. Perfumes, soap, incense, and more are made here inside its Renaissance HQ. Borgo Santa Croce 6. www.aquaflor.it. ✆ **055/234-3471.** Bus: 23.

Il Torchio ★★   This small Oltrarno workshop sells hand-bound notebooks and marbleized paper. Bespoke designs available. Via de' Bardi 17. www.legatoriail torchio.com. ✆ **055/234-2862.** Closed weekends. Bus: C3 or C4.

Madova ★★★   For a century, this has been the best city retailer of hand-made leather gloves, lined with silk, cashmere, or lambs' wool. You'll pay between 50€ and 80€ for a pair. Madova is the real deal, even this close to the Ponte Vecchio. Closed Sundays. Via Guicciardini 1R. www.madova.com. ✆ **055/239-6526.** Bus: C3 or D.

Marioluca Giusti ★★   The boutique of this renowned Florentine designer sells only his trademark synthetic acrylic crystal. The range includes colorful reinventions of cocktail and wine glasses, jugs, and tumblers—every piece tough, lightweight, and chic. Via della Spada 20R. www.mariolucagiusti.it. © **055/214-583.** Bus: 6 or 11. Also at Via della Vigna Nuova 88R.

Officina Profumo-Farmaceutica di Santa Maria Novella ★★★

An iconic temple of scents and skincare, this is Florence's historic herbal pharmacy, founded in the 13th century, when Dominican friars founded the adjacent convent of Santa Maria Novella. Nothing is cheap, but the perfumes, moisturizers, and candles are handmade from the finest natural ingredients and packaged exquisitely. Via della Scala 16. www.smnovella.com. © **055/216-276.** Bus: C2.

Parione ★

A traditional Florentine stationer which celebrated its 100th birthday in 2023. It stocks notebooks, marbleized paper, fine pens, and souvenirs like wooden music boxes and playing cards with 17th-century Florentine designs. Closed Sundays. Via dello Studio 11R. www.parione.it. © **055/215-684.** Bus: C1 or C2.

Scuola del Cuoio ★

Florence's leading leather school is also an open house for visitors. You can watch trainee leatherworkers and gilders at work (Mon–Fri), then visit the small store to buy portable items like wallets, belts, and bags. Closed Sundays in low season. Via San Giuseppe 5R (behind Santa Croce church). www.scuoladelcuoio.com. © **055/244-534.** Bus: C3.

Gilding a leather book at Scuola del Cuoio.

ENTERTAINMENT & NIGHTLIFE

Florence has several listings publications including *Informacittà* (www. informacitta.net), which is strong on theater, concerts, and one-off markets. Younger and hipper *Zero* (www.zero.eu/firenze) has the latest eating, drinking, lifestyle, and edgy nightlife. *Firenze Spettacolo,* a 2€ Italian-language monthly sold at newsstands, is the most comprehensive listing of nightlife, arts, and entertainment.

To wander and see what grabs you, start by exploring the tourist-oriented action in bars close to the city's main squares, many with outdoor piazza seating. For something livelier—with a more local focus—visit **Borgo San Frediano, Piazza Santo Spirito,** or the northern end of **Via de' Macci,** near where it meets Via Pietrapiana. **Via de' Benci** is usually buzzing around *aperitivo* time and is popular with an expat crowd. **Via de' Renai** and the bars of San Niccolò around the **Porta San Miniato** are often lively too, with a mixed clientele of tourists and locals hovering around outdoor tables.

Performing Arts & Live Music

Florence does not have the classical musical cachet of Milan, Venice, Naples, or Rome, but there are two symphony orchestras and a fine music school in Fiesole, as well as a modern opera house (see p. 247). The city's theaters are respectable, and most major touring companies stop in town. Buy tickets to cultural events online or in person from **Box Office,** Via delle Vecchie Carceri 1 (www.boxofficetoscana.it).

Many classical music performances are sponsored by the **Amici della Musica** (www.amicimusicafirenze.it; *C* **055/607-440**), so check the website to see what's on. Its venue is often **Teatro della Pergola,** where Verdi's opera "Macbeth" premiered in 1847; prices range 15€ to 30€. Florence's **Chamber Orchestra** runs an annual concert program, including in churches and other historic spaces in the city: See **orchestracamerafiorentina.it.** Restored and reopened in 2023, the Art Deco **Odeon Firenze ★,** Piazza Strozzi (www. odeonfirenze.com; *C* **055/214-068**) theater shows the latest movies in their original language (10€).

Libreria-Café La Cité ★★   A relaxed cafe-bookshop by day, after dark this place becomes a bar and small-scale live music venue. The lineup is eclectic, often offbeat or world music, one night forrò or swing, the next Italian folk or chanteuse. Borgo San Frediano 20R. *C* **055/210-387.** Bus: C3, C4, 6, 11, 36, 37.

Opera di Firenze ★★   This vast new concert hall and arts complex seats up to 1,800 in daring postmodernist surrounds on the edge of the Cascine Park. Its program incorporates opera, ballet, and orchestral music: Restricted-view or "listening only" seats can be very cheap. Each May and June, the venue hosts the **Maggio Musicale Fiorentino,** one of Italy's most prestigious music festivals. Piazzale Vittorio Gui. www.operadifirenze.it. *C* **055/277-9309.** Tickets 15€–200€. Tram: T1.

Volume ★   After nightly *aperitivo* from 6:30pm, Volume becomes a buzzing cocktail bar with live acoustic sets. Piazza Santo Spirito 5R. www.volumefirenze.com. ⓒ **055/238-1460.** Bus: C3, 11, 36, 37.

Cafes

Florence no longer has a glitterati or intellectuals' cafe scene, and when it did—from the late-19th-century Risorgimento era through 1950s *Dolce Vita*—it was basically copying Paris. Although they're often overpriced tourist spots today—especially around **Piazza della Repubblica**—Florence's few remaining high-toned piazza cafes are fine if you want pastries while you sit and people-watch. These cafes are on the Florence restaurants map, p. 194.

Cantinetta dei Verrazzano ★★   One of the coziest little cafe-bars in the center is decked out with antique wooden wine cabinets, in genuine *enoteca* style. Wines come from their own first-rate Verrazzano estate in Chianti. Light breakfast and morning cappuccino is a delight. Closed evenings. Via dei Tavolini 18R. www.verrazzano.com. ⓒ **055/268-590.** Bus: C2.

Ditta Artigianale ★★   This on-trend spot inside a Michelucci-designed modernist building offers a bit of everything, at any time of day. The highlight is fantastic coffee from their own small-batch roastery in Arezzo. (You can buy beans to take home.) There's daily brunch, wines by the glass, and artisan

The cafes around Piazza della Repubblica.

beers. Via dello Sprone 5R. www.dittaartigianale.it. ✆ **055/045-7163.** Bus: C3 or C4. Also at Via dei Neri 32R; Via G. Carducci 4R; Lungarno Soderini 7R.

La Menagère ★ In the former premises of a vast 19th-century home-wares store, this lively all-day cafe can hook you up with breakfast, brunch, lunch, a caffeine pick-me-up, aperitif, or even a bunch of fresh flowers. Via de' Ginori 8R. www.lamenagere.it. ✆ **055/0750-600.** Bus: C1.

Procacci ★★ The second you walk through the door, you're hit with the perfume of Procacci's specialty: panini *tartufati,* brioche rolls spread with truffle butter. Via Tornabuoni 64R. www.procacci1885.it. ✆ **055/211-656.** Bus: C3.

Rivoire ★ If you pick one pricey sidewalk cafe in Florence, make it this one. The steep charges (6€ for a cappuccino) help pay the rent beside one of the prettiest slices of real estate on the planet. Piazza della Signoria 5R. www.rivoire.it. ✆ **055/214-412.** Bus: C2.

Tosca & Nino ★ The prices, like the rooftop perch, are a little elevated (3€–5€ for a coffee). But you get to enjoy your drink or light lunch on a hidden terrace in the sky, with just medieval towers and Brunelleschi's dome for company. Top floor of La Rinascente, Piazza della Repubblica. www.toscanino.com. ✆ **055/4933-468.** Bus: C2.

Beer, Wine & Cocktail Bars

Florence's iconic cocktail is the **Negroni,** invented in the city in 1919.

Fermento ★ Directly opposite the Medici Chapels, this tiny bar with outdoor tables serves Italian and Belgian craft beers in every style from IPA to stout, simple cocktails like a spritz or Americano (9€), plus carb-rich food to soak it up. Via Canto dei Nelli 38R. http://fermentofirenze.com. ✆ **055/013-8064.** Bus: C1.

Il Santino ★★ This snug wine bar stocks niche labels from across Italy and serves exquisite "Florentine tapas" to munch while you sip. Via Santo Spirito 60R. ilsantobevitore.com. ✆ **055/230-2820.** Bus: C4, 11, 36, 37.

Love Craft ★★ The bar is the star at this snazzy little spot dedicated to everything whiskey (and whisky). Global blends and single malts, cocktails, and flights are all good prices. Borgo San Frediano 24R. www.lovecraft firenze.it. No phone. Bus: C3, C4, 6, 11, 36, 37.

The Negroni.

Mayday is an ever-cool Florentine hangout spot.

Manifattura ★★★ Clientele skews young and casual at this creative cocktail bar in the old center. Drinks are mixed with Italian spirits only, so expect plenty of invention—like a Sazerac without rye or bourbon (!)—and multiple seasonal takes on Florence's icon, the Negroni. Piazza San Pancrazio 1R. www.manifatturafirenze.it. **No phone.** Bus: C3, 6, 11.

Mayday ★★ A Florence original, this laidback bar offers signature cocktails commemorating famous Tuscans and events in 20th-century history. It's delightfully decked out like a mismatched junk store, with everything from old school desks to low-watt lamps dangling from the ceiling. Via Dante Alighieri 16R. www.maydayclub.it. ✆ **055/238-1290.** Bus: C2.

Mostodolce ★ Burgers, pizza, snacks, Wi-Fi, and sports on the screen—so far, so good. And Mostodolce also has its own artisan beers on tap, brewed just outside Florence at Prato (some are very strong). Via Nazionale 114R. www. mostodolce.it. ✆ **055/230-2928.** Bus: 1, 6, 11, 14, 17, 23.

Rasputin Secret Bar ★★ Book via the website to learn the address of this "secret" candle-lit basement speakeasy. Persian rugs, antique furnishings, and gentle jazz give the bar the feel of a comfortable prewar officers' club. The cocktail list is creative-to-wacky but they also nail the classics if you prefer. Secret location in the Santo Spirito neighborhood. rasputinsecretbar.com. ✆ **055/760-9957.** Bus: C3, 11, 36, 37.

Rifrullo ★ This friendly San Niccolò bar is one of Florence's most popular *aperitivo* spots, perennially popular with locals and visitors. Choose a

Wear purple (or not) to any Fiorentina football match.

cocktail, spritz, or glass of wine and enjoy crostini, seasonal salads, and more, including vegan and gluten-free options. You won't need dinner reservations afterward. Via San Niccolò 55R. www.ilrifrullo.com. ✆ **055/234-2621.** Bus: C4 or 23.

Sant'Ambrogio ★   This wine and cocktail bar is in a lively part of the center, northeast of Santa Croce. It is popular with locals without being too achingly hip. In summer, everyone spills out onto the little piazza and church steps outside. Piazza Sant'Ambrogio 7R. www.caffesantambrogio.it. ✆ **055/257-7277.** Bus: C2 or C3.

Spectator Sports

There's only one game in town when it comes to spectator sports: *calcio*. To Italians, soccer/football is akin to a second religion, and an afternoon at the stadium offers more insight into local culture than a lifetime in the Uffizi. Florence's team, **Fiorentina ★** (nicknamed *i viola,* "the purples"), usually plays in Italy's top league, *Serie A.* You can generally catch them alternate Sundays from September through May at the **Stadio Comunale Artemio Franchi,** Via Manfredo Fanti 4 (www.violachannel.tv). Book tickets online at **acffiorentina.ticketone.it** or head to the official ticket office (with photo ID in hand) on arrival, at Via dei Sette Santi 28R, open from 10am matchdays. With kids, get seats in a Tribuna (stand) rather than a Curva, where the fanatics sit.

To reach the stadium, take matchday bus no. 52 or no. 17 from Santa Maria Novella. You can get kitted out in home colors at **AleViola,** Via del Corso 58R (✆ **055/295-306**), or at stalls around the ground on matchday.

DAY TRIPS FROM FLORENCE

By Donald Strachan

Even for other Italians, Tuscany epitomizes everything good about their country. As Tuscany's transportation hub, Florence is perfectly situated within easy day trip range of all of the sites listed in this chapter: You don't even need to switch hotels to see these highlights of central Italy. With these day trips, you'll pass through beguiling landscapes dotted with cypresses and carpeted with vineyards, dine on delicious food and wine, and explore some of the greatest art and architecture of the Renaissance—including the Leaning Tower of Pisa, Siena's Palazzo Pubblico, and the perfectly preserved Gothic hill town of San Gimignano.

FIESOLE ★★

7km (4 miles) NE of Florence

An oasis of cultivated greenery separates hilltop Fiesole from Florence. Fiesole preserves the character of a Tuscan small town, which makes it a perfect escape from peak-season crowds. As you sit at a cafe on Piazza Mino, sipping an iced cappuccino, the lines at the Uffizi and throng around the Duomo seem very distant indeed.

Fiesole predates Florence by centuries. Etruscans from Arezzo probably founded a town here in the 6th century B.C., on the site of an earlier Bronze Age settlement. *Faesulae* grew into the most important Etruscan center in the region, and although it became a Roman town in 90 B.C., it retained a bit of otherness. A place in late Roman history was ensured when, in A.D. 406, Ostrogoth King Radagaisus was defeated and executed near Fiesole, after an unsuccessful siege of Florence. Following later barbarian invasions, in the 9th century Fiesole became part of Florence's administrative district yet continued to struggle for self-government. Florence settled things in 1125 by attacking and razing the entire settlement. Archeologists have since unearthed several structures from the Roman and Etruscan eras.

The Tuscan countryside.

Essentials

ARRIVING   Bus no. 7 from Florence departs from Largo Fratelli Alinari, at the station end of Via Nazionale. The journey to Fiesole takes 25 minutes, arriving in Fiesole's main square, Piazza Mino. The one-way fare is 1.50€.

VISITOR INFORMATION   The Fiesole **tourist office** is at Via Portigiani 3 (www.fiesoleforyou.it; ✆ **055/596-1311**). Opening hours vary year to year; generally it's open daily from March to October (Apr–Sept 9am–7pm; Mar and Oct 10am–6pm). November through February is low season, when typical hours are weekends from 10am to 3pm. At the tourist office, you can buy a single admission ticket to all of Fiesole's linked sights for 12€ adults, 8€ for children 7 to 18; family ticket 24€. It's 2€ per person less without the Museum Bandini (which is missable). A **Firenzecard** (p. 205) is valid in Fiesole. For more information, visit **www.museidifiesole.it** or call ✆ **055/596-1293**.

Exploring Fiesole

Uphill from Piazza Mino, the high point of the town is occupied by a tiny 14th-century church and monastery, **San Francesco ★**, Via San Francesco 13 (www.fratifiesole.it; ✆ **055/59-175;** free admission; Mon–Sat 10am–noon and 2–6pm, Sun 2–5pm). At the end of a small nave hung with devotional works—Piero di Cosimo and Cenni di Francesco are both represented—is a fine "Crucifixion and Saints" altarpiece by Neri di Bicci. Off the cloisters, a quirky little ethnographic museum stuffed with objects picked up by Franciscan missionaries displays an Egyptian mummy and Chinese jade and ceramics. Entrance to the church's painted, vaulted crypt is through the museum. To reach San Francesco, you will climb a sharp hill—pause close to the top,

Day Trips from Florence

where a balcony provides perhaps the best **view ★★★** of Florence and the wine hills of the Chianti beyond.

Terraced into a hill with views over the olive groves and forests north of Florence, Fiesole's romantically overgrown **archaeological area** (enter at Via Portigiani 1) is scattered with sections of columns, broken friezes, and other ancient remnants, with prize exhibits on display in a small museum. Beyond the **Roman Theater ★★** (which seated 1,500 in its heyday), three rebuilt arches mark the remains of 1st-century-A.D. **baths.** Near the arches, a cement balcony over the far edge of the archaeological park offers a view of the best remaining stretch of Fiesole's 4th-century-B.C. **Etruscan walls.** At the other end of the park from the baths, the floor and steps of a 1st-century-B.C.

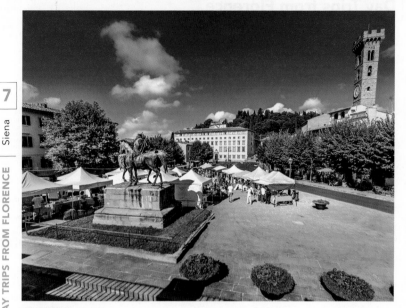

Piazza Mino in Fiesole.

Roman Temple were built atop a 4th-century-B.C. Etruscan one dedicated to Minerva. To the left are oblong **Lombard tombs** from the 7th century A.D., when this part of Fiesole was a necropolis. The archaeological area is open year-round: April to September daily 9am to 7pm; March and October daily 10am to 6pm; and November to February Wednesday through Monday 10am to 3pm.

SIENA ★★★

70km (43 miles) S of Florence

With a uniquely preserved medieval core, Siena is for many admirers the most beautiful town in Italy. Viewed from the summit of the Palazzo Pubblico's tower, a sea of roof tiles and red brick blends into a labyrinth of steep, twisting stone alleys. This cityscape hides dozens of Gothic palaces and pastry shops galore, longstanding neighborhood rivalries, and painted altarpieces of unsurpassed elegance.

Founded as a Roman colony by Emperor Augustus, Siena enjoyed its heyday in the 13th and 14th centuries. In 1270, Sienese merchants established the Council of Nine, an oligarchy that ruled through Siena's great republican era, when civic projects and artistic prowess reached their heights. Artists such as Duccio di Buoninsegna, Simone Martini, and the Lorenzetti brothers invented a distinctive Sienese art, a highly developed Gothic style that became an artistic foil to the emerging Florentine Renaissance. Then in 1348, a plague known as the "Black Death" hit the city, killing perhaps three-quarters of its 100,000

Sienna seen from above.

population, destroying the social fabric and devastating the economy. Siena never recovered. Much of it has barely changed since.

Essentials

ARRIVING The **bus** is more convenient than the train, because Siena's rail station is way outside of town. **Autolinee Toscane** (www.at-bus.it) runs express

Bell tower of the Palazzo Pubblico in Siena.

(*rapida*; 75 min.) and slower buses (*ordinaria*; 100 min.) from Florence's main bus station to Siena's Piazza Gramsci. It costs around 9€ each way and there is no need to reserve ahead. Buses run at least hourly in the morning. Try not to make the trip on Sundays when the service is much reduced. The last bus back usually departs at 8:45pm (7:10pm is generally the last express service on weekends; but check ahead as schedules change).

If you have a **car,** a fast road direct from Florence (it has no route number; follow the green or blue signs toward Siena) is about a 90-minute drive. The more scenic route, down the **Chiantigiana wine road,** the **SS222,** takes 2 hours or so. But for day trips, the bus makes more sense than driving.

VISITOR INFORMATION The **tourist office** is at Piazza del Campo 7 (www.terresiena.it/en/siena; ✆ **0577/29-2222**). It is open daily from 9am to

5pm. An information kiosk also operates 9am to 2pm in summer at Piazza Gramsci, where buses from Florence terminate.

PARKING   Siena's most convenient **parking lots** (www.sienaparcheggi. com; ✆ **0577/228-711**) charge around 2€ per hour. All lots are well marked, and locations are just outside the city gates. An especially handy lot is **Santa Caterina,** where escalators whisk you up to town.

Exploring Siena

Be prepared for one *seriously* busy day (and even then, you can't see it all). Stepped alleys lead down into **Piazza del Campo** ★★ ("Il Campo"), arguably the most beautiful piazza in Italy. Crafted like a sloping scallop shell, the Campo was first laid out in the 1100s on the former site of the Roman forum. The herringbone brick pavement is divided by white marble lines into nine sections representing the city's medieval ruling body, the Council of Nine.

Overlooking the Campo, the crenellated town hall, **Palazzo Pubblico** ★★★ (built 1297–1310), is the city's finest Gothic palace (many would say Tuscany's finest), and the **Museo Civico** inside (✆ **0577/292-615**) is home to Siena's best artworks. Frescoed on the wall of the Sala del Mappamondo, Simone Martini's 1315 **"Maestà"** ★★ honors the Virgin Mary, Siena's saintly protector. Next door, in the Sala della Pace, Ambrogio Lorenzetti covered the walls in his **"Allegories of Good and Bad Government"** ★★★ (1338), full of detail of medieval Sienese life; it was painted to provide encouragement to the city's governing body, which met inside the room. The frescoes are undergoing a major multiyear restoration. The museum is open daily from 10am to 7pm (until 6m Nov–Feb). Admission costs 10€, 9€ for students and seniors, free for children 10 and under. Reduced admission (6€) is offered while Lorenzetti's art is hidden from view.

Having seen Siena's civic heart, next visit its religious monuments on **Piazza del Duomo** (operaduomo.siena.it; ✆ **0577/286-300**) on a single ticket, the **Opa Si Pass** (13€, or 15€ when the cathedral floor is visible; 2€ children 7 to 11), sold at the Museo dell'Opera (see below). The treasure inside Siena's **Duomo** ★★ include Bernini's **Cappella Chigi** ★ (1659) and the **Libreria Piccolomini** ★★, frescoed in 1507 with scenes from the life of Sienese Pope Pius II, by Pinturicchio. If you are visiting in July or from mid-August to mid-October, you will find the **Cathedral Floor** ★★★ uncovered; its 59 etched and inlaid marble panels were created between 1372 and 1547 by Siena's top artists, including Domenico di Bartolo, Matteo di Giovanni, Pinturicchio, and especially Domenico Beccafumi. The **Battistero** ★★ (Baptistery) has a baptismal font (1417–30) with gilded brass panels cast by the foremost Sienese and Florentine sculptors of the early Renaissance, including Jacopo della Quercia, Lorenzo Ghiberti, and Donatello. Inside the **Museo dell'Opera del Duomo** ★ is Siena's most precious work of art, Duccio di Buoninsegna's 1311 **"Maestà"** ★★★. It shows the Virgin and Child in majesty, adored by a litany of saints including St. Paul (holding the sword) and St. John the Baptist (pointing at Jesus and wearing animal skins). From the museum, climb to the top of the **Facciatone** ★★ for the best view in Siena, over the rooftops and

Mosaic floors inside Siena's Cathedral can usually be viewed July and mid-August to October.

down into the Campo. Opening hours for most of the Duomo sights are 10am to 5:30pm, stretching to 7pm in summer. Most of these sites are closed to visitors on Sunday mornings.

You also just about have time for **Santa Maria della Scala** ★★ (www.santamariadellascala.com; ⓒ **0577/228-744**), facing the cathedral facade. It's always much less busy than other sites in the city—and we have no idea why. An "old hospital" might not sound too enticing, but this huge building has treasures hidden away in its eerie corridors. The **Pellegrinaio** ★★ was frescoed in the 1440s with sometimes grisly scenes of life in this medieval hospital; the Old Sacristy has an even more gruesome **"Massacre of the Innocents"** ★★, painted in 1482 by Matteo di Giovanni. Also here is the spooky oratory where St. Catherine of Siena used to pray during the night; the city's **National Archaeological Museum** occupies a labyrinthine lower floor; in **Bambimus,** art is displayed at child's-eye height. Admission costs 9€, or 7€ for anyone 12 to 19 or 65 and over. Discounted combo tickets for Santa Maria Della Scala and the Museo Civico cost 14€. Santa Maria Della Scala is open 10am to 7pm; November through March it closes at 5pm Monday, Wednesday, Thursday, and Friday, plus all day Tuesday.

Where to Eat in Siena

Sienese cooking is rustic and simple, making liberal use of meat from the local *Cinta Senese* breed of pig. **L'Osteria dei Rossi** ★★, Via de' Rossi 81 (ⓒ **0577/287-592**), does a mean line in local grilled meats, including veal and *Cinta;* main courses range from 10€ to 17€. Close to the cathedral the **Osteria del Gusto** ★, Via dei Fusari 13 (www.osteriadelgusto.it; ⓒ **0577/271-076**), serves great-value, seasonal pasta dishes in filling portions. Think *pici* (fat,

---

REAL flavors OF THE CITY

Taste Siena ★★ (www.sienafoodtour.com) runs a culinary adventure in the streets of the city. A 3-hour guided walk provides five unique encounters with traditional Sienese cuisine—with stops for breakfast *bomboloni* (donuts), light lunch, *panforte* (a dense honey and nut cake), artisan cheese, wine, and more. Along the way, you'll hear lively insight into the history and culture of this little city. Tours run daily from 10am. It costs 85€ per person (55€ for children 11 and under), all tastings included.

hand-rolled spaghetti) served with a *ragù* of *Cinta* and porcini mushrooms for around the 10€ to 12€ mark.

If you prefer a sandwich to a sit-down meal, walk around the back of the Palazzo Pubblico to **Gino Cacino di Angelo ★★**, Piazza del Mercato 31 (ginocacinodiangelo.blogspot.com; ✆ **0577/223-076**). Sublime offerings include aged pecorino cheese, Tuscan salami, anchovies, porchetta, and pretty much anything else that can go on bread or a tasting platter, all carefully sourced. It is open daily until 8pm, but often closes for a couple of weeks in August. The best gelato in the city is churned at **Kopakabana ★**, Via de' Rossi 52–54 (✆ **0577/284-124**); it's open daily 11am to midnight mid-February through October.

PISA ★★

76km (47 miles) W of Florence

On a grassy lawn against the northwest corner of the city walls, medieval Pisans created one of the most dramatic (and now most photographed) squares in the world. Dubbed the **Campo dei Miracoli** (or "Field of Miracles"), Piazza del Duomo contains an array of elegant buildings that heralded the Pisan-Romanesque style—including the *Torre Pendente,* better known as the **Leaning Tower of Pisa.**

Founded as a seaside settlement around 1000 B.C., Pisa expanded into a naval trading port under the Romans in the 2nd century B.C. By the 11th century, it had grown into one of Europe's most powerful maritime republics. Extensive

Visiting Pisa's Campo dei Miracoli, you can see the Leaning Tower as part of a whole elegant ensemble.

trading in the Middle East helped Pisa import Arab ideas—decorative and scientific—to Italy. In 1284, Pisa's battle fleet was destroyed by Genoa at Meloria, off Livorno, a staggering defeat that helped the Genoese take control of the Tyrrhenian Sea and forced Pisa's long gradual slide into twilight. Florence took Pisa in 1406 and, despite a few minor rebellions, remained in charge until Italian unification in the 1860s.

Essentials

ARRIVING   From Florence's Santa Maria Novella station, around 50 daily **trains** make the trip (50–90 min.; 9€ one-way) to Pisa Centrale station. The last fast connection back to Florence departs around 9:30pm, but check **www. trenitalia.com** for timetable updates. There's also a fast, direct, and (for now) free **road**—the so-called *FI–PI–LI*—from Florence to Pisa along the Arno valley. Journey time is usually around 1¼ hours, subject to traffic.

VISITOR INFORMATION   The most convenient tourist office for the sights is at Piazza del Duomo 7 (www.turismo.pisa.it; *C* **050/550-100**). It is usually open daily 10am to 4pm.

GETTING AROUND   It's a long walk from the main station to the major sights. Every 10 minutes a LAM Rossa **bus** (www.at-bus.it) runs from the train station to the "Torre" stop near the Leaning Tower (10 min.; 1.50€). Buy tickets from the station newsstand or the automatic machine; it's 2.50€ per person if you purchase a ticket onboard.

PARKING   Much of central Pisa is a controlled traffic zone. However, city-managed lots are conveniently located within walking distance of the Campo, along Via Cammeo and Via Piave (3€/hr.). See **www.pisamo.it**.

Exploring Pisa

At the **Campo dei Miracoli ★★★**, your likely main destination in Pisa, monuments are linked on various combo tickets. The cathedral plus any other site except the Tower costs 7€; to access everything except the Leaning Tower costs 10€. The **Leaning Tower** costs 20€ (includes cathedral admission; no reductions). To enter everything on the square costs 27€. Accompanied children under 10 do not pay, except at the Tower.

Tower admission is via timed half-hour slots. To buy tickets and book a slot, visit **www.opapisa.it**. *You should reserve up to 20 days ahead of arrival in peak season, or if you are on an inflexible schedule.* Anyone under 18 must be accompanied by an adult; children 8 and under are not allowed in the Tower. Ticket offices are dotted around the square: If you have no Tower reservation, head to one of them immediately to book for later in the day.

First, spend a moment looking at the layout of **Piazza del Duomo.** A hidden part of the square's appeal is its spatial geometry: If you take an aerial photo of the square and draw connect-the-dot lines between the centers, doors, and other focal points, you'll come up with an array of perfect triangles and tangential lines of mathematical grace.

The facade of the duomo in Pisa.

Buscheto, the architect who laid the **duomo**'s first stone in 1063, kicked off a new era in art by building what was to become the model for the Pisan–Romanesque style. All its key elements are here on the **facade ★★**, designed and built by Buscheto's successor, Rainaldo: alternating light and dark banding, rounded blind arches with Moorish-inspired lozenges at the top and colored marble inlay designs, and Lombard-style open galleries of mismatched columns, stacked to make the facade much higher than the roof. The **main door** was cast by students of Giambologna after a 1595 fire destroyed the original (the last surviving original door, which you can see in the **Museo dell'Opera,** was cast by Bonnano Pisano in 1180). On the back of the right transept, across from the bell tower, is a 2008 cast of the bronze **Door of San Ranieri ★★★**. Inside the Cathedral, on the north side of the nave, is Giovanni Pisano's masterpiece **pulpit ★★★** (1302–1311)—it's the last and perhaps greatest of the Pisano pulpits. Head over to the **Battistero (Baptistery) ★** to see its prototype: a carved stone **pulpit ★★** by Nicola Pisano (1255–60), Giovanni's father. This father-and-son team created multiple masterful pulpits over the years, following this model. Heavily influenced by classical works, Nicola's high-relief panels (a synopsis of Christ's life) include pagan gods converted to Christianity as Madonnas and saints.

Now on to the main attraction. Why does the **Torre Pendente (Leaning Tower) ★★★** lean? The main problem—and the bane of local engineers for eight centuries—is that you can't stack this much heavy marble on shifting subsoil and keep it all upright. Building began in 1173 under Guglielmo and Bonnano Pisano, who also cast the Duomo's doors (see above). They reached the third level in 1185 when they noticed a lean, at that point only about 3.8cm (1½ in.). Work stopped until 1275, under Giovanni di Simone. He tried to correct the tilt by curving the structure back toward the perpendicular, giving the tower its slight "banana" shape. In 1284, work stopped yet again. In 1360, Tommaso di Andrea da Pontedera capped it off at about 51m (167 ft.) with a vaguely Gothic belfry. In 2018, scientists discovered the lean was 4cm (1½ in.) less than originally thought.

The walls of the **Camposanto ★★**, or cemetery, were once covered with important 14th- and 15th-century frescoes by Taddeo Gaddi, Spinello Aretino, and Benozzo Gozzoli, among others. On July 27, 1944, however, American warplanes launched an attack against the city (which was still in German hands) and the Camposanto was accidentally bombed. The most fascinating panel to survive the bombing is a 1341 **"Triumph of Death" ★**, attributed to Florentine Buonamico Buffalmacco.

Where to Eat in Pisa

If you want a genuine taste of Pisa, get away from the crowds around the Tower. Head south on Via Santa Maria as far as Piazza Cavalotti, then along Via dei Mille into Piazza dei Cavalieri. Continue through this vast, polygonal square to the center of the "real" city—less than a 10-minute walk away. At **Osteria dei Cavalieri ★★**, Via San Frediano 16 (www.osteriacavalieri.pisa. it; ℂ **050/580-858**), you'll find grilled meats, hearty dishes such as wild boar stewed in Chianti, daily fresh fish, and traditional Pisan cuisine like rabbit stewed with oregano. Main courses range from 13€ to 18€. Osteria dei Cavalieri is closed Wednesdays and for 3 weeks in August. Just across the River Arno, you'll find a great-value lunch at **La Taverna di Pulcinella ★**, Via Garofani 10 (ℂ **050/520-2704**). Wood-oven pizzas cost around 10€, including a range of vegan versions, or you can opt for a value 12€ two-course Pisan menu, which may be the likes of spelt with garbanzo beans and porcini mushrooms followed by a rustic pork steak with garlic and rosemary. It's closed Sundays.

For pizza or *cecina* (warm chickpea-flour flatbread) and a cold beer, stop at **Il Montino ★★**, Vicolo del Monte 1 (ℂ **050/598-695**), an eat-in or takeout spot often busy with students.

SAN GIMIGNANO ★★★

52km (32 miles) SW of Florence

An otherworldly scene hits you when you pass through the Porta San Giovanni gate, inside the walls of **San Gimignano:** a thoroughly medieval center peppered with the tall towers which made *San Gimignano delle Belle Torri* ("of the beautiful towers") the poster child for Italian hill towns everywhere. At one time, around 70 of the things spiked the sky above this outsized village. Today, only a dozen or so remain. The towers first rose in the bad old days of the 1200s, partly to defend against outside invaders but mostly as "command centers" for San Gimignano's warring families. As successive waves of plague

Piazza del Duomo, San Gimignano.

swept through (1348, 1464, and 1631 were bad), the economy—then based on textiles and hospitality for pilgrims walking the Via Francigena to Rome—crumbled. San Gimignano slowly became a provincial backwater. As a result, when tourism picked up in the 19th century, visitors found a delightfully preserved medieval village of decaying stone towers.

Essentials

ARRIVING Your best bet is the **bus.** From Florence's main bus station, **Autolinee Toscane** (www.at-bus.it) runs buses for most of the day, a 50-minute journey to Poggibonsi, where many services are timed to connect on to San Gimignano (a further 20–25 min.). Buy through-tickets for the whole journey in Florence (around 7€). The last bus back usually departs around 8:30pm, but check when you leave Florence or in San Gimignano's tourist information office. *Tip:* Avoid making this trip on a Sunday when bus service is much reduced.

Arriving by **car,** take the Poggibonsi Nord exit off the Florence–Siena highway or the SS2. San Gimignano is 12km (7½ miles) from Poggibonsi, through very pretty countryside.

VISITOR INFORMATION The friendly **tourist office** at Piazza Duomo 1 (www.sangimignano.com/en; ✆ **0577/940-008**) is open daily 10am to 1pm and 3 to 7pm (closed Sun afternoon).

PARKING The most convenient parking is at Parcheggio Montemaggio (signposted "P2"), outside the Porta San Giovanni (2.50€ an hour, 15€ per day).

You can stroll into town from here. P1 (Giubileo), the farthest lot from town, is the cheapest (1.50€ an hour, 6€ per day). Drive up to the town gate, drop any passengers, then return to park—it is a stiff uphill walk of 7 to 10 minutes back from P1.

Exploring San Gimignano

Anchoring the town at the top of Via San Giovanni are interlocking triangular *piazze:* **Piazza della Cisterna ★★**, with a 1237 well as its centerpiece, and **Piazza del Duomo,** flanked by the city's main church and civic palace. It is easy to find them: From any direction, just walk uphill.

The town's key art site is the **Collegiata ★★**, Piazza del Duomo (www.duomosangimignano.it; *⌀* **0577/286-300**). The right wall of this collegiate church was frescoed from 1333 to 1341—most likely by Lippo Memmi—with three levels of **New Testament scenes** (22 in all) on the life and Passion of Christ. In 1367, Bartolo di Fredi frescoed the left wall with 26 scenes from the **Old Testament;** Taddeo di Bartolo added a **"Last Judgment"** peppered with gruesome details (just above and left of the main door) in 1410.

In 1468, Giuliano da Maiano built the **Cappella di Santa Fina ★★★** off the right aisle; his brother Benedetto carved relief panels for the altar. Florentine painter Domenico Ghirlandaio decorated the tiny chapel's walls with some of his finest, airiest works, including two scenes depicting the life of

The medieval towers of San Gimignano.

Santa Fina, a local girl who, although never officially canonized, is one of San Gimignano's patron saints. Admission to the Collegiata costs 5€, 3€ for children 6 to 17. From April through October it's open Monday to Friday 10am to 7:30pm, Saturday 10am to 5pm, and Sunday 12:30 to 7:30pm; November to March hours are Monday to Saturday 10am to 5pm, Sunday 12:30 to 5pm. It's closed the second half of November and the second half of January.

The town's small **Museo Civico** ★ (Civic Art Museum), Piazza del Duomo 2 (www.sangimignanomusei.it; ℂ **0577/286-300**), inside the Palazzo Comunale, houses a **"Maestà"** ★★ (1317) by Sienese painter Lippo Memmi and rather racy medieval "wedding night" frescoes by Lippo's father, Memmo di Filippuccio. Admission costs 9€. The same ticket gets you up the tallest tower still standing, the **Torre Grossa** ★★. From 54m (175 ft.) up, you can gaze for miles across hills and grapevines. The museum and tower are open daily 11am to 6pm (Apr–Oct 10am–7:30pm). *Tip:* A **San Gimignano Pass** combo ticket gets you into all the above sites. It costs 13€—grand savings of 1€.

At **Sant Agostino,** Piazza Sant'Agostino (ℂ **0577/907-012**), Florentine painter Benozzo Gozzoli spent two years frescoing the walls behind the main altar floor to ceiling with scenes rich in architectural detail from the **"Life of St. Augustine"** ★★. The church is generally open daily 10am to noon and 3 to 7pm (Nov–Mar it closes at 6pm; Jan–Mar it's sometimes closed Mon mornings). Admission is free.

Where to Eat in San Gimignano

The most convenient restaurant for daytrippers, **Chiribiri** ★, Piazzetta della Madonna 1 (ℂ **0577/941-948**), is open all day—you can dine early before heading for the bus or car parks. It is a small place, with a simple, well-executed menu of Italian and Tuscan classics such as lasagne, *osso buco,* and wild boar stew. Main courses are priced fairly at 10€ to 18€. The town's essential foodie stop, however, isn't a restaurant, but the **Gelateria Dondoli** ★★, Piazza della Cisterna 4 (www.gelateriadondoli.com; ℂ **0577/942-244**), for creative combinations like raspberry and rosemary (it works) and their signature *crema di Santa Fina,* made with saffron and pine nuts. Unusual for the Tuscan hills, the local wine here is white: delicate, straw-colored Vernaccia di San Gimignano DOCG.

VENICE

By Stephen Keeling

No other place in the world looks quite like Venice. This vast, floating city of grand *palazzi*, elegant bridges, gondolas, and canals is a magnificent spectacle, truly magical when approached by sea for the first time, when its golden domes and soaring bell towers seem to rise straight from the sea. While it can sometimes appear that Venice is little more than an open-air museum where tourists outnumber locals—by a large margin—it is still surprisingly easy to lose the crowds. Indeed, the best way to enjoy Venice is simply to get lost in its labyrinth of narrow streets, stumbling upon a quiet *campo* (square), market stall, or cafe far off the beaten track, where even the humblest medieval church might contain masterful work by Tiepolo, Titian, or Tintoretto.

The origins of Venice—known as "La Serenissima" for centuries—are as muddy as parts of the lagoon it now occupies, but most histories begin with the arrival of refugees from Attila the Hun's invasion of Italy in the mid-5th century (though the official foundation date is A.D. 421). The mudflats were gradually built over and linked together, channels and streams eventually becoming canals. By the 11th century, Venice had emerged as a major independent trading city, and by the 13th century a seaborne empire (which included Crete, Corfu, and Cyprus) was held together by a huge navy and commercial fleet. Though embroiled with wars against rival Italian city Genoa and the Ottoman Turks for much of the ensuing centuries, these were golden years for Venice, when booming trade with the Far East funded much of its grand architecture and art. Although it remained an outwardly rich city, by the 1700s the good times were over, and in 1797 Napoleon dissolved the Venetian Republic without a shot (handing it over to the Austrians shortly afterward). You'll gain a sense of some of this history touring **Piazza San Marco** and **St. Mark's Basilica,** or by visiting the **Accademia,** one of Italy's great art galleries, but only when you wander the back

Colorful facades of Venice's floating palaces.

calli (streets) will you encounter the true, living, breathing side of Venice, still redolent of those glory days.

STRATEGIES FOR SEEING VENICE

Wandering aimlessly off the beaten path is a marvelous way to experience Venice, but you'll still want to hit all the must-see sights—preferably without over-spending or getting stuck in San Marco tourist gridlock. These strategies and time-tested tips will help you make the most of your time here.

o **Avoid the lines:** It pays to book ahead (online) for the Palazzo Ducale and the Accademia, which guarantees you an entry time. Venice offers several discount cards (see p. 319) that also let you skip ticketing lines (the **Museum Pass** is recommended).

o **Plan your sightseeing around lunch:** Some sights do close for lunch in Venice (12:30–3pm), but most (including the churches) stay open, meaning a lot fewer people at each location.

o **Walk:** Aside from on boats, the only way to explore Venice is on foot. Though the layout of the city is confusing, getting lost in its streets is part of the fun. Indeed, explore the far reaches of the city and you'll be guaranteed to lose the crowds, even in summer—most folks rarely stray beyond the main routes. See p. 270 for tips on getting around Venice.

o **Be prepared for Sunday closures:** While most sights in Venice are open every day (some museums close on Tues), much of the city's art is in

Piazza San Marco (St. Mark's Square).

churches, and many of those are closed to tourists on Sundays, either for the morning or all day. There's one way to get around this: Attend a Sunday service as a worshipper. You may not be able to study the art at length, but it's the best way to put this great religious art in context.

o **Avoid the crowds:** Late February and March, just after Carnevale, is a great time to visit; it can be cool and misty, but you'll have the streets and canals (largely) to yourself. Otherwise, get up at sunrise in summer at least once, just to wander the city before the crowds emerge—it's a magical experience.

o **Save money on meals:** Eating in Venice can be expensive, but plenty of budget options persist (see p. 304). You'll save loads by frequenting neighborhood bars known as *bàcari* (normally 5–7pm), where you can stand or sit with small plates of *cicchetti* (tapas-like finger foods), washed down with a small glass of wine. Anywhere near Piazza San Marco is likely to be expensive; it's best to avoid places with *menù turistico* options.

ESSENTIALS

Arriving

BY PLANE From North America, the cheapest flights to Venice tend to route through Rome or Milan via **ITA Airways,** though **Swissair** (via Zurich),

TRAVEL DISRUPTIONS IN venice

In 2020, Venice was rocked by the Covid-19 pandemic, which shuttered businesses and devastated the tourist industry. The city fared better than other areas of Italy, however, and by 2021 Venice had largely reopened for business. At the time of writing, it is no longer mandatory to wear a face mask on public transport, but its use indoors and in all cases of crowded outdoor events is highly recommended. Masks are still likely to be required in hospitals and health clinics, so bring some just in case. Check with your hotel or the Venezia Unica website for the latest.

For details on Italy protocols, see chapter 10.

Lufthansa (via Frankfurt), **KLM** (via Amsterdam), and **Air France** (via Paris) usually offer cheap fares in low season (code-sharing with U.S. carriers). If traveling in the peak spring and summer seasons, however, it's worth considering far more convenient seasonal nonstop flights, which are often priced competitively—assuming you buy far enough in advance. **Delta Airlines** (www.delta.com) flies from Atlanta (late Jun–Aug) and New York-JFK (Apr–Sep); **United Airlines** (www.united.com) from Newark (Jun–late Sep); and **American Airlines** (www.aa.com) from Philadelphia (May–Oct). For those already in Europe, numerous budget airlines serve Venice, offering rock-bottom prices. No-frills **easyJet** (www.easyjet.com) flies from Amsterdam, Berlin, London-Gatwick, Manchester, and Paris; while **Ryanair** (www.ryanair.com) flies from Birmingham (UK), Barcelona, and London-Stansted, with many other flights routed through nearby **Treviso** (a 1-hr. bus ride to Venice).

Water taxis and vaporetti along the Canal Grande.

Flights land at the **Aeroporto di Venezia Marco Polo (VCE),** 7km (4¼ miles) north of the city on the mainland (www.veniceairport.it; ☎ **041/2609260**). The cheapest way to get to town is by **bus,** though this is not recommended if you have heavy luggage; buses can't drive into Venice itself, so you'll have to walk to or from the final stop, Piazzale Roma, to the nearby *vaporetto* (water bus) stop for the final connection to your hotel. (See "The Vaporetto Lowdown," p. 267.) It's rare to find porters who'll help with luggage, so pack light.

The **ATVO airport shuttle bus** (www.atvo.it; ☎ **0421/594672**) runs between Piazzale Roma and the airport about every 20 minutes, costing 10€ (18€ roundtrip); the trip takes about 20 minutes. Buy tickets at the automatic ticket machines in the arrival baggage hall, or the Public Transport ticket office (daily 8am–midnight). The local **ACTV bus no. 5** (actv.avmspa.it; ☎ **041/2424**) also costs 10€, also takes 20 minutes, and runs between two and four times an hour depending on the time of day; the best option here is to buy the combined ACTV and "Rete Unica" ticket for 18€ (valid for 90 min.), which includes your first *vaporetto* ride at a slight discount. Buy tickets at machines just outside the airport terminal.

It's also possible to take a **land taxi** (www.radiotaxivenezia.com; ☎ **041/ 5964**) from the airport to Piazzale Roma (where you get the *vaporetto*) for a fixed 40€ (it's 35€ to Mestre). While this is more convenient and a bit faster (15 min.) than the bus, it still doesn't take you to your hotel (unless you're staying right by Piazzale Roma)—you are better off spending the extra euros on water transport.

The most evocative and traditional way to arrive in Venice is by sea. For 15€, the **Cooperative San Marco/Alilaguna** (www.alilaguna.it; ☎ **041/2401701**) operates a large *motoscafo* (shuttle boat) service from the airport boathouse (a short, covered walk from the terminal) with two primary routes. The *Linea Blu* (blue line) runs almost every 30 minutes from 5:20am to 12:20am, stopping at Murano (8€) and the Lido before arriving, after about 1 hour and 30 minutes, in Piazza San Marco. The *Linea Arancio* (orange line) runs almost every 30 minutes from 8:05am to 10:50pm, taking 1 hour and 20 minutes to arrive at San Marco, but gets there through the Grand Canal, which is much more spectacular and offers the possibility to get off at one of the stops along the way. This might be convenient to your hotel and could save you from having to take another means of transportation. If you arrive at Piazza San Marco and your hotel isn't in the area, you'll have to make a connection at the *vaporetto* launches. (If you're booking a hotel in advance, ask for specific advice how to get there.)

A good alternative is the **Venice Shuttle** (www.venicelink.com; daily 4am–11pm; minimum two people for reservations), a shared water taxi (carrying six to eight people) that will whisk you directly from the airport to many hotels and most of the major locations in the city for 32€ (add 6€ after 8pm). You must reserve online in advance.

A **private water taxi** (20–30 min. to/from the airport) is the most convenient option but costly—a trip to the city costs 122€ (discounted rates at www. venicelink.com) for up to four passengers with one bag each (10€ more for each extra person up to a maximum of 10, 5€ for each extra suitcase, and another 10€ for trips 10pm–7am). It's worth considering if you're pressed for time, have an early flight (taxis run 24 hr.), are carrying a lot of luggage (a Venice no-no), or can split the cost with a friend or two. It may be able to drop you off at the front (or side) door of your hotel or as close as it can maneuver given your hotel's location (check with the hotel before arriving). Your taxi captain should be able to tell you before boarding just how close he can get you. Try **Corsorzio Motoscafi Venezia** (www.motoscafivenezia.it; ✆ **041/5222303**) or **Venezia Taxi** (www.veneziataxi.it; ✆ **041/723112**).

BY TRAIN   High-speed **Frecciarossa** or **Frecciargento** trains (www.tren italia.com) or rival high-speed trains operated by **Italo** (www.italotreno.it) from Rome (4 hr.), Milan (2½ hr.), Florence (2¼ hr.), and all over Europe arrive at the **Stazione Venezia Santa Lucia.** To get there, all must pass through (although not necessarily stop at) a station marked Venezia-Mestre. Don't be confused: Mestre is a charmless industrial city that's the last major stop on the mainland (some trains also stop at the next station, Venezia Porto Marghera, before continuing to Venice proper). Occasionally trains end in Mestre, in which case you'll have to catch one of the frequent 10-minute shuttles connecting with Venice; it's inconvenient, so when you book your ticket, confirm that the final destination is Venezia Santa Lucia.

La Serenissima rises from a muddy lagoon in the Adriatic Sea.

THE vaporetto LOWDOWN

Whether you're arriving by train, bus, or car, your first challenge when you get to \Venice will be to take a *vaporetto* (water bus) on to your destination. The *vaporetto* is the seagoing streetcar of Venice, going to all parts of the city. Here's how to do it right.

Finding the right boat is a little easier if you're arriving by bus or car, because you'll be in Piazzale Roma, the route **no. 1** *vaporetto* terminus, and all these boats will be going the right direction. (See "By Vaporetto," p. 271, for information on tickets.) Exiting the train station, however, you'll find the Grand Canal immediately in front of you, with the docks for several *vaporetti* lines to your left and right. Head to the booths to your left, near the bridge, to buy tickets, then head for the docks farther to your right. The most useful routes are the two lines plying the Grand Canal: the **no. 2 express** (from bay "B"), which stops only at the San Marcuola, Rialto Bridge, San Tomà, San Samuele, and Accademia before hitting San Marco (30 min. total); and the slower

no. 1 (from bay "E"), which makes 13 stops before arriving at San Marco (a 36-min. trip). Both leave every 10 minutes or so, but before 9am and after 8pm, the no. 2 sometimes stops short at Rialto, meaning you'll have to disembark and hop on the next no. 1 or 2 that comes along to continue to San Marco.

Word to the wise: The *vaporetti* go in two directions from the train station. Those heading left go down the Grand Canal toward San Marco—which is the (relatively) fast and scenic way. The no. 2 route heading right also eventually gets you to San Marco (at the San Zaccaria stop) but takes more than twice as long because it goes the long way around Dorsoduro (this line serves mainly commuters). As for the no. 1 line going to the right from the train station, it will go only one more stop before it hits its terminus at Piazzale Roma. **Make sure the vaporetto you get on is heading to the left.** Departing from **Piazzale Roma, make sure no. 2 is going to the right** (no.1 will only go right).

BY BUS Although rail travel is more convenient and commonplace, Venice is serviced by long-distance buses from all over mainland Italy and some international cities. Most regional buses terminate at Piazzale Roma, where you'll need to pick up *vaporetto* no. 1 or no. 2 (see box above) to connect you with stops in the heart of Venice and along the Grand Canal. **Eurolines** (www.euro lines.eu) buses drop off on the adjacent island of **Tronchetto,** which is a much longer walk from the action. Buses stop at the Tronchetto **People Mover** station where a light railway whisks you to Piazzale Roma in just 3 minutes (1.50€ one-way), though you will mostly likely need onward transportation from there. *Vaporetto* line 2 does stop at Tronchetto (facing the water, boats depart left to the train station and Grand Canal, right to San Marco).

BY CAR The only wheels you'll see in Venice are those attached to luggage. **No cars are allowed,** or more to the point, no cars could drive through the narrow streets and over the footbridges—even the police, fire department, and ambulance services use boats. You can drive across the Ponte della Libertà from Mestre to Venice, but you can go no farther than Piazzale Roma at the Venice end, where many garages eagerly await your euros (and in high season are often full). The **Autorimessa Comunale garage** (avm.avmspa.it; ℂ **041/2727301**) charges 35€ for a 24-hour period (30€ on-line), while **Garage San Marco** (www.garagesanmarco.it; ☎ **041/5232213**) costs 45€ for 24 hours. From Piazzale Roma, you can catch *vaporetti* lines 1 and 2 (see box p. 267), which go down the Grand Canal to the train station and, eventually, Piazza San Marco. Cheaper (and in some cases free) parking is available on the adjacent island of **Tronchetto** (see "By Bus," above), first right as you cross the Ponte della Libertà.

Visitor Information

TOURIST OFFICES   The most central **Venezia Unica** (www.veneziaunica.it) information office lies in the arcade at the western end of **Piazza San Marco,** Calle Larga de l'Ascensione 71F, near Museo Correr (daily 7am–7pm; ☎ **041/ 2424**). Offices are also at **Piazzale Roma** (kiosk near Ponte della Costituzione; daily 7am–8pm), the **train station** (opposite platforms 2 and 3; daily 7am–9pm), and in the arrivals hall at **Marco Polo Airport** (daily 8:30am–7pm). These offices do not offer free maps—they charge 3€.

The info-packed monthly *Un Ospite di Venezia* (www.unospitedivenezia.it) is a useful source of information (published in Italian and English); most hotels have free copies. Also useful is *VeNews* (www.venezianews.it), a monthly (3€) sold at newsstands all over the city (also in English and Italian).

City Layout

Even armed with the best map or a hefty smartphone data plan, expect to get a little bit lost in Venice, at least some of the time (GPS directions are notoriously

---

Tourist Tax: New Start for Venice?

Pre-Covid-19, Venice was attracting an astounding 30 million visitors a year, or around 80,000 visitors per day—dwarfing the local population of just 50,000. The 2020 lockdown resulted in less pollution and crystal-clear canals for the first time in decades. Though most Venetians recognize the importance of tourism to the local economy, few want to return to the pre-lockdown bad old days of overtourism. Organizations such as the **Venetian Heritage Foundation** (www.venetianheritage.org) and **Save Venice** (www.savevenice.org) have called for restrictions on Airbnb apartments in Venice and support for cheaper long-term rentals to encourage locals to come back from the mainland. In a move widely applauded, cruise ships were banned from the inner lagoon in August 2021 (with ships diverted to the ports of Monfalcone or Marghera, or eventually to a new permanent passenger terminal at the Lido). And to encourage "slow tourism" and longer stays—as opposed to *"mordi e fuggi,"* or "hit-and-run" tourism—the city also plans to charge entry fees for day-trippers. The plan has been delayed many times, but should be in place sometime in 2023, when even the diverted cruise-ship passengers will pay a flat 5€ fee (eventually rising to 7€). For everyone else, the rate will vary according to season and demand, ranging from 3€ to 10€ per day. Day-trippers will also have to make an online booking just to *enter* Venice (entry will be monitored via electronic turnstiles). Check the city's information website for the latest.

A Note on Addresses

Within each *sestiere* is a most original system of numbering the *palazzi,* using one continuous string of 6,000 or so numbers. The format for addresses in this chapter is, where possible, the number with the actual street or *campo* on which you'll find that address. But official mailing addresses (and what you'll see written down in most places), are simply the *sestiere* name followed by the building number, which isn't especially helpful—for example, San Marco 1471 may not necessarily be found close to San Marco 1473. Many buildings aren't numbered at all.

unreliable here). Just view it as an opportunity to stumble across Venice's most intriguing corners. Keep in mind as you wander seemingly hopelessly among the *calli* (streets) and *campi* (squares) that the city wasn't built to make sense to those on foot but rather to those plying its canals.

Venice lies 4km (2½ miles) from terra firma, connected to the mainland burg of Mestre by the Ponte della Libertà, which leads to Piazzale Roma. Snaking through the city is the **Grand Canal,** the wide main artery of aquatic Venice. "Central Venice" refers to the built-up block of islands in the lagoon's center, the six main *sestieri* (districts) that make up the bulk of the tourist city. "Greater Venice" includes all the inhabited islands of the lagoon—central Venice plus Murano, Burano, Torcello, and the Lido.

In summer, the beaches of the Lido offer a cool escape.

Venice Neighborhoods in Brief

San Marco The most visited, and most central, *sestiere* is anchored by the magnificent Piazza San Marco and St. Mark's Basilica to the south and the Rialto Bridge to the north. This has been the commercial, religious, and political heart of the city for more than a millennium. Unfortunately, ever-rising rents have persuaded most locals to look for housing in other neighborhoods, but the area is laced with first-class hotels. See p. 280 for suggestions on where to stay in the heart of Venice without going broke.

Castello Just east of Piazza San Marco, Castello's tony waterside esplanade Riva degli Schiavoni follows the Bacino di San Marco (St. Mark's Basin), skirting Venice's most congested area to the north and east. Riva degli Schiavoni is often thronged, but if you head farther east in the direction of the Arsenale or inland away from the *bacino*, the crowds thin out. Here you'll find such major sights as Campo SS. Giovanni e Paolo and the Scuola di San Giorgio.

Dorsoduro Residential Dorsoduro, the largest of the *sestieri*, lies across the Accademia Bridge from San Marco. Home to the Accademia and Peggy Guggenheim museums, it was known as an artists' haven until rising rents forced many residents to relocate. Come here for good neighborhood restaurants, a charming gondola boatyard, lively Campo Santa Margherita, and the sunny canalside quay of le Zattere.

San Polo This mixed bag of residential corners and tourist sights stretches northwest of the Rialto Bridge to the church of Santa Maria dei Frari. At the foot of the bridge, you'll find the bustling Rialto Market. Some of the city's best restaurants flourish here, alongside some of its worst tourist traps. Spacious Campo San Polo is the main piazza.

Santa Croce North and northwest of the San Polo district and across the Grand Canal from the train station, Santa Croce stretches all the way to Piazzale Roma. Less lively than San Polo but just as authentic, it feels light-years away from San Marco; its little-visited eastern section is a great place for curious visitors to explore. Quiet, lovely Campo San Giacomo dell'Orio is its heart.

Cannaregio On the same side of the Grand Canal as San Marco and Castello, Cannaregio stretches north and east from the train station to include the old Jewish Ghetto. One-quarter of Venice's ever-shrinking population of 50,000 lives here. Many one-star hotels are clustered about the train station—not a dangerous neighborhood but not known for its charm, either. Strada Nova is Cannaregio's main thoroughfare, leading to the Rialto bridge.

La Giudecca Across the Giudecca Canal from Piazza San Marco and Dorsoduro, tranquil La Giudecca is a residential island where you'll find a youth hostel and a few hotels (including the deluxe Cipriani; see p. 288).

Lido di Venezia This slim, 11km-long (6¾-mile) island, the only spot in the Venetian lagoon where cars circulate, is the city's beach, fronting the open sea. It's also the home of the annual Venice Film Festival.

Getting Around Venice

Aside from traveling by boat, the only way to explore Venice is by walking—and by getting lost repeatedly. You'll navigate many twisting streets whose names change constantly and don't appear on any map, and streets that may very well end in a blind alley or spill abruptly into a canal. You'll also cross dozens of footbridges. Treat getting bewilderingly lost in Venice as part of the fun, and budget more time than you'd think necessary to get wherever you're going.

STREET MAPS & SIGNAGE The map sold by the tourist office (3€) and free maps provided by most hotels don't always show—much less name or index—all the *calli* (streets) and pathways of Venice. For that, pick up a more detailed map (ask for a *pianta della città* at news kiosks—especially those at the train station and around San Marco or most bookstores). The best (and most expensive) is the highly detailed **Touring Club Italiano map,** available in a variety of forms (folding from 8.50€) and scales. If using your phone, note that GPS directions are often unreliable in Venice, though Google Maps has definitely improved in recent years (and has added its "streetview" option to the city).

Still, Venice's confusing layout confounds even the best maps and navigators. You're often better off just stopping and asking a local to point you in the right direction (always know the name of the *campo*/square or major sight closest to the address you're looking for and ask for that).

As you wander, look for the ubiquitous yellow signs (well, *usually* yellow) whose destinations and arrows direct you toward five major landmarks: **Ferrovia** (the train station), **Piazzale Roma** (the parking garage), **Rialto** (one of the four bridges over the Grand Canal), **San Marco** (the city's main square), and the **Accademia** (the southernmost Grand Canal bridge).

BY VAPORETTO The various *sestieri* are linked by a comprehensive *vaporetto* (water bus/ferry) system of about a dozen lines operated by the **Azienda del Consorzio Trasporti Veneziano** (**ACTV;** actv.avmspa.it; *©* **041/5287886**). Transit maps are available at the tourist office and most ACTV ticket offices. It's easier to get around the center on foot, as the

A vaporetto cruises up the Grand Canal.

CRUISING THE canals

A leisurely cruise along the **Grand Canal ★★★** (p. 309) from Piazza San Marco to the train station (Ferrovia)—or the reverse—is one of Venice's must-dos. It's the world's most unusual Main Street, a watery boulevard whose *palazzi* have been converted into condos. Lower water-lapped floors are now deserted, but the higher floors are still coveted by the city's titled families, who have inhabited these glorious residences for centuries; others have become the summertime dream homes of privileged expats, drawn here as irresistibly as the romantic Venetians-by-adoption who preceded them: Richard Wagner, Henry James, Robert Browning, and Lord Byron among them.

As much a symbol of Venice as the winged lion, the **gondola ★★★** is one of Europe's great traditions, incredibly and inexplicably expensive but truly as romantic as it looks (detractors who write it off as too touristy have most likely never tried it). The official fixed rate is 80€ for a 30-minute gondola tour for up to six passengers. The rate bumps up to 100€ from 7pm to 8am (for 35 min.), and it's 40€ for every additional 20 minutes (50€ at night). That's not a typo: 150€ for a 1-hour evening cruise. ***Note:*** Although the price is fixed by the city, a good negotiator at the right time of day (when business is slow) can sometimes grab a small discount for a shorter ride. And at these ridiculously inflated prices, there is no need to tip the gondolier. You might also find **discounts online.**

Aim for late afternoon before sundown, when the light does its magic on the canal reflections (and bring a bottle of prosecco and glasses). If the gondola price is too high, find someone—other hotel guests, say—to share it. Though the price is "fixed," before setting off establish with the gondolier the cost, time, and route (back canals are preferable to the trafficked and often choppy Grand Canal). They're regulated by the **Ente Gondola** (www.gondolavenezia.it; *C* 041/5285075), so call if you have any questions or complaints.

And what of the serenading gondolier immortalized in film? Frankly, you're better off without. But if warbling is de rigueur for you, here's the scoop. An ensemble of accordion player and tenor is so expensive that it's shared among several gondolas traveling together. Several travel agents around town book the evening serenades for around 50€ per person.

Venice has 12 gondola stations, including Piazzale Roma, the train station, the Rialto Bridge, and Piazza San Marco. There are also a number of smaller stations, with *gondolieri* in striped shirts standing alongside their sleek 11m (36-ft.) black wonders looking for passengers. All speak enough English to communicate the necessary details. Remember, if you just want a quick taste of being in a gondola, you can take a cheap *traghetto* across the Grand Canal.

vaporetti principally serve the Grand Canal, the outskirts, and the outer islands. The crisscross network of small canals is the province of delivery vessels, gondolas, and private boats.

A *vaporetto* ticket (good for 75 min. after validation) is a steep 9.50€, while the 24-hour **ACTV travel card** is 25€—it only takes three rides to begin saving money with the card. (For even more savings, there are also ACTV travel cards for 48 hr. [35€] and 72 hr. [45€]). Most lines run every 10 to 15 minutes from 7am to midnight, and then hourly until morning. Most *vaporetto* docks have timetables posted. You can buy tickets at Venezia Unica offices, authorized

Gondolas waiting outside Church of Saint Mary of Nazareth.

retailers displaying the ACTV/Venezia Unica sticker, and usually at the dock itself, though not all have machines or kiosks that sell tickets. If you haven't bought a pass or tickets beforehand, you can pay the conductors onboard (find them immediately upon boarding—they won't come looking for you) or risk a stiff on-the-spot fine of at least 61€, no excuses accepted. You **must validate** (stamp) all tickets in the yellow machines at the docks before getting aboard. *Tip:* If you're staying in Venice for more than a week and intend to use the *vaporetto* service a lot, it makes sense to get a **Venezia Unica City Pass** (see "Venice Discounts," p. 319), which lets you buy *vaporetto* tickets for 1.50€.

BY TRAGHETTO   Just four bridges span the Grand Canal, and to fill in the gaps, *traghetti* skiffs (oversize gondolas rowed by two standing *gondolieri*) cross the Grand Canal at several intermediate points (during daylight hours only). You'll find a station at the end of any street named Calle del Traghetto on your map (though not all of them have active ferries today; ask a local before walking to the canal), indicated by a yellow sign with the black gondola symbol. These days only a handful operate regularly, primarily at San Tomà, Santa Maria del Giglio, and Santa Sofia (check with a local if in doubt). The fare is 2€, which you hand to the gondolier when boarding. Most Venetians cross standing up. For the experience, try the Santa Sofia crossing (Mon–Sat 7:30am–7pm, Sun 9am–7pm; Oct–Mar last crossing 6:30pm) that connects the Ca' d'Oro and the Pescheria fish market, opposite each other on the Grand Canal just north of the Rialto Bridge—the gondoliers expertly dodge water traffic at this point of the canal, where it's the busiest and most heart-stopping.

BY WATER TAXI   *Taxi acquei* (water taxis) charge high prices and aren't for visitors watching their euros. Trips in town are likely to cost at least 50€ to 90€, depending on distance, time of day, and whether you've booked in advance or just hired on the spot. Each trip includes allowance for up to four to five pieces of luggage—beyond that there's a surcharge of 3€ to 5€ per piece (rates differ slightly according to company and how you reserve a trip). Plus there's a 20€ supplement for service from 10pm to 7am, and a 5€ charge for taxis on-call. Those rates cover up to four people; if any more squeeze in, it's another 5€ to 10€ per extra passenger (maximum 10 people). Taking a water taxi from the train station to Piazza San Marco or any of the hotels in

A gondola near the Rialto Bridge.

the area will put you back about 90€ (the Lido is around 100€), while fixed fees to the airport range 120€ to 130€ (for up to four people). Taxis to Burano or Torcello will be at least 140€. Note that only taxi boats with a yellow strip are the official operators sanctioned by the city. You can book trips with Consorzio Moscafi Venezia online at **www.motoscafivenezia.it** or call ☎ **041/ 5222303.** Six water-taxi stations serve key points in the city: the Ferrovia, Piazzale Roma, the Rialto Bridge, Piazza San Marco, the Lido, and Marco Polo Airport.

BY GONDOLA　If you've come all this way and don't indulge in a gondola ride, you might be kicking yourself long after you have returned home. Yes, it's touristy, and, yes, it's expensive (see "Cruising the Canals" on p. 272), but only those with a heart of stone will be unmoved by the quintessential Venetian experience. Don't initiate your trip, however, until you have agreed on a price and synchronized watches. Oh, and don't ask them to sing.

[FastFACTS] VENICE

Doctors & Hospitals The **Ospedale Civile Santi Giovanni e Paolo** (☎ 041/ 5294111), on Campo Santi Giovanni e Paolo, has English-speaking staff and provides emergency service (go to the emergency room,

pronto soccorso) 24 hours a day (*vaporetto* Ospedale).

Emergencies The best number to call with a **general emergency** is ☎ 112; this connects you to the military-trained (and English-speaking) **Carabinieri** who will transfer your call as

needed. For the local **police,** dial ☎ 113; for a medical emergency and to call an **ambulance,** the number is ☎ 118; for the **fire department,** call ☎ 115. All are free calls.

Internet Access Venice offers citywide Wi-Fi through

the **Wi-Fi Venezia** (www.
veneziaunica.it) network of
200 hotspots. Buy packages
online (5€/24 hr., 15€/3 days,
or 20€/7 days); access codes
are then sent via e-mail.

Mail   The most convenient post offices are: **Venezia Centro** at Calle de la
Acque, San Marco (© **041/
2404149;** Mon–Fri 8:25pm–
7:10pm and Sat 8:25am–
12:35pm); **Venezia 4** at
Calle de l'Ascension 1241
(© **041/2446711**), off the

west side of Piazza San
Marco (Tues–Fri 8:25am–
1:35pm, Sat 8:25am–
12:35pm); and **Venezia 3**
at Campo San Polo 2012
(© **041/5200315;** same
hours as Venezia 4).

Pharmacies   Venice's
pharmacies take turns staying open all night. To find
out which one is on call in
your area, ask at your hotel
or check the rotational duty
signs posted outside all
pharmacies.

Safety   Be aware of pickpocketing on crowded
vaporetti, particularly on
tourist routes, where passengers are more intent on
the passing scenery than on
watching their bags. Ven-
ice's often deserted back
streets are virtually crime-
free, though occasional
tales of theft have circu-
lated. Generally speaking,
Venice is one of Italy's safest
cities.

WHERE TO STAY IN VENICE

Few cities boast as long a high season as that of Venice, beginning with the
Easter period—for most hotels it runs mid-March through November,
includes weekends year-round, Christmas and New Year, and carnival. This
leaves the few weeks between late November and late December, January, and
the week or so after carnival in early March to capture the low season rates.
May, June, and September are the best months weather-wise and, therefore the

---

COME HELL OR high water

During the tidal *acqua alta* (high water)
floods, Venice's lagoon rises until it
engulfs the city, leaving up to 1.5 to
1.8m (5–6 ft.) of water in the lowest-lying
streets. Piazza San Marco, as the lowest
point in the city, goes first. As many as
50 floods a year have been recorded
since they first started keeping track in
the late 1700s. One of the most devastating was in 1966, though the second-
highest occurred in November 2019, and
they seem to be getting worse—in 2021
flooding affected the city in August,
much earlier than usual.

Significant *acqua alta* can begin as
early as late September or October, but
usually takes place November to March
(there is no way to predict them in
advance). Remember, though, the waters
usually recede after just a few hours—
there is no need to get wet and the city
doesn't shut down. Walkways are set up

along the main routes, but if you intend
to wander around, do as the locals do
and buy rubber wading boots, available
from most stores from 20€ (for about
10€, souvenir shops and stands in Piazza
San Marco also sell disposable knee-high
plastic waterproof slippers, good for a
couple of days). A complex system of
hydraulic gates—the Modulo Sperimen-
tale Elettromeccanico or **MOSE**—began
operating in 2021, though it won't be
fully complete until 2025. MOSE is controversial because of its environmental
impact—keeping the gates closed for
long periods could result in parts of the
lagoon becoming stagnant, for example—but in the short run, key sights such
as St. Mark's Square will be spared the
worst of the flooding. Note however,
MOSE is only activated to block tides of
more than 110cm (3 ft., 7 in.), which
means light flooding is still likely to occur.

Ai Due Fanali **3**
Al Piave **18**
Al Ponte Antico **14**
Al Ponte Mocenigo **5**
American Dinesen **8**
Antica Locanda al Gambero **17**
Antiche Figure **2**
Arcadia **4**
Baglioni Hotel Luna **23**
B&B San Marco **20**
Bloom B&B **10**
Ca' Barba B&B **12**
Casa Verardo **19**
Cipriani, A Belmond Hotel **25**
Combo, Venezia **16**
Corte Di Gabriela **11**
Galleria **7**
Generator Venice **24**
Giorgione **15**
Locanda Fiorita **9**
Londra Palace **22**
Metropole **21**
Moresco **1**
Pensione Accademia **6**
Pensione Guerrato **13**

Venice Hotels

most crowded. July and August are hot (few of the one- and two-star hotels offer air-conditioning, and when they do, it usually costs extra). Like everything else, hotels are more expensive here than in any other Italian city, with no apparent upgrade in amenities—since the end of the COVID-19 pandemic rates have skyrocketed. The least special of those below are clean and functional; at best, they're charming and thoroughly enjoyable, with the serenade of a passing gondolier thrown in for good measure. Some may even provide you with your best stay in all of Europe. Try to reserve your lodging as far in advance as possible, even in the off-season.

Hotels by Price

EXPENSIVE

Al Ponte Antico ★★★, p. 287
Antiche Figure ★★★, p. 286
Baglioni Hotel Luna ★★★, p. 279
Bloom B&B ★★★, p. 279
Cipriani, A Belmond Hotel ★★★, p. 288
Corte Di Gabriela ★★★, p. 280
Londra Palace ★★, p. 281
Metropole ★★★, p. 281
Moresco ★★★, p. 283

American Dinesen ★★, p. 283
Antica Locanda al Gambero ★, p. 280
Arcadia ★★★, p. 287
Ca' Barba B&B ★★, p. 284
Casa Verardo ★★★, p. 282
Galleria ★★, p. 283
Giorgione ★★, p. 288
Locanda Fiorita ★★, p. 280
Pensione Accademia ★★, p. 284
Pensione Guerrato ★★★, p. 285

INEXPENSIVE

B&B San Marco ★★★, p. 282
Combo, Venezia ★★, p. 288
Generator Venice ★, p. 289

MODERATE

Ai Due Fanali ★★, p. 286
Al Piave ★★, p. 281
Al Ponte Mocenigo ★★★, p. 286

Self-Catering Apartments

Anyone looking to get into the local swing of things in Venice should stay in a **short-term rental apartment.** For the same price or less than a hotel room, you could have your own one-bedroom apartment with a washing machine, air-conditioning, and a fridge to keep your wine in. Properties of all sizes and styles, in every price range, are available for stays of 3 nights to several weeks.

In terms of **location,** San Marco is the most convenient part of the city, though anywhere near the Grand Canal will allow you easy access to the best of Venice. Apartments in the farther reaches of Santa Croce, Cannaregio, Giudecca, and Castello may be slightly cheaper and allow a glimpse of residential life in the city, but getting to and from the main sights will take a lot of time.

For those renting apartments, rather than staying in hotels, secure **luggage storage facilities** are available through Radical Storage (which acts as an agent for businesses prepared to look after your bags throughout the city), from 5€ per day (radicalstorage.com).

RECOMMENDED AGENCIES

Airbnb (www.airbnb.com), **VRBO.com**, and **Homeaway.com** are now major players in Venice, each with hundreds of properties listed. On Airbnb you can rent a room in someone's home from just 30€ per night. **Couchsurfing** (www.couchsurfing.com) is also popular and generally safe in Venice, though take the usual precautions (for those who don't know the company, it allows locals to offer free rooms to travelers). **Cities Reference** (www.citiesreference.com; ✆ **06/48903612**) is the best traditional rental agency for Venice, with around 50 properties listed. The company's no-surprises property descriptions come with helpful information and lots of photos. **Cross Pollinate** (www.cross-pollinate.com; ✆ **06/99369799**) is a multi-destination agency with a decent roster of personally inspected apartments and B&Bs in Venice, created by the American owners of the Beehive hotel in Rome (p. 78). **Rental in Venice** (www.rentalinvenice.com; ✆ **041/718981**) has an alluring website—with video clips of the apartments—and the widest selection of mid-range and luxury apartments in the prime San Marco zone (it lists less expensive ones, too).

It's standard practice for local rental agencies to collect 30% of the total rental amount upfront to secure a booking. When you check in, the balance of your rental fee is normally payable in cash only, so make sure you have enough euros in hand. Upon booking, the agency should provide you with detailed check-in procedures. Most apartments provide a list of nearby shops and services; beyond that, you're on your own, which is what makes an apartment stay a great way to do as the Venetians do.

San Marco
EXPENSIVE
Baglioni Hotel Luna ★★★   Perfectly situated on the lagoon just around the corner from the bustle of Piazza San Marco, this is the oldest hotel in Venice, housed in a building from 1118 that was once a church before Napoleon destroyed its sacristy. Today, the boutique property, a member of Leading Hotels of the World, is a cocoon of privacy and comfort; the bright lobby with Murano chandeliers gives way to plush rooms decorated with antique furnishings, brocade, and original artwork from the 1700s. The breakfast room is especially noteworthy: With a room-length mural and intricately painted ceiling frescoes created in the 18th century by students of Tiepolo, it makes every cup of coffee feel like a regal break. Staff here is especially attentive and professional.

San Marco, 1243. www.baglionihotels.com. ✆ **041/5289840.** 91 units. 300€–780€ double. *Vaporetto:* San Marco. **Amenities:** Restaurant; lounge; babysitting; concierge; free Wi-Fi.

Bloom B&B ★★★   Right in the heart of San Marco, just off one of its most interesting piazzas, this relatively new boutique hotel is a romantic hideaway blending classical Venetian style and modern design. Each room is uniquely decorated with lavish color schemes that range from crimson to purple and include exposed-brick, baroque wallpaper, and lots of silky curtains—look at rooms carefully online if you have a preference. All rooms are air conditioned and feature a mini-bar and LCD TV. The best feature is the rooftop terrace, with sensational views of the city, and the adjacent reading room. Note, however, there is no elevator.

Campo Santo Stefano 3470. www.bloom-venice.com. ⓒ **340/1498872.** 6 units. 180€– 300€ double. Breakfast included. *Vaporetto:* Sant'Angelo (walk to tall brick building and go around it, turn right into Ramo Narisi; at small bridge turn left and follow Calle del Pestrin to Campiello Novo on your right—the hotel is opposite the church of Santo Stefano). **Amenities:** Concierge; room service (limited hours); Free Wi-Fi.

Corte Di Gabriela ★★★ This gorgeous boutique hotel just a short walk from Piazza San Marco combines contemporary design and classical Venetian style—ceiling murals, marble pillars, and exposed brick blend with designer furniture and appliances (including free use of iPads, strong Wi-Fi, and satellite TV). The fully renovated property dates from 1870, once serving as the home and offices of Venetian lawyers. Breakfast is one of the highlights and well worth lingering over: fresh pastries made by the owners the night before, crepes and omelets made upon request, and decent espresso.

Calle degli Avvocati 3836. www.cortedigabriela.com. ⓒ **041/5235077.** 10 units. 270€–920€ double. Breakfast included. *Vaporetto:* Sant' Angelo. **Amenities:** Bar; babysitting; concierge; room service (limited hours); free Wi-Fi.

MODERATE

Antica Locanda al Gambero ★ The best attribute of this small, typically cute Venetian hotel is the location, just a 2-minute walk from Piazza San Marco. Rooms are dressed in a bright rococo style with modern extras like satellite TV and air-conditioning, and most have lovely views of the local canal (but not all—check when you book to avoid disappointment). It has no elevator (remember that a "fourth floor" room in Italy is actually on the fifth floor, quite a climb) and the breakfast buffet is small, but it does have free Internet terminals in the lobby and a small rooftop patio that few guests seem to use.

Calle dei Fabbri 4687. www.locandaalgambero.com. ⓒ **041/5224384.** 30 units. 85€– 240€ double. Breakfast included. *Vaporetto:* Rialto (turn right along canal, cross bridge over Rio San Salvador, then left onto Calle Bembo/Calle dei Fabbri; hotel is five blocks ahead on left). **Amenities:** Restaurant; bar; concierge; free Wi-Fi.

Locanda Fiorita ★★ Hard to imagine a more picturesque location for this little hotel, a charming, quiet *campiello* draped in vines and blossoms— no wonder it's a favorite of professional photographers. Standard rooms are small (bathrooms are tiny), but all are furnished in an elegant 18th-century style, with wooden floors, shuttered windows, and richly patterned fittings (air-conditioning and satellite TV are included). The helpful staff more than make up for any deficiencies, and breakfast is a real pleasure, especially when taken outside on the *campiello.*

Campiello Novo 3457a. www.locandafiorita.com. ⓒ **041/5234754.** 10 units. 145€–240€ double. Breakfast included. *Vaporetto:* Sant'Angelo (walk to tall brick building and go around it, turn right into Ramo Narisi; at small bridge turn left and follow Calle del Pestrin to Campiello Novo on your right. **Amenities:** Babysitting; concierge; room service; free Wi-Fi.

Castello

EXPENSIVE

Londra Palace ★★ This white-marble beauty, part of the Relais & Chateaux stable, occupies a prime location overlooking the waterfront promenade—get a room with a balcony to make the most of the spectacular views. All rooms are spacious, with lofty ceilings, 19th-century Biedermeier-style furniture, and satellite TV. This is another place with an intriguing history: The core of the hotel dates to 1853 when it was the Hotel d'Angleterre, beefed up in the 1860s by a "neolombardesque-style" extension. Tchaikovsky was a guest here in December 1877; legend has it he composed the first three movements of his Symphony No. 4 in room no. 106.

The Londra Palace, one of Venice's grande dame hotels.

Riva degli Schiavoni 4171. www.londra palace.com. ☏ **041/5200533.** 53 units. 390€–650€ double. Breakfast included. *Vaporetto:* San Zaccaria. **Amenities:** Restaurant; bar; babysitting; concierge; room service; free Wi-Fi.

Metropole ★★★ This five-star behemoth with a waterfront location is part luxury hotel, part eclectic art museum, with antiques, Asian artworks, and tapestries dotted throughout. But it's no dusty grand dame; on the contrary, the hotel is a chic boutique with rooms opulently furnished in white, red, and gold color schemes. It began life in the Middle Ages as the Ospedale della Pietà, serving as a charitable institution for orphans and abandoned girls, and later became the music school where Vivaldi taught violin in the early 1700s. After it was converted into a hotel in 1895, Sigmund Freud was an early guest, as was Thomas Mann, who allegedly wrote parts of *Death in Venice* here.

Riva degli Schiavoni 4149. www.hotelmetropole.com. ☏ **041/5205044.** 67 units. 320€–701€ double. Breakfast included. *Vaporetto:* San Zaccaria (walk along Riva degli Schiavoni to right; hotel is next to La Pietà church). **Amenities:** Restaurant; bar; babysitting; concierge; room service; free Wi-Fi.

MODERATE

Al Piave ★★ Al Piave is a cozy, old-fashioned family-run hotel just 5 minutes from Piazza San Marco. Rooms are simply but attractively furnished with richly woven rugs, marble floors, and original wood beams exposed (some come with a terrace). Family suites are good value for groups. Bathrooms are relatively big, and the air-conditioning is a welcome bonus in the summer, but the four-floor hotel has no elevators, so be prepared if you get a

Guestroom at Casa Verardo in Castello.

higher floor. Outside of peak months (May, July, Sept), Piave offers exceptionally good value, given its proximity to the *piazza*.

Ruga Giuffa 4838. www.hotelalpiave.com. © **041/5285174.** 20 units. 145€–300€ double. Breakfast included. Closed Jan 7–Carnevale. *Vaporetto:* San Zaccaria (beyond Palazzo Danieli, find Calle delle Rasse and walk to end of street; turn left and then immediately right; cross tiny Ponte Storto, continue to Ruga Giuffa—hotel is on left). **Amenities:** Babysitting; concierge; free Wi-Fi.

Casa Verardo ★★★   Tucked away across a small bridge in the warren of central Castello, this enchanting hotel occupies a 16th-century *palazzo*, though it's been a hotel since 1911. Rooms sport an old-fashioned Venetian style, with Florentine furniture, hand-painted beds, and colorful textiles (antiques and paintings are scattered throughout), but are updated with air-conditioning and satellite TV. Some rooms have a view over a canal, others over the shady courtyard and the city.

Calle Drio La Chiesa 4765 (at foot of Ponte Storto). www.casaverardo.it. © **041/5286138.** 25 units. 135€–220€ double. Breakfast included. *Vaporetto:* San Zaccaria (walk straight on Calle delle Rasse to Campo SS. Filippo e Giacomo; cross *campo* to Calle della Sacrestia, then Calle Drio La Chiesa to Ponte Storto, look for hotel on left). **Amenities:** Bar; babysitting; concierge; room service; free Wi-Fi.

INEXPENSIVE

B&B San Marco ★★★   With just three rooms, this exquisite B&B in a peaceful residential neighborhood fills up fast, so book ahead. It's a comfortable, charming, yet convenient option, not too far from the main sights. Your hosts are the bubbly Marco and Alice Scurati, who live in the attic upstairs and are always happy to provide help and advice. Rooms, which are furnished with antiques, overlook the Scuola di San Giorgio degli Schiavoni and offer wonderful views of the canal. Two rooms share a bathroom; the third has private facilities. Breakfast is self-service in the shared kitchen, a spread of yogurts, pastries, espresso, cappuccino, juice, and tea.

Fondamenta San Giorgio dei Schiavoni 3385. www.realvenice.it. ℂ **041/5227589.** 3 units. 75€–130€ double. Breakfast included. Closed Aug and Jan 7–Carnevale. *Vaporetto:* San Zaccaria (walk on Calle delle Rasse to Campo SS. Filippo e Giacomo; cross *campo* to Calle della Sacrestia, cross canal and turn left at Campo S Provolo along Fondamenta Osmarin; turn left where canal ends, walk to bridge that connects to Calle Lion; at end of street turn left along canal onto Fondamenta San Giorgio dei Schiavoni). **Amenities:** Babysitting; free Wi-Fi.

Dorsoduro

EXPENSIVE

Moresco ★★★   An incredibly attentive staff, a decadent breakfast that includes prosecco (to mix with orange juice, ahem), and lavish 19th-century Venetian decor make this a popular choice, away from the tourist hubbub. Rooms seamlessly blend Venetian style with modern design. Some have a terrace (with canal or garden views), while others have spa bathtubs; all come with flatscreen TVs with satellite channels. If the weather cooperates, take breakfast in the courtyard garden. The hotel is a 5- to 10-minute walk from Piazzale Roma and the train station, but you'll have several bridges and stairs to negotiate along the way.

Fondamenta del Rio Novo 3499, Dorsoduro. www.hotelmorescovenice.com. ℂ **041/2440202.** 23 units. 170€–450€ double. Breakfast included. *Vaporetto:* Ferrovia/Piazzale Roma (from train station walk SW along Fondamenta Santa Lucia, cross Ponte della Costituzione, turn left onto Fondamenta Santa Chiara; cross Ponte Santa Chiara and turn right onto Fondamenta Papadopoli; continue across Campiello Lavadori then along Fondamenta del Rio Novo). **Amenities:** Bar; concierge; free trips to Murano; room service; free Wi-Fi.

MODERATE/EXPENSIVE

American Dinesen ★★   Overlooking the San Vio Canal close to the Accademia, this 17th-century Venetian town house offers elegant rooms decorated in a classical Venetian style, with all the usual modern amenities including LCD TV. All the "superior canal"–view rooms have picture-perfect vistas of the San Vio, many with a balcony (check if this is important to you), and even partial views of the Grand Canal. Cheaper, modern "dependence rooms" are in the annex next door and do not include breakfast.

San Vio 628 (on Fondamenta Bragadin). www.hotelamerican.it. ℂ **041/5204733.** 30 units. 148€–330€ double. Some rates include breakfast. *Vaporetto:* Accademia (veer left around Accademia, take 1st left turn, go straight to cross 1st small footbridge; turn right along Fondamenta Bragadin; hotel is on left). **Amenities:** Bar; babysitting; concierge; room service; free Murano trips; free Wi-Fi.

Galleria ★★   Just around the corner from the Accademia, right on the Grand Canal, this hotel occupies a 19th-century *palazzo* in one of the most inviting locations in the city. It's been a hotel since the 1800s, hosting poet Robert Browning in 1878, and maintains an 18th-century Venetian theme in

A character-filled room at the Hotel Galleria.

the rooms, with wood furniture and rococo decor. Hosts Luciano and Lucio serve a simple breakfast in your room. The smallest rooms here really are tiny, and there is no TV or air-conditioning (rooms are supplied with fans when it gets hot), but the fridge of free water and sodas is a lifesaver in summer. Choose from Grand Canal (more expensive) or Accademia Bridge views.

Dorsoduro 878a (at foot of Accademia Bridge). www.hotelgalleria.it. ℂ **041/5232489.** 10 units. 100€–290€ double. Breakfast included. *Vaporetto:* Accademia (with Accademia Bridge behind you, hotel is just to your left). **Amenities:** Babysitting; concierge; room service; free Wi-Fi.

Pensione Accademia ★★ This spellbinding hotel with a tranquil blossom-filled garden has a fascinating history. The Gothic-style Villa Maravege was built in the 17th century as a family residence but served as the Russian Embassy between World Wars I and II before becoming a hotel in 1950. If that's not enticing enough, the rooms are fitted with Venetian-style antique reproductions, wood furnishings, handsome tapestries, and air-conditioning, with views over either the Rio San Trovaso or the garden. Breakfast is served in your room, in the dining hall, or on the patio.

Fondamenta Bollani 1058. www.pensioneaccademia.it. ℂ **041/5210188.** 27 units. 145€–370€ double. Breakfast included. *Vaporetto:* Accademia (turn right down Calle Gambara/Calle Corfu, which ends at a side canal; walk left to cross over bridge, turn right back toward Grand Canal and the hotel). **Amenities:** Bar; babysitting; concierge; room service; free Wi-Fi.

San Polo
MODERATE/INEXPENSIVE
Ca' Barba B&B ★★ What you'll remember most about Ca' Barba may well be the host, Alessandro, who usually meets guests at the Rialto *vaporetto* stop; inspires daily wanderings with tips, maps, and books; and provides fresh

breads and pastries from the local bakery for breakfast. Of the four rooms, no. 201 is the largest and brightest, with a Jacuzzi tub (no. 202 also has one). All rooms come with antique furniture, 19th-century paintings, wood-beamed ceilings, LCD TVs, air-conditioning, and strong Wi-Fi.

Calle Campanile Castello 1825. www.cabarba.com. ⓒ **041/5242816.** 4 units. 95€–140€ double. Breakfast included. *Vaporetto:* Rialto (walk back along Grand Canal, turn left at Calle Campanile Castello). **Amenities:** Concierge; free Wi-Fi.

Pensione Guerrato ★★★ Dating, incredibly, from 1227, this is definitely one of the city's most historic places to stay. The building's long history—it was once the "Inn of the Monkey," run by nuns, with the original structure mostly destroyed by fire in 1513—is worth delving into (the owners have all the details). Rooms are simply but classically furnished, with wood floors, exposed beams, air-conditioning, and private baths—many with original frescos that may date from the medieval inn. Note that the cheapest rooms have shared bathrooms and some are on the seventh floor—and there's no elevator.

Calle Drio La Scimia 240a (near the Rialto Market). www.hotelguerrato.com. ⓒ **041/ 5227131.** 20 units. 125€–170€ double. Breakfast included. Closed Dec 22–26 and Jan 8–early Feb. *Vaporetto:* Rialto (from N side of Ponte Rialto, walk through the market to corner with UniCredit Banca; go one more short block and turn right; hotel is halfway along Calle Drio La Scimia). **Amenities:** Babysitting; concierge; free Wi-Fi.

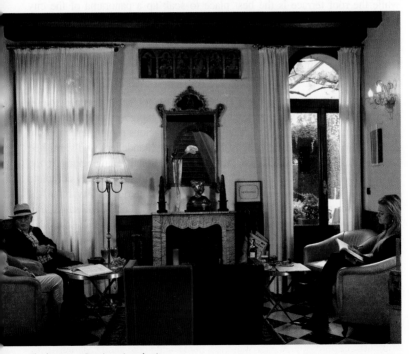

The lounge at Pensione Accademia.

Santa Croce

EXPENSIVE

Antiche Figure ★★★　The most convenient luxury hotel in Venice lies directly across the Grand Canal from the train station, a captivating 15th-century *palazzo* adjacent to an ancient gondola workshop. History aside, this is a very plush choice, its rooms decorated in neoclassical Venetian style with gold leaf, antique furniture, red carpets, silk tapestries, and aging Murano glass and chandeliers, but also LCD satellite TVs and decent Wi-Fi. There is an elevator, just in case you were wondering.

Fondamenta San Simeone Piccolo 687. www.hotelantichefigure.it. ⓒ **041/2759486.** 22 units. 142€–420€ double. Breakfast included. *Vaporetto:* Ferrovia (from train station, cross Scalzi Bridge on your left and turn right). **Amenities:** Restaurant; bar; babysitting; concierge; room service; free Wi-Fi.

MODERATE

Ai Due Fanali ★　Originally a wooden oratory frequented by fishermen and farmers (later rebuilt), this beguiling hotel features small but artsy rooms, even for Venice: Headboards have been hand-painted by a local artist, exposed wood beams crisscross the ceiling, and vintage drapes and curtains add a cozy feel (work by Jacopo Palma the Younger, the 16th-century Mannerist painter, adorns the public areas). The bathrooms are embellished with terracotta tiles and Carrera marble. The location is excellent for proximity to the train station, while the roof terrace is the best place to soak up a panorama of the city (breakfast is served here). It's incredibly popular—book months ahead.

Campo San Simeon Profeta 946. www.aiduefanali.com. ⓒ **041/718490.** 16 units. 85€–165€ double. Breakfast included. Closed most of Jan. *Vaporetto:* Ferrovia (cross Scalzi bridge over Grand Canal, continue straight, take second left, keep walking to Campo San Simeon Profeta). **Amenities:** Bar; concierge; room service; free Wi-Fi.

Al Ponte Mocenigo ★★★　This gem of a hotel shows it is possible to live that Golden Age Venetian fantasy without breaking the bank (rates are a real bargain in the low season). The especially spacious rooms here are pure 18th-century Venice, with big beds, Murano glass chandeliers, and varnished furniture in pastel greens, creams, and golds. Traditional ceiling beams (in the second-floor rooms) and original Venetian wood and stone floors complete the effect. Breakfasts—served in an enchanting interior courtyard when weather allows—are substantial, with bacon, scrambled eggs, and sausage in addition to all the usual cheeses, fruits, and cold cuts. Another huge plus: It's steps away from the Stan Stae *vaporetto* stop, meaning easy transfers to/from the airport and elsewhere along the Grand Canal. Advanced reservations highly recommended. Note that there is usually a discount for paying in cash.

Fondamenta Mocenigo 2063. alpontemocenigo.com. ⓒ **041/5244797.** 10 units. 100€–225€ double. Breakfast included. *Vaporetto:* San Stae. **Amenities:** Bar; babysitting; concierge (24 hr.); free Wi-Fi.

Cannaregio

EXPENSIVE

Al Ponte Antico ★★★ Yes, it's expensive, but this is one of the most exclusive hotels in Venice, steps from the Rialto Bridge, with a private wharf on the Grand Canal—to indulge your James Bond fantasy, look no further. Part of the attraction is its relatively small size: With just seven rooms, it feels far more intimate than most hotels in this price range, and service is always superior. Rococo wallpaper, rare tapestries, elegant beds, and Louis XV–style furnishings make this place seem like Versailles on the water. The building was originally a 16th-century *palazzo;* one of the many highlights is the charming balcony where breakfast is served and where Bellinis are offered in the evenings.

Calle dell'Aseo 5768. www.alponteantico.com. *☎* **041/2411944.** 7 units. 250€–620€ double. Breakfast included. *Vaporetto:* Rialto (walk up Calle Large Mazzini, take second left to cross Campo San Bartolomeo; walk north on Salizada S.G. Grisostomo to Calle dell'Aseo on left). **Amenities:** Bar; concierge; room service; free Wi-Fi.

MODERATE

Arcadia ★★★ This sensational, modestly advertised boutique lodging set in a 17th-century *palazzo* has an appealing blend of old and new: The theme is Byzantium east-meets-west, combining elements of Venetian and Asian style, but the rooms are full of cool, modern touches: rainfall showers,

Breakfast at one of the most exclusive hotels in Venice: Al Ponte Antico.

air-conditioning, flatscreen TVs, bathrobes, and posh toiletries. The lobby is crowned with a Murano glass chandelier. It's just a 5-minute walk from the train station.

Rio Terà San Leonardo 1333, Cannaregio. www.hotelarcadia.net. © **041/717355.** 17 units. 119€–360€ double. Breakfast included. *Vaporetto:* Guglie (take left into Rio Terà San Leonardo; Arcadia is 30m [98 ft.] on left). **Amenities:** Bar; concierge; room service; free Wi-Fi.

Giorgione ★★   Set in a grand 18th-century building, the Giorgione is an elegant gem of a hotel—staying here really is like taking a trip back to old Venice. The combination of old and new works well, where antique furniture, Venetian decor, sumptuous fabrics, and Murano glass chandeliers meet satellite TV and air-conditioning. Rooms are a little worn, but that only adds to the historic ambience. In the summer, a generous breakfast is served in the pretty fountain courtyard.

Campo SS. Apostoli 4587. www.hotelgiorgione.com. © **041/5225810.** 76 units. 160€–250€ double. Breakfast included. *Vaporetto:* Ca' d'Oro (walk up Calle Ca' d'Oro and turn right onto Strada Nuova, which ends in Campo SS Apostoli). **Amenities:** Bar; babysitting; concierge; room service; free Wi-Fi.

INEXPENSIVE

Combo, Venezia ★★   This excellent hostel is tucked away at the northern end of Cannaregio in the restored Ex-Convento dei Crociferi. It's a quiet spot a little out the way, but only a 10–15-minute stroll from the Rialto and the Grand Canal. The elegant, cloistered courtyard is a tranquil place to hang out, while the on-site bar-restaurant usually offers good deals (especially on *cicchetti*). When it comes to the rooms, it's more like a budget boutique hotel than a traditional hostel. All the rooms (twins, doubles, and apartments, from 136€) have individual beds and an ensuite bathroom with shower, while some also have their own kitchenettes (it does have dorms, but these have been closed since the COVID epidemic—check the website for the latest).

Campo dei Gesuiti 4878. thisiscombo.com/it/location/venezia. © **041/5286103.** 130 units. 85€–178€ double. Breakfast included. *Vaporetto:* Fondamente Nove (walk straight up Campo dei Gesuit and it's on the left). **Amenities:** Concierge; bar; self-service laundry; shared kitchen; free Wi-Fi.

Giudecca

A quick ferry straight across from the cacophony of Piazza San Marco brings you to the quiet charms of Giudecca Island and its spectacular views across the lagoon to Venice. This is where you'll find **Cipriani, A Belmond Hotel ★★★**, Giudecca 10 (www.belmond.com; © **041/240801**), the most famous hotel in Venice, if not all of northern Italy (founded in 1958 by Giuseppe Cipriani, of Harry's Bar fame), with its enormous saltwater pool, decadent spa, and rambling gardens. It's extremely expensive but keep an eye out for shoulder-season deals (the hotel is closed Nov–late Mar). Or just ferry over to Giudecca for a meal or cocktail at the hotel's waterside **Cip's Club ★★** (late Mar–Oct daily 12:30–2:30pm and 7:30–10:30pm) where dinner comes with a sparkling view of Piazza San Marco.

INEXPENSIVE

Generator Venice ★   It's also worth the trek over to Giudecca to stay in one of the city's best hostels. Set inside an old warehouse on the waterfront, Generator offers relatively stylish dorms with bunks (one dorm is female-only), as well as comfy en-suite doubles with A/C and canal views. There are also private 3-bed and 4-bed rooms, with shared bathrooms, that work out a bit cheaper. The bar, restaurant, and waterside terrace are great places to hangout, with happy hour daily 6:30 to 8:30pm.

Fondamenta Zitelle 86. staygenerator.com. ℂ **041/8778288.** 26 units. 80€–250 € double; 15€–56 dorm. Breakfast included. *Vaporetto:* Zitelle (walk right along the canal side, Fondamenta Croce/Zitelle for about 525ft/160m and the hostel will be on the left, overlooking the water). **Amenities:** Bar; restaurant; concierge; free Wi-Fi.

WHERE TO EAT IN VENICE

Eating cheaply in Venice is not easy, though it's by no means impossible. The city's reputation for mass-produced menus, bad service, and wildly overpriced food is, sadly, well-warranted, and if you've been traveling in other parts of the country, you may be a little disappointed here. Having said that, everything is relative—this is still Italy after all—and you'll find plenty of excellent dining options in Venice. As a basic rule, value for money tends to increase the farther you travel *away* from Piazza San Marco, and anything described as a *menù turistico,* while cheaper than a la carte, is rarely any good in Venice (exceptions listed below). Note also that compared with Rome and other points south, Venice is a city of early meals: You should be seated by 7:30 to 8:30pm. Most kitchens close at 10 or 10:30pm, even though the restaurant may stay open later.

While most restaurants in Italy include a cover charge *(coperto)* that usually runs 1.50€ to 5€, in Venice they tend to instead tack on 10% to 12% to the bill

---

bàcari **& CICCHETTI**

One of the essential culinary experiences of Venice is trawling the countless neighborhood bars known as **bàcari,** where you can stand or sit with *tramezzini* (small, triangular white-bread half-sandwiches filled with everything from thinly sliced meats and tuna salad to cheeses and vegetables), and *cicchetti* (tapas-like finger foods, such as calamari rings, speared fried olives, potato croquettes, or grilled polenta squares), traditionally washed down with a small glass of wine, Veneto Prosecco, or spritz (a fluorescent cocktail of Prosecco and orange-flavored Aperol). All of the above will cost approximately 1.50€ to 6€ if you stand at the bar, as much as double when seated. Bar food is displayed on the countertop or in glass counters and usually sells out by late afternoon, so though it can make a great lunch, don't rely on it for a light dinner. A concentration of popular, well-stocked bars can be found along the **Mercerie** shopping strip that connects Piazza San Marco with the Rialto Bridge; on the always lively **Campo San Luca** (look for Bar Torino, Bar Black Jack, or the character-filled Leon Bianco wine bar); and on **Campo Santa Margherita.**

Ai Mercanti **28**
Al Covo **33**
Alle Corone **23**
Antico Forno **18**
Bacareto De Lele **5**
Bistrot de Venise **26**
Caffè dei Frari **7**
Caffè Florian **30**
Cantina Arnaldi **8**
Dama **1**
Do Mori **20**
Do Spade **19**
Gelato Fantasy **25**
Gritti Terrace **29**
Il Caffè
  (Caffè Rosso) **11**
Il Doge **12**
La Bottiglia **6**
La Fornace **21**

290

Venice Restaurants

0 — 1/8 mi
0 — 200 m

Information *i*

CANNAREGIO

Pal. Giovanelli

S. Felice

Rio di la Sensa

Pal. Fontana

Ca' d'Oro

Ca' d'Oro

Pal. Brandolin

Pal. Sagredo

Strada Nuova

S. Sofia

Pescaria

Ss. Apostoli

Pal. Widman

Fondamente Nove

To Murano and Burano **21**

Calle d'Fumo

Calle d'Squero

Pal. Mangilli

Ca' da Mosto

Pal. Falier

Rio di S.ta Sofia

S. Canciano

Pal. Grifalconi

C. larga G. Gallina

Ospedale Civile

H

S. Maria d. Pianto

Calle d. Botteri

Fàbbriche Nuove

S. Giovanni Crisostomo

Rio di S. Cristoforo

S. Maria d. Miracoli

Pal. Soranzo-Van Axel

Ss. Giovanni e Paolo (S. Zanipolo)

19 **20**

Palazzo Dieci Savi

Teatro Malibran

Fondaco d. Tedeschi

Pal. Cavazza-Foscari

Pal. Pisani

Campo S. Marina

Rio di S. Marina

Pal. Donà

Pal. Morosini

Pal. Muazzo

18

Aponal

Riva del Vin

Ponte di Rialto

Rialto

S. Bartolomeo

Palazzo Dolfin-Manin

S. Lio

Palazzo Ruzzini

Pal. Cavignis

Palazzo Cappello

S. Lorenzo

S. Silvestro

S. Silvestro

Riva del Carbon

Pal. Bembo

C. Stagneri

S. Maria della Fava

Campo S. Maria Formosa

S. Maria Formosa

Pal. Donà

22

23

M. S. Salvador

S. Salvador

Pal. Tasca Papafava

24

C. Bande

Pal. Querini Stampalia

Ruga Giuffa

CASTELLO

Palazzo Grimani

Ca' Farsetti

27

Campo S. Luca

C. del Teatro

C. Goldoni

C. Guerra

C. Fabbri

Pal. Zorzi

Questura

S. Luca

Campo Manin

28

Palazzo Contarini d. Bovolo

S. Zulian

C. Spadaria

Mercerie Orologio

Palazzo Soranzo

C. Canonica

S. Giovanni Novo

Palazzo Trevisan-Cappello

Pal. Priuli

S. Giorgio dei Greci

31

32

Cinema Rossini

S. Mandola

Riva del Bacaranza

26

25

SAN MARCO

S. Gallo

Torre d. Orologio

Basilica di San Marco

S. Zaccaria

Convento

La Pietà

33

Ateneo Veneto

S. Fantin

Frezzaria

Campanile

Palazzo Ducale (Doge's Palace)

Pal. d. Prigioni

Teatro La Fenice

S. Moisè

S. S. Moisè

C. Vallaresso

Piazza San Marco

30

i

Museo Correr

Piazzetta

Molo

Pal. d. Prigioni

Riva

d. Schiavoni

S. Zaccaria

C. Larga XXII Marzo

Rio di S. Moisè

Giardini ex Reali

Capo di Porto

S. Marco

Ponte d. Sospiri (Bridge of Sighs)

29

Palazzi Contarini

Pal. Gritti

Palazzo Tiepolo

Palazzo Treves d. Bonfili

Bacino di San Marco

Pal. Genovese

Salute

S. Maria d. Salute

Dogana da Mar

Seminario Patriarcale

Punta d. Dogana

Ex Ospizio

Mixed seafood is a special treat in Venice.

for "taxes and service." Some places in Venice will very annoyingly charge you a cover of 5€ and still add on 12%. A menu should state clearly what extras the restaurant charges (sometimes you'll find it in fine print at the bottom) and if it doesn't, take your business elsewhere.

VENETIAN CUISINE   Venice has a distinguished culinary history, much of it based on its geographical position on the sea. For first courses, both pasta and risotto are commonly prepared with fish or seafood: Risotto *al nero di seppia* or *alle seppioline* (tinted black by the ink of cuttlefish, also called *risotto nero* or black risotto) or *spaghetti alle vongole* (with clams; clams without their shells are not a good sign) are two specialties. Both appear with *frutti di mare* ("fruit of the sea"), which is mixed shellfish. *Bigoli,* a thick spaghetti that's perfect for catching lots of sauce, is a Venetian staple, as is creamy polenta, often served with *gamberetti* (small shrimp) or tiny shrimp called *schie,* or as an accompaniment to *fegato alla veneziana* (calf's liver cooked with onions and white wine). Some of the fish and seafood dishes Venice does particularly well include *branzino* (a kind of seabass), *rombo* (turbot or brill), *moeche* (soft-shelled crab) or *granseola* (crab), and *sarde in saor* (sardines in onions, vinegar, pine nuts, and raisins).

Try the dry white Tocai and pinot from the Friuli region to the northeast of Venice and the light, sparkling prosecco that Venetians consume almost like a soft drink. Popular local red wines include Bardolino, Valpolicella, and Soave, all of which come from the surrounding Veneto region. *Grappa,* the local firewater, is an acquired taste and is often offered in many variations.

Restaurants by Cuisine

CAFE

DELI

GELATO

ITALIAN

PIZZA

SEAFOOD

VEGETARIAN

VENETIAN

WINE BAR

San Marco
EXPENSIVE

Bistrot de Venise ★★★ VENETIAN   It may look a bit like a wood-paneled French bistro, but the menu here is old-school Venetian, specializing in rare wines and historical recipes from the 14th to 18th centuries. It's gimmicky but it works; think fried soft crabs with artichoke salad; scallops with fennel and squid ink mayonnaise; and suckling pig with *civiro* (spices), quince, and bitter orange compote. The "historical" tasting menu is a splurge, but we recommend it as the best introduction.

4685 Calle dei Fabbri. www.bistrotdevenise.com. © **041/5236651.** Entrees 26€–42€; 4-course tasting menu 94€; 7-course menu 150€. Daily noon–3pm and 7–11:30pm (bar 11am–11pm). *Vaporetto:* Rialto (turn right along canal, cross footbridge over Rio San Salvador, turn left onto Calle Bembo, which becomes Calle dei Fabbri; Bistrot is about 5 blocks ahead).

tours **FOR FOODIES**

While it's relatively easy to explore Venice's culinary scene solo, it can be fun and more enlightening to enlist the services of a local guide. Indie outfit **The Roman Guy** (theromanguy.com; ✆ **06/94804747**) offers more focused evening food tours in Cannaregio (85€ for 2½ hr.), while **Food Tours of Venice** (foodtoursofvenice.com; ✆ **393/1670961**) offers Rialto and Jewish Ghetto culinary tours (from 89€). **Cesarine** (cesarine.com), Italy's oldest network of home cooks, runs excellent cooking classes in Venice, as well as lunches in local homes, market tours, and wine tastings.

Gritti Terrace ★★★ ITALIAN   One of the city's most famous restaurants remains one of its most magical experiences, despite the high prices. First-time Venice visitors in particular should not miss the chance to dine on this venerable deck overlooking the Grand Canal on a sunny day, or especially, on a clear evening, when the city lights begin to reflect off the water. The view across to Punta della Dogana and Santa Maria della Salute is spectacular (the signature "Basil-i-ca" cocktail was inspired by the latter church). The menu features light salads, pasta, risotto, and platters of seasonal seafood. A sumptuous afternoon tea is also served, along with the usual selection of champagne, Bellini, and Negroni cocktails. Reservations required.

Campo Santa Maria del Giglio 2467 (Gritti Palace Hotel). www.clubdeldoge.com. ✆ **041/794611.** Entrees 24€–60€. Apr–Oct daily noon–10:30pm; closed Nov–Mar. *Vaporetto:* Santa Maria del Giglio.

MODERATE

Ai Mercanti ★★★ VENETIAN/INTERNATIONAL   Nadia Locatello's lauded restaurant pioneered the "gastrosteria" concept (based on the French "bistronomie"), where gourmet dishes are created from relatively simple (and cheap-ish) ingredients. Though it's not a budget restaurant, you'll definitely get your money's worth here, with creative dishes such as croaker fish with cauliflower and candied lemon, cod in coconut and lemongrass spicy soup, and their signature "apparently crispy" egg a little cheaper than they'd be at similarly feted spots. Dinner is served in two shifts: tables are available at 7 and 7:30pm for 2 hours, with a second sitting at 9 and 9:30pm (reservations required online). Another plus: they offer excellent wines by the glass, not just the "house" pours.

Corte Coppo 4346/a (off Calle dei Fuseri). www.aimercanti.it. ✆ **041/5238269.** Entrees 14€–28€. Tues–Sat 12:30–3pm & 7–10pm (closed Jan). *Vaporetto:* Rialto.

INEXPENSIVE

Rosticceria San Bartolomeo ★ DELI/VENETIAN   Also known as Rosticceria Gislon, this no-frills spot is incredibly popular with locals, with a handful of small tables and bar stools and bigger tables in the upstairs dining room (which tends to be quieter). Don't be fooled by appearances—the food here is excellent, with a range of grilled fish and cheap seafood pastas and a tasty *"mozzarella in carrozza"* (fried cheese sandwich; 2.50€). Note that the food displayed on the countertop is reheated to order, but still tastes good. Otherwise just sit at the counter and soak up the animated scene, as cooks chop, customers chat, and people come and go.

Calle della Bissa 5424. ✆ **041/5223569.** Entrees 11€–20€ (pasta downstairs 7€–11€, *cicchetti* 2€–4€). Daily 9am–9:30pm. *Vaporetto:* Rialto (with bridge at your back on San Marco side, walk straight to Campo San Bartolomeo; take underpass to your left marked SOTTOPORTEGO DELLA BISSA; *rosticceria* is on first corner on your right; look for GISLON above the entrance).

Castello
EXPENSIVE

Al Covo ★★ SEAFOOD/VENETIAN For years, this high-quality Venetian restaurant from Diane and Cesare Benelli has been deservedly popular with American food writers and TV chefs, so expect to be eating with plenty of fellow tourists. It features two cozy dining rooms adorned with art (plus some outdoor seating in summer), but it's the food that takes center stage here: fresh fish from the lagoon or the Adriatic, fruits and vegetables from local farms, and meat sourced from the esteemed Falaschi butchery. The pasta, desserts, and sauces are all homemade. Begin with Venetian *saor* (sweet-and-sour fish and shellfish), or fried zucchini flowers, followed by salt cod in cocotte, taggiasca olives, salina capers, and rosemary, or Piemontese beef tagliata with

Al Covo chef Cesare Benelli preparing Carmelli Veneziani, a dessert of caramelized fruits and nuts.

potato fries, chicory sprouts, and homemade ketchup. Diane's desserts might include rustic pear and prune cake with grappa-cinnamon sauce or green apple sorbet with Calvados.

Campiello della Pescheria 3968. www.ristorantealcovo.com. ✆ **041/5223812.** Reservations required. Entrees 22€–31€. Thurs–Mon 12:30–3:30pm (kitchen closes 2pm) and 7:30pm–midnight (kitchen closes 10pm); closed usually in Jan and 10 days in Aug. *Vaporetto:* Piazza San Marco (walk along Riva degli Schiavoni toward Arsenale, take third narrow street left [Calle della Pescaria] after Hotel Metropole).

Alle Corone ★★★ SEAFOOD/VENETIAN   This is one of Venice's finest restaurants, an elegant 19th-century dining room inside the Hotel Ai Reali and overlooking the canal. Start with grilled artichokes with blueberry gel and chicory (26€) before moving on to risotto with saffron, pigeon and coffee powder (28€) or main courses such as turbot fillet in pistacchio crust with cauliflower cream, or guinea fowl leg with red onion, Roman cabbage, and tangerines. To finish, the homemade tiramisu or crème brulée are spectacular. Reservations recommended.

Campo della Fava 5527 (Hotel Ai Reali). www.ristoranteallecorone.com. ✆ **041/2410253.** Entrees 26€–35€; 6-course tasting menu 100€. Thurs–Tues noon–2:30pm and 7–10:30pm (closed in Jan). *Vaporetto:* Rialto (walk east along Calle Larga Mazzini, turn left at Merceria then right on Calle Stella until you reach hotel).

Local ★★★ SEAFOOD/VENETIAN   One of several newish, contemporary restaurants in Venice serving inventive menus. In an elegant space with mint green walls and original timbered ceilings, Chef Salvatore Sodano serves a 7-course (110€) or 9-course seasonal menu (150€) that might feature traditional *cicchetti*, sushi, blue crab, and entrees such as risotto with smoked butter, eel and herring caviar, or duck with black cabbage and persimmon.

Salizzada dei Greci 3303. www.ristorantelocal.com. ✆ **041/2411128.** 7-course tasting menu 110€. Mon & Fri–Sat noon–2pm & 7–10:30pm, Thurs & Sun 7–10:30pm (closed Tues & Wed). *Vaporetto:* S. Marco-San Zaccaria A (walk north along Calle de la Pietà then Calle Bosello and turn right on Salizzada dei Greci—the restaurant is on the left just before the canal.)

Osteria Alle Testiere ★★★ ITALIAN/VENETIAN   This tiny restaurant (with only nine tables) is the connoisseur's choice (and an alleged favorite of Meryl Streep, Emily Blunt, and Stanley Tucci) for fresh fish and seafood, with a menu that changes daily. Dinner is served at two seatings, where you choose from appetizers such as scallops with orange and leeks, or grilled razor clams that seem to have been plucked straight from the sea. Fresh seabass fillet with capers and Ligurian black olives is always an exceptional main choice, and seasonal pastas—like pumpkin-and-ricotta ravioli with prawns, or spaghetti with clams—are all superb. Finish off with homemade peach pie or chestnut pudding. In peak season, make reservations at least 1 month ahead, and note that the second seating offers a less-rushed experience.

Calle del Mondo Novo 5801. www.osterialletestiere.it. ✆ **041/5227220.** Entrees 25€–55€; many types of fish sold by weight. Tues–Sat 12:30–1:30pm; dinner seatings 7pm and 9:30pm; closed in Jan. *Vaporetto:* Rialto or San Marco (look for Salizada San Lio west of Campo Santa Maria Formosa; from there ask for Calle del Mondo Novo).

Dorsoduro
EXPENSIVE
Osteria Enoteca Ai Artisti ★★★ VENETIAN   This unpretentious family-owned osteria enoteca is one of the best dining experiences in Venice, with a menu that changes daily according to what's available at the market (no fish is served on Monday, when the fish market is closed). Grab a table by the canal and feast on octopus salad, swordfish steak, or an amazing buttery beef cheek with corn polenta. Or opt for one of the wonderful pastas, such as fettuccine with spider crab. Reservations recommended—this tiny place has seating for just 20.

Fondamenta della Toletta 1169A. www.enotecaartisti.com. ℃ **041/5238944.** Entrees 25€–29€. Tues–Sat 12:45–2:45pm; dinner seatings 7–9pm and 9:30–11pm. *Vaporetto:* Accademia (walk around Accademia, turn right onto Calle Gambara; at Rio di San Trovaso, turn left onto Fondamenta Priuli; take first bridge onto road that leads into Fondamenta della Toletta).

Locanda Montin ★★ VENETIAN   Montin was the famous ex-hangout of Peggy Guggenheim in the 1950s and later frequented by Jimmy Carter, Robert De Niro, and Brad Pitt, among many other celebrities, but is the food still any good? Well, yes. Grab a table in the wonderfully serene back garden (covered by an arching trellis), itself a good reason to visit, and sample Venetian classics such as sardines in *saor* (a local marinade of vinegar, wine, onion, and

Canalside dining at Osteria Enoteca Ai Artisti.

raisins) or an exquisite *seppie in nero* (cuttlefish cooked in its ink). For a main course, it's hard to beat the crispy seabass *(branzino)* or legendary monkfish, while the lemon sorbet with vodka is a perfect, tangy conclusion to any meal.

Fondamenta di Borgo 1147. www.locandamontin.com. ✆ **041/5227151.** Entrees 21€–30€. Daily 12:15–2:30pm and 7:15–10pm (usually closed Nov–Feb). *Vaporetto:* Ca'Rezzonico (walk straight along Calle Lunga San Barnaba, then turn left along Fondamenta di Borgo).

INEXPENSIVE

Osteria Al Squero ★★★ WINE BAR/VENETIAN   Perhaps the most beguiling view in Venice is from this enticing *osteria,* right opposite the Squero di San Trovaso (p. 322). Sip coffee or wine and nibble *cicchetti* while observing the activity at the medieval gondola boatyard and workshop, on the other side of the Rio di San Trovaso (drinks served in glasses inside, but in plastic cups if you want to stand outside). It's essentially a place for a light lunch or *aperitivi* rather than a full meal. Snack on such delights as Carnia smoked sausage, baccalà crostini (cod), anchovies, blue cheese, tuna, and sardines in *saor* for a total of around 13€ to 16€ per person. Spritz from 2.50€.

Fondamenta Nani 943–944. https://osteriaalsquero.wordpress.com/. ✆ **335/6007513.** *Cicchetti* 1.50€–2.80€ per piece. Thurs–Tues 11am–8:30pm. *Vaporetto:* Zattere (walk west along waterside to Rio di San Trovaso, then turn right up Fondamenta Nani).

San Polo

EXPENSIVE

Wistèria ★★★ VENETIAN   One of the city's newer batch of Michelin-starred restaurants, Wistèria was established by partners Andrea Martin and Massimiliano (Max) Rossetti in 2019, with Chef Valerio Dallamano in the kitchen, and an outdoor space enhanced by blossoming wisteria in the spring. The menu is known for experimentation and innovation—expect lots of unusual shapes, colors, ingredients, and incredible flavors. For dinner there's usually a choice of two menus: the signature "Serendipity" eight-course menu, and a slightly cheaper, six-course tasting menu. Lunch is cheaper but includes two courses, chosen by the chef (including a glass of wine and bottle of water). Menus change seasonally, but usually have a Venetian theme, with riffs on traditional *cicchetti* and *castradina*, a traditional soup, as well as "liquid ravioli milanese style"; pink oyster and pomegranate; capon, hazelnut, and calamansi; and boiled salami, red chicory, and horseradish—you get the picture.

Fondamenta del Forner 2908. www.wisteria-restaurant.com. ✆ **041/5243373.** Lunch (2 courses) 50€. Tasting menu (6 courses) 150€; Serendipity menu (8 courses) 180€. Mon & Tues 7–9pm, Fri–Sun noon–1:30pm and 7–9pm, usually closed in Jan. *Vaporetto:* San Tomà (with your back to Grand Canal, walk up Calle del Traghetto Vecchio, and turn left on Calle del Campanile; at the canal turn right on Fondamenta del Forner, and the restaurant will be ahead on the right).

MODERATE

Do Spade ★ VENETIAN   It's tough to find something so authentic this close to the Rialto Bridge these days but Do Spade ("Two Swords") has been around since 1448; Casanova ate here. Most locals come for the *cicchetti* small plates such as fried calamari, its famed *polpetta di spianata calabra* (meatballs of Calabrian sausage, smoked cheese. and potatoes), and salted cod (1.50€–3.50€), as well as decent Italian wines (3€ a glass). The more formal restaurant section is also worth a try, with seafood highlights including a delicately prepared monkfish, scallops served with fresh zucchini, and a rich seafood lasagna. The seasonal pumpkin ravioli is one of the best dishes in the city.

Calle de le Do Spade 860. www.cantinadospade.com. ℂ **041/5210574.** Entrees 15€–24€. Daily 10am–3pm and 6–10pm. *Vaporetto:* Rialto Mercato (with your back to Grand Canal, walk up Ruga Vecchia San Giovanni, turn right on Ruga dei Spezieri; at end turn left on Calle de le Beccarie O Panataria; take second right onto covered Sottoportego do Spade).

INEXPENSIVE

Antico Forno ★★★ ITALIAN/PIZZA   Venice is not known for pizza, partly because fire codes restrict the use of traditional wood-burning ovens, but the big, fluffy-crusted pies here are the best in the city. Little more than a hole-in-the-wall (take-out only), Antico Forno has been selling thick and thin crust pizza by the slice (as well as excellent craft beers) since 2001. Its "La Pizzaccia-style" pizza is a soft focaccia topped with fresh chopped tomatoes, *mozzarella fior di latte* (from Treviso farms), and everything from Trevisan sausage to gorgonzola and mushrooms.

Ruga Rialto 973. www.anticofornovenezia.it. ℂ **041/5204110.** Pizza slices 5.50€–9€. Daily 11:30am–9:30pm, usually closed in Jan. *Vaporetto:* Rialto Mercato (walk into Campo de la Pescaria, follow Ruga Vecchia San Giovanni for around 300m [32 yds.], just beyond Calle del Paradiso).

Do Mori ★★★ WINE BAR/VENETIAN   Serving good wine and *cicchetti* since 1462 (check out the antique copper pots hanging from the ceiling), Do Mori is above all a fun place to have a genuine Venetian experience, a small, dimly lit *bàcari* that can barely accommodate 10 people standing up. Sample the baby octopus and ham on mango, lard-smothered *crostini,* and pickled onions speared with salty anchovies, or opt for the *tramezzini* (tiny sandwiches). Local TV (and BBC) star Francesco Da Mosto is a regular, but note that this institution is very much on the well-trodden tourist trail—plenty of *cicchetti* tours stop by in the early evening. Sip local wine for 3€ to 5€ a glass. Cash only.

Calle Do Mori 429 (also Calle Galeazza 401). ℂ **041/5225401.** *Tramezzini* and *cicchetti* 2€–3.50€ per piece. Mon–Fri 8am–7:30pm, Sat 8am–5pm (June–Aug closed daily 2–4:30pm). *Vaporetto:* Rialto Mercato (with your back to Grand Canal, walk straight up Ruga Vecchia San Giovanni and turn right on Calle Galeazza).

La Bottiglia ★★ WINE BAR/VENETIAN   This more contemporary *bàcari* features wonderful cheese and meat boards, a well-curated wine list (exceptional Amarone red wine is served here) and excellent panini sandwiches stuffed with prosciutto and cheeses. As you might expect, it's a tiny place, with a few tables outside near the Rio San Stin and just five bar stools inside (most visitors stand).

Campo San Stin (Calle de la Chiesa) 2537. www.facebook.com/labottigliavenice/. ℂ **041/4762426.** Sandwiches from 7€. Daily 10am–11pm. *Vaporetto:* Ferrovia or San Tomà.

Santa Croce

EXPENSIVE

Zanze XVI ★★★ ITALIAN/VENETIAN   Contemporary osteria with a simple but elegant dining room featuring exposed wood beams and wood block tables. It's helmed by Chef Nicola Dinato, whose dishes are created daily depending on fresh ingredients available at local markets and gardens: the menu usually includes fresh fish, with dishes such as pilchard tortelli with chard and pecorino cheese; risotto with oysters and prosecco; and sea bass in black squid ink.

Fondamenta dei Tolentini 231. zanze.it ✆ **041/715394.** Entrees 25€–40€; tasing menu: (5 courses) 110€, 7 courses 130€. Tues–Sun noon–2pm and 7:30–10pm. *Vaporetto:* Piazzale Roma (turn left and walk along the Grand Canal, crossing two bridges before turning right on Fondamenta dei Tolentini).

MODERATE

Osteria La Zucca ★★ ITALIAN/VEGETARIAN   Though not specifically a vegetarian restaurant, the romantic, canal-side dining room of La Zucca (aka "the pumpkin") does offer a huge range of high-quality vegetable dishes, from the signature pumpkin-and-ricotta flan and potato cakes to zucchini-and-almond lasagne. The seasonal menu (Italian only, but the staff speak English) also includes plenty of meat dishes, such as succulent rabbit with white wine, and lamb with spices. End with one of the homemade cakes—pear cake with ginger or the "spices tart" with red wine and raspberry.

Calle dello Spezier 1762. lazucca.it ✆ **041/5241570.** Reservations recommended by phone 11am–noon & 6–7pm, up 20 days in advance. Entrees 9€–24€; Mon–Sat 12:30–2:30pm and 7–10:30pm. *Vaporetto:* San Stae (walk straight down Salizada San Stae, turn right on Calle del Tentor; turn left at Calle Del Meglio and follow it as it turns right).

INEXPENSIVE

Bacareto Da Lele ★★★ WINE BAR/VENETIAN   This tiny hole-in-the-wall *bàcaro* is worth seeking out for its cheap, fresh snacks, sandwiches, and *cicchetti*. Tiny glasses, or *ombras,* of wine and Prosecco are just 1€ to 1.70€. There are no seats, so do as the locals do and grab a space on the nearby Tolentini church steps, or outside by the canal, while you sip and nibble. Opt for a tiny porchetta and mustard or the bacon and artichoke panini (1€–2.50€), antipasti plates (cheese and salami; from 1.50€), or a simple, freshly baked crostini for 1.60€ to 2.50€. Expect long lines here in peak season; the secret is definitely out.

Campo dei Tolentini 183. No phone. *Cicchetti* 1.60€–2.50€ per piece. Mon–Fri 6am–8pm; Sat 6am–2pm. *Vaporetto:* Piazzale Roma (walk left along Grand Canal past Ponte della Costituzione, into Giardino Papadopoli; turn right on Fondamenta Papadopoli, then left. Cross park at first bridge; at next canal [Rio del Tolentini] cross bridge to campo; Da Lele is on SW corner).

Cantina Arnaldi ★★★ WINE BAR/VENETIAN   This welcoming *bàcaro* offers some of the freshest snacks in the city, washed down with quality wines, spritz, and Prosecco (3€–7€). The thing to order is the delicious board of cheese and cold cuts, all sourced from the region and enhanced with fresh

The classic hole-in-the-wall wine bar Bacareto Da Lele.

fruits, fig jam, local bread, and a small pot of roasted potatoes. The extensive wine list includes natural/organic options as well as some of the best cellars from Italy. It's a small place, so reservations are recommended if you want a table (there are also a handful of barstools).

Salizada San Pantalon 35. ℰ **041/718989.** *Cicchetti* 2€–6€ per piece, focaccias 18€–22€. Thurs–Tues 11:30am–midnight. *Vaporetto:* San Tomà (walk up Calle Traghetto Vecchio Galeazza, turn left at Calle del Campanile and right on Fondamenta del Forner; turn left and cross canal on Calle Gozzi, follow to Calle Crosera; turn right and walk straight, crossing Rio de San Pantalon and on to Salizada San Pantalon).

Cannaregio
EXPENSIVE

Dama ★★★ VENETIAN/SEAFOOD Overlooking the busy Canale di Cannaregio in the historic Hotel Ca' Bonfadini (and less than 10 min. walk from the station), this contemporary Venetian kitchen is one of the best in the city. Chef Lorenzo Cogo focuses on local seafood, using modern techniques and creative combinations; think langoustine with hazelnuts miso and sesame to start, black macaroni and spiked squid with ginseng and buffalo stracciatella for first course, and confit mullet with sweet and sour sauce, vermouth and plum and rosemary for an entree. The long tables inside have been fashioned from old Venetian mooring posts.

Fondamenta Savorgnan 461. www.damavenice.com. ℰ **041/0986297.** Entrees 25€–40€; tasting menus 90€–140€. Daily 12:20–2:30pm and 7:30–10pm. *Vaporetto:* Crea (walk left along the canal, with the water on your left, and the restaurant is around 750ft/200m on the right).

La Giudecca

MODERATE

La Palanca ★★ SEAFOOD/VENETIAN   For simple, no-frills Venetian cuisine with a stellar view across to the spires of Dorsoduro, this Giudecca spot, well off the tourist trail, is hard to beat. Grab a table on the waterside for coffee and cake (most locals take breakfast standing at the bar), or have a sandwich, a more substantial lunch, or sunset spritz (meals usually served noon to 2:30pm; it's just *cicchetti* and drinks thereafter). Standouts include the tuna tartare, swordfish carpaccio, and anchovies with pink peppercorns. Some of the friendliest staff in the city seem to work here.

Fondamenta Sant'Eufemia 448. ✆ **041/5287719.** Entrees 9€–20€. Mon–Sat 7am–9pm. Reserve for lunch. *Vaporetto:* Palanca (restaurant is 80m [260 ft.] along canal to left).

Murano & Burano

The glass-making island of **Murano** isn't especially known for its food, though there are plenty of decent trattorias scattered along the main streets. For a real treat, make for **La Fornace** ★★, Fondamenta Manin 1 (lafornace murano.it; ✆ **041/5275408;** Mon & Wed noon–6pm, Thurs–Sun noon–5:30pm and 6:30–10pm), a spacious, contemporary restaurant in a restored glass furnace, with gorgeous views of the lagoon. It's best known for traditional Venetian dishes and fresh seafood.

The island of **Burano** makes a wonderful culinary excursion for its seafood restaurants, notably **Trattoria al Gatto Nero** ★★, the "Black Cat", Fondamenta della Giudecca 88 (www.gattonero.com; ✆ **041/730120;** Tues–Sat 12:30–3pm and 7–9:30pm, Sun 12:30–3pm; usually closed Nov), which has been around since the 1960s. Signature dishes include Burano-style risotto (made with *ghiozzi,* a small, long-bodied fish from the lagoon), local turbot and seabass, and the tagliolini with spider crab. Another favorite is **Trattoria da Romano** ★★, Via Baldassarre Galuppi 221 (daromano.it; ✆ **041/730030;** Mon and Wed–Sat noon–3pm and 6:30–11:30pm, Sun noon–3pm), its dining room adorned with more than 400 artworks donated by visiting artists since the 1940s. Rolling Stone Keith Richards, designer Philippe Starck, and actor Sylvester Stallone have been regulars here for years.

Gelato

Is the gelato any good in Venice? Italians might demur, but by international standards, the answer is most definitely yes. As always, remember that gelato parlors aimed exclusively at tourists are notorious for poor quality and extortionate prices, especially in Venice. Try to avoid places near Piazza San Marco altogether. Below are some of our favorite spots in the city. Each generally opens midmorning and closes late. Winter hours are more erratic.

Gelato Fantasy ★   Since 1998, this tiny gelato shop has been doling out tasty scoops dangerously close to Piazza San Marco, but the quality remains high and portions generous. Fresh, strong flavors, with standouts including the pistachio, tiramisu, and strawberry cheesecake. Calle dei Fabbri 929, San Marco. www.gelatofantasy.com. © **041/5225993.** Cones and cups 4€–8€. Daily 10am–11:30pm, usually closed in Jan. Vaporetto: Rialto or San Marco.

Il Doge ★★ A definite contender for best gelato in Venice, with a great location at the southern end of the Campo Santa Margherita since 1986. These guys use only natural, homemade flavors and ingredients, from an exceptional spicy chocolate to their specialty, "Crema de Doge," a rich concoction of eggs, cream, and real oranges. Try a refreshing *granita* in summer. Campo Santa Margherita, Dorsoduro. © **041/5234607.** Cones and cups 2€–6€. Open daily 11am–10pm, usually closed late Dec–Jan. Vaporetto: Ca'Rezzonico.

La Mela Verde ★★ The popular rival to Il Doge for best scoop in the city, with sharp flavors and all the classics done sensationally well: pistachio, chocolate, *nocciola* (hazelnut), and a mind-blowing lemon-and-basil. The overall champions: *mela verde* (green apple), like creamy, frozen fruit served in a cup, and the addictive tiramisu. Fondamenta de L'Osmarin, Castello. www.facebook.com/lamelaverdevenezia. © **349/1957924.** Cones and cups from 2€. Daily 11am–11pm. Usually closed mid-Nov to mid-Feb. Vaporetto: Zaccaria.

Nico ★ Founded in 1937, this is one of the city's more historic gelato counters, with a handful of chairs on the waterfront (these are only for "table

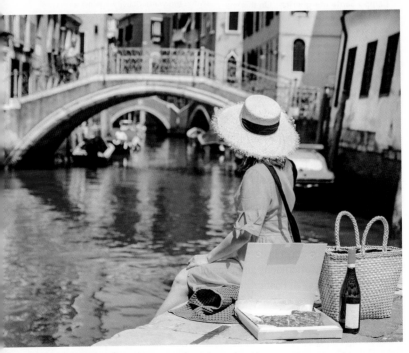

A picnic, Venetian style.

EATING alfresco IN VENICE

You don't have to eat in a fancy restaurant to enjoy good food in Venice. Prepare a picnic, and while you eat alfresco, you can observe the life in the city's *campi* or the aquatic parade on its main thoroughfare, the Grand Canal.

Mercato Rialto Venice's principal open-air market has two parts, beginning with the produce section, with many stalls unfolding north on the San Polo side of the Rialto Bridge. Vendors are here Monday to Saturday 7am to 1pm, with some staying on in the afternoon. Behind these stalls are a few permanent food stores that sell cheese, cold cuts, and bread. At the market's farthest point, you'll find the covered **fish market,** still redolent of the days when it was one of the Mediterranean's great fish bazaars. The fish merchants take Monday off and work mornings only.

Campo Santa Margherita On this spacious *campo* in Dorsoduro, Tuesday through Saturday from 8:30am to 1pm, open-air stalls set up, selling fresh fruit and vegetables. A conventional supermarket, **Conad City** (Mon–Sat 7:30am–8:30pm, Sun 9am–2pm & 4–7:30pm), is just off the *campo* in the direction of the quasi-adjacent *campo* San Barnaba, at no. 3017.

San Barnaba Venice's heavily photographed **floating market** (mostly fruit and vegetables), now operates from just one boat moored off San Barnaba at the Ponte dei Pugni in Dorsoduro. This market is open daily 8am to 1pm and 3:30 to 7:30pm, except Wednesday afternoon and Sunday.

The Best Picnic Spots Given its aquatic roots, you won't find much in the way of green space in Venice (if you are really desperate for green, walk 30 minutes past San Marco along the water to the **Giardini Pubblici,** Venice's only green park). An easier alternative is to find one of the larger *campi* that have park benches, such as Campo San Giacomo dell'Orio (in the quiet *sestiere* of Santa Croce). The two most central are **Campo Santa Margherita** in Dorsoduro and **Campo San Polo** in San Polo.

The **Punta della Dogana** (Customs House; see p. 320) is a prime viewing site at the mouth of the Grand Canal. Perch on the embankment here and watch the water activity against a backdrop deserving of the Accademia Museum. In this same area, **Campo San Vio** (near the Guggenheim), is another superb spot directly on the Grand Canal; it boasts two benches and the option of sitting on an untrafficked small bridge.

A bit farther afield, you can take the *vaporetto* to Burano and then a 5-minute ride on no. 9 to the near-deserted island of **Torcello.** Bring a basketful of bread, cheese, and wine to reenact the romantic scene between Katharine Hepburn and Rossano Brazzi from the 1955 film *Summertime.*

service," at extra charge). Quality is good (the mint, amaretto, and the signature *gianduiotto,* a chocolate and nut blend, are crazy good), but lines are always long in the afternoons and evenings, and service can be a little surly. Fondamenta Zattere al Ponte Longo 922, Dorsoduro. www.gelaterianico.com. ℂ **041/5225293.** Cones and cups 2.50€–3.50€. Daily 7:30am–11pm (Oct–Mar 'til 9pm). Vaporetto: Zattere.

EXPLORING VENICE

Venice is notorious for changing and extending the opening hours of its museums and, to a lesser degree, its churches (often due to special events). Before you begin your exploration of Venice's sights, ask at the tourist office for the season's list of museum and church hours.

San Marco

Basilica di San Marco (St. Mark's Cathedral) ★★★ CATHEDRAL

This cathedral is one of Western Europe's grandest, and certainly the most heavily influenced by the cultures of the eastern Mediterranean. **Basilica di San Marco** is a treasure heap of Venetian art and all sorts of booty garnered from the eastern Mediterranean. Legend has it that **St. Mark,** on his way to Rome in the 1st century A.D., was told by an angel his body would rest near the lagoon that would one day become Venice. Hundreds of years later, the city fathers were looking to replace their original patron St. Theodore with a saint of high stature, someone more in keeping with their lofty aspirations. In 828 the prophecy was fulfilled when Venetian merchants stole the body of St. Mark from Alexandria in Egypt (the story goes that the body was packed in pickled pork to avoid the attention of the Muslim guards). Today the high altar's green marble canopy on alabaster columns is believed to cover the remains of St. Mark (despite a devastating fire in 976), and continues to be the focus of the basilica, at least for the faithful.

Modeled on Constantinople's Church of the Twelve Apostles, the original shrine of St. Mark was consecrated in 832, but in 976 the church burned down. The present incarnation was completed in 1094, then extended and embellished over the years it served as the doge's personal church. Today San Marco looks more Byzantine cathedral than Roman Catholic church, with a cavernous interior gilded with Byzantine mosaics added over 7 centuries, covering every inch of both ceiling and pavement.

For a closer look at many of the most remarkable ceiling mosaics and a better view of the Oriental-carpet-like patterns of the pavement mosaics, pay the admission to go upstairs to the **Museo di San Marco** (the entrance is in the atrium at the principal entrance); this was originally the women's gallery, or *matroneum,* and includes access to the outdoor **Loggia dei Cavalli.** Here you can admire a

The facade and dome of the Basilica di San Marco, reflected in acqua alta floodwaters.

KNOW BEFORE YOU go

- **Access:** Full access to St. Mark's resumed in 2021 after being limited during the Covid-19 pandemic, but it's prudent to check the latest opening times and regulations on the **Basilica website** (www.basilicasanmarco.it) or **VenetoInsider** (www.venetoinside.com). The latter website normally offers "Skip the Line" entry April through October, for an additional 3€

- fee—well worth it—but this was suspended indefinitely in 2020.

- **Attire:** The guards at St. Mark's entrance are serious about forbidding entry to anyone in inappropriate attire: shorts, sleeveless shirts, cropped tops, and skirts above the knee. Note also that you also cannot enter the basilica with luggage.

- **Photos:** Photos and filming inside the basilica are forbidden.

panoramic view of the piazza below and replicas of the celebrated *Triumphal Quadriga,* four gilded bronze horses dating from the 2nd or 3rd century A.D.; the Roman originals were moved inside in the 1980s for preservation. (The word *quadriga* refers to a car or chariot pulled by four horses, though in this case there only the horses.) The horses were transported to Venice from Constantinople in 1204, along with lots of other loot from the Fourth Crusade.

The basilica's greatest treasure is the magnificent altarpiece known as the **Pala d'Oro** (Golden Altarpiece), a Gothic masterpiece encrusted with over 2,000 precious gems and 83 enameled panels. It was created in 10th-century Constantinople and embellished by Venetian and Byzantine artisans between the 12th and 14th centuries. Second to the Pala d'Oro in importance is the 10th-century **"Madonna di Nicopeia,"** a bejeweled icon also purloined from Constantinople and exhibited in its own chapel. Also worth a visit is the **Tesoro** (Treasury), a collection of crusaders' plunder from Constantinople and other icons and relics amassed over the years. Much of the loot has been incorporated into the interior and exterior of the basilica in the form of marble, columns, capitals, and statuary.

Guided tours (1-hour) normally run Monday to Saturday (at least one daily, at 10:45am; guides speak English), and are well worth considering if you'd like to get a better understanding of the Basilica's treasures. Book tours (from 40€) online at www.venetoinside.com. The church also normally also organizes free tours, in English Monday to Friday at 11am, April to October only.

Piazza San Marco. www.basilicasanmarco.it. ⦿ **041/2708311.** Basilica 3€; Museo di San Marco (includes Loggia dei Cavalli) 7€, Pala d'Oro 5€, Tesoro 5€. Basilica Mon–Sat 9:30am–5:15pm, Sun 2–5pm (Nov–mid-Apr closes 4:30pm Sun). Tesoro and Pala d'Oro Mon–Sat 9:45am–5pm, Sun 2–5pm (Nov–mid-Apr Mon–Sat 9:45am–4:45pm, Sun 2–4:30pm). Museo di San Marco daily 9:30am–5:15pm (Nov–mid-Apr 9:45am–4:45pm). *Vaporetto:* San Marco.

Campanile di San Marco (Bell Tower) ★★★ LANDMARK   An elevator whisks you to the top of this 97m (318-ft.) brown brick bell tower, where you get an awe-inspiring view of St. Mark's cupolas. With a gilded angel atop its spire, the bell tower is the highest structure in the city, offering a pigeon's-eye panorama that includes the lagoon, neighboring islands, and the red roof-tops and church domes and bell towers of Venice. Originally built in the 9th century, the bell tower was reconstructed in the 12th, 14th, and 16th centuries, when the pretty marble loggia at its base was added by Jacopo Sansovino. It collapsed in 1902, miraculously hurting no one except a cat. Nine years later it was rebuilt exactly as before, using most of the same materials, even one of the five historical bells still in play today. Check www.venetoinside.com to see if "Skip the Line" tickets, which were suspended indefinitely in 2020 due to Covid-19, have been reinstated. *Tip:* If you have limited time, the view from the bell tower of San Giorgio Maggiore (p. 327) is much better (you get a wider panorama of the whole city) and is a couple of euros cheaper, though you need to take a *vaporetto* to get there.

Piazza San Marco. www.basilicasanmarco.it. © **041/2708311.** 10€. Daily: mid-Apr–Sept 9:30am–9:15pm; Oct–Mar 9:30am–5pm; Apr 1–mid-Apr 9:30am–5:30pm (closes Jan for maintenance). *Vaporetto:* San Marco.

Canal Grande (Grand Canal) ★★★ LANDMARK   A leisurely cruise along the "Canalazzo" from Piazza San Marco to the Ferrovia (train station), or the reverse, is one of Venice's (and life's) must-do experiences (see box, p. 272). Hop on the **no. 1** *vaporetto* in the late afternoon (try to get a coveted outdoor seat in the prow), when the soft light reflects on canal's rippling waters and warms the weather-worn colors of the former homes of Venice's merchant elite. The busy traffic of delivery boats, *vaporetti*, and gondolas that fills the city's main thoroughfare tends to ease up somewhat (if it's still too busy at that time, get on the boat first thing in the morning to beat the crowds).

> ### St. Mark's & the Doge's Palace in 1 Day?
>
> Yes, it is possible (and not too exhaust-ing) to see the Basilica di San Marco and the Palazzo Ducale in 1 day. Start at the church, arriving 30 minutes before open-ing (ideally get an online reservation in advance; see p. 308). Take a break before heading across to the Doge's Palace, where you can spend the rest of the day. You can buy palace tickets in advance online (**muve.vivaticket.it**). Your palace ticket also includes entry to the Museo Correr, Museo Archeologico Nazionale, and Biblioteca Nazionale Marciana, but it's safe to save these for another day—tickets are valid for up to 3 months.

Best stations to start/end a tour of the Grand Canal are Ferrovia (train station) or Piazzale Roma on the NW side of the canal and Piazza San Marco in the SE. Tickets 9.50€.

Palazzo Ducale ★★★ PALACE   The pink-and-white marble Gothic-Renaissance **Palazzo Ducale** (Doge's Palace), residence of the doges who ruled Venice for more than 1,000 years, stands between the Basilica di San Marco and the sea. A symbol of prosperity and power, the original was destroyed by a succession of fires, with the current building started in 1340, extended in the 1420s, and redesigned again after a fire in 1483. If you want

The spectacular ceiling paintings of the Sala del Collegio, in the Palazzo Ducale.

to understand something of this magnificent place, the fascinating history of the thousand-year-old maritime republic, and the intrigue of the government that ruled it, take the **Secret Itineraries tour ★★★** (see box, p. 312). Failing that, at least download the free iPhone/Android app (see the website) or shell out for the audioguide tour (available at entrance, 5€) to help make sense of it all. Unless you can tag along with an English-speaking tour group, you may otherwise miss out on the importance of much of what you're seeing.

The 15th-century **Porta della Carta** (Paper Gate) opens onto a splendid inner courtyard with a double row of Renaissance arches (today visitors enter through a doorway on the lagoon side of the palace). The self-guided route through the palace begins on the main courtyard, where the **Museo dell'Opera** contains assorted bits of masonry preserved from the Palazzo's exterior. Beyond here, the first major room you'll come to is the spacious **Sala delle Quattro Porte** (Hall of the Four Doors), with a worn ceiling by Tintoretto. The

museums **OF SAN MARCO**

Your ticket to the Palazzo Ducale also includes entry to several other museums around Piazza San Marco, though these are recommended for ancient-history and art aficionados only—with limited time you won't miss a lot by skipping them. Much of the **Museo Correr** (correr.visitmuve.it; ✆ **041-2405211;** daily 10am–5pm) is dull, comprising lesser-known artworks, archaeological remains, and odd bits and pieces from the city's later history, but it

does have one spark of gold: the "Courtesans" **★★**, a captivating painting by **Vittore Carpaccio. The Museo Archeologico Nazionale** (✆ **041-2967663;** same hours) contains a collection of Roman and Greek bits and pieces, while the ticket also includes a look at the two original reading rooms of the **Biblioteca Nazionale Marciana** (same hours), accessed via the Museo Correr—the current library is next door in the old mint of the Republic of Venice.

Sala dell'Anticollegio, where foreign ambassadors waited to be received by the doge and his council, is covered in four works by Tintoretto, including "Mercury & the Three Graces" and **"Bacchus and Ariadne"** ★★, the latter deemed one of his best by some critics. The Tintorettos are outshone, however, by Veronese's **"Rape of Europa"** ★★, one of the palazzo's finest paintings.

The highlight of the adjacent **Sala del Collegio** (the Council Chamber itself) is the spectacular cycle of **ceiling paintings** ★★, a Veronese masterpiece completed between 1575 and 1578. Next door lies the most impressive of the interior rooms, the richly adorned **Sala del Senato** (Senate Chamber), with Tintoretto's ceiling painting "The Triumph of Venice." After passing again through the Sala delle Quattro Porte, you'll enter the Veronese-decorated **Stanza del Consiglio dei Dieci** (Room of the Council of Ten), where justice was dispensed and decapitations ordered by the Republic's dreaded security police. Formed in the 14th century to deal with emergency situations, the Ten became more powerful than the Senate and feared by all. In the **Sala della Bussola** (the Compass Chamber), notice the **Bocca dei Leoni** (Lion's Mouth),

The Bridge of Sighs.

a slit in the wall into which secret denunciations and accusations of enemies of the state were placed for quick action by the much-feared Council.

The main sight on the next level down—indeed, the main sight in the entire palace—is the **Sala del Maggior Consiglio** (Great Council Hall). This enormous space is animated by Tintoretto's huge **"Paradiso"** ★ at the far end of the hall above the doge's seat. Measuring 7×23m (23×75 ft.), it is said to be the world's largest oil painting; together with Veronese's gorgeous **"Il Trionfo di Venezia"** ★★ ("The Triumph of Venice") in the oval panel on the ceiling, it affirms the power emanating from the council sessions held here. Tintoretto also did the portraits of the 76 doges encircling the top of this chamber; note that the picture of the Doge Marin Falier, who was convicted of treason and beheaded in 1355, has been blacked out—Venice has never forgiven him. Tours culminate at the enclosed **Ponte dei Sospiri** (Bridge of Sighs), built in 1600, which connects the Doge's Palace with the grim **Palazzo delle Prigioni** (Prison). The bridge took its current name in the 19th century—Lord Byron popularized it in his epic poem "Childe Harold's Pilgrimage" (1812–1818), romantically imagining the prisoners' final breath of resignation upon viewing the outside world one last time. Some attribute the name to Casanova, who, following his arrest in 1755 (he was accused of being a Freemason and spreading antireligious propaganda), crossed this very

secrets **OF THE PALAZZO DUCALE**

The **Itinerari Segreti ★★★ (Secret Itineraries)** guided tours of the Palazzo Ducale are a must-see for any visit to Venice of more than 1 day. The tours offer an unparalleled look into the world of Venetian politics over the centuries and are the only way to access otherwise restricted quarters and hidden passageways of this enormous palace, such as the doges' private chambers and the torture chambers where prisoners were interrogated. The tour must be reserved in advance online (**muve.vivaticket.it**), by phone (*©* **041/4273-0892**), or in person at the ticket desk. Tours often sell out at least a few days ahead, especially from spring through fall. Tours in English are daily at 10am, 11:30am and 1pm, and cost 32€ for adults, 20€ for ages 6 to 14, seniors, and students 15 to 25. Tours in Italian are at 11am and 12:30pm, and French at 10:30am and noon. The tour lasts about 75 minutes.

bridge. One of the rare few to escape, he did so 15 months after his imprisonment began; it was 20 years before he dared return to Venice. Some of the cells still have the original graffiti of past prisoners, many of them locked up interminably for petty crimes.

San Marco, Piazza San Marco. www.palazzoducale.visitmuve.it. *©* **041/2715911.** Admission only with San Marco Museum Pass (30€; reduced to 25€ if purchased 30 days in advance online). For Secret Itineraries tour in English, see box above. Daily 9am–6pm (last entrance 5pm). *Vaporetto:* San Marco.

Piazza San Marco ★★★ SQUARE   Dubbed "the finest drawing-room in Europe" by Napoleon, San Marco Square is undeniably one of Italy's most beautiful spaces, despite being terribly congested in high season (and often flooded during *acqua alta*). Today, the square is a focal point for Carnevale, as well as the spectacular Basilica and the most **historic cafes** in Venice—it's worth spending time in at least one of them for the ambience alone. The oldest (1720) is **Caffè Florian** (see p. 338), with compact **Caffè Lavena ★** (founded on the opposite side of the *piazza* in 1750) said to be Wagner's favorite (look for the plaque inside) and the hangout of fellow composer Franz Liszt in the 19th century. The final member of the San Marco "big three," **Gran Caffè Quadri ★** opened in 1638 as "Il Rimedio" ("The Remedy"), but it was more of a retail coffee operation at first, with the cafe upstairs added in 1830. It's been revitalized by chef Max Alajmo of Le Calandre restaurant in Padua, who added a fancy restaurant (**Ristorante Quadri;** https://alajmo.it). Expect the same high prices and surcharges at all three.

Vaporetto: San Marco-Vallaresso.

Ponte del Rialto (Rialto Bridge) ★★ LANDMARK   This graceful arch over the Grand Canal, linking the San Marco and San Polo districts, is lined with overpriced boutiques and teeming with tourists and overflow from the daily market on the San Polo side. Until the 19th century, it was the only bridge across the Grand Canal, originally built as a pontoon bridge at the canal's narrowest point. Wooden versions of the bridge followed; the 1444 incarnation was the first to include shops, interrupted by a drawbridge in the center. In 1592, this graceful stone span was finished to the designs of Antonio da Ponte (whose last name fittingly enough means "bridge"), who beat out Sansovino, Palladio, and Michelangelo with plans that called for a single, vast, 28m-wide (92-ft.) arch in the center to allow trading ships to pass.

Ponte del Rialto. *Vaporetto:* Rialto.

Scala Contarini del Bovolo ★★ VIEW
Part of a palazzo built in the late 15th century, this multi-arch spiral staircase (a mini-Tower of Pisa) was artfully restored in 2016, featuring a belvedere with fabulous views of Venice. Halfway up, the **Sala del Tintoretto** (Tintoretto Room) contains the rare portrait of Lazzaro Zen, an African who converted to Christianity in Venice in 1770, as well as a preparatory painting by Tintoretto of his monumental "Paradise" (the final version is in the Palazzo Ducale). You can buy **timed entry tickets** in advance at www.ticketlandia.com (advisable in peak season).

Corte Contarini del Bovolo 4299, San Marco. www.gioiellinascostidivenezia.it. ℂ **041/3096605.** 8€. Daily 10am–6pm (Nov–Feb 9:30am–5:30pm). Vaporetto: Rialto.

Teatro La Fenice ★★★ THEATER
One of Italy's most famous opera houses (it ranks third after La Scala in Milan and San Carlo in Naples), La Fenice was originally completed in 1792 but has been completely rebuilt twice after devastating fires; in 1837 and most recently in 2004. Self-guided tours (audio guides included) take in the opulent main theater, ornate side rooms, the gilded "royal box," and a small exhibit dedicated to feted soprano Maria Callas. For tickets to performances, see p. 337.

Campo San Fantin 1965, San Marco. www.teatrolafenice.it. Buy tour tickets on-site or in advance at festfenice.com. ℂ **041/2424.** 12€. Daily 9:30am–6pm. Vaporetto: Giglio.

Teatro La Fenice, fully rebuilt in 2004 after a destructive fire.

T Fondaco dei Tedeschi ★★ STORE/VIEW   The Harrods of Italy? In 2016, architect Rem Koolhaas and friends converted one of the city's great 16th-century *palazzi* (originally headquarters of the city's German or *Tedeschi* merchants) into a posh department store, centered on an elegant courtyard (featuring cafe/restaurant **AMO,** run by the Alajmo brothers). The **Rooftop Terrace** has rotating art exhibitions and quite possibly the greatest view of Venice. Reservations for the terrace are required and can be made on the store website up to 21 days in advance. The building is actually owned by Benetton and leased by the LVMH–owned luxury travel company DFS.

Calle de Fontego dei Tedeschi, Ponte di Rialto, San Marco. www.dfs.com/en/venice. ✆ **041/3142000.** Daily 10am–7:30pm. Roof deck (free) daily 10:15am–7pm; visits limited to 15 min. Vaporetto: Rialto.

Torre dell'Orologio (Clock Tower) ★★ MONUMENT   As you enter the magnificent **Piazza San Marco,** this Renaissance clock tower is one of the first things you see, standing on the north side, the centerpiece of the stately white **Procuratie Vecchie** (the ancient administration buildings for the Republic). With its distinctive blue face ringed by astrological symbols, the tower was built between 1496 and 1506, and the clock still keeps perfect time (although most of its original workings have been replaced). On top, two bronze figures, known as "Moors" because of the dark color of the bronze, pivot to strike the hour. Visits inside are by guided tour only (included in the price of admission), but unless you are interested in the clock's history, these are easily skipped, especially if you've already been up the Campanile di San Marco.

Piazza San Marco. www.torreorologio.visitmuve.it. ✆ **848/082000** or 041/42730892. 14€, 11€ ages 6–14 and students 15–25; ticket also includes Museo Correr, Museo Archeologico Nazionale, and Biblioteca Nazionale Marciana (but not Palazzo Ducale). Tours in English at: 11am (Mon, Fri, Sun); noon (Tues, Wed, Thurs); 2pm (Mon–Wed, Fri, Sat); 4pm (Fri, Sat); must be reserved in advance online; tours start at Museo Correr ticket office. Tours also in Italian and French. *Vaporetto:* San Marco.

Castello

While the highlight of this neighborhood is the huge **Santi Giovanni e Paolo** (see below), within a few minutes' walk from here are two more magnificent

---

The Biennale

Venice hosts the latest in contemporary art and sculpture from dozens of countries during the prestigious **Biennale d'Arte** ★★★ (www.labiennale.org; ✆ **041/5218711**), one of the world's top international art shows. It fills the pavilions of the **Giardini** (public gardens) at the east end of **Castello** and at the **Arsenale,** as well as in other spaces around the city from April to November on even years. (The next Biennale should take place in 2024, then 2026, etc.) It's usually open Tuesday to Sunday 10am to 6pm; tickets cost around 25€, 20€ seniors 65 and over, 16€ students and ages 26 and under. The **Biennale Architettura** (international architecture exhibition) takes place in alternate years (2025, 2027, and so on).

Renaissance churches: **Santa Maria Formosa** (3€; Mon–Sat 10:30am–4:30pm), on Campo Santa Maria Formosa, and **San Zaccaria** (free admission; Mon–Sat 10am–noon and 4–6pm, Sun 4–6pm), at Campo San Zaccaria, which contains Giovanni Bellini's exceptional **San Zaccaria Altarpiece ★★**. Pay 3€ to enter the side chapels for Tintoretto's "Birth of St. John the Baptist" and the creepy flooded crypt, which houses the bodies of eight doges.

Several attractions lie on the far eastern side of Castello. The sprawling **Museo Storico Navale di Venezia,** Riva San Biasio 2148 (www.marina.difesa.it) is worthwhile for folks with a deep interest in maritime history, but can be skipped by most others. Nearby is the **Ponte del Paradiso** and the famous twin-towered entrance to the **Arsenale** (only open during the Biennale).

Basilica Santi Giovanni e Paolo ★ CHURCH   Built by the Dominican order from the 13th to the 15th century, this massive Gothic church, together with the Frari Church in San Polo, is second in size only to the Basilica di San Marco. An unofficial Pantheon where 25 doges are buried (a few tombs are part of the unfinished facade), the church, commonly known as Zanipolo in Venetian dialect, is also home to many artistic treasures. The brilliantly colored **"Polyptych of St. Vincent Ferrer"** (ca. 1465), attributed to a young Giovanni Bellini, is in the right aisle. You'll also see the mummified foot of St. Catherine of Siena—considered a holy relic—encased in glass near here. Visit the **Cappella del Rosario ★,** through a glass door off the left transept, to see three restored ceiling canvases and one oil painting by Paolo Veronese, particularly "The Assumption of the Madonna."

Anchoring the large and impressive *campo* outside the church, a popular crossroads for this area of Castello, is the **statue of Bartolomeo Colleoni ★★,** the Renaissance *condottiere* (mercenary) who defended Venice's interests at the height of its power until his death in 1475. The 15th-century sculpture by the Florentine **Andrea Verrocchio** is considered one of the world's great equestrian monuments and Verrocchio's best.

Campo Santi Giovanni e Paolo 6363. santigiovanniepaolo.it. ⓒ **041/5235913.** 3.50€. Daily 7:30am–7pm (open to tourists Mon–Sat 9am–6pm, Sun noon–6pm). *Vaporetto:* Rialto.

Scuola di San Giorgio degli Schiavoni ★★ MUSEUM   One of the most mesmerizing spaces in Europe, the tiny main hall of this *scuola* once served as a meeting house for Venice's Dalmatian community (Dalmatia is a region of Croatia, and *schiavoni* means "Slavs"). Venetian *scuole,* or schools, were Middle Age guilds that brought together merchants and craftspeople from certain trades or similar religious devotions. Guilds functioned as social clubs, credit unions, even sources of spiritual guidance, and many commissioned elaborate headquarters, hiring the best artists of the day to decorate them. The *scuole* that remain in Venice today house some of the city's finest art treasures. Built beside its sister church, San Giovanni di Malta, in the early 16th century, San Giorgio degli Schiavoni offers a big reason to visit: to

Basilica Santi Giovanni e Paolo, resting place of 25 Venetian doges.

admire the awe-inspiring cycle of paintings on its walls, created by Renaissance master Vittore Carpaccio between 1502 and 1509. The paintings depict the lives of the Dalmatian patron saints George (of dragon-slaying fame), Tryphon, and Jerome. In the upper hall (Sala dell'Albergo), you'll also find Carpaccio's masterful "Vision of St. Augustine."

Calle dei Furlani 3259A. www.scuoladalmatavenezia.com/en. ℗ **041/5228828.** 6€ (cash only). Wed–Mon 10am–5:30pm (last entry 5pm); Reservations required in advance at segreteria@scuoladalmatavenezia.com. *Vaporetto:* Rialto.

Dorsoduro

Ca' Rezzonico ★★★ MUSEUM   Overlooking the Grand Canal, the palatial **Ca' Rezzonico** has a storied history that begins in the 1750s with the noble Rezzonico family. Later tenants included the poet Robert Browning (who died here in 1889) and Cole Porter, who rented the premises from 1926 to 1927. Today its lavish rooms pay tribute to 18th-century Venetian art and decor, with works by Tintoretto, four major ceiling frescoes by Tiepolo (plus his wonderfully preserved **Frescoes from the Villa at Zianigo ★★**), a couple of masterpieces from Francesco Guardi, and rare paintings by Francesco Maffei. The museum closed for a major renovation in 2022; it should be open again by the end of 2023, but check the website for the latest.

Calle San Bernardo 3136. carezzonico.visitmuve.it. ℗ **041/2410100.** 11€. Daily April–Oct 10:30am–6pm, Nov–March 10:30am–5pm. *Vaporetto:* Ca' Rezzonico.

Gallerie dell'Accademia (Academy Gallery) ★★★ MUSEUM

Along with San Marco and the Palazzo Ducale, the **Accademia** is one of the highlights of Venice, a magnificent collection of European art and especially Venetian painting from the 14th to the 18th centuries. There's a lot to take in here, so buy a catalog in the store, as these contain detailed descriptions of the core paintings and plenty of context—the audio guides are a little muddled and not worth 6€. Note also that one of the museum's prize holdings, Da Vinci's iconic **Vitruvian Man** ★★★ ("L'Uomo Vitruviano"), is an extremely fragile ink drawing and rarely displayed in public; check the website before you visit, as exhibitions featuring the drawing are rare but well publicized.

Visitors are currently limited to 300 at a time and lines can be long in high season—so advance reservations are essential (these are timed entry, letting you skip the line). In general, the least crowded times tend to be at opening in the morning, and around 2 hours before closing.

Rooms are laid out in rough chronological order, though renovations and closures mean some rooms may be off-limits when you visit (call ahead to check on specific paintings or check the website, which is updated monthly). Work began on the second-floor galleries in 2018—rooms 12 to 17 and 22 to 24 are likely to be closed at some point before the work is complete in 2024 or 2025. The following artworks should be on display somewhere in the museum, though locations will change (again, check the website for the latest).

Visits normally begin upstairs on the second floor, where room 1 (the grand meeting room of the Scuola Grande della Carità) displays a beautifully presented collection of lavish medieval and early Renaissance art, primarily religious images and altarpieces on wood panels from 1300 to 1450. The giant

"Feast in the House of Levi" in the Academy Gallery.

canvases in room 2 include Carpaccio's "Presentation of Jesus in the Temple," and works by Giovanni Bellini (Bellini is also the focus of rooms 4 and 5). Room 7 features the unsettling, surreal paintings of Hieronymus Bosch, while Giorgione's "The Tempest" and "The Old Woman" are displayed in Room 8. Room 9 showcases Venetian heavyweights Titian and Lorenzo Lotto, while Room 10 is dominated by Paolo Veronese's mammoth **"Feast in the House of Levi"** ★★. Other vast Veronese canvases make up the rest of the room. Room 11 contains work by another Venetian legend, Tintoretto, including **"The Miracle of the Slave"** ★★, along with several paintings by Tiepolo, the master of 18th-century Venetian art, and Titian's last painting, a "Pietà" intended for his own tomb.

Room 20 is usually filled by Gentile Bellini's cycle of **"The Miracles of the Relic of the Cross"** ★, painted around 1500. Room 21 normally contains a monumental cycle of nine paintings by Carpaccio illustrating the **Story of St. Ursula** ★★; most of these continue to undergo restoration, with "Arrival in Cologne" the only one likely to be displayed for some time.

While renovations are ongoing, room 23 will contain some of the museum's most famous paintings—check with the museum information desk (or online) if there's a particular work you want to see. Finally, room 24 is adorned with Titian's "Presentation of the Virgin," actually created to hang in this space between 1534 and 1538.

Downstairs, the renovated ground-floor galleries cover the late 18th to 19th centuries, a far more mediocre collection of baroque and romantic works, though delicate paintings by Tiepolo share space with his large tondo "Feast of the Cross" in gallery 2, along with Veronese's "Venice Receives Homage from Hercules and Ceres." Sculpture galleries (featuring the work of Canova) should also be open on this level.

Campo della Carità 1050, at foot of Accademia bridge. www.gallerieaccademia.it. © **041/5200345.** 12€ adults (admission price subject to change during temporary exhibitions). 1.50€ reservation charge by phone or online. Daily 8:15am–7:15pm (Mon until 2pm). *Vaporetto:* Accademia.

I Gesuati (Santa Maria del Rosario) ★ CHURCH   Built from 1724 to 1743 by Giorgio Massari to mirror the Redentore across the Canale della Giudecca, this cavernous church counters the latter's Palladian sobriety with rococo flair. The interior is graced by airy 1738–39 ceiling frescoes (some of the first in Venice) by **Giambattista Tiepolo.** Tiepolo also created the "Virgin with Saints Rosa of Lima, Catherine of Siena, and Agnes of Montepulciano" on the first altar on the right. The third altar on the left is adorned with a Tintoretto "Crucifixion" (1565).

Fondamenta delle Zattere ai Gesuati. © **041/2750462.** 3€ adults, free for children 5 and under. Mon–Sat 10am–4:30pm. *Vaporetto:* Zattere.

Peggy Guggenheim Collection ★★ MUSEUM   Though this is one of the best museums in Italy exhibiting American and European art of the 20th century, you might find the experience a little jarring, given its location in a city so heavily associated with the High Renaissance and the baroque.

VENICE discounts

Venice offers a somewhat bewildering range of passes and discount cards. For short stays, we recommend buying a 1-day to 7-day **ACTV travel card** (p. 272) and combining that with one of the first two passes listed below. The more complex Venezia Unica card scheme is recommended if you intend to stay up to 7 days and do a lot of sightseeing. The **Venezia Unica website** (www.veneziaunica.it) is a one-stop shop for all the passes listed below.

The **Museum Pass (MUVE)** grants admission to all city-run museums over a 6-month period, and also lets you skip ticketing lines, a useful perk in high season. The pass covers the museums of St. Mark's Square—**Palazzo Ducale, Museo Correr, Museo Archeologico Nazionale,** the **Biblioteca Nazionale Marciana** (it's 25–30€ to visit just these museums with a San Marco Museum Pass)—as well as the **Museo di Palazzo Mocenigo** (Costume Museum), **Ca' Rezzonico, Ca' Pesaro,** the **Museo del Vetro** (Glass Museum) on Murano, and the **Museo del Merletto** (Lace Museum) on Burano. The Museum Pass is available online (for an extra 1€), or at any participating museum. It costs 40€ for adults and 22€ for students under 26, kids ages 6 to 14, and seniors over 65. It's a good deal, as the Doge's Palace alone will set you back 30€; visit two more of the larger museums (e.g., Palazzo Mocenigo, 10€, and Ca' Pesaro, 14€) and you've made a decent saving.

The **Chorus Pass** (www.chorusvenezia. org) grants admission to almost every major church in Venice, 18 in all, for 12€ (8€ for students under 30), for up to 1 year. For 24€, the **Chorus Pass Family** gives you the same perks for a family of two adults and their children up to 18 years old. Most churches charge 3€ admission, which means you'll need to visit more than four to make this pass worthwhile.

The **Venezia Unica card** (www. veneziaunica.it) combines the above passes, transport, discounts, and even Internet access on one card via a "made-to-order" online system, in which you choose the services you want. Of these, the 7-day passes (if available) are the best value. You can also buy various transportation packages from Venezia Unica (1-, 2-, 3- and 7-day ACTV passes 25€–65€), which cover all *vaporetto* and bus travel, or just Wi-Fi access (from 5€ for 24 hr.).

For visitors between the ages of 6 and 29, the **Rolling Venice card** (also available at www.veneziaunica.it) costs just 6€. Valid through the end of the year in which you buy it, it entitles the bearer to significant (20%–30%) discounts at participating restaurants (cardholder's meal only) and discounted ACTV travel cards (27€ for 3 days), along with discounts in museums, stores, hotels, and bars across the city (it comes with a thick booklet listing all the places you're entitled to get discounts).

Nevertheless, art aficionados will find some fascinating work here, and the galleries occupy Peggy Guggenheim's wonderful former home, the 18th-century Palazzo Venier dei Leoni, right on the Grand Canal (you can access the waterfront from the main building). Guggenheim bought the mansion in 1949 and lived here, on and off, until her death in 1979 (the history of this once-derelict palace is wonderfully brought to life in Judith Mackrell's *The Unfinished Palazzo*). Today the entire villa has been converted into galleries. Highlights include Picasso's extremely abstract "Poet" and his more gentle "On the Beach," several works by Kandinsky ("Landscape with Red Spots No.

2" and "White Cross"), Miró's expressionistic "Seated Woman II," Klee's mystical "Magic Garden," and some unsettling works by Max Ernst ("The Kiss," "Attirement of the Bride"), who was briefly married to Guggenheim in the 1940s. Look for Magritte's "Empire of Light," Dalí's typically surreal "Birth of Liquid Desires," and a couple of gems from Pollock (who was especially championed by Guggenheim): his early "Moon Woman," which recalls Picasso, and "Alchemy," a more typical "poured" painting. The Italian Futurists are also well represented here, with a rare portrait from Modigliani ("Portrait of the Painter Frank Haviland"). Adjacent buildings added later to the complex (serving as temporary exhibition space, a cafe, and a shop) are connected to the main

"Developable Surface," a 1941 sculpture by Antoine Pevsner made of bronze rods, is on display at the Peggy Guggenheim Collection.

building by the pleasantly shady **Nasher Sculpture Garden;** Guggenheim is buried in the corner, marked by a simple headstone. Free presentations on aspects of the collection are given daily in the museum galleries or garden (check the website for times). Guided tours can be arranged in advance and cost 95€, for a group of up to 20 people. *Tip:* It's not a good idea to visit the Guggenheim and St. Mark's on the same day—it's a fairly long walk between the two. We also don't advise seeing it on the same day as the Accademia, even though they are only 10 minutes apart; the artistic overload is likely to prove too much for even the most avid art aficionado.

Fondamenta Venier dai Leon 704. www.guggenheim-venice.it. © **041/2405411.** 16€ adults, 14€ 65 and over; 9€ students 10–26; audio guide 7€. Advance purchase online recommended. Wed–Mon 10am–6pm. *Vaporetto:* Accademia (walk around left side of Accademia, take first left, and walk straight ahead following the signs).

Punta della Dogana ★★★ MUSEUM   The eastern tip *(punta)* of Dorsoduro is crowned by the distinctive triangle of the 17th-century **Dogana di Mare** (Customs House), which once monitored all boats entering the Grand Canal. Transformed by architect Tadao Ando into a beautiful exhibition space, it's now a showcase for the contemporary art collection of billionaire François Pinault (officially dubbed the **Centro d'Arte Contemporanea Punta della Dogana**). It's pricey, but expect to see quality work from Cindy Sherman, Cy Twombly, Jeff Koons, and Marlene Dumas, among many others.

Fondamenta della Dogana alla Salute 2. www.palazzograssi.it. © **041/2719031.** 15€– 20€ (includes admission to Palazzo Grassi). Wed–Mon 10am–7pm (usually closed Jan– late March; check ahead). *Vaporetto:* Salute.

San Sebastiano ★★ CHURCH   Lose the crowds as you make a pilgrimage to the parish church of **Paolo Veronese,** home to some of his finest work. Veronese painted the coffered nave ceiling with the florid "Scenes from the Life of St. Esther." In the 1560s he also decorated the organ shutters and panels in the chancel with scenes from the life of St. Sebastian. Although Veronese is the main event here, don't miss Titian's sensitive "St. Nicholas" (just inside the church on the right). Veronese's sepulchral monument (with bust by Mattia Carneri) is to the left of the altar. The real highlight is the sacristy (go through the door under the organ), a tiny jewel box of a room adorned with more wonderful Veronese paintings of the "Coronation of the Virgin" and the "Four Evangelists."

Campo San Sebastiano. ✆ **041/2750462.** 3€. Mon–Sat 10:30am–4:30pm. *Vaporetto:* San Basilio.

Santa Maria della Salute ★ CHURCH   The church of the Virgin Mary of Good Health, known as "La Salute," is a crown jewel of 17th-century baroque architecture, proudly reigning over a landmark point, almost directly across from the Piazza San Marco, where the Grand Canal empties into the lagoon.

The first stone was laid in 1631 after the Senate decided to honor the Virgin Mary for delivering Venice from a plague that had killed around 95,000 people. They accepted the revolutionary plans of a young, relatively unknown architect, Baldassare Longhena. He dedicated the next 50 years of his life to overseeing its progress (he would die 1 year after its inauguration but 5 years before its completion). Today the dome of the church is an iconic presence on the Venice skyline, recognized for its exuberant exterior of volutes, scrolls, and more than 125 statues. The most revered image inside is the **Madonna della Salute,** a rare, black-faced sculpture of Mary brought back in 1670 from Candia in Crete as war booty. The otherwise sober interior is enlivened by the **sacristy,** with several important ceiling paintings and portraits by **Titian.** On the right wall of the sacristy (6€ admission) is Tintoretto's **"Marriage at Cana"** ★, often considered one of his best paintings. It's also now possible to climb 150 steps up the dome

Inside Santa Maria della Salute.

("Cupola") for 8€ (generally Fri–Sun only but check the website), for a unique panorama of the city from the south.

Campo della Salute. www.basilicasalutevenezia.it. © **041/5225558.** Church free admission; sacristy 6€. Daily: Apr–Oct 9am–noon & 3–5:30pm, Nov–Mar 9:30am–12:30pm and 3–5:30pm; **sacristy:** Apr–Oct Tues 2–3:30pm & 4:40–5:30pm, Wed–Fri 10am–12:30pm, 2–3:30pm & 4:40–5:30pm, Sat 10am–12:30pm & 2–5:30pm, Sun 10–10:30am & 2–5:30pm; Nov–Mar Mon–Fri 10am–noon, 3–3:30pm & 4:40–5:30pm, Sat 10am–noon & 2–5:30pm, Sun 10–10:30am & 2–5:30pm. *Vaporetto:* Salute.

Scuola Grande dei Carmini ★★ CHURCH   The former Venetian base of the Carmelite religious order, finished in the 18th century, is now a shrine of sorts to **Giambattista Tiepolo,** who painted the ceiling of the upstairs hall between 1739 and 1744. It's truly a magnificent sight. Tiepolo's elaborate rococo interpretation of "Simon Stock Receiving the Scapular" is now fully restored along with various panels throughout the building.

Campo San Margherita 2617. www.scuolagrandecarmini.it. © **041/5289420.** 7€. Daily 10am–5pm. *Vaporetto:* San Basilio.

Squero di San Trovaso ★★ HISTORIC SITE   One of the most intriguing sights in Venice is this small *squero* (boatyard), which first opened in the 17th century on the narrow Rio San Trovaso (not far from the Accademia Bridge). It is surrounded by Tyrolean-looking wooden structures (a true rarity

---

THE ART OF THE gondola

Putting together one of these sleek black boats is a fascinatingly exact science that is still done in the revered traditional manner at boatyards such as the **Squero di San Trovaso** (see p. 322). Gondolas have been painted black since the 16th century, when local legislators passed a law designed to restrict the gaudy outlandishness so prevalent at the time.

Propelled by the strength of a single *gondoliere,* these boats, unique to Venice, have no modern equipment. They move with no great speed but with unrivaled grace. The right side of the gondola is lower because the *gondoliere* always stands in the back of the boat on the left.

The San Trovaso *squero,* or boatyard, is the city's oldest and one of only three remaining (the other two are immeasurably more difficult to find). Its predominant focus is on maintenance and repair, although they will occasionally build a new gondola (which takes some 40–45 working days), carefully crafting it from the seven types of wood—mahogany, cherry, fir, walnut, oak, elm, and lime—necessary to give the shallow and asymmetrical boat its various characteristics. After all the pieces are put together, the painting, the *ferro* (the iron symbol of the city affixed to the bow), and the woodcarving that secures the oar are commissioned out to various local artisans.

Although some 10,000 of these elegant boats floated on the canals of Venice in the 16th century, today there are only around 425, almost all catering to the tourist trade. The job of *gondoliere* remains a coveted profession, passed down from father to son over the centuries, but nowadays it's open to anyone who can pass 400 hours of rigorous training—including Giorgia Boscolo, who passed the exam in 2010 and became the first-ever *gondoliera;* her father was also in the profession.

in this city of stone built on water) that are home to the multigenerational owners and original workshops for traditional Venetian boats (see "The Art of the Gondola," p. 322). Aware that they have become a tourist site themselves, the gondoliers don't mind if you watch them at work from across the narrow Rio di San Trovaso, but don't try to invite yourself in. *Tip:* It's the perfect midway photo op after a visit to the Accademia and a trip to **Gelateria Nico,** Zattere 922, where the chocolate *gianduiotto* is a decadent delight.

Dorsoduro 1097 (on the Rio San Trovaso, SW of the Accademia). *Vaporetto:* Zattere.

San Polo & Santa Croce

The eastern portion of Santa Croce contains several minor attractions. The grand **Museo di Palazzo Mocenigo,** Salizada San Stae 1992 (mocenigo.visitmuve.it) is worthwhile for visitors with a keen interest in historic costumes and perfumes, but can be skipped by most others, while the nearby **Museo di Ca' Pesaro,** Fondamenta de Ca' Pesaro 2076 (capesaro.visitmuve.it) is home to modernist work from the likes of Rodin and Klimt, plus a large Asian art collection. The **Museo di Storia Naturale,** Salizada del Fontego dei Turchi 1730 (msn.visitmuve.it) is a well-presented natural history museum aimed squarely at children. Lesser visited churches include **San Stae,** Salizada San Stae 1982 (Mon–Sat 1:45–4:30pm), a cavernous, all-white space on the Grand Canal that contains an early Tiepolo, the *Martyrdom of St. Bartholemew,* and **San Nicola da Tolentino,** Campo dei Tolentini (free admission; Mon–Wed, Fri, Sat 3:30–6pm, Sun 10am–12:30pm), home to the funeral monument of Francesco Morosini, a baroque masterpiece.

Santa Maria Gloriosa dei Frari (Church of the Frari) ★★

CHURCH   Known simply as "i Frari," this immense 14th-century Gothic

basilica was built by the Franciscans and is the largest church in Venice after San Marco. It houses several important artworks, including two Titian masterpieces: the **"Assumption of the Virgin"** ★★ over the main altar, painted when the artist was only in his late 20s, and "Virgin of the Pesaro Family" in the left nave. For the latter work, Titian's wife posed for the figure of Mary (and died soon afterward in childbirth). Don't miss Giovanni Bellini's **"Madonna & Child"** ★★ over the altar in the sacristy, of which novelist Henry James wrote, "it is as solemn as it is gorgeous." The grand **mausoleum of Titian** is on the right as you enter the church, opposite the incongruous

The mausoleum of the painter Titian, in Santa Maria Gloriosa dei Frari.

18th-century monument to sculptor **Antonio Canova,** shaped like a pyramid—designed by Canova himself, this was originally supposed to be Titian's tomb.

Campo dei Frari. www.basilicadeifrari.it. (℗) **041/2728611.** 5€; audio guide 2€. Mon–Sat 9am–6pm; Sun 1–6pm (extended hours Jun–Sep, see website). *Vaporetto:* San Tomà (walk straight on Calle del Traghetto, turn right and immediately left across Campo San Tomà; walk straight on Ramo Mandoler, then Calle Larga Prima, turn right at beginning of Salizada San Rocco).

Scuola Grande di San Rocco ★★★ MUSEUM Like many medieval saints, French-born San Rocco (St. Roch) died young, but thanks to his work healing the sick in the 14th century, his cult became associated with the power to cure the plague and other serious illnesses. When his body was brought to Venice in 1485, this *scuola* began to reap the benefits, and by 1560 the current complex was completed. Work soon began on more than 50 paintings by **Tintoretto,** and today the *scuola* is primarily a shrine to the masterful Venetian artist. You enter at the **Ground Floor Hall** (Sala Terrena), where the paintings were created between 1583 and 1587, led by one of the most frenzied "Annunciations" ever made. The "Flight into Egypt" here is undeniably one of Tintoretto's greatest works. Upstairs is the **Great Upper Hall** (Sala Superiore), where Old Testament scenes such as "Moses Striking Water from the Rock" cover the ceiling. The paintings around the walls, based on the New Testament, are generally regarded as a master class of perspective, shadow, and color. In the **Sala dell'Albergo,** an entire wall is adorned by Tintoretto's mind-blowing "Crucifixion" (as well as his "Glorification of St. Roch," on the ceiling, the painting that actually won him the contract to paint the *scuola*). Way up in the loft, the **Tesoro** (Treasury) is a tiny space dedicated primarily to gold reliquaries containing venerated relics such as the fingers of St. Peter and St. Andrew, and one of the thorns that crowned Christ during the crucifixion.

Campo San Rocco 3052, adjacent to Campo dei Frari. www.scuolagrandesanrocco.it. (℗) **041/5234864.** 10€ adults, 8€ ages 18–26 and over 65, free for children 18 and under; audio guide 3€. Daily 9:30am–5:30pm. *Vaporetto:* San Tomà (walk straight ahead on Calle del Traghetto, turn right and immediately left across Campo San Tomà; walk straight on Ramo Mandoler, Calle Larga Prima, and Salizada San Rocco, which leads into the *campo*—look for the crimson sign behind Frari Church).

Cannaregio

Lesser-visited gems in this district include the soaring church of **Madonna dell'Orto,** Fondamenta Madonna de l'Orto 3512 (3€; Mon–Sat 10am–5pm, Sun noon–5pm), where Tintoretto is buried, crammed with his work (including a revered *Last Judgement*), and the nearby church of **Sant'Alvise,** Campo Sant'Alvise (3€; Mon–Sat 10:30–1:30pm and 2:30–5pm), with a sensational frescoed ceiling and several works by Tiepolo, including *The Way to Calvary.*

Galleria Giorgio Franchetti alla Ca' d'Oro ★★ MUSEUM A magnificent *palazzo* overlooking the Grand Canal, the "golden house," was built between 1428 and 1430 for the noble Contarini family. Baron Giorgio Franchetti bought the place in 1894, and it now serves as an atmospheric art

The Venice Ghetto is the oldest Jewish ghetto in Europe.

gallery for his exceptional collection (mostly early Renaissance Italian and Flemish). The highlight is **"St. Sebastian"** ★★ by Paduan artist Andrea Mantegna, displayed in its own marble chapel. The so-called "St. Sebastian of Venice" was the third and final painting of the saint by Mantegna, created around 1490 and quite a contrast to the other two (in Vienna and Paris, respectively); it's a bold, deeply pessimistic work, with none of Mantegna's usual background details to detract from the saint's suffering. Don't miss three panels from Carpaccio's "Stories of the Virgin" series on the second floor.

Strada Nuova 3932. Polomusealeveneto.beniculturali.it. 🕿 **041/520-0345.** 6€; free audio guide available online. Tues–Sun 9am–7pm. *Vaporetto*: Ca' d'Oro.

Museo Ebraico di Venezia ★ MUSEUM/SYNAGOGUE   In the heart of the Ghetto Nuovo, the Jewish Museum contains a small but precious collection of artifacts related to the long history of the Jews in Venice. The museum closed for a major restoration in 2021 that should be complete in 2023 or 2024. Until then, tours of the Scuola Levantina synagogue (and the Luzzatto midrash) will depart a temporary location from the Campo del Ghetto Nuovo (visitors must have shoulders covered and men must have heads covered; no photos). The new museum is slated to expand into three new buildings on the campo, and will include space for temporary exhibits as well as the permanent collection that includes historic chandeliers, goblets, and spice holders used to celebrate Shabbat, Shofàrs (ram's horns), and a Séfer Torà (Scroll of Divine Law). But for many, the real highlight will be the chance to tour the area's historic synagogues (all hidden from view on the top floor of otherwise normal-looking Venetian tenements): **German** (Scuola Grande Tedesca), founded in 1528; **Italian** (Scuola Italiana), founded in 1575; **Sephardic** (Scuola Levantina), founded in 1541 but rebuilt in the 17th century; **Spanish** (Scuola Spagnola), rebuilt in the first half of the 17th century; and the baroque-style **Scuola Canton**, established in 1532 (likely by French Provençal Jews) but largely rebuilt in the 18th century. The Canton, German and Italian synagogues are undergoing various stages of restoration that

Il Ghetto & the Jews of Venice

Jews began settling in Venice in great numbers in the 15th century, and the Republic soon came to value their services as moneylenders, physicians, and traders. In 1516, however, fearing their growing influence, the Venetians forced the Jewish population to live on an island with an abandoned foundry (*ghetto* is old Venetian dialect for "foundry"), and drawbridges were raised to enforce a nighttime curfew. By the end of the 17th century, as many as 5,000 Jews lived in the Ghetto's cramped confines. Napoleon tore down the Ghetto gates in 1797, but it wasn't until the unification of Italy in 1866 that Jews achieved equal status. Il Ghetto remains the spiritual center for Venice's ever-diminishing community of Jewish families, with two

synagogues and a Chabad House; although accounts vary widely, it's said that anywhere from 450 to 2,000 Jews live in all of Venice and Mestre, though very few now live in the Ghetto.

Aside from its historic interest, this is also one of the less touristy neighborhoods in Venice and makes for a pleasant and scenic place to stroll. Venice's first kosher restaurant, **Gam Gam**, opened here in 1996, at 1122 Ghetto Vecchio right on the canal (www.gamgamkosher.com; ✆ **366/2504505**), close to the Guglie *vaporetto* stop. Run by Orthodox Jews, it is open Sunday to Thursday noon to 10pm, Friday noon to 2 hours before Shabbat begins at sunset, and Saturday from 1 hour after sunset until 11pm (excluding summer).

should also be complete by 2024 (depending on funding) and will be part of the new museum experience. The Levantina and Spanish synagogues are used regularly for services, but will also be open for tours at certain times.

Campo del Ghetto Nuovo. www.ghettovenezia.com. ✆ **041/715359.** Museum/tour 10€ adults, 8€ kids and students ages 6–26. For tour times and the latest on the museum, check the website. Closed Jewish holidays. *Vaporetto:* Guglie.

Santa Maria dei Miracoli ★ CHURCH   Hidden in a quiet corner of the residential section of Cannaregio northeast of the Rialto Bridge, the small and exceedingly attractive 15th-century Miracoli has one side of its precious polychrome-marbled façade running alongside a canal, creating colorful and shimmering reflections. It was built from 1481 to 1489 by Pietro Lombardo, a local artisan whose background in monuments and tombs is obvious. He would go on to become one of the founding fathers of the Venetian Renaissance.

The less romantic are inclined to compare it to a large tomb with a dome, but untold couples have made this jewel-like church their choice for weddings. The small square in front is the perfect place for gondolas to drop off and pick up the newlyweds, and inside is decorated with early Renaissance reliefs in a pastel palette of pink, gray, and white marble, an elegant nuptial setting. The church was constructed for a venerated image of the Virgin Mary, credited with working miracles—including bringing back to life someone who'd spent half an hour at the bottom of the Giudecca Canal. The icon is now displayed over the main altar.

Campiello di Miracoli, Rio di Miracoli. No phone. 3€. Mon–Sat 10:30am–4:30pm. *Vaporetto:* Rialto (located midway btw. Rialto Bridge and Campo SS. Giovanni e Paolo).

Giudecca

Il Redentore ★★ CHURCH   Many consider this the finest church ever designed by Andrea Palladio, the great Renaissance architect from nearby Padua most known for his country villas built for Venice's wealthy merchant families. It was commissioned by Venice to give thanks for being delivered from the great plague (1575–77), which claimed over a quarter of the population (some 46,000 people). The doge established a tradition of visiting this church by crossing a long pontoon bridge made up of boats from the Dorsoduro's Zattere, every third Sunday of July, a tradition that survived the demise of the doges and remains one of Venice's most popular festivals ("Festa del Redentore," see p. 50). The interior is done in austere but elegant classical Palladian style. The artworks tend to be workshop pieces (from the studios or schools, but not the actual brushes, of Tintoretto and Veronese), but there is a fine "Baptism of Christ" by Veronese himself in the sacristy (accessed through a door in the last chapel on the right), which also contains Alvise Vivarini's "Madonna with Child & Angels" alongside works by Jacopo da Bassano and Palma il Giovane.

Campo del Redentore 195. ⓒ **041/5231415**. 3€. Mon–Sat 10:30am–4:30pm. *Vaporetto:* Redentore.

San Giorgio Maggiore

Sitting on the little island of San Giorgio Maggiore across from Piazza San Marco are a handful of intriguing sights, not least its namesake church, another Palladio masterpiece.

Fondazione Giorgio Cini ★★ MUSEUM   Founded by the wealthy Cini family in 1951, the Fondazione Giorgio Cini occupies the old San Giorgio Monastery near the church. Its art galleries host traveling exhibitions and items from its extensive collection of rare manuscripts. You can also explore the foundation's Borges Labyrinth (a maze), the 10 "Vatican Chapels," and the open-air Teatro Verde.

San Giorgio Maggiore 30124. www.visitcini.com. ⓒ **0366/4202181**. 15€. Thurs–Tues 11am–7pm. Vaporetto: Take Giudecca-bound vaporetto no. 2 from Riva degli Schiavoni (San Marco/San Zaccaria) and get off at first stop.

San Giorgio Maggiore ★★ CHURCH   Palladio designed this magnificent church in 1565 and it was completed in 1610. To impose a classical front on the traditional church structure, Palladio designed two interlocking facades, with repeating triangles, rectangles, and columns harmoniously proportioned. Palladio also reinterpreted the interior with whitewashed stucco surfaces, an unadorned but harmonious space. The main altar is flanked by two epic paintings by Tintoretto, "The Fall of Manna," to the left, and the more noteworthy **"Last Supper" ★★** to the right, famous for its chiaroscuro. Accessed by free guided tour only (usually Apr–Oct only; times vary), the adjacent Cappella dei Morti (Chapel of the Dead) contains Tintoretto's "Deposition," and the upper chapel contains Carpaccio's "St. George Killing the Dragon." To the left of the choir is an elevator that you can take to the top of the 1791 campanile—for a charge of 8€—to experience an unforgettable view of the island, the lagoon, and the Palazzo Ducale and Piazza San Marco across the way.

San Giorgio Maggiore Island. ℂ **041/5227827.** Free admission. Daily Apr–Oct 9am– 7pm, Nov–Mar 8:30am–6pm. *Vaporetto:* Take Giudecca-bound *vaporetto* no. 2 from Riva degli Schiavoni (San Marco/San Zaccaria) and get off at first stop.

Stanze del Vetro ★ MUSEUM   Next door to the church and designed by Selldorf Architects, the stylish Stanze del Vetro hosts traveling exhibitions dedicated to the art of glassmaking. It's usually closed between shows, so check the website for the latest.

San Giorgio Maggiore 8. lestanzedelvetro.org. ℂ **041/5229138**. Free admission. Thurs–Tues 10am–7pm. *Vaporetto:* Take Giudecca-bound *vaporetto* no. 2 from Riva degli Schiavoni (San Marco/San Zaccaria) and get off at first stop.

Exploring Venice's Islands

Venice shares its lagoon with four other principal islands: **Murano, Burano, Torcello,** and the **Lido.** Guided tours of the first three are available (30€–45€ for 3 to 4 hours). While these can be informative, unless you are very short of time you'll enjoy exploring the islands in far more leisurely fashion on your own, easily done using the *vaporetti.*

Line nos. 4.1 and 4.2 make the journey to **Murano** from Fondamente Nove (on the north side of Castello). For **Murano, Burano,** and **Torcello,** line no. 12 departs Fondamente Nove every 30 minutes (for Torcello, change to the line 9 shuttle boat that runs from Burano, timed to match the arrivals from Venice; it zips between the two islands every 15 minutes). The islands are small and easy to navigate, but check the schedule for the next island-to-island departure (usually hourly) and plan your return so that you don't spend most of your day waiting for connections.

Vaporetto line nos. 1, 2, 5.1, 5.2, and LN cross the lagoon to the **Lido** from the San Zaccaria–Danieli stop near San Marco. Note that the Lido becomes chilly, windswept, and more or less deserted from October to April.

MURANO ★★

The island of **Murano** has long been famous throughout the world for the products of its glass factories. The illuminating **Museo del Vetro (Museum of Glass)** ★★, Fondamenta Giustinian 8 (www.museovetro.visitmuve.it; ℂ **041/739586**), provides context, charting the history of the island's glass-making; it's definitely worthwhile if you intend to purchase a lot of glassware, providing plenty of background so you know what you're buying in the stores outside. Normally it's open daily 10am to 5pm (last entry at 4pm); admission is 10€ adults, 7.50€ ages 6 to 14 and students 25 and under.

Dozens of *fornaci* (kilns) offer free (or cheap) shows of mouth-blown glassmaking, almost invariably hitched to a hard-sell tour of their factory outlet. Once you're on the island, you can't miss these places; they're pretty much of equal quality. A dependable choice is **Original Murano Glass**

Traditional glassblowing in Murano.

(Feb–Oct normally open daily 10am–3pm; reserve 5€ tours and demonstrations at www.visitmuranoglassfactory.com), at the Ellegi Glass *fornaci,* Fondamenta San Giovanni dei Battuti 4, a few minutes' walk from the Murano Faro *vaporetti* stop. Almost all shops will ship their goods, although that often doubles the price. On the other hand, these pieces are instant heirlooms.

Murano is also graced by two worthy churches (both free admission): the largely 15th-century **San Pietro Martire** ★ (Mon–Sat 9am–5:30pm, Sun noon–5:30pm), with its paintings by Veronese and Giovanni Bellini, and the ancient **Santa Maria e Donato** ★ (Mon–Sat 9am–6pm, Sun 12:30–6pm), with its intricate Byzantine exterior apse, 6th-century pulpit, stunning mosaic of Mary over the altar, and a fantastic 12th-century mosaic inlaid floor.

BURANO ★★★

Lace is the claim to fame of tiny, historic **Burano,** a craft kept alive for centuries by the wives of fishermen waiting for their husbands to return from the sea. Sadly, most of the lace sold on the island these days is made by machine elsewhere. It's still worth a trip if you have time to stroll the back streets of the island, whose canals are lined with the brightly colored, simple homes of the Buranesi fishermen—it's quite unlike anything in Venice or Murano. The local government continues its attempt to keep its centuries-old lace legacy alive with subsidized classes.

Visit the **Museo del Merletto (Museum of Lace Making)** ★, Piazza Galuppi 187 (www.museomerletto.visitmuve.it; ✆ **041/730034**), to understand why something so exquisite should not be allowed to fade into extinction. It's normally open Tuesday to Sunday 10am to 5pm (Nov–Mar to 4pm); admission is 5€ adults, 3.50€ ages 6 to 14 and students 25 and under.

Butter biscuits known simply as *buranelli* are also a famous product of the island—expect to be offered them in almost every store.

TORCELLO ★★

Torcello is perhaps the most charming of the islands, though today it consists of little more than one long canal leading from the *vaporetto* landing to a clump of buildings at its center (a 10-min. walk). Hard to imagine this was

Lace is a traditional Venetian craft.

once a thriving city in its own right, with at least 20,000 inhabitants in the 16th century.

Torcello boasts the oldest Venetian monument, the **Basilica di Santa Maria dell'Assunta ★★★**, whose foundation dates from the 7th century (*©* **041/ 2702464**). It's justly famous for its spectacular 11th- to 12th-century Byzantine mosaics—a "Madonna and Child" in the apse and a monumental "Last Judgment" on the west wall—rivaling those of Ravenna's and St. Mark's basilicas. Note that taking photos inside is forbidden. The cathedral is open daily 10:30am to 6pm (Nov–Feb to 5pm), and admission is 5€ (audio guide an extra 2€; the separate bell tower closes 15–30 min. earlier than the Basilica and costs 5€, or 9€ combined with the Basilica). Also of interest is the adjacent 11th-century church of **Santa Fosca** (free admission), a simple Byzantine brick chapel with a plain interior, and the **Museo di Torcello** (*©* **041/ 730761**), with two small galleries showcasing archaeological artifacts from the Iron Age to the medieval era, many found on the island. The church closes 30 minutes before the basilica, and the museum is open Tuesday to Sunday 10:30am to 5:30pm (Nov–Feb 10am–5pm). Museum admission is 3€. You must buy tickets for all attractions at the Basilica entrance (museum, cathedral, and bell tower is 12€).

Peaceful Torcello is now uninhabited except for a handful of families and is a favorite picnic spot. You'll have to bring food in from Venice—there are no stores on the island and only a handful of bars/trattorias along the canal plus one fabulous destination restaurant, **Locanda Cipriani ★★★** (Wed–Mon noon–3pm and 7–9pm; closed Jan to mid-Feb; www.locandacipriani.com), of Hemingway fame; Queen Elizabeth II, Winston Churchill, and Princess Diana all dined here too). Opened in 1935 by Giuseppe Cipriani (it's still owned by the family), this spot is definitely worth a splurge (reservations recommended). Once the tour groups have left, the island offers a very special moment of solitude and escape.

THE LIDO ★

Although a convenient 15-minute *vaporetto* ride away from San Marco (see transport details above), Venice's **Lido beaches** are not much to write home about and certainly no longer a chic destination (the Grand Hotel des Bains depicted in Thomas Mann's *Death in Venice* closed in 2010). But the parade of wealthy Italians and foreign tourists (plus a good number of Venetian families) who still frequent this coastal area make interesting people watching indeed—in summer it feels more like the south of France than Venice.

The Lido has two main beach areas. **Blue Moon** (Piazzale Bucintoro) is at the opposite end of Gran Viale Santa Maria Elisabetta (the main drag and referred to as the Gran Viale) from the *vaporetto* station Santa Elisabetta. It's a 10-minute stroll; walk straight ahead along Gran Viale to reach the beach (Gran Viale is lined with seafood restaurants and bars). **San Nicolò,** about 1.5km (1 mile) north, can be reached by bus B from Santa Elisabetta. The

The Lido beach in summer.

THE film FESTIVAL

The **Venice International Film Festival** ★, in late August and early September, is the most respected celebration of celluloid in Europe after Cannes (pared-down versions were held in 2020 and 2021 despite the Covid-19 pandemic). Films from all over the world are shown in the **Palazzo del Cinema** on the Lido as well as at various venues—and occasionally in some of the *campi*. Ticket prices vary, but those for the less-sought-after films are usually modest. See **www.labiennale.org/en/cinema** for details.

beaches tend to get narrower to the south, though **Alberoni** at the southern tip is a wilder, less developed stretch backed by dunes. At the main beach areas, lounge chairs and umbrellas can cost from 10€ to 20€ per person (per day) depending on the time of year (it's just 1€ to use the public showers and bathrooms). Keep in mind that if you stay at any of the hotels on the Lido, most have some kind of agreement with the different *bagni* (private beach establishments). Note that the restored **Ancient Jewish Cemetery** (Antico Cimitero Ebraico), on the Lido (established in 1386), is open to the public but best appreciated on a tour from the Museo Ebraico (p. 325).

Organized Tours

Because of the sheer number of sights to see in Venice, some first-time visitors like to start out with an organized tour. Although few things can really be covered in any depth on these overviews, they're sometimes useful for getting your bearings. **Avventure Bellissime** (www.tours-italy.com; ✆ **041/970499**) coordinates a plethora of trips (in English), by boat and gondola, though the walking tours are the best value, covering all the main sights around Piazza San Marco in 2 hours for 45€ (includes "skip the line" tickets to St Mark's Basilica).

For those with more energy, learn to "row like a Venetian" (yes, literally standing up) at **Row Venice** (www.rowvenice.com; ✆ **347/7250637**), where 1½-hour lessons take place in traditional, hand-built "shrimp-tail," or *batele coda di gambero* boats for 85€ for up to 2 people. Or you could abandon tradition altogether and opt for a **Venice Kayak** tour (www.venicekayak.com; ✆ **346/4771327**), a truly enchanting way to see the city from the water. The company offers a variety of tours from April to early November, from 2-hour loops to a full day (110€–160€). **SUP in Venice** (www.supinvenice.com; ✆ **389/9851866**) offers guided SUP (standup paddleboard) trips (Apr–Oct), with 1-hour, 40-minute sessions starting at 70€.

Especially for Kids

It goes without saying that a **gondola ride** (p. 272) will be the thrill of a life-time for any child (or adult). If that's too expensive, consider the far cheaper alternative: a **ride on the no. 1** *vaporetto* (p. 267).

The Venetian Carnevale is a colorful party that draws visitors from around the world.

Judging from the squeals of delight, **feeding the pigeons in Piazza San Marco** could be the high point of your child's visit to Venice, and it's the ultimate photo op. Purchase a bag of corn and you'll be draped in pigeons in a nanosecond. Be sure your child won't be startled by all the fluttering and flapping.

A jaunt to the neighboring **island of Murano** (p. 302) can be as educational as it is recreational—follow the signs to any *fornace* (kiln), where a glassblowing performance of the island's thousand-year-old art is free entertainment. But be ready for the guaranteed sales pitch that follows.

Take the elevator to the **top of the Campanile di San Marco** (p. 308) for a scintillating view of Venice's rooftops and cupolas, or get up close and personal with the four bronze horses on the facade of the Basilica San Marco. The view from its **outdoor loggia** is something you and your children won't forget. Scaling the **Torre dell'Orologio** (p. 314) or the bell tower at **San Giorgio Maggiore** (p. 327) is also lots of fun.

Feeding the pigeons in Piazza San Marco.

carnevale **A VENEZIA**

Carnevale traditionally was the celebration preceding Lent, the period of penitence and abstinence prior to Easter; its name is derived from the Latin *carnem levare,* meaning "to take meat away." In Venice, the heyday of Carnevale was the 18th century; it was outlawed in 1797 and only revived in 1979 to boost winter tourism. Today Carnevale in Venice builds for a whole month until the big blowout, Shrove Tuesday, when fireworks illuminate the Grand Canal, and Piazza San Marco is turned into a giant open-air ballroom for the masses. The festival is a harlequin patchwork of cultural events, many of them free of charge, which appeals to all ages, tastes, nationalities, and budgets. Musical events from reggae and zydeco to jazz and baroque are staged in dozens of *piazze.* Book your hotel months ahead, especially for the two weekends prior to Shrove Tuesday. Check **www.carnevale.venezia.it/en** for details on upcoming events.

The **winged lion,** said to have been a kind of mascot to St. Mark, patron saint of Venice, was the very symbol of the Serene Republic and to this day appears on everything from cafe napkins to T-shirts. Keep a running tab of who can spot the most flying lions—you'll find them on facades, atop columns, over doorways, as pavement mosaics, on government stamps, and on the local flag.

SHOPPING

In a city that for centuries has thrived almost exclusively on tourism, remember this: **Where you buy cheap, you get cheap.** Venetians, centuries-old merchants, aren't known for bargaining. You'll stand a better chance of getting a good deal if you pay in cash or buy more than one item. In our limited space below, we've listed some of the more reputable places to stock up on classic Venetian items.

Shopping Streets & Markets

A mix of low-end trinket stores and mid-market-to-upscale boutiques lines the narrow zigzagging **Mercerie** running north between Piazza San Marco and the Rialto Bridge. More expensive boutiques make for great window-shopping on **Calle Larga XXII Marzo,** the wide street that begins west of Piazza San Marco and wends its way to the expansive Campo Santo Stefano near the Accademia Bridge. Narrow **Calle Frezzaria,** which runs north-south just west of Piazza San Marco, offers bars, souvenir shops, and tony clothing stores like Louis Vuitton and Versace. The non-produce part of the **Rialto Market** is as good as it gets for basic souvenirs, such as cheap T-shirts, glow-in-the-dark plastic gondolas, and tawdry glass trinkets. The 3-day professional antiques market **Mercatino dell'Antiquariato** (www.mercatinocamposan maurizio.it) takes place four to five times a year (usually Mar–Apr, May, Sept, Oct, and Dec; check website for dates), in Campo San Maurizio, San Marco.

Many, many shops in Venice sell Carnevale masks and accessories year-round.

Arts & Crafts

Venice is uniquely famous for local crafts that have been produced here for centuries and are hard to get elsewhere: the **glassware** from Murano, the **delicate lace** from Burano, and the *cartapesta* (**papier-mâché**) **Carnevale masks** you'll find in endless *botteghe* (shops), where you can watch artisans paint amid their wares.

Now here's the bad news: There is such an overwhelming sea of cheap glass that buying **Venetian glass** can become something of a turnoff (shipping and insurance costs make most things unaffordable; the alternative is to hand-carry anything fragile). Plus, there are so few women left on Burano willing to spend countless tedious hours keeping alive the art of **lace-making** that the few pieces you'll see not produced by machine in China are sold at stratospheric prices; ditto the truly high-quality glass (although trinkets can be cheap and fun). The best place to buy glass is Murano itself—the **"Vetro Artistico Murano"** trademark guarantees its origin, but expect to pay as much as 60€ for just a wine glass.

Atelier Segalin di Daniela Ghezzo ★★ Founded in 1932 by master cobbler Antonio Segalin and his son Rolando, this old leather shoe store is now run by Daniela Ghezzo (Rolando's star apprentice), maker of exuberant handmade shoes and boots, from basic flats to crazy footwear designed for Carnevale (custom footwear from 650€). Calle dei Fuseri 4365, San Marco. www.danielaghezzo.it. ⓒ **041/5222115.** Mon–Fri 10am–1pm and 3–7pm; Sat 10am–1pm. Vaporetto: San Marco.

Ca' del Sol Maschere ★★ Run by a group of artists since 1986, this shop is a treasure trove of Venetian masks (prices 35€–360€), along with elaborate 18th-century costumes; you can even take mask-making courses here. Fondamenta de l'Osmarin 4964, Castello. www.cadelsolmascherevenezia.com. ⓒ **041/5285549.** Daily 10am–8pm. Vaporetto: San Zaccaria.

Il Grifone ★★★ Toni Peressin's handmade leather briefcases, satchels, bound notebooks, belts, and soft-leather purses have garnered quite a following, and justly so—his craftsmanship is truly magnificent (he makes everything in the workshop out back). Small items start at around 25€. Fondamenta del Gaffaro 3516, Dorsoduro. www.ilgrifonevenezia.it. ✆ **041/5229452.** Tues and Fri 10am–6pm; Wed, Thurs, Sat 10am–1pm and 4–7pm. Vaporetto: Piazzale Roma.

Kartaruga ★★ Remember the creepy orgy scenes in Stanley Kubrick's film *Eyes Wide Shut*? The ornate masks used in the movie were made by the owners of this vaunted store. The artisans craft all manner of traditional, feathered, and animal masks in the on-site workshop. Calle delle Bande 5369 (near Campo Santa Maria Formosa), Castello. kartaruga.it. ✆ **041/5210393.** Daily 10am–7pm. Vaporetto: San Zaccaria.

La Bottega dei Mascareri ★★ High-quality, creative masks—some based on Tiepolo paintings—have been crafted by the brothers Sergio and Massimo Boldrin since 1984. Basic masks start at around 20€, but you'll pay over 75€ for a more innovative piece. The smaller, original branch lies at the foot of the Rialto Bridge (San Polo 80; ✆ **041/5223857**). Calle dei Saoneri 2720, San Polo. www.mascarer.com. ✆ **041/5242887.** Both locations daily 9am–6pm. Vaporetto: Rialto.

Marco Polo International ★ This vast showroom, just west of the Piazza San Marco, displays quality glass direct from Murano (although it's more expensive than going to the island yourself), including plenty of easy-to-carry items such as paperweights and small dishes. Frezzaria 1644, San Marco. www.marcopolointernational.it. ✆ **041/5229295.** Daily 10am–7pm. Vaporetto: San Marco.

Books

Libreria Acqua Alta ★★★ Like a set on a Harry Potter movie, this venerable bookshop has become a tourist attraction thanks to its museum-like atmosphere. Note the gondola filled with paperbacks and the friendly resident cats. It is still a great place to pick up rare and used tomes (in Italian or English). Get there early to avoid long lines. Calle Longa Santa Maria Formosa 5176b. ✆ **041/2960841.** Daily 9am–7:30pm. Vaporetto: San Marco or Ospedale.

ENTERTAINMENT & NIGHTLIFE

If you're looking for serious nocturnal action, you're in the wrong town—Verona and Padua are far livelier. Your best bet is to sit in the moonlit Piazza San Marco and listen to the cafes' outdoor orchestras, with the illuminated basilica before you—the perfect opera set—though this pleasure comes with a hefty price tag. Other popular spots to hang out include **Campo San Bartolomeo,** at the foot of the Rialto Bridge (admittedly a zoo in high season), and nearby **Campo San Luca.** In late-night hours, for low prices and low pretension, the absolute best place to go is **Campo Santa Margherita,** a huge open *campo* about halfway between the train station and the Accademia Bridge.

Visit one of the tourist information centers for current English-language schedules of the month's special events. The monthly *Ospite di Venezia* is distributed free or online at **www.unospitedivenezia.it** and is extremely helpful, but it's usually available only in the more expensive hotels.

Performing Arts & Live Music

Venice has a long and rich tradition of classical music; this was, after all, the home of Vivaldi. People dressed in period costumes stand around in heavily trafficked spots near San Marco and Rialto passing out brochures advertising classical music concerts, so you'll have no trouble finding up-to-date information.

Santa Maria della Pietà ★★   The so-called "Vivaldi Church," built between 1745 and 1760, holds concerts throughout the year, mostly performed by lauded ensemble **I Virtuosi Italiani;** check the website for specific dates. Full-price tickets are usually 28€ to 35€ (with discounts online). Riva degli Schiavoni 3701, Castello. www.ivirtuositaliani.eu/chiesa-di-vivaldi. © **041/5221120.** Vaporetto: San Zaccaria.

Teatro La Fenice ★★★   The opera season runs from late November through June, but La Fenice also hosts ballet performances and classical concerts. Tickets are expensive for the major productions (110€–210€ for the gallery and 190€ to 240€ for a decent seat). Those on a budget can opt for obstructed-view seats (from 35€). Campo San Fantin 1965, San Marco. www.teatro lafenice.it. © **041/2424.** Vaporetto: Giglio.

Inside La Fenice.

Cafes

For tourists and locals alike, Venetian nightlife mainly centers on the many cafes in one of the world's most remarkable *piazze:* Piazza San Marco. It is also a most expensive and touristed place to linger over a **spritz** (the Venetian classic cocktail of Prosecco and orange-flavored Aperol), but it's a splurge that should not be dismissed too readily. These cafes are on the Venice restaurants map, p. 290–291.

Caffè dei Frari ★★★   Established in 1870, this inviting bar and cafe overlooking the Frari church has walls adorned with original murals, an antique wooden bar, and a wrought-iron balcony upstairs. The seafood is especially good here, and at least three excellent German beers are usually on tap. The whole place morphs into **Il Mercante Cocktail Bar** in the evenings (Tues–Thurs 6pm–1am; Fri and Sat 6pm–2am; Sun 6pm–midnight). Fondamenta dei Frari 2564, San Polo. www.ilmercantevenezia.com. ℂ **041/5241877.** Tues–Sat 9am–5pm. Vaporetto: San Tomà.

Caffè Florian ★★   Occupying prime *piazza* real estate since 1720, this is one of the world's oldest coffee shops, with a florid interior of 18th-century mirrors, frescoes, and statuary. Sitting at a table, expect to pay 11.50€ for a cappuccino, 22€ for a Bellini (Prosecco and fresh peach nectar in season), and 16€ for a spritz—add another 6€ per person if the orchestra plays (Mar–Nov). Standing or sitting at the bar is much cheaper (5.50€ for a cappuccino, 11.50€ for a Bellini, etc.). Piazza San Marco 57. www.caffeflorian.com. ℂ **041/5205641.** Mon–Thurs 10am–9pm; Fri & Sat 9am–11pm; Sun 9am–9pm. Vaporetto: San Marco.

Caffè Florian, one of the world's oldest coffee shops, on Piazza San Marco.

Il Caffè (aka Caffè Rosso) ★★★   Established in the late 19th century, Il Caffè has a history almost as colorful as its clientele, a mixture of students, aging regulars, and lost tourists. This is an old-fashioned, no-nonsense Venetian cafe/bar, with reasonably priced drinks (spritz 3.50€) and sandwiches, and plenty of seating on the *campo* (plus small seating area inside). Cash only. Santa Margherita 2963, Dorsoduro. www.cafferosso.it. ℂ **041/5287998.** Mon–Sat 7am–1am. Vaporetto: Ca'Rezzonico.

Marchini Time ★★   The outlet for the famed Marchini *pasticcerie* (it opened in 1938), this plush modern cafe offers a range of addictive pastries, *biscotti*, chocolates, coffees, cakes, and savory *pizzette*. Campo San Luca 4589, San Marco. www.facebook.com/pasticceriamarchini/. ℗ **041/2413087.** Mon–Sat 7:30am–8pm, Sun 8am–8pm. Vaporetto: Rialto.

Pasticceria Nobile ★★   Founded in the 1930s, this is the most happening cafe in this section of town, celebrated for its tempting range of sweets, snacks, pastries, and chocolate. Locals congregate here for breakfast and for *aperitivo* after work. Calle del Pistor 1818, Cannaregio. www.facebook.com/PasticceriaNobile/. ℗ **041/720731.** Daily 6am–8.30pm (closed July). Vaporetto: San Marcuola.

Pasticceria Tonolo ★   This tiny bakery has had a cult following since 1886, thanks to its deep-fried sweet treats (*frittelle*, Italian-style doughnuts, 1.30€–1.80€), plus a vast range of sumptuous cakes and cookies. Coffee is served in charming, antique blue German porcelain cups (standing room only). Calle San Pantalon 3764, Dorsoduro. https://pasticceria-tonolo-venezia. business.site/. ℗ **041/5237209.** Tues–Sat 7:30am–7pm; Sun 7:30pm–1pm (often closed through Aug). Vaporetto: San Tomà.

Beer, Wine & Cocktail Bars

Venice has never been a late-night clubbing hotspot. Evenings are better spent lingering over a late dinner or nursing a glass of Prosecco in one of the outdoor bars and cafes in Piazza San Marco or Campo Santa Margherita. It's also worth considering dressing up for a visit to one of the **historic bars** in Venice's grand-dame hotels, at least for a cocktail. It will be an expensive but memorable experience, often with mesmerizing views and impeccable service to match. You should also visit the neighborhood bars known as *bàcari* at least once (see p. 289).

Al Prosecco ★★   Get acquainted with all things bubbly at this local enoteca, a specialist, as you'd expect, in Veneto Prosecco. It features plenty of tasty *cicchetti* to wash down the various brands, and plenty of outdoor tables from which to observe the laid-back Campo San Giacomo da l'Orio. Most drinks run 3€ to 5€. Campo San Giacomo da l'Orio 1503, Santa Croce. www.al prosecco.com. ℗ **041/5240222.** Mon–Sat 10am–10:30pm (closes 8pm in winter; closed Aug and Jan). Vaporetto: San Stae.

Bar Dandolo ★★   Doge Dandolo built his glorious Venetian Gothic palace three doors down from the Palazzo Ducale in the 14th century, and current occupier Hotel Danieli has been one of the most sumptuous hotels in Venice since 1822. Nestled amid marble columns on the ground floor of the *palazzo*, this classic Venice bar serves everything from velvety cappuccinos and a traditional afternoon tea (daily 3–6pm) to a decadent Vesper Martini cocktail.

You can also opt for an alfresco drink on the rooftop **Bar Terrazza Danieli** (Apr–Oct daily 3–11pm) in the same hotel. Riva degli Schiavoni 4196, Castello. www.hoteldanieli.com/en/dining.html. ℗ **041/5226480.** Daily 6:30am–1am (pianist plays daily 7pm–12:30am), usually closed in Jan. Vaporetto: San Zaccaria.

Bar Longhi ★★★ The Gritti Palace Hotel really was the 16th-century palace of Doge Andrea Gritti, whose portrait graces one of its antiques-filled lounges (it remains the city's most expensive hotel since opening in 1895). Bar Longhi is the quintessential Venetian watering hole, with lavish decor (hand-sculptured mirrors, Murano glass appliqués, and a marble bar counter), plus paintings belonging to the school of the celebrated 18th-century Venetian artist Pietro Longhi. Afternoon tea, cocktails, and champagne served. Campo Santa Maria del Giglio 2467 (Gritti Palace Hotel), San

Bar Dandolo at the Hotel Danieli.

Marco. www.marriott.com. ℗ **041/794611.** Daily 11am–1am. Vaporetto: Santa Maria del Giglio.

Harry's Bar ★ Possibly the most famous bar in Venice (and now a global chain), Harry's was established in 1931 by Giuseppe Cipriani and frequented by the likes of Ernest Hemingway, Charlie Chaplin, and Truman Capote. The Bellini was invented here in 1948 (along with *carpaccio* 2 years later), and you can sip the signature concoction of freshly squeezed peach juice and Prosecco for a mere 22€. Go for the history, but don't expect a five-star experience—most first-timers are surprised just how ordinary it looks inside (though the bow-tied waitstaff still look the part). It's more restaurant than bar these days, serving very expensive food (main courses 40€–45€), but just stick to the drinks. Calle Vallaresso 1323, San Marco. www.cipriani.com. ℗ **041/5285777.** Daily 10am–midnight, usually closed in Jan. Vaporetto: Vallaresso.

Il Santo Bevitore ★★ Beer aficionados will be pleased to learn that Italy has a growing craft beer scene, with this local spot showcasing the best brews from all over the country (many on tap). Sample Milan's Birrificio Lambrate and Birrificio Extraomnes, Parma's Birra Toccalmatto, Udine's Borderline Brewery, and Veneto's very own Mesh Brewery. The small bar overlooks the Rio de Servi just off the main drag (Strada Nova), with a few benches outside for warmer days. Fondamenta Diedo 2393, Cannaregio. www.ilsantobevitore pub.com. ℰ **335/8415771.** Daily 4pm–2am. Vaporetto: San Marcuola.

Margaret DuChamp ★★ This popular student and *fashionista* hangout has plenty of chairs on the *campo* for people-watching, cocktails, and a spritz or two (spritz is 4€). It also serves decent club sandwiches (from 7€) and *piadina* (Italian flatbread) filled with ham and cheese (from 5€), and has free Wi-Fi. They now also run a burger bar and pizzeria next door (open 'til 1am). Campo Santa Margherita 3019, Dorsoduro. www.facebook.com/MargaretDuchamp Venezia/. ℰ **041/5286255.** Mon–Sat 9am–2am. Vaporetto: Ca' Rezzonico.

DAY TRIPS FROM VENICE

By Stephen Keeling

If you only have 3 days or so, you will probably want to spend them in the center of Venice. If, however, you are here for a week—or on your second visit to the city—head over to the mainland to see some fascinating old towns in the historic Veneto region.

9

PADUA ★★★

40km (25 mi) W of Venice

Tucked away within the ancient heart of **Padua** lies one of the greatest artistic treasures in all Italy, the precious Giotto frescoes of the **Cappella degli Scrovegni.** Although the city itself is not especially attractive (it was largely rebuilt after bombing during World War II), don't be put off by the urban sprawl that now surrounds it; central Padua is refreshingly bereft of tourist crowds, a workaday Veneto town with a large student population and a small but intriguing ensemble of historic sights.

Like much of the region, Padua prospered in the Middle Ages, and Italy's second-oldest university was founded here in 1222. Its fortunes grew further when St. Antony of Padua died in the city in 1231, making it a place of pilgrimage ever since. In the 14th century, the da Carrara family presided over the city's golden age, but in 1405 Padua was conquered and absorbed by Venice, losing its independence. With the fall of the Venetian Republic in 1797, Napoleon ruled the city and it then became part of the Austrian Empire in 1814. Finally annexed to Italy in 1866, the city boomed again after World War II, becoming the industrial dynamo of northeast Italy.

Essentials

ARRIVING The most efficient way to reach Padua (and the other destinations in this chapter) is to take the train from Venice's Santa Lucia station. Trains depart every 10 to 20 minutes and take 26 to 50 minutes depending on the class (tickets 4.70€–19€ one-way). The main Padua station ("Padova" in Italian) is a short walk north up Corso del Popolo from the Cappella degli Scrovegni and the old city.

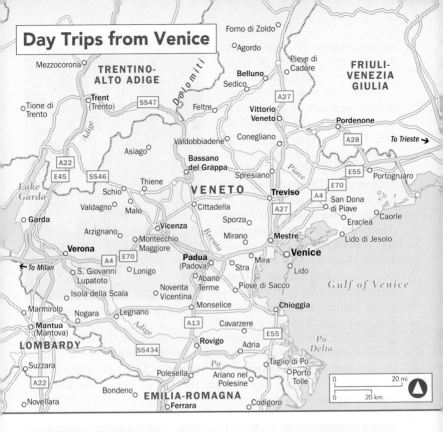

Day Trips from Venice

Exploring Padua

The one unmissable sight in Padua is the **Cappella degli Scrovegni ★★★** (www.cappelladegliscrovegni.it; *☎* **049/2010020;** daily 9am–7pm) at Piazza Eremitani, an outwardly unassuming chapel commissioned in 1303 by Enrico Scrovegni, a wealthy banker. Inside, however, the chapel is gloriously decorated with an astonishing cycle of frescoes by Florentine genius **Giotto.** The frescoes depict the life of the Virgin Mary and the life of Jesus, culminating with the Ascension and Last Judgment. Seeing Giotto's powerful work in the flesh is spine-tingling; this is where he made the decisive break with Byzantine art, taking the first important steps toward the realism and humanism that would characterize the Renaissance in Italy.

Entrance to the chapel is limited, involving groups of 25 visitors spending 15 minutes in a climate-controlled airlock, used to stabilize the temperature, before going inside for another 15 to 20 minutes. To visit the chapel, you must **make a reservation at least 24 hours in advance.** You must then arrive 45 minutes before the time on your ticket. Tickets cost 14€ (5€ for kids ages 6–17 and students under 27).

If you have time, try to take in Padua's other historic highlights. The vast **Palazzo della Ragione** on Piazza delle Erbe (7€; Tues–Sun 9am–7pm, closes 6pm Nov–Jan) is an architectural marvel, a cavernous town hall completed in 1219 and decorated with frescoes by Nicola Miretto in the 15th century. The **Basilica di Sant'Antonio** (Piazza del Santo; www.santantonio. org; ✆ **049/8225652;** free admission; daily 6:15am–7:30pm), is the stately resting place of **St. Anthony of Padua,** the Portuguese Franciscan best known as the patron saint of finding lost things or people. While the exterior of

Giotto's frescos in Capella degli Scrovegni.

the church is a bizarre 14th-century mix of Byzantine, Romanesque, and Gothic styles, the interior is richly adorned with statuary and murals. In the piazza outside, don't miss **Donatello**'s stupendous 1453 equestrian statue of the Venetian *condottiere* **Gattamelata** (Erasmo da Narni), the first large bronze sculpture of the Renaissance.

Donatello's imposing 1453 equestrian statue, the first large bronze sculpture of the Renaissance, in the piazza outside the Palazzo della Ragione, Padua.

The Basilica of St. Anthony of Padua.

Where to Eat in Padua

Padua offers plenty of places to eat and drink (Aperol was created here in 1919), and you'll especially appreciate the overall drop in prices compared with Venice. It's hard to match the location of **Bar Nazionale ★★**, Piazza delle Erbe 40 (Tues, Thurs, and Fri 7am–11:30am; Mon and Sat 7am–10:30pm; Sun 9am–9:30pm; Wed 7am–midnight), on the steps leading up to Palazzo della Ragione, though it's best for drinks and snacks (excellent *tramezzini* from 3€, panini from 4.50€, spritz 3.50€, and glasses of wine 3.50–4€) rather than a full meal. For that, make for **Belle Parti ★★★**, Via Belle Parti 11, a short walk from Piazza dei Signori (www.ristorantebelleparti.it; ☏ **049/8751822;** Mon–Sat 12:30–2:30pm and 7:30–10:30pm), one of Padua's best restaurants. Set within the historic Palazzo Prosdocimi, it serves classic Veneto dishes and seafood (entrees 18€–28€).

VERONA ★★

115km (71 mi) W of Venice

The affluent city of **Verona,** with its Roman ruins and gorgeous medieval buildings in red and peach hues, is one of Italy's major tourist draws, though its appeal owes more to William Shakespeare than real history. He immortalized the city in his (totally fictional) *Romeo and Juliet, The Two Gentlemen of Verona,* and *The Taming of the Shrew.* Despite its popularity with tourists, Verona is not Venice; it's a booming commercial center with vibrant science and technology sectors.

Verona emerged as a city-state in the 12th century, ruled primarily by the bloodthirsty (and, in Renaissance tradition, art-loving) Scaligeri family until 1387. After a brief period of Milanese rule, Verona fell under the control of Venice in 1405. Like the rest of the region, the city was occupied by Napoleon in 1797, then Austria, and became part of Italy in 1866.

Essentials

ARRIVING   The best way to reach Verona from Venice is by **train.** Direct
services depart every 30 minutes and take anywhere from 1 hour and 10 minutes to 2 hours and 20 minutes, depending on the type of train you catch (one-
way tickets 10€–28€). From Verona station (Verona Porta Nuova), it's a
15-minute walk to the historic center.

VISITOR INFORMATION   The **Visit Verona** tourist office at Via Leoncino
61 (Palazzo Barbieri) in Piazza Bra (www.visitverona.it; ℂ **045/8068680;**
Mon–Sat 9am–5pm, Sun 10am–4pm) has maps and guided tour information.

Exploring Verona

"Two households, both alike in dignity, in fair Verona…" So go the immortal
opening lines of *Romeo and Juliet,* ensuring that the city has been a target for
love-sick romantics ever since. Though Verona is crammed with genuine historic goodies, one of the most popular sites is the ersatz **Casa di Giulietta,**
Via Cappello 23 (6€; Tues–Sun 9am–7pm; also open Mon Jun–Sep; reserve
tickets at museiverona.com), a 14th-century house (with balcony, naturally),
claiming to be the Capulets' home. In the courtyard, the chest of a bronze
statue of Juliet has been polished to a gleaming sheen thanks to a legend
claiming that stroking her right breast brings good fortune. **Juliet's Wall,** at
the entrance, is quite a spectacle, covered with the scribbles of star-crossed
lovers (though the corridor is periodically scrubbed clean of graffiti and gum);
love letters placed here are taken down and, along with 5,000 letters annually,
are answered by the Club di Giulietta (a group of locally based volunteers).

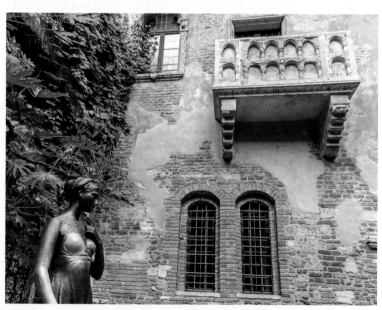

"Juliet" statue and balcony at Casa di Giulietta.

Verona's arena in Piazza Bra.

There's not much to see inside the house, though plenty of visitors line up for a chance of a selfie on the balcony.

Once you've made the obligatory Juliet pilgrimage, focus on actual historic sights. The 1st-century **Arena di Verona** ★ (10€; Mon 1:30–7:30pm and Tues–Sun 8:30am–7:30pm), in the spacious Piazza Bra, is the third-largest classical arena in Italy after Rome's Colosseum and the arena at Capua—it could seat some 25,000 spectators and still hosts performances today (see www.arena.it).

To the northwest on Piazza San Zeno, the **Basilica di San Zeno Maggiore** ★★ (www.basilicasanzeno.it; 4€, includes audioguide; Mar–Oct Mon–Fri 9:30am–6pm, Sat 9am–6pm, Sun 1–6pm; Nov–Feb Mon–Fri 10am–5pm, Sat 9am–6pm, Sun 1–6pm) is the greatest Romanesque church in northern Italy. The present structure was completed around 1135 over a 4th-century shrine to Verona's patron saint, St. Zeno (who died in 380). The church's massive rose window represents the Wheel of Fortune, lintels above the portal represent the months of the year. The highlight of the interior is Mantegna's "Madonna and Saints" above the altar.

Where to Eat in Verona

The most authentic central Verona restaurant is **Antica Bottega del Vino,** Via Scudo di Francia 3 (bottegavini.it; ℂ **045/8004535;** daily 11am–midnight, restaurant Mon–Fri 12:30–2:40pm and 6:30–10:40pm; Sat and Sun 12:30–10:40pm), open since 1890. Dishes range from risotto with Amarone wine and tortellini with black truffle and crispy parmesan, to pigeon with broccoli and Venetian-style veal liver with toasted polenta (14€–26€). **Caffè Monte Baldo,** Via Rosa 12 (www.osteriamontebaldo.com; ℂ **045/8030579;** Mon,

Wed, Thurs 11am–3pm and 6–11:30pm, Fri 11am–midnight, Sat and Sun 10am–midnight), an old-fashioned cafe (open since 1909) transformed into a trendy *osteria,* serves classic pastas and scrumptious *crostini* with wine in the evenings.

TREVISO ★★

30km (19 mi) N of Venice

Long overshadowed by Venice, **Treviso** is a small, prosperous city of narrow medieval streets, Gothic churches, and an enchanting network of canals, replete with weeping willows and waterwheels (it's known as "*piccola Venezia,*" or "little Venice"). Giotto's follower **Tomaso da Modena** (1326–79) frescoed many of its churches, and its maze of back streets makes for pleasant, often tourist-free exploring.

Essentials

ARRIVING   Trains run two to four times an hour from Venice's Santa Lucia station; it's a 30- to 40-minute trip, definitely your fastest option. Tickets start at 3.80€ one-way. Arriving at Treviso Centrale station, you'll have an easy 10- to 15-minute walk to Piazza dei Signori, north across the River Sile

Treviso is often called "Little Venice" because of its many canals.

Treviso's San Nicolò church.

(follow signs to "Centro"). Note also that most Ryanair **budget flights to Venice** actually arrive at Treviso airport (p. 264).

VISITOR INFORMATION The **Visit Treviso** tourist office at Via Fiumicelli 30 (www.visittreviso.it; © **0422/547-632**) is open Monday from 10am to 1pm, Tuesday to Saturday 10am to 5pm, and Sunday 10am to 4pm.

Exploring Treviso

The historic heart of Treviso, **Piazza dei Signori ★** is anchored by the **Palazzo del Podestà,** rebuilt in the 1870s with a tall clock tower, and the **Palazzo dei Trecento,** the 13th-century town council hall (chic **Bar Beltrame** nestles beneath the arches). Just beyond the square, on adjacent Piazza San Vito, sit two handsome medieval churches: **Santa Lucia ★** (www.santaluciatreviso.it; © **0422/5457200**), with a superb Tomaso da Modena fresco of the "Madonna del Pavegio" in the first shrine on the right; and **San Vito ★,** with its fine 13th-century Byzantine-style frescoes. Both are open Monday to Friday 9am to noon, and Saturday and Sunday 9am to noon and 3:30 to 6pm; admission is free.

Historic **Via Calmaggiore,** lined with posh boutiques, runs northwest from Piazza dei Signori toward Treviso's **Duomo ★** (free admission; Mon–Sat 7:30am–noon and 3:30–7pm, Sun 8am–1pm and 3:30–8pm). Its relatively dull neoclassical facade dates only from 1836, but its flanking Romanesque lions and seven Venetian-Byzantine–style green copper domes testify to the cathedral's 12th-century origins. The crypt is the most compelling part of the interior, with tombs of the city's bishops amid a forest of columns and fragments of 14th-century frescoes and mosaics. The cathedral also has a fine 1520 Titian altarpiece, the "Malchiostro Annunciation." Stroll southwest from the Duomo to the massive Italian Gothic **San Nicolò church** ★ (free admission; daily 8am–noon & 3:30–6pm), with its intriguing Gothic frescoes. Tomaso da Modena and his school decorated the huge, round columns with a series of saints, notably St. Jerome and St. Agnes. Antonio da Treviso painted the gargantuan St. Christopher—his .9m-long (3-ft.) feet strolling over biting fish—in 1410.

East of Piazza dei Signori, in Piazzetta Mario Botter, the **Museo di Santa Caterina** (www.museicivicitreviso.it; ✆ **0422/658442;** 6€; Tues–Sun 10am–6pm) is housed in a deconsecrated church. Its highlight is another fresco cycle by Tomaso da Modena, the "Story of the Life of Saint Ursula" (detached from a now-destroyed church and preserved here). There's also a cache of local archaeological finds, plus minor works by Titian, Lorenzo Lotto, and Francesco Guardi. South of there, the 15th-century church of **Santa Maria Maggiore** (free admission; daily 8am–noon and 3:30–6pm) houses a venerated frescoed image of Mary (the "Madonna Granda"), an ancient Byzantine-style image later touched up by Tomaso and members of his school.

Where to Eat in Treviso

For atmosphere it's hard to beat the **Hostaria Dai Naneti** ★★, Vicolo Broli 2 (✆ **3403/783158;** Mon–Sat 9am–2:30pm and 5:30–9pm, Sun 11am–2pm and 5–9pm; closed Sun May–Sept), a cozy tavern, deli, and cheese shop where you can grab a delicious baguette and glass of wine, or just snack at the bar for around 6€ (standing-room only).

For a full meal in the center, reserve a table at **Trattoria All'Antico Portico** ★★, overlooking the church at Piazza Santa Maria Maggiore 18 (www.anticoportico.it; ✆ **0422/545259;** Mon 9am–4pm, Wed–Sun 9am–11pm), which serves local specialties such as radicchio risotto and *baccalà alla veneziana* (salt cod); main courses are 11€ to 22€.

PLANNING YOUR TRIP

By Donald Strachan

This chapter provides a variety of planning tools, including information on how to get to Italy, how to get around in safety and comfort, and the inside track on local resources you can consult for up-to-date advice. If you do your homework, pick the right place for the right season, and pack for the climate, preparing for a trip to Italy should be as pleasant and uncomplicated as ever. For "When to Go" advice, see p. 46.

ARRIVING

By Plane

If you're flying across an ocean, you'll most likely land at Rome's upgraded **Leonardo da Vinci–Fiumicino Airport** (FCO; www.adr.it/fiumicino), 40km (25 miles) from the center. This is almost always the cheapest intercontinental destination. Rome's much smaller **Ciampino Airport** (CIA; www.adr.it/ciampino) serves low-cost airlines connecting to European cities and some destinations within Italy. For information on getting to central Rome from its airports, see p. 52. Travelers can also board a direct high-speed train from Fiumicino to Florence or Venice **without** passing through central Rome.

Carriers within Europe fly direct to many smaller Italian cities, including Venice's **Marco Polo Airport** (VCE; www.veniceairport.it), **Florence Airport** (FLR; www.aeroporto.firenze.it/en), Bologna's **Marconi Airport** (BLQ; www.bologna-airport.it), and Pisa's **Galileo Galilei Airport** (PSA; www.pisa-airport.com). For information on getting into central Venice from the airport, see p. 263. For reaching central Florence from the airport—and from Pisa airport—see p. 174.

By Train

Italy's major cities are well-connected to Europe's rail hubs. You can arrive in Milan on direct trains from France—including Paris and Lyon—by **TGV** (www.sncf-connect.com), or on a Swiss intercity service from Zurich (www.sbb.ch/en) and connect in Milan to Venice or Rome (see "Getting Around," below). **Nightjet** rail routes (www.nightjet.com/en) depart Munich, Germany and Vienna, Austria to Venice, Florence, and Rome. Direct trains from elsewhere in central Europe also arrive at Verona and Venice.

You can book European rail travel in advance online with an agent such as **Rail Europe** (www.raileurope.com).

Note: Rail Europe keeps its website updated with public health–related regulations for rail travel.

GETTING AROUND
By Train

Italy, especially the north, has one of the best train systems in Europe, with most destinations connected. Consequently, the train is an excellent option to visit major sites without the hassle of driving. Almost all lines are run by state-owned **Ferrovie dello Stato,** or **Trenitalia** (www.trenitalia.com; © 89/2021). Private operator **Italo** (www.italotreno.it; © 06/0708, or 89/2020) serves a few key long-distance routes, including the main Milan–Florence–Rome–Naples high-speed line and branches north from Bologna to Padua/Venice and Verona/Trento.

Travel Times Between Major Cities

CITIES	DISTANCE	(FASTEST) TRAIN TRAVEL TIME	DRIVING TIME
Florence to Venice	261km/162 miles	2 hr.	3 hr.
Rome to Florence	277km/172 miles	1½ hr.	3 hr.
Rome to Venice	528km/327 miles	3hr., 20 min.	5¼ hr.

Travel durations and ticket prices vary considerably depending on the type of train you choose. The country's principal north–south high-speed line links Milan to Bologna, Florence, Rome, and Naples. Milan to Rome, for example, takes around 3 hours on the fast train, and costs around 90€—although you can find tickets as low as 20€ if you buy ahead and travel in off-peak hours. *Tip:* To grab the cheapest fares on high-speed trains, **book around 100 to 120 days before your travel dates.** The **Italo newsletter** (and homepage) regularly advertises limited-time promo code discounts offering up to 50% off advanced fares—making them crazy cheap. You can also book on Trenitalia and Italo via **Trainline** (www.thetrainline.com/trains/italy).

TYPES OF TRAIN   The speed, cleanliness, and overall quality of Italian trains vary. **High-speed trains** usually have four classes: Standard, Premium, Business, and Executive on Trenitalia; Smart, Comfort, Prima, and Club Executive on Italo. The cheapest of these, on both operators, is perfectly comfortable, even on long legs of a journey. *Tip:* Business class on Trenitalia's Frecciarossa is worth paying extra for if it's reduced for advance ticket purchase.

The **Frecciarossa,** as well as Italo's rival high-speed train, is the fastest of the fast, Italy's bullet train. These trains operate on lines connecting both Milan and Venice with Florence–Rome–Naples, and run up to 300 kmph (186 mph). Frecciarossa services also connect Milan with Venice (with halts in Verona and Vicenza). The **Frecciargento** uses lesser hardware and is a bit slower; it links Naples, Rome, and Florence with Pisa and Verona at speeds of up to 250 kmph (155 mph). Speed and cleanliness come at a price, however, with tickets for any of these high-speed trains usually around three times the cheapest, standard "regional" train. On all Freccia services you **must make a seat reservation** when you buy a ticket. If you are traveling with a rail pass (see p. 355), you also pay a 10€ reservation fee to ride (which you can do from automated Trenitalia ticket machines in stations, as well by queuing at a teller window). Rail passes are not valid on Italo trains.

Intercity **(IC)** trains are a step down, in both speed and comfort; specific seat reservations are compulsory. The slower *Regionale* **(R)** and *Regionale Veloce* **(RV)** make many stops and are occasionally on the grimy side, but are also cheap: A Venice–Verona second-class ticket will put you back only 10€ compared with 29€ on a high-speed service. There's no need to book R or RV trains ahead of time, and no price advantage in doing so. Just turn up, buy a ticket, and go.

KEY ITALY bookmarks

www.italia.it/en: Official English-language portal for visitors to Italy

www.arttrav.com: Cultural travel, exhibitions, and openings, especially in Florence

www.summerinitaly.com/traveltips/transport-strikes-in-italy: Updated with the latest rail, bus, and airline strikes

www.prezzibenzina.it: Find the cheapest fuel close to your lodgings (also a free mobile app)

www.thelocal.it: Easily digested news from around Italy—in English

www.frommers.com/destinations/italy: Frommer's expert advice on the country

ETIAS: **EUROPE'S NEW ENTRY REQUIREMENT**

Travelers planning to visit Italy anytime from 2024 onward will encounter a new hoop to jump through: the European Travel Information and Authorization System, or **ETIAS.** This electronic visa waiver is essentially the European Union equivalent to the USA's Electronic System for Travel Authorization (ESTA). ETIAS registration will be mandatory for travelers who don't otherwise need a visa to enter Europe's Schengen Area, which includes 22 European Union countries plus Iceland, Liechtenstein, Norway, and Switzerland. The scheme applies to the citizens of around 60 visa-exempt countries, including the United States, Canada, Mexico, the United Kingdom, Australia, Japan, much of the Caribbean, and most of South America.

The online application process is fast and easy and includes the following requirements:

- Personal data, including name, date of birth, address
- Passport info
- Name of first Schengen country of intended stay
- Answers to background questions about criminal record, any past deportations, and past travel to zones experiencing conflict or infectious disease epidemics

Unless the applicant is flagged on one of the EU's watch lists, e-mail approval of ETIAS should arrive within minutes. The proposed fee for ETIAS registration is 7€ (about $7) per applicant between the ages of 18 and 70. All travelers, regardless of age, must register with ETIAS, but those under 18 and over 70 are presumably exempt from paying the fee.

Once approved, ETIAS registration is **valid for 3 years.** However, if your passport expires during that time, you'll need to apply for a new ETIAS waiver. Consistent with current tourist visa rules, ETIAS is intended for stays of 90 days or less within a 180-day period.

When should travelers planning a trip to Italy apply for ETIAS status? While the EU promises nearly instant approval for most travelers, in some cases processing can take up to 30 days. So it's best to play it safe and secure your ETIAS status a few weeks before your trip. And keep in mind: starting in 2024, if you show up for your international flight to Italy without a valid ETIAS document, you will be denied boarding or entry.

As the deadline for implementation keeps shifting, stay up to date with complete information at https://travel-europe.europa.eu/etias_en.

Old *Regionale* rolling stock is slowly being replaced, and comfort is improving. However, **overcrowding** is still a problem on some services (that is, not the pre-bookable trains) on Friday evenings, weekends, and holidays, especially in and out of big cities, or just after a strike.

TRAIN TRAVEL TIPS   If you don't have a reservation for a specific train, then you must **validate any paper ticket by stamping it in the little yellow box** on the platform before boarding the train. If you board a train without a ticket, or without having validated, you'll have to pay a hefty fine on top of the ticket or supplement, which the conductor will sell you. If you board a train without a ticket or realize once aboard that you have the wrong type, your best bet is to let the conductor know; she is likely to be more forgiving because you sought her out and made it clear you weren't trying to ride for free.

Rail **apps** for state and Italo services offer **paperless ticketing and convenient in-app payment** for tickets via credit card or PayPal. These represent the simplest, contactless way to buy and carry rail tickets—for both high-speed and regular services. They are available, in English, from the usual app stores. You can just show a copy (paper or electronic) of your booking confirmation email, which has a unique PNR code.

In big cities and tourist destinations, ticketing lines can be dreadfully long. Don't be intimidated by **automatic ticket machines.** These are easy to navigate, provide instructions in English, accept cash and credit cards, and save the stress of waiting in a slow line. *One caveat:* You cannot buy international tickets at automatic machines. Best bet? Use the apps.

Schedules for all trains leaving a given station are printed on yellow posters tacked up on the station wall (a white poster lists arrivals). These are good for general information. Keep your eye on electronic boards and screens updated with delays and track *(binario)* changes. You can get official schedules (also in English) at www.trenitalia.com and www.italotreno.it.

RAIL PASSES & DISCOUNTS   To buy the **Eurail Italy Pass,** available only outside Europe and priced in U.S. dollars, contact **Rail Europe** (www.raileurope.com) or **Eurail** (www.eurail.com). The pass gives you a month to use the train a set number of days; the base number of days is 3, and you can add up to 5 more. For adults, the first-class pass costs $181, second class is $142. Additional days each cost $35 to $40 more for first class, around $30 for second class. For youth tickets (27 and under), a 3-day second-class pass is $118 and additional days about $20 each. **Buying your pass early** in the year is often rewarded with an extra day's travel at no additional cost (such as, pay for 3 days, get 4) or significant discounts: We have seen up to 35% off some Eurail passes. The **Eurail Global Pass** covers rail travel in Italy, all its neighbors, and most of the rest of Europe (33 countries). The electronic **Trenitalia Pass** costs slightly more than an Italy Eurail Pass, but seat reservations are free, and you can buy it in Italy or online at www.trenitalia.com.

Note: Booking individual rail journeys online ahead of arrival may often beat a pass on price, especially if you factor in the cost (and hassle) of making compulsory seat reservations on every high-speed train. However, the cheapest online fares are nonrefundable: You gain flexibility with a pass.

Children 14 and under ride half-price on Italian trains, and kids 3 and under don't pay—although they do not have the right to their own seat. On state railways, there are sometimes **free tickets for children 14 and under** traveling with a paying adult; ask about "Bimbi gratis" when buying your ticket (this option will appear automatically when available in-app or on automatic ticket machines). The **Italo Famiglia** fare, available at least 2 days before travel at the station or online, includes free travel for kids 13 and under accompanying an adult (in Smart [standard] class only).

By Bus

Although trains are quicker, you can get just about anywhere in Italy on a network of local, provincial, and regional bus lines. In bigger cities, the **bus station** for intercity trips is usually near the main train station. A small town's **bus stop** is generally in the main square or on the edge of town. If there's no office, tickets are usually sold at the nearest newsstand or *tabacchi* (a sign with a white T) or occasionally a bar. Buses in cities often have the technology to accept **fare payment via contactless credit card or mobile phone**—a major convenience boost.

Two useful long-distance bus routes are the efficient **Florence–Siena** service and slightly more awkward **Florence–San Gimignano** run (see p. 258). If you are traveling on a tight budget, check intercity fares for **FlixBus** (www. flixbus.it). They often significantly undercut train prices. For comparing time-tables and prices across different modes of transport, **www.rome2rio.com** is useful. A long-distance bus is *un pullman*.

For details on urban bus transportation, see individual chapters—for Rome, p. 63; for Florence, p. 179; and for Venice's water buses, p. 267.

By Car

Much of Italy is accessible by public transportation, but to explore vineyards, countryside, and smaller towns, a car is essential. You may also feel more comfortable in a private car than a shared train carriage—although Italy's train operators have implemented strict hygiene protocols since the pandemic. You'll get the **best rental rate** if you book your car far ahead of arrival. Try the website **AutoSlash.com**, which applies any coupons on the market to your rental; and then monitors your booking. If the price drops, they'll make you a new reservation. We've found AutoSlash to be the best search engine for rentals by far, though it's a bit clunky to use: You must wait for a return e-mail

---

INFLATION hesitation?

Prices have risen. There's no sugarcoating things: Like pretty much everywhere else in the world, Italy is experiencing sustained **inflation** unlike anything seen for more than three decades. 2023 started out with the rate topping 12%. However, inflation is not evenly spread and tends to be more obvious in energy-intensive sectors. Yet even this rule of thumb is only a guideline. While a few **museum prices** have risen sharply, hotel rates offer a mixed picture: Some have leapt, especially at the budget and mid-range level, while others have hardly moved. **Gas** prices have skyrocketed (though are already falling) but the cost of **train travel** is almost unchanged. On top of this, travelers from the U.S. are shielded from the brunt of inflation by a dollar which remains strong against the euro. Indeed, the price of Italy rail passes (sold in dollars) has fallen over the last couple of editions of this guide. Naturally, Italy's inflation situation is fluid: If you are concerned, use the tools and advice in this chapter—as well as Google—to check ahead.

before you can see the options, but thankfully it usually comes within minutes of your request. Car-rental search companies generally report the **lowest rates available between 6 and 8 weeks ahead** of arrival. Rent the smallest car possible and request a diesel rather than petrol engine to minimize fuel costs. You must be 25 or older to rent from many agencies (although some accept ages 21 and up, at a premium price).

The legalities and contractual obligations of renting a car in Italy (where accident rates are high) are more complicated than those in almost any other country in Europe. You also must have nerves of steel, a sense of humor, a valid driver's license, and strictly speaking (for non-Europeans), an **International Driving Permit** (see below). Insurance on all vehicles is compulsory. *Tip:* If you're planning to rent a car in Italy during high season, you should **book farther in advance than you usually would.** It's not unheard of to arrive at Rome airport in June or July to find that every agent is out of cars, perhaps for the whole week.

It can sometimes be tricky to get to the *autostrada* (fast highway) from a city center or airport, so consider renting or bringing a GPS-enabled device or installing an offline navigation app on your smartphone. In bigger cities you will first have to get to the *tangenziale*, or beltway. The beltway in Rome is known as the *Grande Raccordo Anulare*, or "Big Ring Road."

The going can be slow on Friday afternoons out of Italian cities and Sunday nights on the way back into town, and an urban rush hour any day of the week can be epic. Gas costs over 1.85€ *per liter* at time of writing; prices have been extremely volatile. Add in the price of the rental, and it's often cheaper to take the train, even for two people. If you are visiting mainly cities, take the train.

PERMITS & AUTO CLUBS   Before leaving home, you can buy an **International Driving Permit** from the **American Automobile Association** (**AAA;** www.aaa.com; © **800/622-7070** or 650/294-7400). In Canada, the permit is available from the **Canadian Automobile Association** (**CAA;** www.caa.ca; © **800/222-4357**). Technically, you need this permit and your driver's license to drive in Italy. Traffic police can fine you for driving without an IDP. Visitors from within the EU need only take their domestic driver's license.

Italy's equivalent of AAA is the **Automobile Club d'Italia** (**ACI;** www.aci.it). They're the people who respond when you place an emergency assistance call to © **803-116** for road breakdowns (© **800/116-800** from an overseas cellphone). Nonmembers are charged for this service.

ROAD TYPES   **Autostrade** are toll highways denoted by green signs and a number prefaced with an *A*, like the A1 from Milan to Florence, Rome, and Naples. A few fast highways aren't numbered and are simply called a *raccordo*, a connecting road between two cities (such as Florence–Siena and Florence–Pisa). Autostrada tolls can get expensive, costing just over 1€ for every 15km (9 miles): it costs around 23€ to drive from Rome to Florence. See **www.autostrade.it** for live traffic updates and a road-toll calculator.

Road Signs

Here's a brief rundown of road signs you'll encounter:

- **Speed limit sign:** Black number inside a red circle on a white background
- **End of a speed zone:** Black and white, with a black slash through the number
- **Yield to oncoming traffic:** Red circle with a white background, a black arrow pointing down, and a red arrow pointing up
- **Yield ahead:** Point-down, red-and-white triangle
- **Pedestrian zone:** Simple white circle with a red border, or the words *zona*

pedonale or *zona a traffico limitato* (if your hotel is in such a zone, ask if you can prearrange to drop baggage off by car; it's often allowed)

- **One-way streets:** White arrow on a blue background
- **Do not enter:** Mostly red circle with a horizontal white slash
- **No parking:** Circular sign in blue with a red circle-slash
- Any image in black on a white background surrounded by a red circle means that whatever is portrayed is **not allowed** (for instance, if the image is two cars next to each other, it means no passing; and so on).

Strade statali (singular, *strada statale*) are state roads, usually without a center divider and two lanes wide (although sometimes they can be a divided four-way highway), indicated by blue signs. The route numbers are prefaced with an *SS,* as in the SS11 from Milan to Venice. On signs, however, these official route numbers are frequently omitted. Usually, you just see blue signs listing destinations by name with arrows pointing in the appropriate directions. It pays to study the map before coming to an intersection, or better yet, download an **offline navigation app** for your smartphone. Because they bisect many towns, the *strade statali* can be frustratingly slow: When feasible, pay the euros and take the autostrada.

DRIVING RULES   Italian drivers aren't maniacs; they only appear to be. Spend any time on a highway and you will have the experience of somebody driving insanely close behind while flashing their headlights. Take a deep breath and don't panic: This is the aggressive signal for you to move to the right so he (it's always a "he") can pass. Until you do he will stay mind-bogglingly close. On a two-lane road, the idiot swerving into your lane to pass someone in oncoming traffic expects you to veer obligingly toward the shoulder so three vehicles can fit. He would do the same for you. Probably. Many Italians seem to think turn signals are optional, so be aware the car in front could be ready to turn at any moment.

A few important rules:

When traveling outside of towns, it is compulsory to **keep your headlights illuminated**—set to dip—even during the day.

The **speed limit** on roads in built-up areas around towns and cities is 50 kmph (31 mph). On two-lane roads it's 90 kmph (56 mph) and on the highway it's 130 kmph (81 mph). Italians have astounding disregard for these limits. However, police can ticket you and collect a fine on the spot.

The **blood-alcohol limit** in Italy is 0.05%, often achieved with less than two drinks; driving above the limit can result in a fine, driving ban, or imprisonment. The blood-alcohol limit is set at zero for anyone who has held a driver's license for less than 3 years.

Seat belts are obligatory in both front and back seats; ditto child seats or special restraints for minors under 1.5m (5 ft.) in height—although this latter regulation is often ignored.

Drivers may not use a **cellphone** while driving. This is another regulation locals treat as optional.

PARKING Even savvy locals struggle to find convenient parking in Italy's cities. Hotels rarely have parking facilities, but many do negotiate deals with private lots. Your hotel should be a first point of contact if you plan to park and leave the car for the duration of a stay. Should you prefer driving to the high-speed train, this is the only sensible option in big cities. On streets, **white lines** indicate free public spaces; **blue lines** are pay spaces; and **yellow lines** indicate spots where only residents may park. Meters don't line the sidewalk; rather, there's usually a machine on the block where you punch in how long you want to park. The machine prints a ticket to place on your dashboard. If you park in an area marked *parcheggio disco orario,* root around in the glove compartment for a cardboard parking disc. With this device, you dial up the hour of your arrival and display it on your dashboard. You're allowed *un'ora* (1 hr.) *due ore* (2 hr.), or whatever the sign advises. If you do not have a disk, **write your arrival time clearly on a sheet of paper and leave it on the dash.**

Parking lots have ticket dispensers, but exit booths are not usually manned. When you return to the lot to depart, first visit the office or automated payment machine to exchange your ticket for a paid receipt. You then use this to pass through the exit gate.

FUEL Gasoline (gas or petrol), *benzina* in Italian, can be bought at pull-in gas stations along major roads and on the outskirts of towns, as well as in 24-hour stations along the autostrada. Almost all are closed for the *riposo* (midday siesta) and on Sundays (except along the autostrada), but most have an automatic machine that accepts cash or card. Unleaded gas is *senza piombo.* Diesel is *gasolio* (or just *diesel*).

[FastFACTS] ITALY

Area Codes The **country code** for Italy is **39.** City codes (Florence is 055, Venice is 041, Rome is 06) are incorporated into the numbers themselves. Therefore, you must dial the entire number, *including the initial zero,* when calling from *anywhere* outside or inside Italy, and within the same town. To call Florence from the United States, dial **011-39-055,** then the rest of the phone number. Numbers in Italy can range anywhere from 6 to 12 digits in length.

ATMs Referred to in Italy as *un bancomat,* ATMs are easy to find in Italian cities; smaller towns usually have one, but it's good practice to fuel up on cash in urban centers before visiting rural areas.

Before traveling, confirm your card is valid for international withdrawals and that you have a four-digit PIN. (Some ATMs in Italy will not accept any other number of digits.) Also, be sure you know your daily withdrawal limit.

If at the ATM you get an on-screen message saying your card isn't valid for international transactions, don't panic: Most likely the bank can't make an electronic connection to check it (occasionally this can be a citywide epidemic). Try another ATM or another town.

Business **Banks** tend to be open Monday through Friday 8:30am to 1:30pm and 2:45 to 4:15pm. General opening hours for **stores, offices,** and **churches** are from 9:30am to noon or 1pm and again from 3 or 3:30pm (or later) to 7:30pm. The early afternoon shutdown is the *riposo,* the Italian siesta (in large cities, downtown stores don't usually close for *riposo*). Most small stores close all day Sunday and some also on Monday (morning only or all day). Some public services and business offices are open to the public only in the morning.

Traditionally, **state museums** are closed Mondays. Most large museums stay open all day otherwise, although some smaller or private collections close for *riposo* or are only open in the morning (9am–2pm is popular). State museums usually offer free admission on the **first Sunday of the month**.

Cellphones See "Mobile Phones," p. 362.

Credit Cards Between them, computerized banking and the pandemic entrenched the triumph of plastic throughout Italy. It remains a good idea to carry some cash—small businesses may accept only cash or even claim their machine is broken to avoid card fees. **Visa** and **Mastercard** are almost universally accepted, and some businesses, typically at the luxe end, take **American Express. Diners Club** tends not to be accepted in Italy. Be sure to let your bank know you'll be traveling abroad to avoid having your card blocked after a few days of purchases far from home.

Note: Many banks assess a 1% to 3% "transaction fee" on **all** charges you incur abroad, whether you're using the local currency or your native currency. If a card machine prompts you to choose between your home currency or euros, pick euros. The "wholesale" exchange rate will be much more favorable. The same rule applies at ATMs.

Customs Foreign visitors arriving by air can bring most items for personal use, including new merchandise bought duty-free for up to 430€. Returning to the United States, U.S. citizens can bring with them up to $800 of goods, including 1 liter of alcohol, but no meats, fresh fruits, or vegetables. Vinegars, oils, preserves, chocolates, and certain cheeses are permissible (vacuum-packed cheeses, yes; raw milk cheese, no).

Disabled Travelers Most museums and churches have ramps at entrances, and many hotels have converted first-floor rooms into accessible units. Otherwise, expect to find some parts of Italy tricky to tackle with a mobility impairment. Builders in the Middle Ages didn't have wheelchairs in mind when they built narrow doorways or spiral staircases, and heritage preservation laws keep Italians from doing much about this in some places.

Public transportation is improving, however. Passengers in wheelchairs are getting better access, particularly on modern local buses and new transit infrastructure like Florence's tram. Dedicated seats or areas cater for those with disabilities, and Italians are quick to give up a place for somebody who looks like they need it. **Trenitalia** has a number for disabled travelers to call for assistance on the rail network: ☏ **323232.** The private rail network **Italo**

has wheelchair spaces on every train: Call ✆ **060708** for any station assistance you need.

Drinking Laws People of any age can legally consume alcohol in Italy, but a person must be 16 years old to be served alcohol in a restaurant or bar. Bars generally close around 2am, although alcohol is served in clubs after that. Supermarkets and small convenience stores sell beer, wine, and liquor.

Electricity Italy operates on a 220-volt AC (50 cycles) system, as opposed to the U.S. 110-volt AC (60 cycles) system. A simple adapter plug makes American flat pegs fit Italian round holes. Most gadgets you carry are dual voltage, so you're unlikely to need an additional converter. Buy all electrical accessories **before** you travel.

Embassies & Consulates Most countries have embassies in Rome. The **U.S. Embassy** is at Via Vittorio Veneto 121 (it.usembassy.gov; ✆ **06/46-741**). There is also a **U.S. Consulate General** in Florence at Lungarno Vespucci 38 (✆ **055/266-951**). The **Canadian Embassy** is at Via Zara 30 (www.italy.gc.ca; ✆ **06/854-441**). The **Australian Embassy** is at Via Antonio Bosio 5 (italy.embassy.gov.au; ✆ **06/852-721**). The **New Zealand Embassy** is at Via Clitunno 44 (www.mfat.govt.nz/en/embassies; ✆ **06/853-7501**). The **U.K. Embassy** is at Via XX Settembre 80a

(www.gov.uk/world/italy; ✆ **06/4220-0001**). Each national embassy website publishes coronavirus-related information for citizens traveling to or from Italy.

Emergencies The best number to call with a **general emergency** is ✆ **112,** which connects you to the **Carabinieri,** who will transfer you as needed. For the **police,** dial ✆ **113;** for a **medical emergency** and to call an **ambulance,** the number is ✆ **118;** for the **fire department,** call ✆ **115.** If your car breaks down, dial ✆ **116** for **roadside aid** courtesy of the Automotive Club of Italy. All are free calls, but roadside assistance is a paid service for nonmembers.

Family Travel Italy is a family-oriented society. A crying baby at a dinner table is greeted with a knowing smile rather than a stern look. Children almost always receive discounts, and maybe a special treat from the waiter, but the availability of such accoutrements as child seats for dinner tables is more the exception than the norm. There are plenty of parks, offbeat museums, markets, ice-cream parlors, and vibrant street life to amuse even the youngest children.

Health & Hospitals The Italian public health care system is generally well regarded. Even if you don't have insurance, **you will be treated in an emergency.** Italy offers universal health care to its citizens and those

of other European Union countries.

Others should be prepared to pay medical bills upfront. Before leaving home, find out what medical services your **health insurance** covers.

Insurance Italy may be one of the safer places for travelers, but accidents and setbacks can happen, from lost luggage to car accidents. We recommend looking at the following online insurance marketplaces: **SquareMouth.com, Insure-MyTrip.com,** and **TravelInsurance.com**. All three allow users to quickly and easily compare policies from different, vetted travel insurance companies. We find the user interface at SquareMouth to be the more intuitive, but all three are excellent resources.

Internet Access For traveling with your own computer or smartphone, you'll find Wi-Fi in almost every accommodation, but if this is essential for your stay, verify before booking. In a pinch, hostels, libraries, many cafes, and some bars offer access. Several spots around Venice, Florence, Rome, and other big cities have free Wi-Fi access provided by local government, but antiterrorism laws make it obligatory to register before you can log on.

High-speed trains and long-distance buses often have free Wi-Fi (but it can be shaky and they throttle Skype/Zoom, streaming, and other data-hungry services). Rome's **Fiumicino Airport** has free Wi-Fi.

LGBT Travelers Italy as a whole, and northern Italy in particular, is LGBT-friendly. Homosexuality is legal and the age of consent is 16. Same-sex civil unions became legal in 2016, although the present government has expressed unwillingness to go any further than civil recognition. Italians are generally more affectionate than North Americans in their friendships, and even straight men occasionally walk down the street with arms around each other. However, kissing anywhere other than on the cheeks may draw attention. Italy's national associations and support networks for gays and lesbians are **Arcigay** (www.arcigay.it) and **Arcilesbica** (www.arcilesbica.it); most cities have a local office. See **www.arcigay.it/en/sedi** for a directory of local affiliates.

Mail & Postage Sending a postcard or letter up to 20g, or a little less than an ounce, costs 1.15€ to European countries, 2.40€ to North America, and a whopping 3.10€ to Australia and New Zealand.

Mobile Phones Pretty much any phone with 4G/5G compatibility will work in Italy. Before traveling, contact your home service provider to activate "international roaming."

But—and it's a *big* but—using roaming can be expensive, especially to access the Internet. It is usually much cheaper, once you arrive, to buy an Italian SIM card. This is an especially good idea if you will be in Italy for more than a week. You can **buy a SIM card** at one of many cellphone shops you pass in every city. The main service providers are **TIM** (www.tim.it), **Vodafone** (www.vodafone.it), and **WINDTRE** (www.windtre.it). With an Italian SIM card, local and national calls will be as low as .10€ per minute and incoming calls are free. Deals on each network change regularly and often include prepaid data; check the individual websites, visit a provider's store, or go into an electronics chain such as **Euronics** (www.euronics.it). *Note:* U.S. contract cellphones are often "locked" and will only work with a SIM card from your own service provider, check first if you have an unlocked phone.

Buying a phone is another option, and you should find one for about 20€. Use it then recycle when you get home. It may save you a fortune versus alternatives such as roaming or using hotel telephones.

Money & Costs Frommer's lists exact prices in local currency. The currency conversions quoted below were correct at press time. However, rates fluctuate, so before departing, consult a currency exchange website, such as **www.oanda.com/currency/converter**, to check up-to-the-minute rates.

THE VALUE OF THE EURO VS. OTHER POPULAR CURRENCIES

€	Aus$	Can$	NZ$	UK£	US$
1	A$1.54	C$1.45	NZ$1.68	£0.88	$1.09

Like 19 other European countries, Italy uses the **euro** as its currency. Euro coins are issued in denominations of .01€, .02€, .05€, .10€, .20€, and .50€, as well as 1€ and 2€; bills come in denominations of 5€, 10€, 20€, 50€, 100€, 200€, and 500€. You'll get the best rate if you **exchange money** at a bank or take cash out from an **ATMs** (see p. 360).

Traveler's checks have gone the way of the Stegosaurus.

Newspapers & Magazines The *New York Times International Edition* and *USA Today* are available at newsstands in big cities. At larger kiosks you can find the *Wall Street Journal Europe*, European editions of *The Economist*, and major European newspapers and magazines.

Pharmacies Pharmacies are ubiquitous (look for the green cross) and serve almost like mini-clinics, where pharmacists diagnose and treat minor ailments, like flu symptoms and general aches and pains, including with over-the-counter drugs. Carry the generic name of any prescription medicines you take, in case a local pharmacist is unfamiliar with your overseas brand. Pharmacies in cities take turns covering the night shift; normally a list is posted at the entrance of each pharmacy informing customers which are open each night of the week. Face masks and hand sanitizer are usually on sale. Many pharmacies still offer certified **antigen and PCR testing** for travelers.

Police For emergencies, call $\mathcal{C}$ **112** or $\mathcal{C}$ **113.** Italy has several different police forces, but you'll likely need to deal with only two. The *Carabinieri* ($\mathcal{C}$ **112;** www.carabinieri.it) normally concern themselves only with serious crimes but point you in the right direction. The *Polizia* ($\mathcal{C}$ **113;** www.poliziadistato.it), whose city headquarters is called a *questura*, is the place to go for help with lost and stolen property or petty crimes.

Safety Italy is a remarkably safe country. The worst threats you'll likely face are pickpockets who sometimes frequent touristy areas and public buses. Keep your hands on a camera and valuables in an under-the-clothes money belt or inside zip-pocket. Don't leave anything valuable in a rental car overnight and leave nothing visible in it at any time. If you are robbed, you can fill out paperwork at the nearest police station (*questura*), but this is mostly for

insurance purposes or to get a passport reissued—don't expect them to hunt down the perpetrator. In general, avoid public parks at night. Streets around the rail station are often unsavory, but rarely any worse.

Senior Travel Seniors and older people are treated with respect and deference, but few specific programs or concessions are made for them. One exception is admission prices for museums and sights, where those ages 60 or 65 and older often get in at a reduced rate or even free. As a senior in Italy, you're *un anziano* (if you're a woman: *un'anziana*). It's a term of respect and you should let people know if you think a discount may be due.

Smoking Smoking has been eradicated from inside restaurants, bars, and most hotels, so smokers tend to take outside tables. If you pick an outdoor table, you are essentially choosing a seat in the smoking section; requesting that your neighbor refrain from smoking may not be politely received.

Student Travelers An **International Student Identity Card (ISIC)** qualifies students for savings on rail passes, plane tickets, entrance fees, and more. The card is valid for 1 year. You can apply at **isicusa.com.** If you are still 26 and under, you can get an **International Youth Travel Card (IYTC)** instead from the same issuer, which entitles you to some discounts. Teachers can carry an

International Teacher Identity Card (ITIC), but an I.D. from home should suffice for educator discounts at museums and the like.

Taxes No sales tax is added to the price tag of purchases in Italy, but a 22% value-added tax (in Italy: IVA) is automatically included in just about everything, except food and a few specific goods and services where rates of 4% or 10% apply. Entertainment, transport, hotels, and dining are among a group of goods taxed at a lower rate of 10%. For major purchases, non–EU residents can get IVA refunded. Several city governments have also introduced an **accommodation tax.** For example, in Florence, you are charged between 3€ and 5€ per person per night depending on the hotel or rental apartment's government-star rating. Children 11 and under are exempt. Venice, Rome, and many other popular destinations levy their own taxes. This tax is not usually included in any published room rate, even those prepaid online.

Tipping In **hotels,** service is usually included in your bill. In family-run operations, additional tips are unnecessary and sometimes considered rude. In fancier places with a hired staff, however, you may want to leave a 1€ daily tip for the maid and pay any porter 1€–2€ per bag. In **restaurants,** a 2€ to 3€ per person "cover charge" is automatically added to the bill, and in some tourist areas, especially Venice, another 10% to 15% is tacked on. Except in the most unscrupulous of places, this will be noted on the menu; if unsure, you should ask, "È incluso il servizio?" It is not necessary to leave extra money on the table, although it is common to leave up to 10€ for good service. Locals often leave nothing. It is not necessary to tip **taxi** drivers, although it is common to round up the fare to the nearest euro or two.

Toilets Aside from toilets in train stations, which sometimes cost .50€ to 1€ to use, and gas/petrol stations, where they are free (with perhaps a basket seeking gratuities for cleaners), public toilets are few and far between. It is advisable to always make use of toilets in a hotel, restaurant, museum, or bar before setting off around town. Public toilets—and often those in bars, too—can be dirty, with no seat or toilet paper. It's best to carry a pack of tissues and hand sanitizer with you, especially if you're traveling with children or teens.

USEFUL ITALIAN PHRASES

English	Italian	Pronunciation
Thank you	Grazie	*graht*-tzee-yey
You're welcome	Prego	*prey*-go
Please	Per favore	pehr fah-*vohr*-eh
Yes	Sì	see
No	No	noh
Good morning/Good day	Buongiorno	bwohn-*djor*-noh
Good evening	Buona sera	*bwohn*-ah *say*-rah
Good night	Buona notte	*bwohn*-ah *noht*-tay
It's a pleasure to meet you.	Piacere di conoscerla.	pyah-*cheh*-reh dee koh-*nohshehr*-lah
My name is ____.	Mi chiamo ____.	mee *kyah*-moh
And yours?	E lei?	eh lay
Do you speak English?	Parla inglese?	*pahr*-lah een-*gleh*-seh
How are you?	Come sta?	*koh*-may *stah*
Very well	Molto bene	*mohl*-toh *behn*-ney
Goodbye	Arrivederci	ahr-ree-vah-*dehr*-chee
Excuse me (to get attention)	Scusi	*skoo*-zee
Excuse me (to get past someone)	Permesso	pehr-*mehs*-soh

GETTING AROUND

English	Italian	Pronunciation
Where is . . . ?	Dov'è . . . ?	*doh*-vey
the station	la stazione	lah stat-tzee-*oh*-neh
a hotel	un albergo	oon ahl-*behr*-goh
a restaurant	un ristorante	oon reest-ohr-*ahnt*-eh
the bathroom	il bagno	eel *bahn*-nyoh
I am looking for . . .	Cerco . . .	*chehr*-koh

English	Italian	Pronunciation
the check-in counter	il check-in	**eel check-in**
the ticket counter	la biglietteria	*lah beel-lyeht-teh-ree-ah*
arrivals	l'area arrivi	*lah*-reh-ah ahr-*ree*-vee
departures	l'area partenze	*lah*-reh-ah pahr-*tehn*-tseh
gate number	l'uscita numero	loo-*shee*-tah *noo*-meh-roh
the restroom	la toilette	lah twa-*leht*
the information booth	l'ufficio informazioni	loof-*fee*-choh een-*fohr*-mah-*tsyoh*-nee
a public telephone	un telefono pubblico	oon teh-*leh*-foh-noh *poob*-blee-koh
an ATM/cashpoint	un bancomat	oon *bahn*-koh-maht
baggage claim	il ritiro bagagli	eel ree-*tee*-roh bah-*gahl*-lyee
a restaurant	un ristorante	oon ree-stoh-*rahn*-teh
a bookstore	una libreria	*oo*-nah lee-breh-*ree*-ah
a pharmacy	una farmacia	*oo*-nah far-ma-*chee*-ah
To the left	A sinistra	ah see-*nees*-tra
To the right	A destra	ah *dehy*-stra
Straight ahead	Avanti (*or* sempre diritto)	ahv-*vahn*-tee (*sehm*-pray dee-*reet*-toh)

DINING

English	Italian	Pronunciation
Breakfast	Prima colazione	*pree*-mah coh-laht-tzee-*ohn*-ay
Lunch	Pranzo	*prahn*-zoh
Dinner	Cena	*chay*-nah
How much is it?	Quanto costa?	*kwan*-toh *coh*-sta
The check, please	Il conto, per favore	eel kon-toh *pehr* fah-*vohr*-eh

A MATTER OF TIME

English	Italian	Pronunciation
When?	Quando?	*kwan*-doh
Yesterday	Ieri	ee-*yehr*-ree
Today	Oggi	*oh*-jee
Tomorrow	Domani	doh-*mah*-nee
What time is it?	Che ore sono?	kay *or*-ay *soh*-noh
It's one o'clock.	È l'una.	eh *loo*-nah
It's two o'clock.	Sono le due.	*soh*-noh leh *doo*-eh
It's two-thirty.	Sono le due e mezzo.	*soh*-noh leh *doo*-eh eh *mehd*-dzoh
It's noon.	mezzogiorno.	*eh* mehd-dzoh-*johr*-noh
It's midnight.	È mezzanotte.	*eh* mehd-dzah-*noht*-teh
in the morning	al mattino	ahl maht-*tee*-noh
in the afternoon	al pomeriggio	ahl poh-meh-*reed*-joh
at night	alla notte	dee *noht*-the

DAYS OF THE WEEK

English	Italian	Pronunciation
Monday	Lunedì	**loo-nay-*dee***
Tuesday	Martedì	**mart-ay-*dee***
Wednesday	Mercoledì	**mehr-cohl-ay-*dee***
Thursday	Giovedì	**joh-vay-*dee***
Friday	Venerdì	**ven-nehr-*dee***
Saturday	Sabato	***sah*-bah-toh**
Sunday	Domenica	**doh-*mehn*-nee-kah**

PLANNING YOUR TRIP | Useful Italian Phrases

Index

Restaurants

Photo Credits

Front cover: DaLiu / Shutterstock.com; title page: Nicola Forenza / Shutterstock; p. iii: Shaiith / Shutterstock; p. 2: claudio zaccherini / Shutterstock.com; p. 3: Andriy Blokhin / Shutterstock.com; p. 4: Jeanette Teare / Shutterstock; p. 5: Courtesy of Villa Spalletti Trivelli; p. 6: Yasonya / Shutterstock; p. 7: Pyty / Shutterstock.com; p. 8: Paolo Paradiso / Shutterstock; p. 9, top: Alfredo Cerra / Shutterstock.com; p. 9, bottom: Nick N A / Shutterstock; p. 10: Alexander Mazurkevich / Shutterstock.com; p. 14, top: SCStock / Shutterstock; p. 14, bottom: Resul Muslu / Shutterstock; p. 15: Viacheslav Lopatin; p. 16: Dreamer4787; p. 18: Jon Chica / Shutterstock; p. 19: Fedor Selivanov / Shutterstock; p. 20: Yasonya; p. 22: Alliance Images; p. 23: Catarina Belova / Shutterstock; p. 24: Obatala-photography / Shutterstock; p. 25: Anna Nahabed / Shutterstock; p. 27: Sopotnicki / Shutterstock; p. 28: Raffaele Conti 88 / Shutterstock; p. 29: fivetonine / Shutterstock; p. 30: footageclips / Shutterstock; p. 31: Vladimir Mucibabic / Shutterstock; p. 32: Nick N A / Shutterstock; p. 34: Cris Foto / Shutterstock; p. 37, top: Katvic; p. 37, bottom: essevu / Shutterstock; p. 38: Javen / Shutterstock; p. 39: Ilia Baksheev / Shutterstock.com; p. 40: Dave & Margie Hill / Kleerup; p. 41: carulmare; p. 43: r.nagy / Shutterstock.com; p. 44: MyVideoimage. com / Shutterstock.com; p. 45: Drop of Light / Shutterstock; p. 47: Bucchi Francesco / Shutterstock; p. 48: Ian Melvin / Shutterstock; p. 49: M. Rohana / Shutterstock; p. 52: Nakasaku / Shutterstock; p. 55: Steve Boyko / Shutterstock; p. 56: cge2010; p. 57: Matteo Gabrieli / Shutterstock; p. 58: Matyas Rehak / Shutterstock.com; p. 62: Phuong D. Nguyen / Shutterstock; p. 66: Alvov / Shutterstock; p. 69: Courtesy of Mama Shelter Roma / FRANCIS AMIAND; p. 70: Courtesy of Villa Laetitia; p. 71: Courtesy of Lancelot Hotel; p. 75: Courtesy of The Inn at the Spanish Steps / MAX LITTERA; p. 79: Courtesy of Hotel San Francesco / MAX LITTERA; p. 82: Courtesy of Taverna Angelica / Chiara Pasqualini; p. 84: natalia_maroz / Shutterstock; p. 86: Courtesy of Pipero Roma / Alberto Di Cesare; p. 89: Courtesy of Al Ceppo / pikorra. com; p. 92: Courtesy of Antico Arco / Andrea Di Lorenzo / www.andreadilorenzo.it; p. 93: Courtesy of Glass Hostaria / Cristiano Pacchiarotti; p. 94: Courtesy of Dar Poeta; p. 97: AlexAnton / Shutterstock; p. 98: Shchipkova Elena / Shutterstock; p. 100: Tyler Bell / Flickr; p. 104: Viacheslav Lopatin / Shutterstock; p. 105: Jurate Buiviene / Shutterstock; p. 110: sancastro / Shutterstock; p. 113: Marco Rubino / Shutterstock; p. 117: Viacheslav Lopatin; p. 122: NICOLA MESSANA PHOTOS / Shutterstock.com; p. 123: Noppasin Wongchum / Shutterstock; p. 124: f11photo / Shutterstock; p. 127: Tomasz Wozniak / Shutterstock; p. 130: Boris-B / Shutterstock; p. 132: lexan / Shutterstock.com; p. 136: lexan / Shutterstock. com; p. 138: Kirk Fisher / Shutterstock; p. 140: V_E / Shutterstock; p. 146: Jannis Tobias Werner; p. 147: Zvonimir Atletic / Shutterstock; p. 150: Heracles Kritikos / Shutterstock; p. 151: Di Gregorio Giulio / Shutterstock; p. 152: Courtesy of Castroni / MP Visual Communication; p. 154: PhotoLife_Style / Shutterstock; p. 155: lornet / Shutterstock; p. 158: Courtesy of Salotto42; p. 159: Courtesy of Stravinskij Bar / Janos Grapow; p. 162: Darryl Brooks / Shutterstock; p. 163: Jakub.it; p. 164: Viacheslav Lopatin / Shutterstock; p. 166: leventina / Shutterstock; p. 167, top: LifeCollectionPhotography / Shutterstock; p. 167, bottom: mgallar; p. 169: Marco Rubino / Shutterstock; p. 170: Marina99; p. 173: StevanZZ / Shutterstock; p. 175: PHOTOCREO Michal Bednarek; p. 176: Dave Z / Shutterstock; p. 179: skovalsky / Shutterstock; p. 180: ArTono / Shutterstock; p. 186: Courtesy of Residenza della Signoria; p. 188: Courtesy of Alessandra Hotel; p. 189: SkandaRamana / Shutterstock.com; p. 192, top: Courtesy of Riva Lofts Hotel / ALESSANDRO MICHELAZZI / Olga Makarova; p. 192, bottom: SvetlanaSF / Shutterstock; p. 196: Courtesy of Coquinarius; p. 199: Courtesy of Trattoria Mario; p. 201: Courtesy of Brac / Anna Positano / Studio Campo; p. 202: Courtesy of iO: Osteria Personale; p. 203: frantic00 / Shutterstock; p. 204: Lasse Johansson / Shutterstock; p. 209: Imago; p. 211: vvoe / Shutterstock.com; p. 212: pio3 / Shutterstock; p. 214: canbedone / Shutterstock; p. 216: StockphotoVideo / Shutterstock; p. 219: S-F; p. 221: FrentaN / Shutterstock; p. 223: Federico Magonio / Shutterstock; p. 225: DinoPh / Shutterstock; p. 228: Anna Pakutina / Shutterstock.com; p. 230: Kamira / Shutterstock; p. 233: Cesare Andrea Ferrari / Shutterstock; p. 236: John_Silver / Shutterstock; p. 238: gvictoria / Shutterstock; p. 240: ColorMaker / Shutterstock; p. 241: Courtesy of Scuola del Cuoio / Michael Calabro Photography; p. 243: Yuriy Biryukov / Shutterstock; p. 244: Maurese / Shutterstock; p. 245: Courtesy of Mayday / Carrie Radford / Radford